third edition

Partners in Play

An Adlerian Approach to Play Therapy

Terry Kottman and Kristin Meany-Walen

AMERICAN COUNSELING
ASSOCIATION
6101 Stevenson Avenue, Suite 600
Alexandria, VA 22304
www.counseling.org

third edition

Partners in Play

An Adlerian Approach to Play Therapy

American Counseling Association
6101 Stevenson Avenue, Suite 600
Alexandria, VA 22304

Associate Publisher   Carolyn C. Baker

Digital and Print Development Editor   Nancy Driver

Production Manager   Bonny E. Gaston

Copy Editor   Kerri L. Tolan

Cover and text design by Bonny E. Gaston

Libarary of Congress Cataloging-in-Publication Data
Kottman, Terry.
    Partners in play: an Adlerian approach to play therapy/by Terry Kottman, Kristin Meany-Walen.—3rd edition.
        pages cm
    Includes bibliographical references and index.
    ISBN 978-1-55620-352-7 (pbk. : alk. paper) 1. Play therapy. 2. Adlerian psychology. I. Meany-Walen, Kristin. II. Title.
RJ505.P6K64 2016
616.89'1653—dc23   2015024590

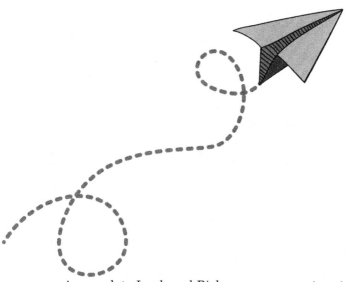

As usual, to Jacob and Rick, my permanent partners in play.

To the memory of Byron Medler, who gave me permission
to be myself.

To Jeff Ashby, who continues to help me figure who that is.

—With love, Terry

• • •

From Kristin:

To Skyler—for inspiring me become a better person, and for giving
me lots of opportunities to practice Adlerian play therapy!

To Terry Walen—for being my partner in life.

To Terry Kottman—for believing in me and trusting me with this book.
I hope to make you proud.

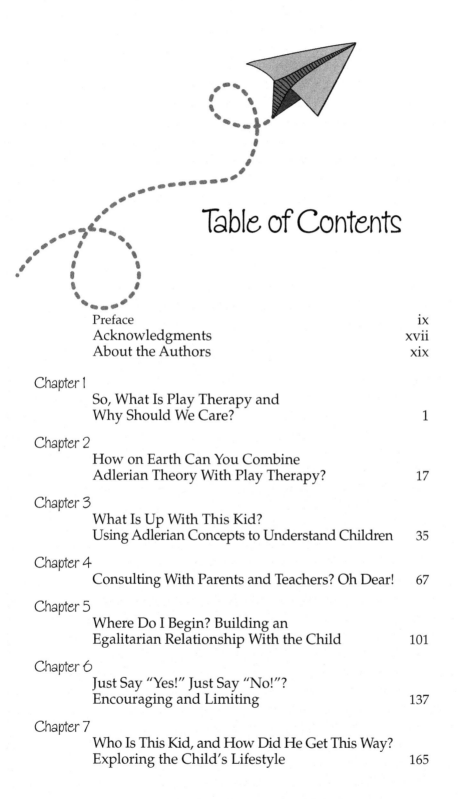

Table of Contents

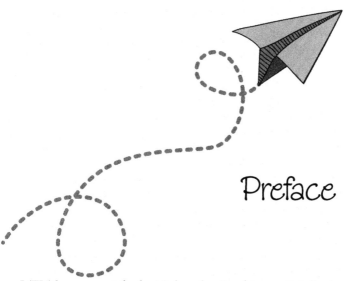

Preface

I (TK) have spent the last 3 decades "making up" Adlerian play therapy—a method for integrating Adlerian concepts and techniques into the practice of play therapy. Helping professionals (mental health counselors, school counselors, social workers, psychologists, psychiatrists, day-care workers, teachers, principals, and any other professionals who interact with children in therapeutic ways) can use Adlerian play therapy in their work with children who are experiencing emotional, behavioral, or academic problems. (Because there are many different professionals who wish to pursue training as play therapists, we simply use the term *counselor* or *play therapist* interchangeably throughout the remainder of the book.) Actually, the book can be adapted to help anyone (including adolescents and adults) who is able and willing to use play as a vehicle for communication, but this book is dedicated to working with children.

Adlerian play therapy is a process in which the counselor (a) builds an egalitarian relationship with the child client; (b) explores the child's lifestyle; (c) develops hypotheses about the intrapersonal and interpersonal dynamics of the child's difficulties (from the perspective of the child and from the perspectives of other people in the child's life); (d) designs a treatment plan for the child and for any other individuals who have a strong influence on the child (e.g., parents and teachers); (e) helps the child gain insight and make new decisions about self, the world, and others; (f) teaches the child new skills for relating to others; (g) helps the child practice new skills for interacting with others; and (h) consults with parents and teachers, working with them to develop more positive perspectives on the child and to learn encouraging strategies for interacting with the child.

There continues to be increased concern about the mental health of young children. Many helping professionals are recognizing a need for increased ability to communicate with children using children's language—the language of play and metaphor. Consequently, the field of play therapy is expanding rapidly. The Association for Play Therapy has grown from a tiny group of friends who got together to talk about working with children to an organization with approximately 6,000 members. The association has established criteria for registration of play therapists and play therapy supervisors. Many professionals who work therapeutically with children all over the world have expressed a desire to acquire the requisite training and supervised experience to become qualified play therapists.

This increased interest in the field of play therapy was one of the primary reasons why I wrote the original version of *Partners in Play: An Adlerian Approach to Play Therapy* (1995). I believed then that practicing counselors and counselors-in-training need practical application-oriented guides for using play to communicate with and help children grow in positive directions. I still believe this. In the ensuing years, I have continued to learn more about children and families (from my son Jacob, from other children, from parents, from teachers, from other counselors, from my students, from workshop participants, and from books describing new, and sometimes old, ways of thinking about and interacting with children and their families). On the basis of these ideas and experiences, Adlerian play therapy has continued to evolve. Since I wrote the first edition of this book, I have added many strategies for conceptualizing children, piloted new techniques for working directly with children and with parents, and developed a systematic method for designing a treatment plan for both children and parents (and for working with teachers and other school personnel when appropriate). This evolution prompted me to write a second edition of *Partners in Play* in 2003. As time has passed, the world of play therapy has continued to grow and evolve, as have Adlerian play therapy and my understanding of children, families, and schools. In the past several years, I have been repeatedly asked to write a third edition of *Partners in Play* but was reluctant to do so—I was afraid I didn't have anything new to offer even though I have relentlessly (obsessively?) studied a wide-ranging plethora of subjects (leadership, life coaching, dance and movement, sand tray therapy, trauma and its effects on children, and energy, just to name a few). I approached one of my former students (now colleague), Kristin Meany-Walen, an amazing young woman who has already made a significant contribution to the field by conducting research studies and writing about Adlerian play therapy. I asked her if she would be willing to collaborate with me on a new edition of the book. And she said, "Yes!" Hint: She wrote the chapter in this book on research, which is not my forte. Writing this book with Kristin has been a delightful experience, with Kristin inspiring me, grounding me, keeping me moving toward completion. In addition, it has turned out that the two of us have a lot to offer. (Who knew?)

Development of Adlerian Play Therapy

Now . . . before we get into the meat (and potatoes for those vegetarians out there), I wanted to include a small story about the genesis of Adlerian play therapy. When I was taking my doctoral practicum class, clients were sparse. One day, the professor asked, "Who in this class has taken a course in play therapy?" We all stared dejectedly at him. None of us had taken a course in play therapy. Next he asked, "Who has taken a course in counseling children?"—still no reply. Finally, looking a little desperate, he asked, "Who has experience working with kids? Aren't any of you teachers?" I raised my hand, rather timidly, having realized that I really did not have the kind of background he wanted me to have. I said, "I used to teach elementary school. Now I counsel in a high school. I have some background in working with young children but not counseling them."

He replied,

> It will have to do. We need this client. We just don't have enough to go around this semester. I'll have a doctoral student who has a lot of experience and training in play therapy supervise you by watching every session. It will be like on-the-job training. You'll do fine.

With that comment, I started on a learning process that I hope will never end. I began to learn about using toys and play to communicate with children.

This particular client, Claire, was a child who lived in a foster family. Her birth parents had decided the previous year that they no longer wanted the responsibility of caring for a child. They had dropped their 7-year-old daughter off at the local shopping center and left town. Child Protective Services had placed the little girl with a foster family. Claire was dealing with her abandonment and her grief and hurt by being aggressive toward the other children in the family. During the years she had lived with her birth parents, Claire had not experienced a great deal of structure and supervision. She had pretty much gotten to do whatever she wanted to do. Now that she was living in the foster home, she was having difficulty adjusting to having structure and rules. She was verbally abusive to her foster parents and blatantly violated all of the family rules.

Although Claire's foster parents wanted her to participate in some form of counseling, they had neither the time nor the resources to get her to the clinic. Part of my responsibility in having Claire as a client was to pick her up at her day-care center and drop her off after we were finished.

Quite truthfully, when I read the intake form on Claire and her life, I was terrified. This reaction was not necessarily rational. I had taught emotionally disturbed children with problems much worse than those described on the intake form. However, teaching them and being their counselor seemed worlds apart, and I was afraid that I would not be able to help Claire. Even worse than that, I was afraid that my lack of training, my not knowing how to do play therapy, might even hurt her.

I spent that entire week trying to become an instant expert on play therapy. I stayed up late every night and spent the entire weekend reading books on play therapy. I borrowed class notes from students who had taken play therapy courses from Dr. Garry Landreth and memorized them. I spent several hours on the telephone talking to the doctoral student who was going to supervise me. I observed experienced students at the counseling center doing play therapy with children. Almost all of the information I gathered was about *nondirective* play therapy, an approach in which the counselor focuses on reflecting what the child is saying, doing, and feeling in the belief that when children's feelings are expressed, identified, and accepted, they can accept their feelings and that frees them up to deal with them (Landreth, 2012). This was 1984, and there was little written in the field, and almost all of it was focused on nondirective strategies.

By the time I drove over to the day-care center to get Claire, I was a walking (driving) encyclopedia on nondirective play therapy. However, I was a little concerned about two things: my personality and my theoretical orientation. From what I had seen in my observations and read about nondirective therapy, I was not sure whether my personality and the way I usually interacted with people—especially children—was consistent with this approach. I tend to be rather bouncy and loud. My interpersonal style and my counseling style tend to be directive and active rather than nondirective. I was also having cognitive dissonance in that I had already decided that Adlerian theory fit the way I conceptualized people and I believed therapy helps people to make changes in their lives. I was not sure how I was going to reconcile those beliefs with the nondirective perspectives on people and change.

I had anticipated that Claire might be hostile and unwilling to go to the university center with me. Contrary to my prediction, she was jumping up and down with anticipation. She was feeling very special about coming to the university. Claire and I had a nice chat in the car on the way to the center, getting to know each other and being a little silly. She told me some about her "real" family and her foster family—who she liked best in each and what she liked to do with them. I think I was more nervous than Claire. We were both going on an adventure, but she was more confident than I was that the adventure would be a positive one.

When we got to the clinic, I took her on a little tour so that she could get used to the facility. We continued to talk and laugh together. Then I took her into the playroom, and I said, "This is our playroom, and you can do many of the things you want to in here." I sat in the chair and watched her explore the playroom. I tracked her behavior and restated the content of the statements she made to me. Whenever I noticed her expressing a feeling, whether it was verbally or nonverbally, I reflected that feeling to her. When Claire asked me to play with her, I told her that I could tell she wanted me to play with her, but this was her time to play by herself. When our time was up, we walked down the hall and back to my car, laughing and talking. We repeated this routine five or six more times.

The feedback from my supervisor and my professor was positive, but I was rather uneasy. I felt uncomfortable and stilted in the playroom, as though I was trying to play a part. I felt that my rapport with Claire was better outside the playroom than it was in the playroom. In the playroom, I felt tense—trying to always say the right thing, the right way—and bored. I was watching her, trying to follow her lead and understand the thoughts and feelings she expressed, but it seemed as though she never allowed herself to show very many of her thoughts and feelings in the playroom.

I was also not always comfortable with letting Claire lead the way. She avoided revealing any thoughts or feelings about her family, her abandonment, or her present situation in both her play and her conversation. She seemed to want to pretend that none of the sad or scary things in her life had ever happened. She liked to pretend that she was a fairy princess who could control all those around her with her magic wand. Even though her foster parents reported that her behavior was still out of control at home, she acted in the playroom as though everything in her very chaotic life was perfectly under control. Although I realized that the play therapy process was gradual, I had a certain sense of urgency. If Claire's behavior did not improve, this foster family was also going to abandon her, and then she would face another rejection and upheaval in her life. I was not sure how to get to all of these problems simply following Claire's lead.

One day, on a drive back to the day-care center, all of my doubts crystallized when Claire said,

> Terry, why do you act like a funny, fun person on the way to the playroom and on the way back to day care, but you act kind of weird in the room with the toys? You don't smile very much, or laugh, or ask any questions. All you do is sit there and tell me what I am doing and saying. It's like you're not a real person in the playroom.

I realized at that moment exactly what the problem was. I was not a real person in the playroom. I was what I thought a nondirective play therapist should be, and that was not the real me. I was leaving my personality and my beliefs about people, my most valuable tools for helping people, outside the door of the playroom. I decided then and there to figure out a way to use both my personality and my beliefs about people in the playroom.

Because I already knew my personality and the way I viewed people fit with Adlerian theory when I was working with adults, I started researching Adlerian views about children. The majority of Adlerian therapists worked with children in the context of the family or schools, in the form of family therapy, parenting information for parents, or classroom management programs for teachers (Bitter, 2014; Lew & Bettner, 1998, 2000; Nelson, 2011; Sweeney, 2009). There were books, chapters, and articles on working directly with children, but none of the authors discussed in detail how to use play therapy from an Adlerian perspective (Adler, 1930/1963; Bordon, 1982; Dinkmeyer & Dinkmeyer, 1977, 1983; Lord, 1982; Nystul, 1980; Yura & Galassi, 1974).

I began to try out ways of bringing my personality and my beliefs about the nature of people into the playroom with Claire and with my subsequent play therapy clients. I took courses and workshops from professionals who were experienced in different approaches to play therapy. I also received extensive supervision in my counseling with children and their parents. Adlerian play therapy evolved from this process. Over the years, I have continued to experiment with ways of integrating the practice of play therapy and the concepts and strategies of Individual Psychology. Adlerian play therapy is not a finished approach; it is still evolving. Kristin and other professionals are helping fuel this evolution. I hope that reading this book helps you to be more real with your clients and that you take the ideas that make sense to you and use them to better understand and help the children with whom you work. It is essential to get training and supervision from experienced professionals, whether you are developing skills in a new area of counseling or perfecting the skills that you have already. Consultation with other therapists can help us continue to grow, both personally and professionally.

Overview of the Chapters

The primary focus of Chapter 1, "So, What Is Play Therapy and Why Should We Care?" is an explication of the various elements of play therapy, such as the rationale for using play and toys as a part of the therapeutic process, toy selection, arrangement of the playroom, and types of clients appropriate for play therapy.

Chapter 2, "How on Earth Can You Combine Adlerian Theory With Play Therapy?" contains a discussion of various concepts essential to the understanding of Individual Psychology, including social embeddedness and social interest, lifestyle, purposiveness of behavior, Crucial Cs (connect, capable, count, and courage), personality priorities, feelings of inferiority, mistaken beliefs, private logic, and creativity and self-determinism. In Chapter 2, we briefly introduce the four stages of Adlerian therapy and the way these phases are operationalized in Adlerian play therapy, the goals of Adlerian play therapy, and the role of the counselor in Adlerian play therapy.

Chapter 3, "What Is Up With This Kid? Using Adlerian Concepts to Understand Children," is a guide to the various Adlerian concepts used in this approach to play therapy to help the counselor gain an understanding of children and their dynamics. The emphasis is on the Crucial Cs, goals of misbehavior, and personality priorities. We use case study vignettes to illustrate concretely how the counselor can apply these concepts with children in play therapy.

In Chapter 4, "Consulting With Parents and Teachers? Oh Dear!" we start with an explanation of the importance of including parents and teachers as active participants in the Adlerian play therapy process and a discussion of techniques for involving parents and teachers and keeping them involved. We explain methods for (a) building a relationship with parents and teachers; (b) exploring the lifestyle of parents and teachers and gathering information about their perceptions of the child's lifestyle; (c) helping parents and teachers gain insight into their lifestyles and into the child's lifestyle; and (d) reorienting and reeducating parents and teachers by teaching encouragement skills, behavior management skills, and communication skills. Personality priorities and Crucial Cs are key elements in this process, so this chapter includes descriptions and examples designed to illustrate how these concepts can be applied to consultation with parents and teachers.

Adlerian therapy depends on an egalitarian relationship between the therapist and the client. Chapter 5, "Where Do I Begin? Building an Egalitarian Relationship With the Child," presents ideas on how to build a democratic relationship with the child in play therapy. It contains a discussion about how you can use (a) tracking, restating content, and reflecting feelings to help the child feel comfortable in the playroom; (b) metacommunicating and returning responsibility to the child to convey understanding and respect to the child; (c) questioning strategies to communicate interest in the child's life; (d) actively interacting with the child, including role-playing techniques and other relational tools to make a strong connection with the child; and (e) cleaning the room together to strengthen the relationship with the child. In the last section of this chapter, we include a case example to illustrate how to use these skills to build a relationship with the child.

Encouragement and limiting are essential elements in Adlerian play therapy. In Chapter 6, "Just Say 'Yes!' Just Say 'No!'? Encouraging and Limiting," you will learn how to use encouragement to build the relationship with the child, help the child gain self-confidence and a sense of self-efficacy, and help cement changes the child has made in his or her behavior and attitudes. This chapter provides an explanation of how you can tailor encouragement strategies on the basis of the Crucial Cs and personality priority of the client. In the second half of this chapter, we provide Adlerian techniques for setting limits, an explanation of appropriate limits, and methods for helping the child learn to generate alternative appropriate behaviors. This chapter closes with case examples designed to illustrate how to integrate the steps in the limit-setting process and a discussion of how to tailor strategies for limiting on the basis of the child's Crucial Cs, goals of misbehavior, and personality priorities.

Adlerian therapists view lifestyle as the individual's characteristic way of understanding situations and interacting with others. As you explore the child's lifestyle, you will begin to understand how the child views self, the world, and others. Chapter 7, "Who Is This Kid, and How Did He Get This Way? Exploring the Child's Lifestyle," contains various strategies you can use to investigate the child's lifestyle, including exploring the atmosphere and birth order in the child's family and early recollections. The case example begun in Chapter 5 is continued, illustrating a practical application of this phase of Adlerian play therapy.

In Chapter 8, "What Do I Do With All This Information? Developing Adlerian Lifestyle Conceptualizations and Treatment Plans," you will learn to take the information gathered in the exploration of the child's lifestyle and the exploration of the parents' lifestyles (and sometimes the teacher's lifestyle) and integrate all of these data into a formal conceptualization of the child (and parents and teacher when appropriate). This chapter also contains an explanation of how you can use this conceptualization and a systematic understanding of the intrapersonal and interpersonal dynamics of the child to develop a treatment plan for the child (and for the parents and the teacher when necessary). Conceptualizations and treatment plans for the child and her parents from the case study begun in Chapter 5 and continued in Chapter 7 help to make these processes more concrete.

Adler believed that clients will not change their behaviors until they gain insight into their lifestyles. The third stage of Adlerian play therapy uses various strategies to help children gain insight into their lifestyles and behavior. Chapter 9, "Lions and Tigers and Bears, Oh My! Helping the Child Gain Insight," details ways to use metacommunication and tentative hypotheses, mutual storytelling and other metaphoric techniques, drawing and art, sand tray activities, dance and movement experiments, and adventure therapy techniques, immediacy, confrontation, and humor to help children begin to understand how they view self, the world, and others and how these perceptions affect their behavior. To help children generalize their learning, you will often point out connections between what happens in the play session and what happens in other places. A continuation of the case example from Chapters 5, 7, and 8 illustrates a practical application of this phase of Adlerian play therapy.

The purpose of the last stage of Adlerian therapy, described in Chapter 10, "How Can I Wind It Down and Wrap It Up? Reorienting–Reeducating," is to help the client learn new ways of viewing self, the world, and others; new ways of behaving in various situations; and new ways of interacting with other people. In this stage, you might use brainstorming and problem-solving strategies to help the child generate alternative perspectives and behaviors. You might also actively teach skills that the child does not possess, such as social skills, negotiation skills, and ways of sharing power. The playroom becomes a laboratory in which the child can practice these new perceptions and skills in a safe, nonthreatening environment. This chapter also contains information about introducing a second child into the play therapy process and terminating the play therapy. A continuation of the case example from the earlier chapters illustrates this phase of Adlerian play therapy.

Chapter 11, "Who Me? Conduct Research?" is designed to encourage you (and anyone else who might be interested) to consider conducting research into Adlerian play therapy. The chapter contains information about the research support for play therapy, in general, and about research supporting Adlerian play therapy. We also explore considerations for conducting research and provide a detailed description of the skills needed in each phase of Adlerian play therapy.

We have compiled some supplemental materials for you to be able to use in your work with children, families, and schools. We have included some of the appendices from this volume and some handouts for parents on working with children with specific goals of misbehavior and those who struggle with specific Crucial Cs. We also included a "cheat sheet" to remind you of what you need to be considering as you conceptualize and develop treatment plans. If you want to do research, we have provided you with the checklists you can use for measuring treatment fidelity. (You could also use them for supervision of Adlerian play therapist if you want.) You can find these supplemental materials with the book in the ACA Online Bookstore at www.counseling.org.

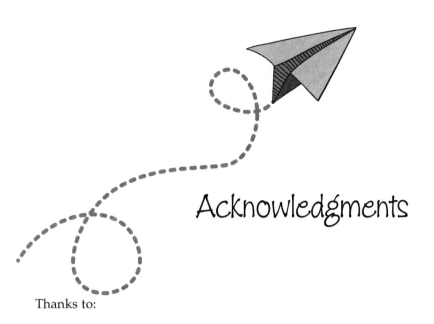

Acknowledgments

Thanks to:

Laura Brown and the rest of Leigh Johnson-Migalski's 2014 Child
and Adolescent class at Adler University in Chicago for helping us
refine our explanation of faulty convictions.

Amy Lew and Betty Lou Bettner for developing and promoting the
Crucial Cs, their gift to the world of understanding children.

Leah, Dawn, Nate, and all the other amazing staff at
Cup of Joe in Cedar Falls, Iowa, the best coffee shop in the universe
for their support, encouragement, and brews.

• • •

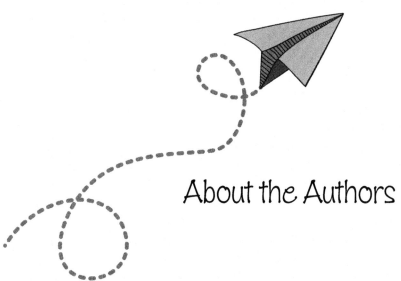

About the Authors

Terry Kottman, PhD, NCC, RPT-S, LMHC, founded The Encouragement Zone, where she provides play therapy training and supervision, life coaching, counseling, and "playshops" for women. Dr. Kottman developed Adlerian play therapy, an approach that combines the ideas and techniques of Individual Psychology and play therapy. She regularly presents workshops and writes about play therapy, activity-based counseling, school counseling, and life coaching. She is the author of *Partners in Play, Play Therapy: Basics and Beyond,* and several other books.

• • •

Kristin Meany-Walen, PhD, LMHC, RPT-S, is an assistant professor of counseling at the University of Northern Iowa. Kristin actively researches and publishes articles that explore the effectiveness and implications of Adlerian play therapy. In addition to researching and teaching, she works with children and adolescents in school-based settings and private practice.

• • •

Chapter 1

So, What Is Play Therapy
and
Why Should We Care?

We are so glad you asked. Officially, according to the Association for Play Therapy (2014), play therapy is "the systematic use of a theoretical model to establish the interpersonal process wherein trained play therapists use the therapeutic powers of play to help clients prevent or resolve psychosocial difficulties and achieve optimal growth and development" (para. 1). Formally, play therapy is an approach to communicating therapeutically with clients using toys, art materials, games, sand trays, and other play media, giving clients a safe and nurturing relationship in which they can explore and express feelings, gain insight into their own motivation and into their interaction with others, and learn and practice socially appropriate behaviors (Henderson & Thompson, 2011; Homeyer & Sweeney, 2011; Kottman, 2011; Landreth, 2012; Ray, 2011; Schaefer, 2011). Informally, play therapy is counseling clients (usually kids, but not always) with toys, stories, and art. VanFleet, Sywulak, and Sniscak (2010) said it most succinctly: "In play therapy, whatever form it takes, *play is the therapy*" (p. 12). The counseling in play therapy uses the natural language of children—play—as the basis for the therapeutic interaction. In the play, much of what the child does and says takes the form of symbolic, metaphoric communication about the relationships and situations in the child's world.

> *A play therapist is not looking for children to be able to discuss cognitively the meaning or content of their play, but recognizes that the subconscious issues of children float to the surface through play.* Also, as the subconscious material arises, children utilize play and the environment created by the play therapist to "work through" issues that they need to address to regain emotional and social health. (VanFleet et al., 2010, p. 12)

Depending on the approach to play therapy, counselors can use many different ways to communicate with the client: free play, directed play, games, art techniques, metaphoric storytelling, bibliotherapy, drama therapy strategies, adventure therapy techniques, sand tray activities, prop-based play interventions, movement and dance, music, or any other creative process therapeutically. In writing this, we realized that if we described all of these strategies in detail, this book could get to be thousands of pages long and prohibitively expensive, so we needed to figure out how to give you access to the information without clogging up the first paragraph of our book with reference after reference. So we have created an appendix (see Appendix A) that lists references and resources for these processes. In Adlerian play therapy, we use all of these modalities in our work with children and their families (and sometimes their teachers too).

Rationale for Play Therapy

What makes play therapy therapeutic? Schaefer and Drewes (2013) listed the "therapeutic powers of play" as facilitating communication (self-expression, access to the unconscious, direct teaching, and indirect teaching); fostering emotional wellness (catharsis, abreaction, positive emotions, counterconditioning fears, stress inoculation, and stress management); enhancing social relationships (therapeutic relationship, attachment formation, social competence, and empathy); and increasing personal strengths (creative problem solving, resiliency, moral development, accelerated psychological development, self-regulation, and self-esteem). If you are interested in learning more about these therapeutic powers, Schaefer and Drewes (2013) have a chapter on each of them in their book.

Play therapy is a particularly appropriate approach to counseling children because play comes naturally to children. This is because most children under the age of 10 have not yet developed the abstract reasoning skills and verbal abilities to sit in the counselor's office and be articulate about their thoughts, emotions, and behaviors. Young children seldom have the ability or the comfort level to talk articulately about what is bothering them, but they are almost always comfortable using toys and play to express themselves through metaphors (Kottman, 2011; Nash & Schaefer, 2011).

Most young children have better developed receptive language skills than expressive language skills, and they can frequently comprehend concepts even when they do not know how to verbalize them. This discrepancy means that the counselor might be able to use words to successfully communicate ideas to children, even when they would not have the abstract verbal reasoning skills or the vocabulary to be able to articulate these ideas themselves. Because of this, the counselor can frequently combine play and verbalizations to communicate with children.

Everything the child does or says in the session communicates information about how the child views himself or herself, the world, and others (Kottman, 2011). The 6-year-old whose father is dying of cancer takes all the toy soldiers, lays them down on the floor, looks at you and says, "They died. Nobody could help them." The 4-year-old bosses you around and is resistant to any suggestion that he should take turns or share power with you. The 8-year-old takes the father doll and has him push the mother doll down the stairs in the dollhouse, laughing while the child doll tries to stop him. The child's play and the child's verbalizations in play are metaphors representing the child's lifestyle and life situation. In Adlerian play therapy, your job is to observe the child in the playroom, understand how the child's lifestyle and life situation are represented through the play, and begin to articulate that understanding to the child. You will use a combination of interactive playing, verbal interpretation, and storytelling to communicate with the child.

For older elementary-age children, adolescents, and adults, who usually do have the capacity for describing what is going on with them, there are other reasons for using play therapy as an intervention. With older elementary-age children (sometimes referred to as "tweens") and teenagers, play can be used to build the relationship simply because it is fun and joy filled (B. Gardner, 2015; Milgrom, 2005). This can sometimes short circuit the natural resistance of adolescents, who are often dragged (sometimes literally kicking and screaming) into therapy. Play therapy also provides a chance to allow adolescents to use the therapy relationship to "move back and forth along the developmental continuum while striving for health individuation and separation from a nonabusive and nonpunative adult" (Milgrom, 2005, p. 4). Being invited to use kinesthetic and visually engaging props, toys, art supplies, and other materials to express themselves also takes some of the pressure of sitting across from someone, making eye contact, and being expected to reveal their innermost secrets. Using play as the vehicle for communication also encourages adolescents to express their creativity and to learn through experience, which can instill a sense of ownership over what they are learning (B. Gardner, 2015; Kottman, Ashby, & DeGraaf, 2001). Being allowed to communicate symbolically through metaphor rather than be forced to communicate directly can help adolescents feel safe to explore and express painful and/or frightening thoughts, emotions, and experiences that they might otherwise want to hide or avoid.

Although most adults enter therapy of their own free will, they too can benefit from play therapy. According to Brown and Vaughn (2009) and Frey (2015), grown-ups need to play too. Play therapy can provide adults the opportunity to develop insight, reduce stress, improve communication, facilitate self-efficacy, and encourage mastery. It can also boost creativity, mind–body integration, happiness, cooperation, insight, and social skills. I (TK) combine play therapy with talk therapy in my sessions with adolescents and adults, and I find that play therapy facilitates relationship building, making the sessions more enjoyable for me and for the clients. Play therapy also helps to create and deepen insight, allowing clients to "get" things they would have normally resisted, and building bridges from the abstract conversations in our sessions to the day-to-day situations in the clients' "real" lives.

Setting for Play Therapy

The "perfect" setting for play therapy is a custom-designed playroom that you get to create for yourself with unlimited space, resources, and support. However, in the real world, it is the rare and lucky counselor who has an opportunity to work in such a setting. No matter where you work, the play space should reflect your personality and your philosophy about children and play therapy. It should also reflect the particular clientele you serve. Some counselors have very few toys and limited visual stimulation in their play space because they work with children who are easily distracted. Other counselors have many costumes and a stage in their play space because they, personally, are dramatic and like to use drama and enactments with their clients. Other counselors who have a need for order and structure, or who have limited space, have everything built in—shelves, kitchen appliances, and/or sandbox.

In Adlerian play therapy, the most important factor in playroom design is the attitude of the counselor. If the counselor feels happy, safe, and comfortable in the playroom, children will feel happy, safe, comfortable, and welcome. It is essential for the Adlerian counselor to remember to use flexibility and imagination to create a space in which the counselor can feel comfortable and clients can feel safe.

The "Ideal" Playroom

Landreth (2012) provided a thorough description of the practical considerations in designing that rare accommodation, the "ideal" playroom. He suggested that the ideal playroom would be approximately 12 feet by 15 feet (3.6 by 4 meters), with an area of between 150 and 200 square feet (approximately 14 by 19 square meters). This area gives the child room to move about, at the same time keeping her or him relatively close to the play therapist. A room this size could comfortably accommodate several children at one time if the play therapist wanted to work with a small group.

It is important to be able to provide the child with privacy in the playroom. In a play space where there are windows or a one-way mirror, it is helpful to have curtains or blinds so that the play therapist or the child can decide whether he or she needs some privacy if something sensitive is happening in the play therapy process.

It is also useful to have washable wall coverings and floors so that children can make messes without fear of negative consequences. Probably the best arrangement is to cover the floors with vinyl tile, which is an easy surface to clean or replace if necessary, and to paint the walls with a neutral color of washable enamel. However, when this is not possible (e.g., if the space is carpeted or you don't have unlimited money), you must consider how you will react if paint or glue or some other messy material is spilled on the floor. If this will be a major problem for you (or will put you in a place where you can't keep on maintaining a positive attitude toward the child who makes a mess), it would be wise to make accommodations (e.g., avoid using finger paints or put plastic on a section of the carpet that is designated as the art area) or set strict limits about these materials.

There should be as many shelves as necessary for accommodating the toys and materials without being chaotic or crowded. So that short children can reach the top shelf, it is helpful if the shelves are no taller than 38 inches (96.5 cm). As a safety precaution, it is advisable that shelves for the toys be secured to the wall. This will prevent accidental occurrences like the shelves being knocked over and purposeful occurrences like an angry child pulling them down on top of you (which also might make it difficult to maintain a positive attitude toward the child; Kottman, 2011; Landreth, 2012).

The ideal playroom contains a sink with cold running water but without potentially dangerous hot water. If possible, having some countertop space (either connected with the sink or separate) is helpful for providing a place for artwork or "schoolwork." A cabinet for storing materials such as paint and clay, extra paper, and so forth is extremely helpful because then you can control access, which might prevent a child from running amok with your supplies. (See Chapter 6 on limiting, just in case you don't have such a cabinet.) A chalkboard or white board attached to a wall or put on an easel provides a safe means for self-expression. A small bathroom opening into the playroom can eliminate power struggles about trips down the hall to the bathroom, but if this is not possible, then a bathroom close to the playroom will work almost as well (Kottman, 2011; Landreth, 2012).

Noise must also be a consideration in the placement and features of a playroom (Kottman, 2011). The playroom should be located as far as possible from other populous areas in the building so that noise will not present a problem—either to other inhabitants of the building or to people passing. It is also helpful if the ceiling of the room can be fitted with acoustical tile to reduce noise; however, again, unless you have an unlimited supply of funding for equipping your playroom, this may not be reasonable.

The furniture in the room should be constructed of wood or molded plastic and designed to accommodate children. If you will be working with parents in the playroom, it is important to have furniture available to accommodate them too. You will need a place to sit. This chair (or pillow) should support your level of comfort without being so relaxing that it would undermine the ability to focus on the child or stay awake when you are talking to parents (Kottman, 2011).

Other (Perfectly Lovely) Spaces for Play Therapy

A counselor does not need an ideal playroom to be able to use play therapy with children. (We would like to mention that neither of us has anywhere close to a "perfect" or even "ideal" setting for play therapy, and we do just fine with our clients.) Kristin brings toys in a bag into an elementary school and works wherever there is a free space that day. Terry relies on the kindness of a school counselor who generously shares her office—a room that has a big table in the middle of it where school personnel have meetings after school. Having a conference table in the middle of your playroom is less than ideal, and yet it works—the kids haven't ever read this book (or any play therapy book), so they don't know anything about an ideal playroom.

Many play therapists "have toys—will travel" (Drewes & Schaefer, 2010; Niel & Landreth, 2001). School counselors frequently travel from school to school, bringing a bag of toys with them. Some counselors who work for community agencies go into children's schools or homes to conduct play therapy sessions. Many counselors who work for hospitals or hospices go into hospital rooms and do play therapy on hospital beds. Counselors who do not have the ideal space for play therapy or even a permanent setting for sessions will need to find a space for sessions that is somewhat quiet, free from distractions, and relatively private. (This is sometimes difficult to do in a crowded home or school, so you need to remember just to give it your best shot and hope for the best.) It is helpful to have a place (a table, a spot on the floor) to set out the toys in a predictable arrangement. To avoid lugging around tons of stuff and injuring yourself, you might even choose to bring different toys to the session depending on what you want to work on with that child in a particular session. Other than those modifications, the play therapy process in a less-than-ideal space is identical to the play therapy process in an ideal space.

Toys Appropriate for Adlerian Play Therapy

Because toys are the medium of communication for the child in play therapy, their selection must be a carefully considered process (which is hard for us because we would buy every toy that has ever been manufactured and stuff it in our playrooms if we could). In evaluating which play materials to include as therapeutic components of a playroom, the counselor should consider whether they (a) facilitate a broad range of creative and emotional expression; (b) allow for both verbal and nonverbal exploration and expression in the playroom; (c) are considered interesting and fun by children; (d) can be used in a projective or metaphoric play; (e) can be used by children across a range of developmental levels; (f) provide experiences for children in which they can feel successful; (g) allow for both individual play and interactive play; (h) would be appropriate across different cultures; and (i) are well made, durable, safe, and sanitary (Kottman, 2011; Landreth, 2012; Ray, 2011).

In the course of the play therapy, the child will use the toys and play media to (a) establish a positive relationship with the counselor, (b) express many different feelings, (c) explore and reenact real-life situations and relationships, (d) test limits, (e) strengthen self-concept, (f) improve self-understanding, and (g) enhance self-control (Landreth, 2012). In Adlerian play therapy, it is essential to have toys that the child can use to (a) explore family constellation and family atmosphere; (b) examine mistaken beliefs, perceived threats, and past traumas; (c) explore control and trust issues; (d) explore and express feelings related to family dynamics and relationships with others; (e) explore and express their unique ways of gaining significance and relating to others; (f) explore and express their creativity and imaginations; and (g) practice new attitudes and behaviors.

To provide toys that allow for all of these aspects of the child's experiences, Adlerian play therapists equip their "tool boxes" with five general categories of toys: family–nurturing toys, scary toys, aggressive toys, expressive toys, and pretend–fantasy toys. It is not necessary to have all of the toys in each of the following lists (and it would be crazy to try—there wouldn't be any room for you and the child in your playroom). It is, however, essential to have representative toys from all five different categories of play media. A study exploring children's use of toys in the playroom suggests that children frequently use toys from each of the general categories (Ray et al., 2013). The more choices children have for expressing themselves, the more likely it is that they will communicate clearly. You will need to balance the need for a wide range of possibilities for the play with the need to have a playroom that is not so crowded that it is overwhelming to you and the child.

Family–Nurturing Toys

Children use these toys to build a relationship with the therapist, explore their understanding of and feelings about family relationships, and recreate events that occur outside the playroom. Many times, Crucial Cs (connection, capability, counting, and courage); goals of misbehavior; and family constellation–birth-order issues (see Chapters 3, 6, and 7 for in-depth discussion of these topics) are expressed and explored with family–nurturing toys. Children frequently use these toys to act out their family atmospheres or to give or ask for nurturing. This category includes the following toys:

- dollhouse
- baby dolls
- a cradle
- animal families
- people puppets
- baby clothes
- baby bottles
- stuffed toys
- child-sized rocking chair
- warm, soft blanket
- pots, pans, dishes, and silverware
- toy cleaning supplies, like a broom and dustpan
- several different families of bendable dolls
- sand in a sandbox, along with various family figures that can be used in the sand
- "humanlike" figures (like clowns) that could be used for a family but are not obviously a family
- empty food containers, like cereal boxes and cans
- wooden or plastic kitchen appliances (if space is available)

Regardless of the racial composition of your client load, it is essential to provide children with dolls from different ethnic groups. This encourages children to explore differences and similarities among various groups of people and to explore their own identities. If possible, it is also important to have several families of each different ethnic group. This allows children who live in stepfamilies or extended families to have enough dolls to recreate their own family structures in the playroom. It also allows children being raised by gay or lesbian couples to have two mother dolls or two father dolls. The clothing of the dolls in the families should be removable (Velcro and elastic construction are appropriate) because many children (especially those who have experienced sexual abuse) will want to disrobe and rerobe the family members. You don't want to have to keep gluing the clothes back on or buying new dolls every time the dolls get naked.

Sometimes a doll family looks too much like a real family, which can be extremely threatening to some children. These children may be more willing to act out family dynamics with the kitchenware or with a family that does not look like a family of human beings. To facilitate this process, we like to have several different species of plastic animal families—with some of the figures being bigger than others so they can represent parents and children. This gives children a way to explore what is happening in their families without directly dealing with the issues inherent in the family. They can even put a family together with members represented by different species. For instance, I (TK) might choose a deer for my sweet husband, a monkey for my mischievous son, and an otter for myself to represent my playfulness.

With some children, exploring family situations is so scary they cannot even use the kitchenware or animal families. We always have several small figures (like clowns or gnomes) that kind of look like people but are not clearly identifiable as a family. This provides children who are extremely protective of their family and children who are anxious about revealing family dynamics an even more indirect vehicle for dealing with family and nurturing issues without having to acknowledge that the subject of their play is a family.

Scary Toys

Children use scary toys to deal with their fears, both reality and fantasy based. They can act out being frightened, and they can protect themselves from whatever they find frightening or ask the counselor to protect them. The following are examples of toys that fit into the scary category:

- plastic snakes
- toy rats
- plastic monsters
- dinosaurs
- insects
- dragons
- sharks
- alligators
- a variety of puppets representing fierce, dangerous, or scary animals (e.g., wolf, bear, alligator)

Children tend to have specific reactions to the scary toys. For instance, to some children, the insects are very frightening, whereas to other children, the insects are fascinating or funny. This makes it important to have a wide variety of scary toys in an effort to have something that is anxiety provoking across the spectrum of children. We also like to have several of each type of scary toy. This way, children can make scary families, combat multiple foes, and have "good" scary toys and "bad" scary toys of the same species.

Although it is not essential to have all of these different scary toys, we think the play therapist should be sure to include several snakes and an alligator or shark with a hollow body and sharp teeth in the collection. Many sexually abused children use the snakes in their play, sometimes directly acting sexual abuse out with the phallic shape of the snake and other times using the snake to act out a sense of menace or threat. They like to put other toys or their fingers into the open mouths and pretend to bite them off with the teeth as a way to act out self-protection themes. Having snakes in the playroom allows children to act out these themes without talking about them directly. It also allows them to do "mean" things to the snakes as a way of dramatizing the punishment of an abuser and practicing their ability to keep themselves safe. It is important to note that many other children also like to play with these toys, so it is not diagnostic of abuse if a child plays with them. Sometimes a snake is just a snake.

If a child has a specific fear or has experienced a particular situation that provokes anxiety, it is frequently helpful to obtain a toy that could more exactly represent the feared object. For example, if DeShawn witnessed a train hitting and killing his little sister, it might be important to have a train in the playroom so that he could process his feelings about this incident. If LeeAnn is having recurrent nightmares about ghosts chasing her, it might be helpful to have ghost puppets in the playroom. Also remember, though, unless you want or need an excuse to buy more "stuff," if a child really needs something to represent a certain fear, he or she can (and will) make something else in the playroom into the desired object. For example, if DeShawn could not find a train in the playroom, he could pretend that a car or a small box was the train.

Aggressive Toys

Children use aggressive toys to express feelings of anger and fear, to learn to act out their aggression symbolically, and to explore issues of power and control. They can also use aggressive toys to protect themselves symbolically from dangers, such as those represented by the scary toys. Toys from this category are also very important for children in building a sense of competence. When children recognize they can keep themselves safe (through symbolic play with the weapons in the play therapy session), they often begin to develop an enhanced sense of self-efficacy in other settings as well. Aggressive toys can also provide a valuable means for children to test limits in a safe environment and to develop self-control. The following is a list of some of the toys in this category:

- a stand-up punching bag–bop bag
- weapons (e.g., dart guns, play pistols, holsters, swords, rubber knives)
- toy soldiers and military vehicles
- small pillows for pillow fights
- rope for tying up
- foam rubber bats
- plastic shields
- handcuffs

We make sure that the weapons in our playrooms do not look like realistic weapons—they are usually brightly colored or ray gun–type guns. We do this to convey that there is a distinction between real weapons that are dangerous and should not be used for aggression toward another person and pretend weapons that we can use to act out aggression symbolically.

Handcuffs and ropes are excellent toys for playing out themes of power and control. They are also useful for exploring trust issues. However, you must be sure to obtain handcuffs that have a catch release built in because children quite frequently appropriate the keys to handcuffs, and they vanish, and you don't want to be handcuffed to a chair in your office for several hours before someone comes to liberate you.

Some counselors prefer not to include aggressive toys or weapons in their offices. This is usually because of their desire to avoid conveying to the child that violence of any kind (whether it is symbolic or actual) is acceptable or their need to comply with the rules of conduct in the setting where they work (e.g., school counselors). You must follow the dictates of your own thinking about this issue. It is certainly possible to do Adlerian play therapy without aggressive toys. Children will find other means to play out the themes of protection and aggression without having the actual toys to represent these factors. For example, if Cassandra wants to act out shooting a monster who is chasing her in a session, she will use her hand or a magic wand or a puppet or anything else that she picks up to make an imaginary gun.

It is also important to examine your own issues with power and control, trust, and fears before stocking the playroom with scary or aggressive toys that you might find personally threatening. Children can sense when certain toys bring up issues for the counselor, and they may use this awareness to try to intimidate or control the course of therapy. You can decide on rules of play for the aggressive toys in advance of the session with the child. For instance, my (TK's) rule is that children can handcuff themselves any way they want, but they can only handcuff me with my hands in front of my body. Because I feel afraid when I do not have control of my hands, I am not comfortable with my hands immobilized behind my body. I use self-disclosure about this feeling when I explain the handcuffing rules with children who want to handcuff me. I no longer have a stand-up punching bag–bop bag in my playroom because I noticed that many of the children with whom I work, who have major anger and aggression issues anyway, just hit the bag the entire session, to the exclusion of anything else. I found myself being bored in these sessions, and when I took the children back to their classrooms after our sessions, they were inevitably less self-regulated and more aggressive than they were at other times—which did not endear me to their teachers.

Expressive Toys

Expressive toys and other art materials are excellent vehicles for getting a picture of how children see themselves, others, and their world. Children use expressive toys to explore relationships, portray self-image, express feelings and cognitions, understand problems, work out solutions, and foster creativity. Expressive toys can also provide an avenue for developing skill mastery, which can enhance self-confidence, self-esteem, and self-control. Most expressive toys are artistic or creative in nature. The following is a sample list of some of the materials in this category:

- an easel and tempera paints
- watercolor paints
- finger paints
- crayons
- markers
- colored pencils
- glue
- glitter glue
- feathers
- pompoms
- newsprint
- Play-Dough or clay
- pencils
- scissors
- Scotch tape
- egg cartons
- pipe cleaners
- stickers
- sequins
- beads
- needles and thread
- socks for puppets
- brown lunch bags
- yarn
- poster board
- construction paper
- butcher paper
- magazines for potential pictures and words for collages

It is important to have a place for children to create with the expressive toys. For many projects, this simply means a large clear space on the floor of the play area. If you are lucky enough to have an actual playroom, a child-size table or desk is the perfect work surface for some projects. (This is really the only time that I [TK] appreciate the conference table sitting in the middle of my playroom—we can spread out when we are doing art–craft projects.) Depending on the age of the children, their overall messiness, and the requirements for neatness in the play setting, you may also want to have a paint smock to protect children's clothing and a large piece of plastic (like a picnic tablecloth) to protect the surfaces in the playroom.

This, too, is an area that you need to consider before you go out and acquire a lot of potentially messy art materials (unless you are obsessed by office supplies like we are). If you are going to be anxious about paint spilling on the floor or glue getting in the carpet, this will be an area of vulnerability that some children will use to control the course of the sessions. You need to be very comfortable with the art materials with which you supply your playroom (and with the consequences should the art materials be misused or an art project gone amok). I (KMW) was initially very anxious about the possibility of paint colors being mixed and the impact that would have on the next client's ability to use the paints. I was challenged to explore my own personal rules (not guidelines—rules) about cleanliness, order, and fairness so that I could be flexible with children who accidentally or intentionally mixed paint colors.

Pretend–Fantasy Toys

Children use pretend–fantasy toys to explore different roles, express feelings, experiment with alternative behaviors and different solutions to problems, pretend to be someone else, and act out situations that they observe in real life. They may also use these toys to explore relationships and ideas metaphorically and to communicate about their attitudes, thoughts, and experiences. Pretend–fantasy toys can include materials from the following list:

- masks
- doctor kit
- magic wands
- blocks and other building materials
- pieces of different colors of fabric
- human figure puppets
- animal puppets
- broom, iron, ironing board
- telephones (two)
- zoo and farm animals
- puppet theater
- knights and a castle of some kind
- big pillows
- figures of alien or outer space creatures
- hats, jewelry, neck ties, purses, costumes, and other dress-up clothes
- cars, trucks, airplanes, and other transportation toys
- fantasy creature puppets (e.g., witch, wizard, unicorn, ghost, princess, alien)

In choosing pretend–fantasy toys, you should try to avoid toys that have a preconceived identity. By eschewing toys associated with television shows, movies, and the like, you can encourage children to use the toys as projective objects, imposing their own ideas and identities on the toys. I (KMW) often bring in my clothes or clothes of my family members that are no longer worn, such as shoes, bridesmaid dresses, belts, suits and ties, and hats. If you have costumes and hats, you will need to consider the possibility of lice and other nasties. Some counselors choose to avoid having these play items because of this pitfall, and others make allowances by using hats and costumes that can be frequently cleaned or disinfected. You will need to decide what is best for you, your clients, and your setting.

Toy Arrangement

It is important to have the toys openly displayed so that children can have ready access to them (Kottman, 2011; Landreth, 2012; Ray, 2011; VanFleet et al., 2010). They should be within easy reach and placed in a predictable place. By keeping toys in the same basic position, the play therapist can establish that the play area is a place where the children can feel safe and expect consistency and routine. (This is often in contrast to what they experience at home and in other settings—and that is sometimes true for us in our lives as well—it is lovely to have a place where you know you can count on things being in a predictable place.) It is easier for children to remember where the toys belong if the toys are arranged by category. If the counselor has a permanent playroom, it is helpful to have shelves for the toys. Many counselors who use play therapy as a modality for working with children have to make do with shared quarters or temporary spaces. This should not have an adverse effect on the counselor's ability to conduct play therapy sessions. For those who have to cart their toys with them, just putting them on the floor or a table in a predictable order will work just fine.

Types of Clients Appropriate for Play Therapy

Most play therapists work with young children—usually between the ages of 3 and 10 years. It is possible to work with children under the age of 3, especially with children who have experienced trauma (Carey, 2006; Gil, 2010; Levine & Kline, 2007; Schaefer, Kelly-Zion, McCormick, & Ohnogi, 2008; Terr, 1990), but the process is slower and more concrete than it is with older children. Depending on the developmental level of the child and the child's ability and inclination to talk about what is happening in his or her life, play therapy can also be used with older children. There are even therapists who use play therapy with adolescents and adults (Ashby, Kottman, & DeGraaf, 2008; Frey, 2015; Gallo-Lopez & Schaefer, 2005; B. Gardner, 2015; Garrett, 2014; E. Green, Drewes, & Kominski, 2013; Ojiambo & Bratton, 2014; Schaefer, 2003; Trice-Black, Bailey, & Riechel, 2013). The playroom will appeal to older preadolescent and adolescent children if it contains more sophisticated toys, such as craft supplies, carpentry materials, office equipment and supplies, and older looking play media, or if the therapist provides a more structured activity-oriented process. (And this will give you a reason to buy more "stuff" if you need an excuse.)

In our experience, Adlerian play therapy works well with a variety of presenting problems. This intervention strategy is especially helpful with children who have (a) power and control issues (e.g., temper tantrums, power struggles with teachers or parents, bullying behavior), (b) experienced some kind of trauma (e.g., sexual abuse, neglect, parental divorce, death of a close friend or family member, natural disaster, adoption), (c) poor self-concepts (e.g., giving up easily, making denigrating remarks about self), (d) difficulty getting along with their families (e.g., sibling rivalry, fights with parents), and (e) poor social skills (e.g., trouble making friends, not getting along with classmates).

Working With Diverse Populations

With ever-changing dynamics of the world today, it is essential for play therapists to become competent to work with children and families of various diverse populations (Chang, Ritter, & Hays, 2005; Gil & Drewes, 2005; Kim & Nahm, 2008; Post & Tillman, 2015; Vaughn, 2012). As part of understanding the impact a child or family's culture has on the development, worldview, and interpersonal behaviors of clients, play therapists learn skills and concepts so that they can be prepared to be responsive to diversity among their play therapy clients and their families (Gil & Drewes, 2005; Post & Tillman, 2015). Diversity can include, but is not limited to, race, ethnicity, faith, spirituality, political views, sexuality, socioeconomic status, age, acculturation, and ability–disability. To become culturally sensitive and culturally responsive, play therapists work to develop an understanding of their own cultural worldviews and an awareness of the impact of culture on clients and their families. A culturally responsive play therapist might have ethnically and culturally diverse dolls, nondescript toys, and multiple representations of faith included in the playroom. Play therapists who work with children from a variety of cultures can also include specific toys that could resonate with those children, such as dolls from specific regions of the world, currency from a variety of countries, and traditional clothing from children's native countries. Another example of cultural responsiveness would be a playroom designed to accommodate children who use a wheelchair, with toys, shelves, and chairs intentionally wheelchair height for easy access.

Different Approaches to Play Therapy

There are many different ways to use play in the counseling of children (and adolescents and adults). Each of the approaches to play therapy has unique methods of conceptualizing people, defining the role of the counselor, and interacting with clients and their parents. Depending on the counselor's beliefs about people, his or her personality, and the client population, the counselor may choose to adhere strictly to one particular theoretical approach to play therapy or to apply different approaches in an eclectic fashion. We believe that play therapists should seek out those approaches that are most congruent with their basic beliefs about people and their personalities. Schaefer (2011) and Crenshaw and Stewart (2015) provide detailed information about the major theoretical approaches to play therapy.

Summary

Play therapy is usually used as an intervention approach for working with young children who lack the abstract verbal abilities to articulate their difficulties clearly enough to receive support and assistance from counselors. Play therapy seems to work with children experiencing a broad range of difficulties. It can also be used as a modality to help older children, adolescents, and adults who would benefit from a fun, nonthreatening, creative expressive arts form of therapy.

When working with young children, the play therapist must carefully select toys that will help them express their thoughts and feelings. The arrangement of the toys and the atmosphere in the play therapy setting must provide comfort and consistency so that children will feel safe in acting out problem situations and relationships. When working with older children, adolescents, and adults, the play therapist will want to adapt the materials used to a more appropriate developmental level.

Although each approach to play therapy has its own philosophy and rationale for the play therapy process and the selection of toys, the Adlerian play therapist uses the play therapy process to help clients gain a better understanding of how they view themselves, others, and the world and to learn new attitudes to replace self-defeating attitudes. The Adlerian play therapist chooses toys designed to facilitate this exploration and to help clients learn new ways of interacting with others. Adlerian play therapy seems to work best with children and adolescents who have issues surrounding power and control; children and adolescents with poor self-concepts and social skills; and children, teens, and adults who have experienced some kind of trauma.

Further Resources

What is play therapy and how does it work?

http://www.a4pt.org/?page=APTYouTubeChannel
http://www.a4pt.org/?page=PTMakesADifference
http://cpt.unt.edu/about-play-therapy/what-play-therapy/
http://ct.counseling.org/2010/11/the-power-of-play/
http://c.ymcdn.com/sites/www.a4pt.org/resource/resmgr/Publications/
  Play_Therapy_Best_Practices.pdf

Playroom setups:
http://cpt.unt.edu/about-play-therapy/playrooms/
http://www.kimscounselingcorner.com/2012/08/20/unique-inexpensive-or-diy-ideas-for-a-play-therapy-or-childs-room/
https://www.pinterest.com/bluedaylily2/my-dream-play-therapy-office/

Play therapy publications:
http://www.a4pt.org/?page=PlayTherapyPub
http://cpt.unt.edu/researchpublications/literature-home/

Theoretical approaches to play therapy:
http://www.journalofplay.org/sites/www.journalofplay.org/files/pdf-articles/1-2-article-play-therapy.pdf
http://potentiality.org/drjwilcoxson/wp-content/uploads/2008/05/PLAY-THERAPY-Menassa.pdf

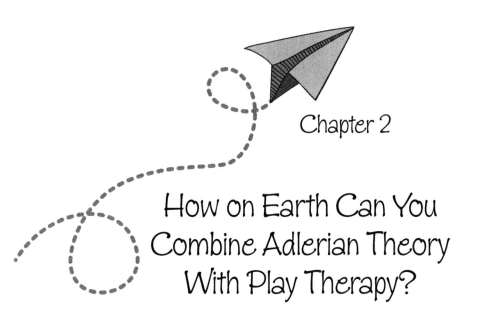

Chapter 2

How on Earth Can You Combine Adlerian Theory With Play Therapy?

The psychological theory developed by Alfred Adler in the early part of the 20th century, Individual Psychology, is the foundation on which Adlerian play therapy rests. The theory provides an explanation (one that makes a lot of sense to us and we hope it does to you too) of the nature of people—how their personalities are formed, how they interact with others, how they are motivated, and how they become maladjusted. We also like the Adlerian definition of the goals of therapy and description of the role of the therapist and have extrapolated them into play therapy.

As you explore the ideas in this chapter, you will need to examine your own beliefs about the nature of people, the goals of therapy, and the role of the therapist. We believe that a counselor should not practice Adlerian play therapy unless his or her basic beliefs about people and the job of the therapist are congruent with the basic tenets of Individual Psychology. These philosophical beliefs do not have to match perfectly at all points; that is unrealistic. However, if you are going to be an Adlerian play therapist, most of your convictions about the nature of people, personality formation, human motivation, and the counseling relationship should resemble those presented in this chapter.

Nature of People

A cornerstone of Adlerian psychology is the belief that people are indivisible, social, creative, decision-making beings whose beliefs and behavior have a purpose. Therefore, the individual is best understood holistically as a total being whose thoughts, feelings, and beliefs are present in a consistent and unified pattern of actions. (Carlson & Slavik, 1997, p. xi)

According to Adler, people are (a) socially embedded, (b) goal directed, (c) subjective, and (d) creative beings who must be viewed from a holistic perspective (Ansbacher & Ansbacher, 1956; Maniacci, Sackett-Maniacci, & Mosak, 2014). These are the basic tenets of Individual Psychology, and everything else in the theory is predicated on the idea that they comprise the key components of human nature. (In other words, we are "acting as if" these ideas are true and can be applied to understanding children, parents, teachers, and other people in the process of play therapy.)

People Are Socially Embedded

To truly understand a person, according to Adlerian theory, the counselor must remember that they are socially embedded—they are a part of a system of connection with other people. Adlerians believe that all human beings have a need to belong (Adler, 2011/1938; Ansbacher & Ansbacher, 1956; Jones-Smith, 2015; Maniacci et al., 2014; Sweeney, 2009), and they gain a place of belonging through their relationships with others. To establish and maintain a sense of belonging, children observe the world to determine a way they can gain significance and fit into different groups. The first group to which children belong is their families. (After all, these are the first people they encounter, other than the doctor who delivered them and the nurses in the delivery room.) As they grow older, children watch to see how the other members of their families react to different behaviors and attitudes. They note which of their behaviors gain attention and which do not, which promote a sense of belonging and which do not. Over time, individuals develop something that Adlerians call lifestyle. (We're sorry—there is a LOT of jargon in Adlerian theory, but if you will bear with us, we promise it will all make sense in the end and even be helpful in your understanding of your clients and your capacity to be helpful to them.)

Lifestyle
According to Maniacci et al. (2014, p. 66),

> Lifestyle (as the Adlerians define it) is the use of the personality, traits, temperament, and psychological and biological processes in order to find a place in the social matrix of life.

If a child cannot establish himself or herself as belonging to the family in a positive, useful way, he or she will determine a way to fit into the family in a negative, useless way. Eventually, this way of establishing his or her belonging becomes his or her lifestyle: the way the child views himself or herself, the world, and others and the repertoire of behaviors based on these views. Lifestyles are the individual's collected patterns of thinking, feeling, and behaving that help him or her navigate through life. They create a predictability and emotional safety. As the child grows and matures, he or she will act out his or her lifestyle in various social contexts: the neighborhood, school, work, dating, and marriage.

A useful tool in gaining insight into a person's lifestyle is the concept of *personality priorities* (Dillman Taylor, 2013; Kfir, 2011; Kottman & Ashby, 2015). Personality priorities constitute the most important aspect in an individual's striving for belonging. According to this typology, there are four possible priorities: comfort, pleasing, control, and superiority. To recognize the person's personality priority, the counselor examines (a) his or her personal reaction to the client, (b) the client's behaviors, (c) the client's presenting problem or complaints about life, (d) the client's goals for life, (e) the client's assets, and (f) the aspects of life the client expresses an interest in avoiding. (See Chapter 3 for more details about using personality priorities in play therapy and Chapter 4 for using them in parent consultation.)

A tricky thing about a person's lifestyle is that most of the time it is not obvious to the individual. Maniacci et al. (2014) described the lifestyle as a map for traveling through life's experiences that usually remains out of a person's awareness. One of the primary tasks of the Adlerian therapist is to observe the various aspects of the client's lifestyle and use a variety of strategies for helping the client become more aware of his or her patterns of thinking, feeling, and behaving.

Psychological "Boxes"

In most families, by the time the child is 6 or 7 years old, the entire family has a fixed idea about who the child is and how the child will behave. By the time the child has been in preschool or school for even a very short time, school personnel may also be locked into a set perspective on who the child is and how he or she will act. (With my [TK] son, Jacob, this happened in the first hour of kindergarten roundup.) These beliefs and expectations constitute a psychological "box" in which the child lives. This box can define who the child is and what the child does, becoming boundaries of the child's lifestyle. The box can be positive or negative, but in either case, it is almost always confining to the child. Examples of different kinds of boxes for a child:

- Mariah's box is being "the wild child." She takes risks and likes adventures. People expect her to be daring and dangerous. She believes she must up the ante and be more courageous and gutsy than others to be accepted and valued. She often accepts challenges and succumbs to peer pressure.
- Kiku's box is being "the smart child." She "must" always act and sound intelligent. Whenever she does something stupid or silly, she feels badly and may be punished. She "must" get perfect scores on schoolwork and score well on standardized tests.
- Armin's box is being "the lazy child." He is an underachiever who never does anything—at school or at home. Because everyone has low expectations for contribution or achievement from him, no one ever asks him to do anything.
- LeShandra's box is being "the good child." She "must" always behave perfectly. She is not allowed to make any kind of mistake, be messy, or whine. If she is ever less than perfect, either she is severely punished or everyone totally ignores her transgression, as if it did not happen.

- Alexander's box is being "the bad child." He believes that he "must" always behave abominably. He is not expected to do anything well, be thoughtful, or be well behaved. Even when he does something nice, he seldom gets credit for a positive thought or behavior because others believe that this is out of character for him, therefore suspect.
- Linnea's box is being "the phobic child." She believes that she "must" always be afraid to gain significance in the family. Other members of the family expect her to be afraid, so family life frequently revolves around protecting Linnea from whatever she fears. Her primary method of getting attention and feeling powerful is through her fear. When family members interact with her, it is usually to reassure her or to chastise her for being afraid.
- Kwazi's box is being "the responsible child." He assumes responsibility for his siblings and friends. Others depend on him to be reliable and prepared. His family expects that he will sacrifice his own fun to take care of the family's needs. The few times he has not made sound and trustworthy decisions, he was harshly ridiculed and punished for his "immature, selfish, and unreliable" behaviors.

What is really difficult about the box is when everyone in the child's life, including the child, begins to act as if these rigid expectations imposed on the child (from within and from the outside) constitute who the child is and must be. In many cases, when the child acts in ways that do not conform to the box, the other members of the family (or school personnel) give the child feedback that he or she must return to the expected patterns. At times when the child who is perceived negatively by others acts in socially appropriate ways, this gets discounted or ignored. If the child who is considered to be a "good kid" acts inappropriately, often other people make excuses for misbehavior (e.g., "She is just having a bad day" or "The other child provoked him").

When people have rigid expectations that dictate their thoughts, attitudes, and behaviors, they can get stuck in a trap. This situation becomes a snare when individuals begin to set up situations in which they re-prove to themselves what they already believe about themselves. They act as if their own internal picture of themselves is true, evoking a reaction from others that confirms that they do, indeed, belong in their box. For example, because Mariah believes that she is the wild child, she engages in dangerous behavior. Other children and adults who interact with her respond by being impressed or alarmed, sending her a message that she deserves praise and attention only when she can excite others with her over-the-top behaviors. This feedback spurs on Mariah to do more exaggerated and risky activities, believing that "typical" behavior will not be enough.

Social Interest

One of the ways we get the need for belonging met is through social interest. (We know—more jargon—sorry.) Adlerians believe people are social beings, born with the innate capacity to develop social interest and a sense of connectedness with other human beings (Kronemyer, 2009; La

Voy, Brand, & McFadden, 2013; Maniacci et al., 2014; Overholser, 2010; Watts, 2012). Social interest is

> the individual's awareness of belonging in the human community and the cosmos of which it is a part, and an understanding of his or her responsibility for the way the life of the community is shaped by her or her actions. It is a fundamental sense of being one amongst the others as a fellow being. Social interest . . . can be thought of as an index to successful adaptation (mental health): The more developed the community feeling, the more diminished the inferiority feeling with its associated sense of alienation, and isolation. (Griffith & Powers, 2007, p. 11)

This innate capacity must be fostered and developed, first by the family and then by other social forces, to flourish. As part of the development of social interest, children must form an attachment with their primary caretaker, who then helps them expand this connection—first to siblings, then to neighborhood children, classmates, teachers, and other people whom they encounter. If given the proper encouragement and stimulation, children eventually generalize their feelings of social interest to the entire human race, to the planet, and the other inhabitants of the planet. Social interest is considered a criterion for mental health (Nelson, Lott, & Glenn, 2007; Sweeney, 2009).

La Voy et al. (2013) stated that "the relationships of the individual to the single other and to the community at large are reciprocal and each contributes to the health and welfare of the other" (p. 282). Social interest or "community feeling" describes a person's connection to and appreciation of others' contributions to the betterment of the entire community. People who strive toward life's goals in ways that benefit others demonstrate social interest. People who selfishly move through life with behaviors that are socially useless or damaging to others demonstrate diminished social interest (Adler, 1927/1954).

Practical Implications for Adlerian Play Therapists

The belief in social embeddedness dictates that an Adlerian play therapist must consider the child and the child's behaviors in the context of other human beings rather than in isolation. Because the child's first social context is the family, you will want to explore the child's relationship with her or his parents and other family members to see how the child gains significance and a sense of belonging in the family. With older children, you will also consider other social contexts, such as the neighborhood, church, day-care center, and school.

Because of our belief that the child is socially embedded, we are reluctant to see a child in play therapy without conjoint parent consultation. We believe that a child's lifestyle can be best understood from the perspective of the child and the perspective of other family members, teachers, or other important adults and people in the child's life. To effect long-lasting changes, it is essential for (a) the child to make shifts in the way he or she sees him- or herself, others, and the world, and (b) the members of the family members to be willing to make adjustments in the way they view and respond to the child. If you work in a school or other setting in which it is sometimes difficult to involve parents, it is helpful to include other significant people in the system as a vehicle for exploring how the child is gaining a sense of belonging in that system.

Through the questions we ask during consultation, we try to understand how the child belongs within the contexts of the family, the neighborhood, and school. We may also go to the child's school or day-care center and observe his or her interactions with peers and teachers or consult with the teacher or the school counselor about the child's behavior and performance at school. We use all of the information that we gather this way to help us understand the child.

To get my own impression of how the child establishes significance in the family and how others in the family react to him or her, I (TK) quite frequently ask the entire family to come to a session or two so I can observe relationships, interactional patterns in the family, and how the personality priorities of each family member are played out within the family. One of the most important aspects of my explorations in this area is related to any rigid beliefs about and expectations of the child held by the child and by important others in the child's life—the child's box.

A huge part of our job in working with children is to avoid colluding with them around their boxes when they try to re-prove what they already believe about themselves. We try to make sure, when children act as if what they believe about themselves is true, that we do not react in a way that reinforces negative self-beliefs (or even positive self-beliefs, which can still be confining). Our purpose in doing this is to evoke the creative genius that lies in all children. In our consultation with significant others in the child's life, we work with parents, other family members, and teachers on changing their patterns of thinking about and reacting to children's self-defeating or self-confining thoughts and behaviors.

Most children who come to play therapy seem to have poorly developed social interest. We see one of our primary responsibilities to children and their families as the enhancement of social interest. We use our connection to children to encourage attachment to other people. We make sure that children know we find a great deal of joy in their company. We treat them with respect and expect them to be respectful to us. If children need nurturing, we are willing to act out nurturing scenarios in the playroom. We can feed one another, feed the dolls, rock in the rocking chair, and perform other loving behaviors. Before we dismiss a child from therapy, we often bring in a second child—a sibling, one of our other clients, or a friend of the child's—or include the child in a group play therapy process so that we can promote expansion of the child's connection to other people.

Keeping in mind that we are not going to be the primary influences in the child's life (after all, we might spend 45–50 minutes a week with a child, as opposed to the other people in the child's life, who spend much more time with the child), we work with parents to increase their sense of connection with the child, to teach them how to foster social interest.

Many times, we have one or both of the parents come into play sessions with the child. In these sessions, we model ways to interact with the child in positive, nurturing ways and invite parents to practice making a connection with the child. We frequently give specific homework to family members, assigning cooperative activities and fun experiences. In our parent consultation, we teach parents how to use encouragement to build a positive relationship with the child. We also teach parents strategies for helping the child to generalize a sense of social interest. These techniques include providing experiences of making connections with siblings, relatives, and neighbors; sharing and taking turns; making charitable contributions and volunteering to help less fortunate people; and acting on a concern about the environment and other species of creatures. When we are working with a child in a school, we also solicit help from teachers in building the child's social interest.

People Are Goal Directed

Another important Adlerian concept is the idea that all human behavior is purposive and goal directed (Adler, 1927/1954; Jones-Smith, 2015; Maniacci et al., 2014; Sweeney, 2009). Adler believed that people are neither motivated by instincts nor formed solely by experience, heredity, temperament, or environment. Although each of these factors has a certain amount of influence in the formation of personality and in determining behavior, the primary motivating force in human life is the movement toward various life goals. People choose their behaviors to move toward their goals. These goals may be out of their awareness, but they are still always moving toward them.

Recognizing Goals

In Adlerian therapy, recognizing a person's goals is one of the keys to understanding the person.

> If we know the goal of a person, we can undertake to explain and to understand what the psychological phenomena want to tell us, why they were created, what a person has made of his innate material, why he has made it just so and not differently, how his character traits, his feelings and emotions, his logic, his morals, and his aesthetics must be constituted in order that he may arrive at his goal. (Ansbacher & Ansbacher, 1956, p. 196)

The Adlerian therapist always looks at the client's behavior to explore the goal of that behavior. When the therapist and the client can understand the purpose of the behavior, this gives them a way to help the client decide whether he or she wants to continue to strive toward that goal and retain that particular behavior in his or her repertoire of behavioral choices. (We cannot emphasize enough how important considering the goals of behavior are—our students get very tired of us harping on this, but it is an essential component in the Adlerian play therapy process. If you can understand the goal of the clients' behavior, you have the key to helping them get their needs met in healthier ways.)

Although there are many different goals for people's behavior, Dreikurs and Soltz (1964) classified the goals of discouraged children's misbehavior into four basic categories: attention, power, revenge, and proving inadequacy. In trying to determine which goal the child is striving toward, you will want to consider several factors: the child's behaviors, other people's reactions to the child's behaviors, and the child's reaction to correction (Dinkmeyer, McKay, & Dinkmeyer, 2007; Dreikurs & Soltz, 1964; Nelson, 2011; Nelson et al., 2007). (See Chapter 3 for more information about these goals.)

As you help children shift away from misbehavior motivated by these four goals, you can also support them in replacing them with one or more of the goals of positive behavior: involvement, independence, fairness, and competence (Dinkmeyer et al., 2007). The first of these is the goal of *involvement*. Children who are motivated by this goal help others, acting out the belief that they can belong by contributing. Children striving toward the second goal, *independence*, believe that they can make responsible decisions and have age-appropriate power. These children are resourceful, exhibit self-discipline and self-control, and take care of themselves. Children moving toward the third goal of *fairness* are interested in cooperating and believe in turning the other cheek. In response to cruelty or hurt, these children return kindness and caring. Children motivated by this goal have usually experienced these values in their interactions with influential adults. The fourth goal is being *competent*. Children motivated by this goal believe that they can succeed. They want to learn to think for themselves and demonstrate competency and trust in themselves.

Another positive configuration of goals has been postulated by Lew and Bettner (1998, 2000), who suggested that children strive toward the Crucial Cs. In this model, children have a need for (a) *connecting* with others (the positive goal of cooperation), (b) being *capable* (the positive goal of self-reliance), (c) *counting* or being significant (the positive goal of contribution), and (d) having *courage* (the positive goal of resiliency). (In Chapter 3, we elaborate on each of these in greater detail—actually, we go on and on about them.)

Practical Implications for Adlerian Play Therapists

Most of the children who come to play therapy are striving toward goals of misbehavior rather than goals of positive behavior. As an Adlerian play therapist, you must be able to recognize both types of goals because the ultimate aim of therapy is to help children move toward the positive goals of behavior rather than the negative goals of misbehavior. Whenever you notice children in the playroom being motivated by the more socially appropriate goals, you can encourage the resultant behavior. You can also use children's gradual letting go of striving to attain the negative goals and moving toward the positive goals as a road to increased happiness and stability and a barometer of improving mental health.

People View Life Subjectively

Adlerian theory is based on a phenomenological perspective, which leads to the belief that people make decisions based on their subjective interpretation of facts rather than on actual facts (Adler, 1927/1954; Ansbacher & Ansbacher, 1956; Eckstein & Kern, 2009; Kronemyer, 2009; Maniacci et al., 2014). People filter reality through the already formed perceptions and conviction in their lifestyles, re-proving to themselves what they already believe about self, others, and the world.

Mistaken Beliefs

Young children are excellent at observing, constantly scanning their atmospheres for perceptions about themselves and the world, but they frequently make inaccurate interpretations of events and interactions (Sweeney, 2009). An example of an inaccurate interpretation would be when LaShandra, a 7-year-old girl, believes that her own misbehavior is the cause of her parents' divorce.

Because young children are egocentric, they tend to believe everything that happens in their lives is somehow about them. This can lead to misperceptions they incorporate into their lifestyles in the form of a set of basic convictions about themselves, others, and the world and the behavior that logically follows from those convictions (Griffith & Powers, 2007). These misperceptions and misinterpretations evolve into a plethora of *mistaken* beliefs—ideas about self, others, and the world that are self-defeating and discouraging. Mistaken beliefs can be convictions about self, others, and the world that are negative (e.g., "I am fat, so nobody will want to be my friend"), or they can be ideas that certain things can and must be true that are based on misconceptions (e.g., "Life is fair and certain" or "I am and must be perfect"). On the basis of these mistaken beliefs, people develop a private logic that frequently remains out of their awareness but that is the foundation for their reasoning and for many of their assumptions, decisions, attitudes, and behaviors. Oberst and Stewart (2003) defined private logic as "a way of interpreting reality as quite different than most people do" (p. 25). Adler suggested that this private logic interferes with the day-to-day functioning of individuals. He believed that it is more helpful for a person to develop common sense—"meanings in which others can share and which others can accept as valid" (Ansbacher & Ansbacher, 1956, p. 253). As LaShandra grows up, she might generalize from her belief that she is responsible for her parents' divorce to the idea that she is to blame every time something goes wrong in her relationships. On the basis of this private logic, she may decide to avoid friendships and other relationships. An Adlerian counselor would work with LaShandra to replace her private logic with common sense.

Feelings of Inferiority

Because there is always a discrepancy between the self-perception and the self-ideal, all people experience feelings of inferiority (Ansbacher & Ansbacher, 1956; Duba, 2012; Kottman & Heston, 2012; Maniacci et al., 2014). There are two types of possible responses to feelings of inferiority: discouragement or inspiration. (Obviously, we would like everyone in the world to go the route of inspiration rather than discouragement, but then we would be out of a job.)

People who are discouraged by their feelings of inferiority usually feel overwhelmed and worthless. In response to these feelings, they may choose a path of giving up or a path of overcompensating. Individuals who just give up and stop trying to act in a constructive manner respond to their feelings of discouragement by simply shutting down. They may look and act depressed or suicidal or they may just be extremely negative and discouraging to themselves and others. The second reaction to feeling overwhelmed by a sense of inferiority involves overcompensating. Individuals who have this reaction frequently develop a "superiority complex." They spend most of their time and energy trying to counter their own feelings of inferiority by proving that they are "in fact" *not* inferior to others—they are better than others. By working hard to be superior to others, they become fixated on outdoing others and letting them know that they have been outdone.

People who choose to be inspired by their feelings of inferiority use the discrepancy between what they want to be and what they perceive they are as a challenge. They work to overcome their feelings of self-doubt by trying to move toward their self-ideals. They do not allow themselves to feel overwhelmed by feelings of inferiority but rather use these feelings as a barometer to help them learn more about themselves and what they want to work toward improving in themselves, their relationships, and other aspects of their lives.

Practical Implications for Adlerian Play Therapists

In Adlerian play therapy, you must be aware of the subjective interpretation of various situations. As you gather information from the parents, the child, and the teacher, it is super helpful to remember that everyone involved in any given situation has a different view of the relationships and the circumstances involved. Sifting through the various perspectives, you will want to remind yourself that there is no one correct interpretation of reality. Because the child is the primary client, it is important to give extra thought to his or her viewpoint by trying to understand how the child is interpreting the events and interactions that he or she observes. This way, you may be able to recognize times when the child is using private logic and incorporating potentially negative, harmful, or self-defeating (mistaken) beliefs into his or her lifestyle.

Presentation is a key in trying to prevent the child from including faulty assumptions or negative interpretations in his or her lifestyle. Because adults are frequently guilty of telling children how they should interpret situations and what they should think about relationships and ideas, you offer your alternative interpretations tentatively. If you see something differently than the child does, it is sometimes helpful to offer "another way of looking at things"—not as a better interpretation but as a possible alternative, a different interpretation. You must pay close attention to your own interpretation of events and your verbal and nonverbal reactions to avoid conveying that the child should see things differently.

As an Adlerian play therapist, you will want to stay alert to indications that children are feeling overwhelmed by their feelings of inferiority and becoming discouraged. Some children act out a sense of discouragement by simply refusing to participate in life. They may act depressed, suicidal, withdrawn, underachieving, or any other form of shutting down. Other children act out a sense of discouragement by overcompensating for their feelings of inadequacy. They may bully others, brag, denigrate others, or otherwise artificially elevate themselves over other people.

One of the best intervention strategies with children who are having difficulty coping with their inferiority feelings is encouragement. (See Chapter 6 for ways to use encouragement in the playroom.) It is also important to teach the parents, teachers, and other adults who come into contact with children how to encourage them and help them learn to use feelings of inferiority as a challenge rather than a defeat.

People Are Creative

According to Beames (1992),

> Individual Psychology is deeply conscious of and rejoices in the uniqueness of each individual member of the human race. This uniqueness is seen to be the expression of a fundamental, mysterious creativity that is innate in each person. It is this creative element that takes the givens of life (heredity, environment) and interprets them, modifies them, expresses them in purely subjective and surprisingly unpredictable personal ways. (p. 34)

In Individual Psychology, the focus is on the special and wonderful qualities of each individual. As part of the quest to celebrate the creativity and uniqueness of each person, Adlerian counselors help their clients explore their assets; goals; Crucial Cs; personality priorities; private logic; and thoughts, emotions, and behaviors. The counselor takes a holistic view of life, examining clients' uniqueness across the five tasks of life: work, friends, love, finding meaning in life (spirituality–existential), and coming to terms with oneself (self–self-regulation); (Adler, 1931/1958; Bitter, 2012; Mosak, 1977).

Self-Determination

Adlerians believe that each human being expresses creative ability by making choices. Self-determination is a key tenet in Individual Psychology because it involves recognition of the human ability to choose unique interpretations of situations and relationships and to act as if those interpretations are true.

> [T]he important thing is not what one is born with, but what use one makes of that equipment. . . .To understand this we find it necessary to assume the existence of still another force, the creative power of the individual. (Ansbacher & Ansbacher, 1956, pp. 86–87)

This also means that human beings are free to make new decisions and interpretations, different from the ones they have made previously. The ability to make choices allows individuals to exercise their creativity and uniqueness constantly throughout their life span (Adler, 1927/1954). Of all the exciting (well, we think they are) concepts in Individual Psychology, this is one of my (TK) favorite ones because it means that people can change—their emotions, attitudes, thoughts, and behaviors—they can even change the direction of their lives, which makes Adlerian theory incredibly optimistic.

Practical Implications for Adlerian Play Therapists

The Adlerian belief in the ability to make new choices and to reinterpret situations provides a vehicle for play therapists to work with children to get out of their boxes, change their lifestyle patterns, increase their social interest, make shifts in the goals of their behavior, and a host of other forums for determining their paths. One of your primary responsibilities as an Adlerian play therapist is to discover how each child expresses his or her special and wonderful self and to convey a sense of celebration in his or her uniqueness to the child, parents, and other people who interact with him or her. Sometimes the child expresses uniqueness in a way that others do not appreciate. For example, Jeremy is frequently in trouble at school for offending others by cursing and using socially inappropriate language. As the counselor, Ms. Barry, gets to know Jeremy, she notices that Jeremy consistently uses language in very creative ways. It becomes Ms. Barry's job to help Jeremy to recognize and celebrate this unique asset and realize that he can use his unique command of language in more constructive, useful ways.

Goals of Therapy

According to Maniacci et al. (2014), the major goals of Adlerian therapy are to help clients to (a) enhance their social interest; (b) decrease their feelings of inferiority; (c) overcome their feelings of discouragement while recognizing and using personal resources; (d) make changes in their life goals and in their mistaken beliefs about self, others, and the world; (e) alter negative motivation or selfish values; (f) gain a sense of equality with others; and (g) become cooperative, contributing members of society. Not all clients need help with every one of these goals. During the initial sessions, the therapist and the client (and/or the client's parents and/or teacher, depending on the circumstances) collaboratively determine which therapeutic goals are appropriate for the client. In play therapy, the Adlerian counselor uses play, stories, art, sand tray, movement and dance, and other therapeutic strategies to move the child from destructive goals and misbehavior toward constructive goals; foster the Crucial Cs; increase the child's social interest; adjust any self-defeating beliefs about self, others, and the world; reduce discouragement; and help the child to acknowledge his or her personal assets (Kottman, 2011).

Four Phases of Adlerian Play Therapy

Individual Psychology includes four phases of the therapy process: (a) building a relationship, (b) exploring the client's lifestyle, (c) helping the client gain insight into his or her lifestyle, and (d) reorienting and reeducating the client (Jones-Smith, 2015; Maniacci et al., 2014; Watts, 2013). In Adlerian play therapy, the counselor goes through the first three phases with the child in the playroom. The fourth phase is practiced within and outside of the playroom with the goal for the child to use his or her positive resources outside of the playroom. The four phases are also used in consultation with important adults in the child's life, such as teachers and parents.

In the first phase, the counselor uses tracking, restatement of content, reflection of feelings, questioning strategies, active interaction with the child, cleaning the room in a collaborative manner, encouragement, and limit setting to build an egalitarian relationship with the child, using the metaphor of the child when appropriate. Simultaneously, the counselor uses strategies such as paraphrasing, feeling reflection, encouragement, and identification of personality priorities and Crucial Cs to build a relationship with the child's parents during parent consultations. If the play therapist is consulting with teachers, these same skills are essential to establish rapport with them as well.

To investigate the child's lifestyle, during the second phase, the play therapist uses observation of play and other interactions, questioning techniques, and art therapy strategies to gather information from both the child and the parents about the goals of the child's behavior, the Crucial Cs, personality priorities, the family constellation, family atmosphere, assets, private logic, and early recollections. The counselor organizes this information into a conceptualization of the child to be shared with the child and the parents during the third phase of therapy: helping the child and his or her parents gain insight into the child's lifestyle. In the parent consultation, the counselor is also exploring parents' ideas about themselves as parents, parenting strategies, marital issues, and personal issues that may be interfering with the parents' ability to positively interact with the child. Treatment plans outlining goals and strategies for working with the child and the parents stem from the understanding developed during the second phase.

As part of the process in the third phase, the counselor uses tentative hypotheses, interpretation, metaphors, art techniques, confrontation, immediacy, and humor to help the child examine his or her attitudes, perceptions, feelings, thoughts, and actions to decide which of these he or she wants to change and which he or she wants to continue. In parent consultation, the counselor uses these same tactics to help parents increase their understanding of the child and his or her motivation, enhance their insight about themselves as parents, and make decisions about parenting strategies to support the changes the child is making.

In the reorientation–reeducation phase, the counselor helps the child and parents operationalize these decisions in play therapy sessions, in the family, and in other settings. The play therapist uses brainstorming, problem solving, and teaching to convey various interactional skills to the child and parenting skills to parents. Practicing the newly acquired knowledge and skills in sessions helps the child and parents consolidate what they have learned before they practice them in other situations, coming back to the play therapist for encouragement and learning to encourage one another.

These phases are not discrete. The counselor continues to build the relationship throughout the process. The counselor may choose to combine techniques to help the client gain insight into his or her private logic or faulty assumptions during the information-gathering process or to teach some new skills (reorientation–reeducation) as the client gains insight. In many circumstances (e.g., school, private practice, agency settings), the counselor may feel pressure to hurry the process and go directly to the reorientation–reeducation phase. It is essential to resist this temptation and go through all four phases without skipping any.

Beware of trying to take a shortcut approach. In our experiences with children and their families, skipping phases simply does not make for an effective, lasting intervention. It is like putting a Band-Aid on the problem. If you do not take the time to build a relationship with the client or to understand the dynamics of the problem, there is little motivation on the client's part and little therapeutic leverage on your part to help the client make meaningful, positive change. If you only establish rapport and explore the problem but do not work to help the client gain insight, the client has no basis for making and sustaining behavior or attitude changes. The cumulative experience of going through each of the four phases is necessary for the client to feel motivated, identify his or her own resources, and constructively put positive changes into action.

Role of the Therapist

The role of the Adlerian therapist is active and directive. The therapist provides information, guidance, positive modeling, reality testing, encouragement, respect, and supportive confrontation (Jones-Smith, 2015). In Adlerian play therapy, the role of the therapist is extremely fluid, changing according to the phase of therapy (Kottman, 2009, 2011). During the first phase, the play therapist is relatively nondirective, acting as a partner who invites the child to share power and responsibility in sessions and inviting parents to feel a sense of collaborative investment in the therapeutic process. A big component of the therapist's role during this phase is to encourage the child and the parents so that they gain self-confidence and a sense of competence.

In the second phase, the role of the play therapist shifts into a more active and directive mode. The therapist acts as a detective, gathering information about the child's and the parents' attitudes, perceptions, thought processes, emotions, interactions, and so forth. At the end of this phase, the therapist develops a conceptualization of the child's lifestyle and a treatment plan for working with the child, parents, and teacher when appropriate (Kottman, 2009, 2011).

The play therapist is again a partner during the third phase—a partner with essential information to communicate to the child and to the parents.

Most of the time during this phase, the play therapist is very directive. The therapist challenges long-held, self-defeating mistaken beliefs about self, others, and the world; invites the child and the parents to make changes in attitudes and perceptions; nudges both the child and the parents to master additional Crucial Cs; encourages increased social interest; and facilitates movement in a host of other facets of the family's functioning (Kottman, 2009, 2011).

In the reorientation–reeducation phase, the play therapist is an active teacher and encourager. The primary function of the therapist during this phase is to help the child and the parents learn and practice new skills for adding to their behavioral repertoire and apply new more positive self-perceptions and perceptions of others in their daily lives. The therapist usually spends time in session teaching and providing opportunities to practice assertiveness skills, negotiation skills, social skills, parenting skills, communication skills, and other useful strategies that the child and the parents can use to interact with others and cope with problem situations (Kottman, 2009, 2011).

Culture: Ahead of His Time

As Adler developed and published his ideas about human nature and how people develop, he was conscious of the role of culture on the creation of lifestyle. However, like other theorists of his time, he drew from his own experiences. Thus, the values of peace, equality, holism, and social interest are not global values, and adaptations may need to be made where values vary significantly (Sperry & Carlson, 2012).

Adler brought attention to gender roles within society with his concept of "masculine protest" (Jones-Smith, 2015; Kottman & Heston, 2012; McBrien, 2012), which was based on Adler's disagreement with Freud's early beliefs about women's drive to be like men. Adler believed that the presumption that the differences between sexes created men to be superior was a social or cultural phenomenon that was, in fact, discouraging to all sexes (Adler, 1927/1954).

Adler also believed that a person could not be understood without understanding of his or her social experience or culture. He was adamant that the climate in which people lived and experienced life produced the challenges and encouragement from which people created their lifestyle. In other words, a person's culture and the perception of one's place in that community and society at large play a role in the person's beliefs about self, others, and the world (Oberst & Stewart, 2003).

The Journal of Individual Psychology took note of the importance of culture around the world and how it intersects with Adlerian theory. A special issue of the journal, edited by Jon Carlson, was devoted to Adlerian theory and various cultures such as Islam (Alizadeh, 2012), Bulgarian (Walton & Stoykova, 2012), Asian (Sun & Bitter, 2012), Greek (Nicoll, Pelonis, & Sperry, 2012), and South African (Brack, Hill, & Brack, 2012). Other, more specific topics related to Adlerian theory and culture have been published as well. Oryan (2014) described the importance of understanding culture when working with parents and families. Duba Sauerheber and Bitter (2013) described implications for religion and spirituality in terms of Adlerian counseling.

Adlerian play therapy works well with a wide spectrum of children from various cultures and ethnic groups (Fallon, 2004; Kottman, Bryant, Alexander, & Kroger, 2009).

> Adlerian concepts are congruent with the values of many ethnic and cultural groups. The congruence exists primarily due to the considerable flexibility of Adlerian cognitive and action-oriented techniques. The Adlerian emphasis on the individual's subjective view and interpretation of his or her world leads to response as well for ethnic values and perceptions. (Herring & Runion, 1994, pp. 218–219)

As an Adlerian play therapist, you will be responsible for continuously learning about and understanding various cultures and the impact that culture may have on your clients (Gil & Drewes, 2005; Hinman, 2003; O'Connor, 2005; Post & Tillman, 2015; Vaughn, 2012). It is important to remember that cultural competence is a journey, not a destination. As a vehicle for continuing to develop cultural competence, you can continue to examine your beliefs and privately, or not-so-privately, held biases about other cultures. For example, some questions you could ask yourself about the beliefs that might affect your ability to work with diverse clients:

- What are your beliefs about the work ethic or intelligence of low-income families?
- What are your beliefs about parenting and discipline styles of Asian or Asian Americans, Europeans or European American, and/or Africans or African Americans?
- What is your initial, internal reaction when you learn that a child is being raised by a grandparent, same-sex parents, single parent, and/or married parents?
- How do you schedule appointments with a child/family whose religious holiday practices are different from yours?
- What resources do you provide to families who do not speak your language?

Consultation, supervision, and personal counseling are productive strategies to increase your self-awareness, knowledge of, and effectiveness with other cultures.

Summary

According to Adlerian theory, people are socially embedded, goal directed, and creative. They view themselves, others, and the world from a subjective perspective. Because they conceptualize the child on the basis of this view of the nature of people, Adlerian play therapists must consider the impact of family and community on the child's personality and interactional patterns. They must also understand the purposes or motivations for the child's behaviors and the individual and unique ways the child gains a sense of belonging and significance. Through the four phases of Adlerian play therapy, counselors build rapport with the child, explore the child's lifestyle, help the child to gain insight into his or her lifestyle, and teach the child new ways of interacting with others, based on his or her altered view of self, others, and the world. During the four phases of Adlerian parent consultation, counselors build an egalitarian relationship with parents, explore parents' perceptions of their child's lifestyle and explore the lifestyle of the parents, help parents gain insight into their own lifestyle and that of their child, and teach them new skills for interacting with their child and seeing themselves as parents from a more positive, proactive framework. The ultimate goal in Adlerian play therapy is for the therapist to use the relationship with the child and his or her parents to help the members of the family enhance their understanding of their intrapersonal and interpersonal dynamics and to invite them to use that insight to make far-reaching, positive, permanent changes in their attitudes, thoughts, emotions, and actions.

Further Resources

Adlerian Psychology:

http://www.alfredadler.org/what-is-an-adlerian
http://alfredadler.edu/about/theory
http://www.goodtherapy.org/adlerian-psychology.html

Adlerian Play Therapy:

http://www.hbftpartnership.com/documents/uploadResources/
    Adlerian_Therapy_Kottman.pdf
https://www.psychotherapy.net/video/adlerian-play-therapy

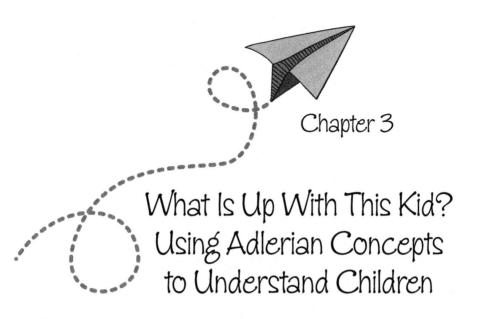

Chapter 3

What Is Up With This Kid? Using Adlerian Concepts to Understand Children

A big part (but not the whole) of doing Adlerian play therapy is using the Adlerian conceptualization process to gain an understanding of children and their dynamics. By considering children's Crucial Cs (Lew & Bettner, 1998, 2000), the goals of their misbehavior (Dinkmeyer et al., 2007; Dreikurs & Soltz, 1964; Nelson, Lott, & Glenn, 2013), and their personality priorities (Henderson & Thompson, 2011; Kfir, 1981, 2011), the Adlerian play therapist can develop a picture of children's lifestyles and how their lifestyles are reflected in the patterns of their behaviors, thoughts, attitudes, and relationships. We believe that all of these concepts can also be applied to adults, and we use these ideas to enhance our understanding in our consultation with parents and teachers and in our supervision and training of play therapists (Kottman, 2011). (See Chapter 4 for more about how to apply these concepts with parents and teachers.)

Crucial Cs

Lew and Bettner (1998, 2000) developed the concept of the Crucial Cs in response to the research, which suggested that children who are successful in life have strong relationships with others, feel valued by others, and have a perception that they have control over some of the facets of their lives. Compared with children who are struggling, children who are successful seem to have four beliefs that serve as unconscious behavioral guides. According to Lew and Bettner (2000), these beliefs are the internal certainty of

- Being *connected* to others, feeling a sense of family and community;
- Being *capable* of taking care of oneself;
- Being valued by others, knowing that one *counts* and makes a difference;
- Having *courage.*

When children have the vital protections provided by the Crucial Cs, they grow up responsible, productive, cooperative, self-reliant, resilient, resourceful, contributing, and happy.

During the first and second phases of Adlerian play therapy, you will observe the child's behavior, ask the child questions (in many different ways), and gather information from parents (and teachers when appropriate) with the goal of understanding whether the child has incorporated each of these beliefs into his or her self-perceptions (Kottman, 1999). On the basis of this investigation, you will make an assessment of whether each of the Crucial Cs could be considered an area of strength or weakness for this particular child. On the basis of this assessment, you can plan ways of fostering the Crucial Cs that the child has not incorporated into his or her belief system, using interactions in the playroom during the third and fourth phases of therapy and helping parents and teachers learn to foster this internal protection within the child.

Connect

Children need to have a sense of belonging, a feeling of connection with others (Lew & Bettner, 1998, 2000). Those who have the desire to connect with others in positive ways, the skills needed to connect with others, and the confidence in their own ability to connect with others feel socially secure and believe that they belong. They can reach out to others and make friends. They can build and maintain cooperative positive relationships with other children and with adults. (These are the kids who don't usually get sent to therapy, so you probably won't ever interact with them professionally.)

When a child who has this sense of belonging comes to play therapy, he or she will quickly build rapport with you, behaving confidently and comfortably in the partnership in the playroom. As you gather information from the child and from parents and teachers, it will become apparent that the child easily makes and keeps friends at school and in the neighborhood and interacts positively with other members of the family.

Although Lew and Bettner (2000) did not address this issue, in our experience there are children who seem to have only partially incorporated a belief in their ability to connect but do not have complete confidence in this ability (Kottman, 1999). These children are usually a little tentative in forming a relationship with the counselor in the initial stages of therapy, but they are open to the possibility of a comfortable connection. According to other-report and self-report, they are able to form relationships with others but may struggle with maintaining friendships and developing a strong social network.

Children who have not learned the value of social interest or have not acquired the skills necessary for connecting with others feel isolated and insecure (Lew & Bettner, 1998, 2000), and they often get sent to play therapy. These children do not believe that they belong and therefore act as if they do not belong. When they act as if they do not belong and expect to be rejected by others, they usually get feedback from others that this belief is accurate, which reinforces their sense of disconnection. Sometimes children who do not connect in constructive ways decide that connecting through negative means is better than not connecting at all. As a result of this decision, these children often seek attention in negative, self-destructive ways to give themselves a way to feel that they have a place in a group or the family, even if it is a negative place.

In the playroom, these children will have difficulty connecting with you, sometimes avoiding eye contact, resisting coming into the playroom, refusing to follow your suggestions about possible collaborative activities, and so forth. As you gather information from parents and teachers about the social interactions of children who do not believe that they can connect or do not have the social skills necessary for connecting, a picture forms of consistent difficulty in making friends and maintaining relationships with others—at home, at school, in the neighborhood. These children tend to be social rejects, social isolates, or scapegoats.

During the first phase of play therapy with children who do not have the confidence or skills necessary to connect with others, you will need to balance working to build the relationship with restraining yourself from pushing them into a relationship before they are ready (or deciding that, really, you don't actually want a relationship with them). You need to re-member this follows their usual pattern of re-proving what they already believe about themselves and others. You will want to avoid conveying disapproval or discouragement about their ability to connect. It is helpful to do more tracking, restating content, reflecting feelings, and encouraging with these children than you do with children who can connect more easily.

Once you feel as though you have begun to build a connection, you can move into the second phase of therapy very slowly, asking just one or two questions and only asking the children to do activities such as drawing or a puppet show if you feel that they will have fun doing them. It is essential to work on strengthening the connection with the child throughout the second phase. If it ever feels as though your exploration of the child's lifestyle would threaten the relationship, you will want to wait on the investigation to make sure that the relationship does not suffer.

During the third phase of Adlerian play therapy, you can use toys, stories, books, or examples from your other relationships or the child's situation to process the value of building relationships, the child's feel-ings and beliefs about connecting, and the child's ability to connect. The following are some examples of these strategies:

- "I am thinking that the octopus is both excited AND scared about making friends with that fish."
- "Those puppets are being very friendly toward one another."
- "I would bet that the little girl in the story is worried that no one likes her. I think that she must feel really lonely."
- "Sometimes I get scared that my friends might like somebody else better than they like me, and I have decided to be friends with them

anyway because I really like having friends, even when I am not their best friend."

- "I have noticed that whenever I talk about other kids in your class, you think that there is no chance they would want to be friends with you. How do you think that keeps you from getting to be friends with them?" (You would only want to do this last one with verbally sophisticated children—because many gifted children fit into the "low in connect" category, this could be a very appropriate way to interact with them.)

With children who have low levels of social interest, we often use interventions that enhance a sense of the value of connection to others (e.g., bibliotherapy, metaphoric storytelling, role-playing, movement). We also work with their parents and teachers on communicating the message that caring about and connecting with others are important values. Some resources that might be helpful to parents and teachers would include *Social Rules for Kids: The Top 100 Social Rules Kids Need to Succeed* (Diamond, 2011), *The New Social Story Book* (Gray & Atwood, 2010), and *How to Make & Keep Friends: Tips for Kids to Overcome 50 Common Social Challenges* (Briggs & Shea, 2011).

In the fourth phase, we provide experiences such as modeling, role-playing, and puppet shows to help children learn and practice social skills. Often, we use activities from *Skillstreaming the Elementary School Child: A Guide for Teaching Prosocial Skills* (McGinnis, 2011) and *My Mouth Is a Volcano Activity and Idea Book* (Cook, 2009). We also teach parents and teachers to provide positive feedback to help children overcome negative beliefs about their ability to connect with others.

Capable

Children need to believe they are capable of taking care of themselves (Lew & Bettner, 1998, 2000). Children who feel capable are grounded in their own competence. They manifest self-control and self-discipline. These children know that they can rely on themselves, and they willingly take responsibility for themselves and for their own behavior. They have a realistic assessment of their own abilities, and when they set their minds to doing something, they have confidence that they can be successful. Because they believe that they are capable, they act with competence and self-assurance. Children with a strong sense of being capable express confidence in their ability to do things in and outside of the playroom. Listening to these children talk about home and school, you will notice that they have a strong sense of self-efficacy and a clear idea of things they can do well.

In the playroom, children who sometimes feel capable are hesitant about their abilities, but they are usually willing to try new things when the therapist encourages them to do so. They may report successful efforts but tend to focus on those times when they struggled rather than those times when they were triumphant. In describing situations in which they demonstrated competence, they frequently sound as if these successes surprise them. These children are open to positive feedback about specific accomplishments but sometimes hesitate to accept global complimentary comments from others. Some children feel situationally capable—my (TK) son struggled in school and rocked at video games. He was super confident about his abilities at Super Mario Bros., and at the same time he felt like a failure at school.

Children who do not feel capable frequently feel inadequate (Lew & Bettner, 2000). Their lack of belief in their own abilities becomes a self-fulfilling prophecy. Because these children do not have confidence in their competency, they repeatedly experience failure. They frequently sabotage their own efforts, making sure that the end results of their exertions prove what they already believe about themselves. Even in situations in which they are successful, they find ways to interpret the end results as confirmation that they have failed. Children who lack confidence in their own competence may try to control others by overpowering them. Sometimes these children use systematic defiance in an effort to communicate to others that they cannot be controlled. Other children who have not incorporated a sense of competence in their beliefs about themselves become overly dependent on others, expecting others to take care of them because they believe that they do not have the skills to take care of themselves.

Children who struggle with believing in their own competence express a great deal of self-doubt in play sessions. In the playroom, these children are quite reluctant to try new activities that require any kind of skill or expertise and are often unwilling to try new ways of playing with toys they "already know how to play with." In describing their experiences in other settings, they consistently provide evidence for their lack of competence, describing their failures in extensive detail and never mentioning any successes they might have had.

Encouragement is your primary intervention tool in all four phases of play (Kottman, 1999). You can concentrate on pointing out the child's assets and skills whenever possible. It is helpful to use your interactions with the child to explore possible areas in which he or she might feel competent and areas in which he or she considers that competence might be a future possibility.

You will want to start making guesses about the child's lack of belief in his or her capability in the third phase. You can "spit in the child's soup" about doubts about his or her ability to be capable, suggesting that this is not the most constructive or accurate stance to take. To do this, sometimes you will communicate through metaphor and want to directly address situations in the child's life. (See Chapter 10 for a detailed discussion of this technique.) Some examples of this strategy would include comments like the following:

- "When things get kind of difficult for that bunny, she decides that she just can't do it. Do you think that she really can't do it?"
- "In this story, the boy was pretty sure that he couldn't kick the ball, so he didn't even try. What do you think he should have done if he wanted to learn to kick the ball?"
- "You didn't want to try putting that dart in the dart gun because you didn't know how it went in there. Once you looked at the insides of the gun barrel, you figured it out."

- "You say that you can't paint pictures, and yet you have made some paintings that most kids who come in here would be very proud of."

Throughout the process, we invite the child to participate in activities in which we believe he or she can experience success (e.g., games that require little or no skill, puppet shows for which we generate the plot, and art projects that need no art talent). We also teach the child specific skills (such as knocking over a pile of blocks with a ball or working the catch release mechanism on the handcuffs) that we can use to help the child gain a sense of competence. We are constantly alert for the smallest sign of progress, a slight willingness to try something new, or an expression of pride or accomplishment and encourage the child for this movement toward a sense of capability. Sometimes it gets tiring to be an encouragement machine in the face of the child's discouragement and resistance to thinking about himself or herself in a more positive light. Don't give up—look for small changes, and remind yourself the child isn't just being a Negative Nancy or Discouraged Doug to frustrate you. The well-worn groove of negativity is hard to leave behind.

Count

Children need to know that they are significant and valuable, that they count without having to earn esteem or love from others (Lew & Bettner, 1998, 2000). Those who believe they count have confidence that they make a difference in the world and constructively contribute to the lives of others. These children feel valuable and valued. They acknowledge their inherent worth as individuals. Because they have faith that they do matter and that they can make a positive contribution, their behavior is constructive and helpful—they act in ways that make a difference in their families, their communities, their schools.

In the playroom, children who know that they count are confident that you will believe that they are special and important (Kottman, 1999). This is not arrogance but assurance that others value them without them having to do anything to get recognition and acceptance. They also recognize their positive contributions in school, at home, and in social situations. They frequently report situations in which they were helpful to others, serving as mentors to younger children, conflict managers on the playground, and so forth.

Other children believe that they only count if they are meeting some specific set of conditions (Kottman, 1999). For instance, they may think that they only count if they are taking care of others; are beautiful, athletic, or strong; or let others make all the decisions. Because their significance is conditional, these children work very hard at whatever it is that they believe makes them valuable. They are extremely anxious because they believe if they do not meet whatever condition that defines their worth, no one will care about them. Both of us tend to fall into this abyss—we tend to believe that we need to keep doing more, faster, and better—that our worth depends on our contributions—so we know it is hard to let go of this pattern.

In the playroom, children who believe that they count only if they meet certain conditions spend much of their time and energy working to make sure that those conditions are met. If you do not respond as these children expect, with comments that reinforce the conditional nature of their significance, these children often become extremely anxious or hostile. As they describe their interactions outside the playroom, these children make it clear that they perceive the only way they can gain acceptance is to comply with their specific set of conditions.

Children who do not believe that they count feel insignificant (Lew & Bettner, 2000). They often believe that no one notices them or hears what they have to say. Most children who feel that they do not count develop poor self-images. They may give up, try to intimidate others, or overcompensate by acting superior. Because these children believe that they do not have the ability to gain acceptance or make a difference in a positive way, they behave in negative ways or they withdraw from interaction with others, ensuring that they will not be accepted or make a constructive contribution.

In the playroom, the behavior of these children is usually designed to prove that they do not count. They may make negative self-statements, refuse to answer questions about their lives outside the therapy setting, perpetually defer to others, refuse to play, make comments about the therapist never listening, and so forth. These children report experiences from outside the play setting that confirm their belief that they are insignificant and worthless.

When building the therapeutic relationship with a child who does not believe that he or she counts, it is essential to convey an honest excitement about the child and that you get to spend time with him or her (Kottman, 1999). Make certain that you are focused on what the child is doing and saying and give the child feedback about how much you value your interaction and his or her opinions and experiences. It will be helpful to make comments that indicate your belief that the child is special and important, and in your consultation sessions, you can teach parents and teachers to do this as well. Some resources that might help them are *A Teaspoon of Courage: The Little Book of Encouragement* (Greive, 2006) and *Lunch Box Letters: Writing Notes of Love and Encouragement to Your Children* (Sperando & Zimmerman, 2007). You can also suggest *The 5 Love Languages of Children* (Chapman & Campbell, 2012), which contains suggestions for how adults can communicate that the child counts.

The child who believes that he or she counts conditionally is constantly scanning relationships for confirmation that people will only value him or her under those conditions. We are very careful to monitor and self-manage our comments and our nonverbal behaviors so that we can convey that our regard for the child is unconditional.

During the second phase, we ask questions designed to explore situations and relationships in which the child has felt significant or special, looking for experiences in which the child has made a difference. In helping the child to gain insight into his or her lifestyle, we metacommunicate about areas in which the child does not feel significant while using encouragement to suggest that there are other areas in which the child has potential for having a strong positive impact. It is sometimes helpful to construct therapeutic metaphors or use bibliotherapy books to inspire the child to believe he or she counts. We spit in the child's soup when the child discounts his or her impact or importance. Some examples of our doing this include the following:

- "I am really happy to see you today. Being with you brightens up my day."
- "When the boy in the story said that he was glad to see his friend, it sounded as if his friend didn't believe him."
- "You know a lot about working with cars. Based on what you told me today, I have a good idea of what is wrong with my Beetle. Thanks for helping me out."
- "When the llama thanked the pig for his help, the pig argued that he had been no help at all. What do you think about that?"
- "Even when you have good ideas in school, it sounds like you think that no one listens to you."
- "Seems like that Barbie thinks people only like her when she has nice clothes on and her hair is perfect. I think that anybody who didn't like her just because she was having a bad hair day wouldn't be a very good friend."

In the fourth phase of therapy, we try to find ways for the child to make a positive contribution in the playroom (e.g., finding a lost toy, helping to sharpen the colored pencils, and giving a younger sibling a tour of the playroom). We also suggest to parents and teachers that they find ways for the child to make a contribution to the family, the school, or the community in the spirit of making a difference in the world (e.g., helping Mom carry in groceries, bringing the milk from the cafeteria for the class snack time, or mentoring a younger child) and work with them to communicate unconditional acceptance and support for the child. I (TK) invite some of the children from the school where I do volunteer play therapy to patrol the school grounds with me and pick up litter. Although at first some of them are reluctant, seeing that we are making a difference has inspired several of them to suggest this as one of our activities during our sessions.

Courage

Children need to be courageous. They must be willing to face life's tasks and take risks even in situations in which they do not know whether they will be successful.

> For children to develop as fully as possible, they must have the courage to press on in the face of failure and fear. Courage is not the absence of fear; courage is the willingness to go forward and do what needs to be done in spite of the fear. (Lew & Bettner, 2000, p. 15)

Children who have courage feel hopeful, confident, and equal to others. Even when they are afraid, these children are willing to take chances because they believe they can handle challenging situations. They are resilient, not giving up or allowing themselves to be overwhelmed by discouragement or unduly influenced by the opinions of others. Children with courage say to themselves, "I know that I can handle what comes my way," and because of this belief, they can.

In play therapy, children manifest courage by being willing to take risks and try new behaviors and experiences (Kottman, 1999). They are flexible thinkers and are willing to share power without feeling threatened or diminished. They report situations outside the play setting in which they persist even when things are not working out the way they expected and in which they stand up for their personal beliefs even when others disagree with them. Parents and teachers of these children have reported courageous behavior and resilience. They have witnessed evidence that their children will not let themselves be overcome by fear.

Children who have some courage but are not completely courageous may be hesitant to try new activities. However, they are usually willing to accept encouragement and positive feedback from adults and peers. As they become more confident about their ability to deal with their own fears, these children gain a sense of hopefulness and equality, which results in increased courage. When this happens, it is incredibly inspiring and encouraging, one of the things that keeps both of us going back to the schools where we volunteer.

Children who do not have courage feel inferior to others, discouraged, hopeless, and inadequate. They are easily overwhelmed by fear and discouragement, avoiding challenging situations in which they might fail. Parents and teachers frequently report that these children give up easily, quite frequently developing poor work habits, school phobia, selective mutism, or depression. Because they do not try new experiences or enter into new relationships, demanding that little or nothing in their lives change, their passage through life confirms what they already believe about themselves—that they are inferior and inadequate.

In play therapy, a lack of courage manifests itself in children who simply will not take any risks or try any play experience that is not a guaranteed success. These children will do little or nothing in a play session, which can become very frustrating to the play therapist. Building a relationship with a child who lacks courage is rather slow going, so the key to this phase is patience (Kottman, 1999). You will want to temper your inviting the child to try new experiences with your willingness to go slowly enough that the child is not overwhelmed by anxiety. When you have a child who struggles with courage, do a lot of returning responsibility to the child. You should avoid doing things for the child that he or she can do alone, and avoid making decisions for the child. It is also helpful to metacommunicate about situations in which the child has taken even a small risk or tried something new.

These children tend to ignore questions during the second phase, making sure that they do not make a mistake in one of their answers. A response of "I don't know" is their usual reply to any other than factual questions. When this happens, I (TK) use a technique I have adapted from Gerald Corey (personal communication, March 1988). First, I say to the child, "If you did know, what would the answer be?" If this does not work, I move to asking for "outside" help. Sometimes, I bring in a fairy or wizard puppet and ask the puppet the question, hoping that the child will answer for the puppet or contradict a nonsensical answer I provide for the puppet. Other times, I ask the child what a favorite teacher, aunt, or grandparent would tell me if I asked one of them the question.

In helping the child gain insight into his or her lifestyle, you can make guesses about how anxiety seems to be preventing the child from having experiences that are potentially fun or from accomplishing things he or she has the capacity for doing. You can also metacommunicate about how courage creates a sense of hopefulness and how lack of courage creates a sense of despair. Some examples of these interventions are as follows:

- "It seems like that flying squirrel was scared about trying to jump from one tree to the other, even though she knew that she could do it just fine. She was pretty sad and a little disappointed in herself because it looked like it would be fun and exciting."
- "The little otter pup wasn't willing to go swimming with the other otter pups. What do you think stopped him from going swimming?"
- "You decided not to finger paint because you were afraid you might make a mistake."
- "I am guessing that you don't want to decide what color to paint the house because you are afraid that it might not be the perfect choice. In here, there is no perfect choice."

During the reorientation–reeducation phase, we find it helpful to break tasks down into small components so that the child's risk of "failure" is reduced. We sometimes set up situations in which we teach the child specific skills necessary for successful mastery of new experiences (e.g., how to test each of the Jenga® pieces before pulling one out, how to make the mouth of a puppet move so that it looks like the puppet is talking). Both of us purposely (and not purposely, which is convenient) make mistakes, modeling "the courage to be imperfect" to demonstrate that taking risks, trying new activities, being embarrassed, or experiencing failure in the playroom is never fatal. To demonstrate that I (TK) am afraid of many things but do not let fear stop me from doing what I want to do, I use self-disclosure, telling stories about situations in my own life in which I have proved to myself that I can successfully face challenges. When I do this, I am careful that these disclosures are relatively short so that the session does not become "all about me." I also monitor how I present my story because I do not want to convey (either verbally or nonverbally) that I am judgmental or disapproving of the child because of his or her fears.

Goals of Misbehavior

In trying to understand and alter the goals of discouraged children, it is essential to remember that children's misbehavior is the result of them trying to get their needs met, albeit in inappropriate ways (Burke, 2008; Lew & Bettner, 2000; Nelson, 2011; Nelson et al., 2013). The goals of discouraged children fall into four primary categories of striving: attention, power, revenge, and proving inadequacy (Dreikurs & Soltz, 1964).

To determine a child's goal, you will want to gather information about the child's feelings and behaviors, the feelings and reactions of adults who interact with him or her, and the child's responses when he or she experiences criticism or punishment. (It is also helpful to notice your own feelings and reactions to the child's misbehavior; at the same time, it is important to remember that your reaction is probably different from the reaction of other adults—at least we hope it is—we play therapists are supposed to be more tolerant than other adults.) Because each of these factors is different for the four goals, you can usually determine toward which goal of misbehavior the child is striving. It is important to make this determination because the intervention strategies in play sessions differ according to the counselor's understanding of the child's goal. Knowing the child's goal is also helpful in planning parent and teacher consultations because the Adlerian techniques used in dealing with misbehavior are somewhat goal specific. Ultimately, you want to come up with solutions that help the child learn to get his or her needs met using appropriate, prosocial behavior. This may also involve helping parents, family members, and school personnel learn to recognize the child's needs and help the child get them met through positive behavior. In some cases this will include changing the way the family and classroom systems work so that misbehavior is no longer "working" for the child.

Attention

Children whose goal is attention believe that the only way they are significant is when they are the center of attention. When others are not paying attention to them, they feel insignificant and unimportant. They feel that they need attention to belong. Children whose goal is attention have four possible routes to get that attention: the active constructive route, passive constructive route, active destructive route, and passive destructive route (Dreikurs, 1948; Lew & Bettner, 2000; Nelson, 2011; Nelson et al., 2013; Pepper, 1980). Children usually try to gain significance through a constructive route first, but if they feel that they have not achieved acceptance and belonging using positive "useful" methods, they switch to the destructive mode. Children use the active or passive mode depending on the level of their personal courage and energy. Children who have a great deal of courage and energy take the active path to gain significance. Children who feel discouraged, defeated, and afraid take the passive path to belonging.

Each of these subcategories has distinctive types of typical behaviors. Children who have elected to take the active constructive path to gaining attention typically have many positive behaviors and mannerisms, all designed to make them the center of attention. These children are usually the teacher's pets or model children who use goodness to get recognition. They are frequently very conscientious and may use tattling as a way to gain attention. Active constructive attention seekers flamboyantly do nice things for other people—drawing attention to their good deeds all the while. These children seldom get sent to counseling—though they may have to go when they are adults because they tend to get locked into meeting the needs of others rather than meeting their own needs. (We both wish the children in our families had this form of the goal of attention, but neither of us is that lucky.)

Children who have elected to take the passive constructive path to gaining attention typically exhibit the same kind of behaviors that active constructive children do (Dreikurs, 1948; Pepper, 1980). The primary difference is that passive constructive children do these behaviors less obviously and then wait wistfully for someone else to notice and give them the attention that they crave. Sometimes passive constructive attention seekers act like clinging vines, expecting others to take care of them. These children may also receive a lot of attention for good looks or charming personalities and frequently develop a desire for admiration and service. Because their behavior is passive and constructive, they seldom get referred to counseling either—too bad because helping them to find better ways to get attention would be an easy success.

Children who have elected to take the active destructive path to gaining attention usually do rather obvious negative things to gain attention (Burke, 2008; Dreikurs, 1948; Pepper, 1980). These children are quite frequently class clowns or family smart alecks. They use negative behaviors in a rather obvious, loud fashion to get attention. They may be silly, argumentative, overly active, easily distracted, or bullying.

Pepper (1980) described several different types of children who fit into this category. The show-off is the child who uses flamboyantly negative behavior to gain attention. He or she likes to shock people and may make statements simply designed to get attention. The obstructive child becomes a nuisance to gain attention and significance. The enfant terrible child purposely breaks rules of tact and convention to get attention. This child interrupts and says rude things. He or she may be witty, sly, and clever in interactions with other children and with adults. The walking question mark child constantly asks questions, even though he or she knows the answer already. The unstable child gives up easily and constantly needs reassurance and bolstering, even though he or she is capable of doing many things. A child who is an active destructive attention seeker may, at one time or another, use any and all of these behaviors to gain attention.

Children who have elected to take the passive destructive path to getting attention are not quite as obvious as active destructive attention seekers (Dreikurs, 1948; Pepper, 1980). These children are frequently characterized as lazy or dependent. They may appear to be shy and use bashfulness to keep other people involved. They may be messy, perpetually late, or unwilling to do chores. These behaviors are passive techniques for gaining attention. Passive destructive attention seekers can also be children who exhibit a great deal of fear and anxiety, constantly needing reassurance and care.

When adults interact with children motivated by attention, they feel mildly annoyed with them. Most of the time, adults give these children attention when they are asking for it—either positively or negatively. With constructive attention seekers, adults initially react favorably. As time passes, the children's constant need for involvement and attention begins to be a strain on the relationship. With destructive attention seekers, adults sometimes try to coax them into more appropriate behavior.

In response to correction, attention-seeking children temporarily reduce or eliminate the annoying behaviors. When others are paying attention to them, they seem to feel content and stop demanding interaction. However, when they stop being the center of attention, their anxiety escalates, and soon they resume the behavior that they typically use to gain attention. Children who crave attention, whether they are using positive or negative behavior to stay in the spotlight, seldom get referred to play therapy because their behavior is not usually upsetting enough to the adults in their lives to warrant it. Because they modify their behavior when corrected, this keeps them from pushing the bounds of appropriate behavior beyond a tolerable level.

To contradict attention-seeking children's belief that they must be the center of attention, you can use three different strategies: ignoring, giving attention, and metacommunicating. It is best to ignore these children when they are asking for attention in inappropriate ways such as being silly or acting needy. By attending to them when they are not seeking attention, you will encourage them to explore other, more positive ways (such as the positive goals of behavior discussed in Chapter 2 or working to develop the Crucial Cs) of gaining significance. You can also metacommunicate about the purpose of their behavior. This intervention strategy is most appropriate for the third phase of Adlerian play therapy as a strategy for helping children gain insight into the goals of their misbehavior. Some examples of metacommunication about the goal of attention would be,

- "You really want me to pay attention to you."
- "It seems like sometimes you're afraid that I don't like you if I'm not paying attention to you when we are together."
- "Sometimes I think that you really like for your mother to stay busy with you and not pay any attention to your brother."

The ultimate goal of intervention is for children to realize that they do not need to be the center of attention to belong or be important. With parents and teachers of attention-seeking children, you can suggest how to use these same techniques to help children generalize this idea to settings other than play sessions.

Power

Children whose goal is power believe that they only count when they are in control (Burke, 2008; Dreikurs, 1948; Nelson, 2011; Pepper, 1980). They believe they need to be in control of themselves (and sometimes of other people and situations), and they believe that they must show others that they cannot be controlled. When they are not in control, they feel worthless and unimportant and try to regain power by any available means. Children who are seeking power to gain significance typically show the rest of the world faces that look self-confident and superior, sometimes even smug. This is not the way they really feel, however. These children have often tried to gain significance in more constructive ways, but they have not achieved a sense of belonging by these means and believe that they must try to achieve power to be safe and secure. At times they do not have age-appropriate power and feel a need to "steal" it from others.

Although there is no constructive form of the goal of control, there are active and passive versions. The primary distinction between the active and passive manifestations of power seeking is in the degree of energy children devote to their behavior. Active power children get into power struggles with authority figures and peers by arguing, fighting, contradicting, and acting with open defiance. Many times they use temper tantrums to get what they want. They may also tell blatant lies, cheat to win at games, and use other forms of dishonesty to stay in control of situations and other people. Passive power children get into power struggles by being disobedient, forgetful, manipulative, stubborn, lazy, and uncooperative. Passive children do not overtly challenge others but get their way in a passive–aggressive manner.

When adults encounter power-seeking children, they usually get angry at them. They tend to feel challenged or threatened by the children's need for control. Adults frequently react to this challenge by engaging in power struggles with these children, threatening them or preaching to induce them to comply with rules and structure. These strategies rarely succeed with children motivated by power. When they are punished, power-seeking children tend to escalate their negative behavior. Active children work harder at being defiant, and passive children work harder at being passive aggressive.

In our experience, the child whose goal is power usually comes from a background in which one of three circumstances exist: (a) the child's family does not allow him or her to have reasonable or appropriate power and responsibility; (b) the child's family permits him or her to have excessive amounts of power and responsibility; or (c) the child's family is chaotic, disorganized, and lacking in a sense of structure and safety. We make a distinction among these three backgrounds because our intervention style in the play session will vary according to this underlying dynamic in the power-seeking child's life.

Background and Play Therapy Intervention Strategies for Children Who Have Too Little Power

Children whose families do not allow them to have any power at all often feel a need to gain some modicum of control over situations and overcompensate by demanding power over all situations. These children's parents are usually overprotective or extremely rigid and authoritarian. The parents do things for these children that they can do for themselves, continuing to brush their children's teeth, dress them, cut their meat, choose their clothes, decide what they can do, where they can go, and who they can befriend. These children have few opportunities to exercise control over themselves and their lives, even when it is developmentally appropriate for them to have some limited power or responsibility. Because they are seldom allowed to make decisions, be responsible, or take control over even small facets of their everyday experiences, these children develop a need to control others, through manipulation or temper tantrums. They become so intent on gaining a small amount of power that every interaction becomes a power struggle, with the children determined to win and gain control.

Our strategy with children who have too little power is to inundate them with control during the initial sessions and then to introduce gradually the idea that we will share the power with them. During the first sessions, we never make any decisions in the playroom. We leave all of the choices up to the children and constantly return responsibility back to them. We sometimes use the "whisper technique" discussed in Chapter 5 to accomplish this.

Frequently, these children have negative reactions to having power shared with them because they are not sure how to deal with it and may even believe that this is some kind of a trap. We have had children scream at us that they cannot make the decisions, that we are the adults and it is our job to decide what happens in the play session. We have had other children simply refuse to make decisions and sit passively waiting for us to take charge. (These same children, if we showed a willingness to assume the control, would try to wrest the power away from us—kind of a "gotcha" approach to interacting.) We metacommunicate about these responses, making guesses about how hard it is for them to trust us and to take responsibility for what happens in the session.

As the relationship develops and the children begin to feel more comfortable with having power as a matter of course, rather than a matter of force, you can begin to ask them to share power with you. You will want to convey the idea that they can be comfortable and safe in the session whether they are in charge or you are. To accomplish this, you will want to set up ways to share power with them. For instance, you can suggest taking turns making the rules for any games you play; you can take role plays in different directions by not using the whisper technique; you can set up a play scenario to enact. It is important to monitor children's reactions to this process to be able to reflect their feelings and metacommunicate about what is going on with them.

In parent consultation, we work with parents to teach them to allow their child to exercise age-appropriate control. Sometimes, parents do not have enough information on child development and simply do not realize what children should be able to do by themselves. When this is the case, we might ask them to read child development books (e.g., *Developmental Milestones of Young Children* (K. Petty, 2009); *Ages and Stages: A Parent's Guide to Normal Childhood Development* (Schaefer & DiGeronimo, 2000); *Ages and Stages: Developmental Descriptions and Activities, Birth Through Eight Years* (Miller, 2001); *Your 5-Year-Old: Sunny and Serene* (Ames & Ilg, 1979); *Your 7-Year-Old: Life in a Minor Key* (Ames & Haber, 1985; or any of the other books that come from the Gesell Institute of Human Development) that contain information about what to expect from "normal" children (are there really any of those in the world?) at specific ages.

Some parents have difficulty sharing power with anyone else because of their own issues. We often refer these parents for personal counseling, but it is difficult to interest them in the counseling process because it would mean giving up some of their control. They may also resist learning new ways of interacting with their children. The most effective way we have found to encourage power-seeking parents to share power with their children is to teach them how to give limited choices. This strategy allows the children to have some control over their lives but does not require the parents really to give up making all the decisions in the family.

Background and Play Therapy Strategies for Children Who Have Too Much Power

Children with excessive power at home come to believe that they need to have that same amount of power in their interactions with others (and the rest of the world—yikes!). Parents of these children may have (a) a laissez-faire attitude toward parenting; (b) so many personal problems that they are absorbed in their own difficulties and do not have the energy to set boundaries and structure, which results in *parentified* children (children who are expected to play the role of a parent in their family); (c) such a strong need to please others that they are reluctant to set limits for their children; and (d) many anxieties, which tend to make them overprotect and inclined to pamper their children. These children make their own decisions about the various aspects of their lives before they are developmentally ready to make those choices. They often take care of themselves and perhaps several siblings. Sometimes they are pampered and expect others to comply with their every desire. When people outside their families do not allow them the control they have learned to expect from others, these children try to wrest that control away from them because they do not feel safe without their usual power. This results in constant power struggles with authority figures, who these children believe to be violating their right to be powerful.

In play sessions with children who have too much power, you will want to establish egalitarian power sharing from the first session. This way, you can help them learn that they can give up demanding complete control over every situation and still survive, feel safe, and be happy. These children usually have a negative reaction to the idea that you are going to share power with one another, and they may try to engage you in a power struggle about it. When this happens, the best thing to do is to use metacommunication about their goals and avoid getting into power struggles with them. Examples of metacommunication with power-seeking children:

- "You want to change the rules so you can win."
- "It seems to be really important to you to get me to do it your way."
- "I'm thinking that you like to be the boss and tell me what to do."

Some methods for avoiding power struggles are to give choices, seek solutions, or set up consequences (see Chapters 4 and 6). These strategies keep the relationship democratic and allow children to have a degree of power without letting them control the entire situation. It is important to avoid taking the children's behavior personally and feeling challenged or threatened in any way. It is often helpful to remind yourself that you (being an adult—even when you don't really feel like one) have more freedom and choices in your life than children do, and you must act like an adult by remaining calm and balanced in your interaction with them.

With parentified children, we make sure that we do not expect them to be overly responsible in our sessions. We frequently avoid asking them to help clean up the room, and we try to engage them in silly and childlike behavior (although these children are often way more serious than we are, so this can be hard work). With pampered children, we avoid pampering them or lowering expectations for them. We want to convey our confidence that they can flourish without being overprotected or getting everything they want.

We work with the parents of children who have too much control on the parenting skills required to establish appropriate boundaries and structure. The parents particularly need to learn how to set up choices and logical consequences, how to seek solutions in which the children do not have too much power, how to determine problem ownership, and how to avoid getting involved in power struggles.

We work with parents on minor personal issues that might be interfering with their parenting, or, if there are major personal issues, we usually refer them for personal counseling. We want individuals who are struggling with their ability to parent effectively to feel empowered and to begin to take on the parental responsibility rather than expecting the child to do this. To accomplish this task, we use encouragement and teach discipline skills. With parents who have personal problems and those who are trying too hard to please their children, we ask them to look at how their difficulties are affecting their relationship with their children. Parents of pampered children need to examine their purpose in pampering and to get additional information on the harm pampering can do to their children's development and self-esteem. A resource that has helped me (TK) with my tendency to overindulge my only child is *Parents Who Love Too Much: How Good Parents Can Learn to Love More Wisely and Develop Children of Character* (Nelson & Erwin, 2000). (Although I did stop speaking to the friend who first gave me the book—just for a couple of months—really.)

Background and Play Therapy Strategies for Children From Chaotic Families

In some families, children have no sense of safety or protection because the entire family is out of control. This may be because of mental illness, drug abuse, poor health, or alcoholism on the part of parents. In some cases, the chaos in the family stems from parents' lack of parenting skills and inability to set up the structure and routine needed to help children feel safe. Many of these families move through different social services, seeking stabilization but never finding it. For these children, the striving for control is a survival skill that they use to protect themselves.

Our intervention strategies with children from chaotic families are similar to those we use with children who have too little power. At first we let them control all of the interactions in the play session, and then we gradually introduce the idea of power sharing so they can have an experience in which they can feel safe even if they are not in control. We want to provide a secure environment in which they can relax and enjoy playing and having fun just being children.

We sometimes make guesses about how it feels to be a part of a family in which there is little order or safety. When we do this, we are careful to avoid seeming critical of parents. This is actually not too hard for us because we believe that the parents in these families (and in all other families) are doing their best to function in ways that make sense to them.

It is difficult to have a major impact on chaotic families, partly because there are so many problems that it seems impossible to make any substantial restructuring. Family members resist help because change seems threatening to them. There are often so many overwhelming problems that family members do not seem to be able to learn enough or get mentally healthy enough to interact in a way that could facilitate effective parenting.

Although we believe that it is important to work systemically with these families, at times it seems more appropriate to teach the child survival skills and methods of gaining control over his or her environment that do not threaten or challenge other individuals. For example, with Lonnie, an 8-year-old boy whose mother is mentally ill, I (TK) might teach him how to recognize the signs that appear when his mother stops taking her medication and how to contact a responsible adult to care for him when this happens.

Revenge

Children motivated by revenge seek to get even or to punish others for pain or injury inflicted on them (Burke, 2008; Dreikurs, 1948; Nelson, 2011; Nelson et al., 2013; Pepper, 1980). Revenge-seeking children have frequently experienced abuse of some kind—physical, sexual, emotional—or neglect, and they want to protect themselves in the future by striking out before anyone else has a chance to hurt them. They have felt so much pain in their lives that they want to hurt other people. In some situations, children have only experienced relationships as being painful and believe that the way to establish and maintain a relationship is to inflict pain. In other situations, children who are motivated by power but thwarted in their attempts to make things go their way lash out at others to exact revenge for the perceived hurts resulting from their frustration. Revenge-seeking children feel that they are unacceptable, unlovable, and unwanted. Many times, these children believe that they deserve to be hurt and expect others to reject them, so they use a preemptive strike and reject others before they can be rejected.

Although there is no constructive form of revenge, there is an active form and a passive form, which manifest in different types of behaviors. Children who engage in active revenge seeking are violent, malicious, and cruel. These children are frequently bullies who hurt other children and adults, either physically or emotionally. When they lose at games, they try to punish those who beat them. Bed wetting and soiling clothes are sometimes exhibited by revenge children. Although encopresis and enuresis can be caused by physical problems, which should be checked out medically, they can also be metaphoric communication of children's feelings to the adults who clean up after them. Actively revenge-oriented children frequently steal favorite possessions of others to hurt them.

Children who are passively striving for revenge exhibit behaviors that are more subtle in their hurtful intent. They are frequently moody, pouty, threatening, or withdrawn. They may refuse to participate in activities or sabotage those they do join. The difference between passive power children and passive revenge children is intent. Power children want control, and revenge children want to hurt others.

Because revenge children are very good at acting on this intention, when adults encounter them, the adults usually feel hurt. Some adults react to this pain by withdrawing from the children to protect themselves, which provides support to the children's belief that they are unlovable. Other adults react to pain inflicted by revenge children by trying to get even with the children for hurting them. This confirms the negative self-image of the children and further inflames their desire to get revenge and protect themselves from future hurts. Whenever they experience any kind of correction or reprimand, these children assume that the punishment is designed to hurt them. Their immediate response is to escalate their efforts to hurt others.

When we work with children motivated by revenge, we often need to keep reminding ourselves that they are trying to hurt us because they have been hurt, not because they like to inflict pain on others. This helps us avoid taking their behavior personally and allows us to stay positive with them despite their efforts to push us away from them.

Patience and consistency are the keys to play therapy with revenge-seeking children. Because these children discount any attempts to encourage them for a long time, you will need to exercise persistence without getting discouraged by their reactions. Work to convey respect and caring in all of your interactions with these children. It is important to make sure that limits are fair and predictable. When you limit, pay even more attention than usual to keeping your verbal and nonverbal communication matter of fact and nonjudgmental. Even with these efforts, revenge children frequently assume that you are using the limiting process to further reject and hurt them. When metacommunicating about the goal of behavior to these children, it is helpful to remember to keep any kind of emotion out of your voice and simply label the goal. The following are examples of metacommunications about the goal of revenge:

- "I'm guessing that you are angry with me because you wanted to shoot the dart gun, so you're stepping on the dart gun to try to get me back."
- "Seems like you want to hurt that boy doll for what he did to the girl doll."
- "Maybe you think if you call me names that you will hurt my feelings and I will go away and not talk to you."

In circumstances in which parents or other family members are responsible for the child's feeling of hurt, you must first assure yourself that any
abuse or neglect is stopped. If the child is in a continuing abusive situation,
it is essential to find a way to make sure the child is removed from the
danger and moved to a place where she or he can feel safe and protected.
You should know the rules for mandatory reporters in your state.

Even in situations in which all parental hurtful behavior has ceased,
repairing a damaged parent–child relationship is slow work. Parents
must learn to be consistently supportive of the child, to limit without
judgment, to resist provocation, and to gain an impersonal perspective on
hurtful behavior. The child must learn to trust parents, begin to believe
that he or she is lovable and important, and explore new and positive
ways to gain his or her significance and keep safe from harm. Your main
function in this process is to encourage both the child and other family
members, not letting them give up on one another or themselves. It is also
important to give parents a place to vent their own feelings of hurt and
frustration and to help them work on their own issues so that no further
harm comes to the child.

In some families, even when parents were not responsible for any hurt
inflicted on the child, the child acts out the need for revenge on them.
This is often because the child feels hurt because adult family members
did not sufficiently protect her or him from harm. In some cases, the
child does not feel safe in acting out negative feelings on the person
who hurt her or him but does feel safe in acting out these feelings on
nonoffending parents.

Proving Inadequacy

Children who are trying to prove that they are inadequate are truly discouraged. They protect themselves from the demands of life by avoiding
activities in which they feel deficient (Burke, 2008; Dinkmeyer et al., 2007;
Dreikurs, 1948; Nelson, 2011; Nelson et al., 2013; Pepper, 1980). Children
sometimes decide that they cannot do things as well as (a) they want to
do, (b) other people can, or (c) they ought to be able to do. Inadequate
behavior is usually passive (e.g., the child who will not try, gives up easily,
or avoids the company of others), but the ultimate form of discouragement is active: suicide.

In certain families, parents have contributed to their children's negative
self-images because of their own personal discouragement, which can
take the form of neglect, overambition, pressure, pessimism, criticism,
and impossibly high standards. Sometimes children get discouraged by
comparing themselves unfavorably with siblings or peers. In cases in
which children have some type of challenging condition, such as learning
disabilities, attention-deficit/hyperactivity disorder (ADHD), physical
disability, or mental retardation, their assessment that they cannot do
as well as others may be accurate. However, in many of these cases, the
resultant discouragement is disproportionate to the problem.

Adults who interact with children striving to prove inadequacy usually feel helpless, hopeless, and just as discouraged as the children. They

do not know what to do to help the children, and even when they make attempts to intervene, the children either do not respond or respond in a passive way. Parents and teachers frequently give up on these children because they tend to get worse rather than improving. If really discouraged children experience failure or correction, they sink even deeper into their despair and give up even small attempts at success or progress.

In play sessions, most children who believe they are inadequate refuse to engage in any kind of play for fear that they will not succeed. We are never critical of their inactivity, nor do we imply (in either our verbal or nonverbal communication) that we think they should be doing something. We seek out information about their assets, usually from conversations with parents and teachers, because the children themselves do not believe that they have any strengths. Encouragement can bolster these children's feelings of competence. We especially look for circumstances in which they put out effort or improve in some activity. It is important to engage them in activities in which they can succeed. This requires low-risk toys or materials. Board games that depend strictly on chance, rather than skill, are sometimes helpful. Chutes and Ladders and Candyland are examples of this type of play media. Finger painting and sand are also excellent intervention tools with this population because it is impossible to make a mistake with them.

Sometimes with children who are working to prove they are inadequate, it is better to have the play session in a room with limited toys and activity choices. Because these children are easily overwhelmed and cannot imagine that they can successfully cope, the ideal playroom may be overpowering to them. If possible, you can bring one or two low-risk items into a room with few distractions or opportunities for failure. Because these children are determined to re-prove what they already believe about themselves, if the playroom contains potentially defeating activities, they seek them out to confirm their perceptions of themselves.

Your primary tool with these children will be unlimited amounts of encouragement and your personal belief in the potential of every human being, which you will need to constantly communicate to the children and their parents. Sometimes metacommunications about their goals are also helpful, although these children seldom have any discernible reaction. Examples of metacommunication with children striving to establish their own inadequacy:

- "Sometimes it seems like you just don't want to try anymore because you don't think you can do things as well as Joseph."
- "I'm guessing that it hurts so much when it doesn't work for you that you just give up."
- "You look like you wish you could do that, and you're kind of afraid to try."

Most parents of children whose goal is proving their own inadequacy are discouraged themselves. Your main job with these parents is to give them a great deal of support to keep them from giving up. Encouraging their efforts and improvements in parenting skills is helpful. You can ask them to eliminate any of their behaviors that might be contributing to their children's discouragement and suggest more positive ways of interacting with the children. They must learn to recognize small increments of improvement in their children and to celebrate any type of risk-taking behavior on the children's parts. This is a slow, sometimes painful process, but with support these parents can learn to encourage their children, resulting in changes in the children's attitudes and behaviors.

Personality Priorities

Kfir (1981, 1989, 2011) conceptualized a typology that she labeled *personality priorities* as one method of developing an understanding of lifestyle. She described the personality priority as a pattern of behavior and reactions that is based on a person's convictions about how he or she acquires belonging, significance, and a sense of mastery. Kfir believed that individuals use personality priorities as a means for coping with or avoiding impasses (perceived traumatic events) and achieving a sense of mastery over fear and feelings of inferiority. Her typology consisted of four personality priorities: controlling, pleasing, being morally superior, and avoiding.

Using Kfir's concepts as a foundation, Pew (1976) expanded the idea of the "number one priority," which he defined as "a manifestation of our self-created, self-consistent style of living, a theme which runs through all of our human transactions" (p. 1) or the usual mode of thinking about situations and conducting relationships with others. He suggested that it is important to look at the stressful experience that each person is working to avoid and the positive purpose he or she is striving to achieve. He labeled the priorities control, pleasing, superiority, and comfort.

Langenfeld and Main (1983) conducted a factor-analytic study to investigate the typology of personality priorities, developing a research instrument to measure the priorities posited by Kfir and Pew. In their study, they found five factors rather than the four factors they had expected. They labeled these factors achieving, outdoing, pleasing, detaching, and avoiding. Dillman Taylor (2013), in her work developing the Adlerian Personality Priority Assessment, an appraisal tool for identifying clients' personality priorities, used factor analysis to provide "strong empirical support for the four-factor structure of personality priorities most commonly used in the literature: superiority, control, comfort, and pleasing" (p. 85).

In using the concept of personality priorities, I (TK) have combined the ideas of Kfir, Pew, Langenfeld and Main, and Dillman Taylor. I emphasize both the avoiding of the negative aspect of each priority and the striving toward the positive aspect of each priority. I use the labels developed by Pew and supported by Dillman Taylor's research, but I add information from the study conducted by Langenfeld and Main and divide the control priority into two subcategories (those who are only invested in control of self and those who are invested in control of everything and everyone) and the superiority priority into two subcategories (achievers, who are interested in being the best that they can be without having a need to put others down in the process, and outdoers, who measure their own worth in comparison with others).

We all live our lives with a smidgen of every priority (control, pleasing, superiority, and comfort), so the division between people with different personality priorities is not always obvious or glaring. What we are looking for when we are investigating the lifestyle of the child (and when we are considering the lifestyles of parents, teachers, and so forth) is which one (or sometimes two, as we frequently see people having a primary personality priority and a secondary personality priority) of these priorities serves as an organizing pattern of coping with situations and relationships. As we think about a child's personality priority, we ask ourselves the following questions (adapted from Dewey, 1978) as a vehicle for discovering whether we believe that the person strives to belong, gain significance, and gain a sense of mastery through control, pleasing, superiority, or comfort:

1. What is this person striving to achieve in life?
2. What does this person need to feel that he or she belongs and is significant?
3. What does this person need to feel a sense of mastery of various situations in life?
4. What are this person's assets? What does he or she do well?
5. What is this person trying to avoid in life?
6. What does this person complain about? What does this person believe he or she lacks in life?
7. What happens when this person just cannot cope any longer?
8. What is the price this person pays for the way he or she interacts with others?
9. What is the price this person pays for the way he or she copes with problems?
10. How do others react to this person?

None of the personality priorities is more advantageous than the other ones. Every personality priority exacts a price from the individual who manifests it, and every one bequeaths advantages as well. Each of the personality priorities has strengths, and each has struggles, so it is not necessary or appropriate to try to change the client's personality priority. We conceptualize individuals functioning somewhere along a continuum from constructive to destructive, and our goal with clients who are functioning in the destructive range of their personality priorities would be to help them move their functioning into the constructive range of that personality priority. To do this, we use metacommunication, storytelling, sand trays, life coaching, movement, and an assortment of play therapy techniques, along with parent and teacher consultation. We may also need to work with the significant adults in child clients' lives to help them shift from the destructive range of their personality priorities into to the more constructive range.

Control

Children whose goal is control gain their significance and sense of belonging and mastery by attempting to maintain control or show others that they cannot control them (Ashby & Kottman, 1998; Eckstein & Kern, 2009; Kfir, 1989, 2011; Nelson et al., 2013). These children feel uncomfortable and powerless in situations and relationships in which they do not perceive that they are in control. They work constantly to avoid feeling or being out of control, because they are convinced that they must be in control to avoid dangerous or humiliating situations. Control children seldom have many friends and quite frequently experience high levels of anxiety, sometimes expressed in psychosomatic symptoms. Because of their powerful need for control, these children have trouble letting go, being free, and playing like other children—they do not feel comfortable just being kids. In their effort to stay in control, they frequently struggle with connecting and courage (especially those whose goal is control of the universe); they push others away and avoid taking any kind of risk. They may use tantrums, withholding, perfectionism, bossiness, or passive-aggressive behaviors to ensure that their striving for control is successful. These behaviors often result in them being rejected or avoided by other children and criticized and overpowered by adults. These children can be very powerful in appropriate ways as well. They are strong leaders, organized, responsible, productive, reliable, and persistent. (Remember, each of the priorities has positive attributes and downfalls.)

In the playroom, children whose personality priority is control are inclined toward getting into power struggles and testing limits. They want to be in charge and have difficulty sharing power. Frequently expressing their dissatisfaction with the play therapy process, they will try to subjugate you and control the unfolding of the relationship. Because this personality priority results in power being these children's goal of misbehavior, their behavior is the same as the behavior described in the section on power-oriented children. Again, it would be important to consider the dynamics of their family backgrounds and life experiences in thinking about these children and designing play therapy interventions for them. The primary thing to remember with control personality priority children is that if you allow them to engage you in a power struggle, you have already lost control of the process. You have to stay centered in your own ability to control yourself, avoid trying to control them, and never take their behaviors personally.

Depending on the child's background, it is usually a useful procedure to establish that eventually (with some sooner, with some later) we will be sharing power in the playroom. We use limited choices with them (e.g., "Would you like to paint a picture of your family or draw a picture of your family?"). (The subtext of this interaction is that we are going to do a picture of the family.) We also take turns "being in charge." If we have an activity that we want them to do (such as a body outline or puppet show), we do what we want to do first, and when we are finished with it (to our satisfaction) then we do what the child wants to do.

These children often refuse to answer questions verbally, so it becomes extremely important to watch their nonverbal reactions (which are usually minimal—after all these children are really good at control). Sometimes when they choose to remain silent in response to one of my questions or guesses, I (TK) just get silly, making up absurd answers to my own questions. If I do not overuse this technique, it is very effective because these children cannot resist setting me straight.

We want to encourage these children just to act like kids, not worrying about making mistakes or staying in control. After we have established a relationship with them and they trust us, we invite them to be more spontaneous and playful. We smear shaving cream on the tables, put our feet in finger paint, make T-shirts by splattering paint, make potions, and so forth.

In our metacommunication, we gently point out their need to be in control and their fears about what it is like when they are not in control. We also make guesses about the relationship between their need to be in control and the price that they pay in their relationships and ability to cope with problems. We give them feedback about how it affects us when they try to control us; without judging or criticizing, we tell them how we feel when this happens. We encourage them for their assets and any efforts they make to take risks and connect with others. We point out progress they make in their willingness to share power and work cooperatively with us and other people in their lives. Some examples of metacommunicating with children whose primary personality is in the dysfunctional range of control might be:

- "You like to be the boss and tell me what you want me to do."
- "I am guessing that sometimes the other kids in your class get irritated with you because you never let them decide what to play."
- "When you talk to me in a grouchy voice, I don't always want to do what you tell me to do. If you talk to me in a friendlier voice, I might be more willing to do what you want."
- "I feel happy and excited when you tell me I get to decide what we are going to do today."

Pleasing

Children who gain their sense of belonging and mastery by pleasing others believe that they can only gain acceptance and love by keeping others happy (Ashby & Kottman, 1998; Kfir, 1981, 1989, 2011; Nelson et al., 2013). Pleasers do not feel confident of their own worth, and they constantly strive to gain the approval of others so that they feel accepted. Children striving to please seem to struggle with courage and believe that they do not count or that they only count if they meet conditions set by others (e.g., taking care of others to impress them with their worthiness as people; trying to be perfect to gain acceptance by others). Because these children fear rejection, they try to avoid anger and conflict by reading the minds of others and giving them "what they want." They also suppress their own anger because they are convinced that if they expressed frustration or hostility they would be rejected.

Pleasers seldom ask for what they need; they don't take the lead in relationships because they are afraid of rejection. They complain about a lack of respect and help from others and a lack of self-respect and self-confidence. The price that they pay for this priority is that they are highly anxious and take on guilt and responsibility for situations that they have not created (like war, famine, poverty, pestilence, and so forth). These children seldom get their own needs met, and even when they have great ideas, others tend to ignore them or take credit for their suggestions without acknowledging their contribution. Initially, other people really like to be around pleasers. After all, they are kind, helpful, nurturing, reliable, responsible, friendly, and cheerful, willing to take on any tasks when asked. However, after a while, the anxiety of pleasers, their struggle with being emotionally congruent, and their constant need for reassurance tend to wear on relationships, resulting in irritation and avoidance. When this happens, pleasers interpret these reactions as rejection and redouble their pleasing efforts.

In the playroom, these children are compliant and cooperative. They are very careful to express only "positive" emotions, and when they do express anger or hurt, they do it covertly and try to retract it later. Pleasers spend a great deal of their interpersonal energy in hypervigilance, watching for the least little indication that they have pleased or displeased you and preparing to react with pleasing behaviors. They clean up the playroom before being asked, they ask permission to do any activity they would like to try, and they apologize over and over again if they spill or break anything. Children striving to please others ask (both implicitly and explicitly) for approval and acknowledgment that they count. In their need to know that you approve of them, they may violate your personal space, standing closer than other children stand. They also ask more questions about the relationship and more personal questions, striving to prove to themselves that they are important to you.

With these children, we use many of the techniques that we would use with children who struggle with the Crucial Cs of courage and count. Encouragement is a real key with these children, but it can be a double-edged sword. We want to let them know that we think they are wonderful and that our regard is unconditional; at the same time we want to convey that they do not have to do anything to gain our acceptance. To achieve this, we are vigilant in our avoidance of evaluative words with pleasers and carefully monitor our nonverbal communication. We reflect their feelings of insecurity about our reactions, and we use self-disclosure about our own struggles with being a pleaser. (If you are not a pleaser, obviously, you don't have to do this—you can use self-disclosure with children whose personality priorities are more similar to your own.) Using metacommunication to point out their checking for permission; concealment of anger, frustration, or aggression; needing to be physically close to us; and guilt for things they have no reason to be guilty about can be extremely helpful to these children. Just as with control children, it is fun

to give permission to pleasing children to be silly and make mistakes—
to play with sand or water, to make a mess and not have to clean it up.
(Speaking of cleaning up, with these children, we often choose to leave
cleaning up the playroom together out of our play therapy with them. It
is quite liberating to pleasing children to have the freedom to just leave
toys and art materials everywhere and walk out the door.) Some examples
of metacommunication that would be helpful with pleasing children who
are in the dysfunctional range are:

- "You are looking at me to make sure it is okay with me if you pour
  water in the sandbox."
- "You seem a little nervous about whether I am mad because you
  got kicked out of school today."
- "I will never be angry at you even if you get in trouble with your
  mom."
- "It's important to you to make sure other people are happy with
  you."
- "You seem to work really hard so other people will like you."

During the reorientation–reeducation phase of play therapy, we teach
pleasing children interpersonal skills in service of them getting what
they want more often. We practice negotiation skills, assertive behaviors,
procedures for asking for what they want and for saying no, and activities that involve expressing feelings that might not be socially acceptable.
We also work with parents of these children on giving them permission
to just be kids and to help them practice assertiveness skills in the family. *The Mouse, the Monster and Me: Assertiveness for Young People* (Palmer,
2009) and *Speak Up and Get Along! Learn the Mighty Might, Thought Chop,
and More Tools to Make Friends, Stop Teasing, and Feel Good About Yourself*
(Cooper, 2005) are great resources for parents who want to help their kids
with these issues.

Superiority

Children who gain a sense of belonging and mastery through superiority
strive toward perfection in everything they do (Ashby & Kottman, 1998;
Kfir, 1981, 1989, 2011; Nelson et al., 2013). They think they have to devote
all of their (considerable) energy to achievement to be accepted by others, especially the important adults in their lives. Superiority children
are running from their own strong feelings of inferiority. Those who
tend toward outdoing compensate for these feelings by trying to prove
that they are "better" than others. Those who tend toward achieving
compensate for these feelings by being the "best" at whatever they do.
Outdoers and achievers both want to avoid a sense of meaninglessness
and futility.

Children whose personality priority is superiority work hard, have high
standards for achievement, and have high levels of social interest; they are
knowledgeable, idealistic, responsible, reliable, and persistent. However,

they often struggle with feeling capable, believing that they count, and connecting with others. They may also lack courage, sticking to projects and relationships in which they are guaranteed success.

Because many of these children are very competitive or appear to others to be trying to set the bar for achievement at such an unreasonable height, other children (and adults) feel inadequate, inferior, or challenged. The price these children pay for working so hard at being "more" is a sense of being overworked, overinvolved, overresponsible, and overwhelmed. They complain of being overextended and overcommitted, lacking time or energy for fun. Because their standards for themselves are impossibly high, they spend an inordinate amount of time wondering, "Was that good enough?" and "Did I do enough?"

In play therapy, these children come into sessions as little adults, mature and serious about working hard to prove that they are more competent, more right, more useful, smarter, better at sports, better at games, better at stacking blocks or putting on puppet shows than anyone else. Achievers want to do better than they have done in the past, competing with themselves. Outdoers want to do better than the other children who come to the playroom, the children in their class or neighborhood, their teachers, their parents, and their play therapist. They use accomplishments to get attention—so their play is usually designed to demonstrate their competence, and their stories about situations and relationships outside of the playroom are designed to illustrate their mastery of various skills. Superiority children interact with the play therapist from a know-it-all perspective. Even young children are experts on whatever their presenting problem or diagnosis is and want to show off their knowledge during play sessions.

The most important thing you need to remember (especially if one of your personality priorities is superiority) is that the best way to build a relationship with these children is to grant them their own areas of expertise and competence. You will want to be sure to keep yourself from getting into struggles with them about whether or not they know more about dinosaurs (or depression or hurricanes or . . .) than you do or are better at making clay sculptures (or building a tower or riding skateboards or . . .) than you are. They need to have a relationship in which they do not have to compete or prove themselves—in which they have inherent value just for being themselves.

Encouragement is important with these children, but presenting it is tricky. It is essential to communicate that you do not have impossibly high standards for them even if they do. You will want to acknowledge their strengths while conveying that you will accept and value them even if they do not live up to their own high standards.

We use a lot of metacommunication with superiority-oriented children: talking about their need to prove themselves, their struggles with feelings of inferiority, their lack of willingness to try experiences that have no guarantee of success. We spit in their soup when they complain about being overwhelmed at the same time they are not willing to let go of being on the soccer team, ballet lessons, the after-school mentoring program, and so forth. Some examples of metacommunication with children whose personality priorities are in the dysfunctional range of superiority are:

- "It's important to you for me to know that you are really good at sports."
- "You seem to really struggle when you can't be the best at something."
- "If you don't get a 100% on an assignment, it is like you think you are not good enough."
- "When you can't do something perfectly, you seem super angry with yourself . . . and with everyone else."
- "When things don't go just the way you want them to go, sometimes you seem to give up because it isn't perfect."

During the third and fourth phases, we teach superiority-oriented children decision-making strategies designed to help them say no more often. We teach them cognitive techniques for stilling the self-talk that suggests that they are inadequate and methods for learning to delegate and ask for help. We practice saying "I don't know," "I am not sure how to do that," "This is good enough," and "I am good enough." (All of which are good for us to practice saying for ourselves as well—play therapy for the clients and play therapy for us—everybody benefits.)

Comfort

Children with the personality priority of comfort seek peace, pleasure, comfort, and fun (Ashby & Kottman, 1998; Eckstein & Kern, 2009; Kfir, 1989, 2011; Nelson et al., 2013). They hope to find others to care for and pamper them. Comfort-seeking children are easygoing, mellow, understanding, predictable, empathic, and nonjudgmental. They connect easily because they make few demands of others and mind their own business.

These children try to avoid stress, tension, responsibility, and making an effort. To minimize these negative factors in their lives, they set very low standards for themselves, dodging expectations from others, "excessive" effort, and responsibility. Because their standards are low, they set themselves up to struggle with the Crucial Cs of capable and count. They do very little to reinforce their belief in their own capabilities and they have little impact on others or situations, limiting their ability to feel as though they make a difference. They may also demonstrate limited courage, not wanting to try new things or take risks. Comfort children sometimes complain of their own lack of productivity and lack of achievement. Adults and other children frequently label comfort children as being lazy, stupid, lacking athletic or musical ability, or just too slow. These children often feel undervalued in relationships: They tend to believe that the strengths they bring to interactions and experiences are not appreciated by others. This is especially true when others express impatience, irritation, and boredom in response to the passivity of comfort children.

In play therapy, building a relationship with comfort children is quite fun. They are spontaneous and willing to try new things as long as they do not take too much effort. Their ability to go with the flow is pleasant and relaxing, and their willingness to follow the playroom rules is refreshing, especially if you have a caseload heavy with children whose personality is control.

Comfort children are usually willing to answer questions in the second phase of therapy. However, if they have to think about their answer, they frequently say that they don't know. They show very little interest in or curiosity about the questions or anything else you want them to do that will take energy. If you ask them to do a puppet show or a drawing, they often say that they would prefer less strenuous activities (like sitting on the pillows and running sand through their fingers). This lack of willingness to commit fully to the therapeutic process may persist through the third and fourth phases (if they continue coming). It is essential with comfort children not to get impatient with their need to take things slowly and to keep stress to the minimum. This means that you will need to tailor your requests so that they are quick and simple to accomplish. These are not children who are going to enthusiastically endorse building a fort or writing and illustrating a book. If you get impatient, irritated, or disapproving, these children will shut down, and the relationship may be over.

We use encouragement to give them positive feedback on their assets and to acknowledge the least little bit of effort or improvement on their part. Returning responsibility to the child is an important skill to use with comfort children because they will try to enlist us in taking care of them and making decisions for them so that they do not have to strain themselves. By metacommunicating about their need for comfort and the consequences for their interactions with others and their sense of accomplishment, we can sometimes motivate them to reevaluate some of their choices or to make more of an effort in specific situations or relationships. Some examples of metacommunication with children in the dysfunctional range of comfort might be:

- "You don't like it when you think people are pressuring you to do better, so you just don't try."
- "I am thinking that you like to do things the easy way, and sometimes your teacher might get mad at you when that happens."
- "It sounds like you think that would be too much trouble, so you don't want to do it."
- "You only like to do things that sound like fun."
- "You seem confused about why your friend gets so upset because you don't let things bother you."

Depending on what we think about comfort children's Crucial Cs, we may use tactics similar to those we would use with children who are unsure about being capable or counting or those who seem to lack courage. Many times, discouraged comfort children are working to prove that they are inadequate. With these children, we use strategies similar to those described in the section of this chapter on working with children whose goal is proof of inadequacy.

Looking for Patterns

Although most of the time there is a pattern across different situations and relationships, children are not always completely consistent in their mastering of the Crucial Cs, their striving for goals of misbehavior, or their expression of their personality priorities. For example, Lindsay might really feel capable at home but struggle with her confidence in her abilities at school; Alonso might strive for power at home and attention at school; Mulan might be pleasing with her parents and controlling with her teachers. The Adlerian play therapist must be alert to shifts in various settings and with different people and adjust therapeutic interventions accordingly.

Although we have presented the Crucial Cs, goals of misbehavior, and personality priorities as discrete systems for understanding children and designing play therapy strategies for working with them, this is somewhat misleading. You may have noticed that these concepts often overlap and frequently dovetail with one another. As you work with children based on the ideas presented in this chapter, you will begin to notice patterns across the systems because they are really complementary, not separate.

Summary

The Adlerian play therapist must learn to recognize children's mastering of the Crucial Cs, their goals of misbehavior, and their personality priorities to conceptualize their lifestyles and design play therapy interventions that are tailored to their needs. By understanding each of the Crucial Cs, the goals of misbehavior, and the personality priorities, the play therapist can choose specific techniques appropriate for play therapy and parent consultation for all four phases of Adlerian play therapy.

Further Resources

Crucial Cs:

http://www.adleriansociety.co.uk/phdi/p3.nsf/imgpages/0939_
    KarenJohn-ASIIPConf-April2011.pdf/$file/KarenJohn-ASIIP-
    Conf-April2011.pdf

http://www.google.com/url?sa=t&rct=j&q=&esrc=s&source=web
    &cd=2&sqi=2&ved=0CCUQFjAB&url=http%3A%2F%2Fwww.
    imdetermined.org%2Ffiles_resources%2F150%2Fa_teachers_
    guide_to_undertanding_and_motivating_students1.doc&ei=-
    hRqVfr0OdGZyASw_IGADw&usg=AFQjCNEzqm9ZFkqRb1A
    DLFHwbLjyF5rzVw&bvm=bv.94455598,d.aWw

Personality priorities:

http://digital.library.unt.edu/ark:/67531/metadc4794/m2/1/high_
    res_d/dissertation.pdf

Child development:

http://www.cdc.gov/ncbddd/childdevelopment/
http://files.eric.ed.gov/fulltext/EJ603020.pdf

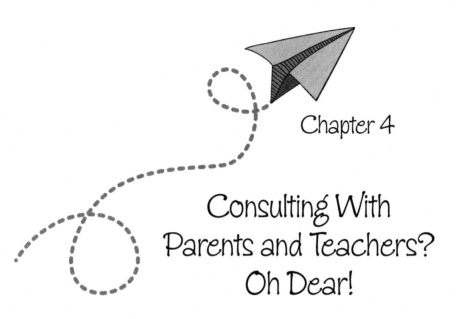

Chapter 4

Consulting With Parents and Teachers? Oh Dear!

The most influential and important people in the social context of children are their parents and teachers. Consulting with parents and teachers is an essential component in Adlerian play therapy because these adults can have a significant impact on children and their lifestyles. Parents and teachers are invaluable sources of information about children's developmental history, learning styles, and interactional patterns. They can also provide support for changes children make during play therapy. As children learn new ways of viewing themselves, others, and the world and begin to develop new attitudes and practice more socially appropriate behaviors, parents and teachers can help them apply their learning to many different situations outside the play session. Quite frequently, parents and teachers need the counselor's help to move in positive directions in the way they view themselves and the children. They may also need to make shifts in their patterns of interacting with other adults and children.

Some children seem to struggle more with relationships and situations at home, some experience the bulk of their problems at school, and others struggle in both places. We base the focus of our consultation with important adults in the child's life on the initial reports of where the child seems to be experiencing the most negative feedback. With a child who is having difficulties with other family members but does not seem to be having similar difficulties at school, we might spend all of our consultation time with parents without consulting with the teacher, the school counselor, or other school personnel. For a child who is really struggling at school (either behaviorally or academically) but seems to be doing well at home, we might concentrate our consultation with teachers or other members of the school staff. If a child is experiencing problems in both settings, we will work to collaborate both with parents and with school personnel to make sure that the child has consistent global support for any changes that he or she decides to make.

In our consultation with parents and teachers, we follow the same four-phase Adlerian model we use in our play therapy. Just as these phases—building the relationship, gathering information about lifestyles, helping clients gain insight into lifestyle, and reorienting–reeducating clients—are not discrete in the play therapy process, they are not discrete in the consultation process either. We continue to work on the relationship throughout the process, regardless of the phase in which we are working, simply because the relationship is the foundation for any changes that might occur during our interaction.

We gauge whether to overlap the other phases on the basis of the clients' readiness and needs. For instance, for the Browns, a family whose members are very discouraged, it might be appropriate to teach the new skill of encouragement during the first or second session if I (KMW) think that the parents would be responsive to this teaching and apply what they have learned with the child. If I (TK) felt that Mrs. Ajabu's personality priorities were negatively affecting her relationships with her students, I might share a guess about this early in our second or third consultation session. However, I would probably wait until later in the relationship to do this if I believed that she would be more open to this feedback after we have developed a stronger rapport.

Many of the counselors we have trained have been a bit intimidated by working with adults (okay . . . sometimes they have been shaking in their metaphorical boots—after all, they did choose to work with kids for a reason). It will be important for you to examine your own feelings about working with adults. If you are one of those people who feel threatened by the idea of building supportive relationships with grown-ups, afraid of confronting them when they are acting in ways that are not in the best interest of their children, or insecure in your ability to help them gain insight and teach them skills, you will need to explore the underlying issues connected to these concerns. If this is too daunting to do by yourself, it might be helpful to do with a supervisor or personal counselor.

Parent Consultation

Parent involvement is a really important component of Adlerian play therapy. Although children can make progress even without parental participation, when parents are active partners in the process, changes are much more likely to be systemic and long lasting. When children know that their parents care enough about them to make changes in their own behavior, it is easier for them to give up a defensive posture and enter wholeheartedly into the relationship with the play therapist. When parents are showing support for the positive changes they observe in their children, the children are often more willing to alter their attitudes and behaviors.

It is not always possible to involve parents in the play therapy process on a weekly basis. The configuration of the parent consultation will vary with each family and the setting of the play therapy. Many school counselors and some agency counselors do not have the time or the resources to include parents in every session with a child, so they have to create a different kind of schedule for their consultation sessions. For instance, to include parents in the process, these counselors might choose to have a 5- to 10-minute telephone conversation with parents every other week or an hour-long meeting once a month. Counselors might require parents of children in play therapy to attend parenting class based on Adlerian principles. These classes often use books such as *Raising Kids Who Can* (Bettner & Lew, 1990, 1998), *A Parent's Guide to Understanding and Motivating Children* (Lew & Bettner, 2000), *The Parent's Handbook: Systematic Training for Effective Parenting* (Dinkmeyer et al., 2007), *Positive Discipline* (Nelson, 2011), *Parent Group Handbook for Calming the Family Storm* (McKay, 2005), or *Active Parenting: A Parent's Guide to Raising Happy and Successful Children* (Popkin, 2014) as the source of information for the class. Sometimes, asking a parent to read a parenting book based on Adlerian principles is the best way to go in the parent consultation–parent education quest. Some examples of books that might appeal to parents are *Ain't Misbehavin': Tactics for Tantrums, Meltdowns, Bedtime Blues, and Other Perfectly Normal Kid Behaviors* (Schafer, 2011); *Honey, I Wrecked the Kids: When Yelling, Screaming, Threats, Bribes, Time-Outs, Sticker Charts and Removing Privileges All Don't Work* (Schafer, 2009); *Encouraging Words for Kids: What to Say to Bring Out a Child's Confidence* (Bartlett, 2012); or *If I Have to Tell You One More Time . . . : The Revolutionary Program That Gets Your Kids to Listen Without Nagging, Reminding, or Yelling* (McCready, 2012). Other counselors use a filial therapy model (Bratton, Landreth, Kellum, & Blackard, 2006; Guerney, 2013; VanFleet, 2009, 2013) to train parents to build a stronger relationship with their children. By thinking creatively, counselors who cannot (or do not want to) require parents to participate in the play therapy process can devise methods to include them.

Tailoring the Parent Consultation to the Family

We tailor the configuration of the parent consultation on our clinical judgments about what would be most likely to meet the needs of the family. Our preference is to talk with parents for at least one entire session to begin to build a relationship with them and hear them talk about the presenting problem before we even meet the child. After this initial session, we usually see parents for 20 minutes of the session and the child for 30 minutes of the session. Depending on schedules, we may see the parents one week and the child the next week. At other times, we might combine the play session and the parent consultation, including the parents or other family members in a play session. With other families, we meet with the child for the entire 50 minutes of two or three sessions and then meet with parents for an entire session the next week. You will want to decide what works for you in your setting and what works best for the families with which you work.

There are many factors to be considered in tailoring the parent consultation to the needs of the family. Some important considerations are the willingness of parents to participate in the play therapy process, the marital status of the child's parents, the severity of the child's problem, the severity of any family problems, the parents' relationship, the parenting skills demonstrated by the parents, and the personal difficulties experienced by the parents.

If the family is a two-parent family, we try to get both parents involved. Often the parent who calls says that the other parent is unwilling or unable to attend sessions because he or she is not interested, does not have the time, disapproves of therapy, or some other reason. Surprisingly, this happens when parents have divorced and in families in which the parents are still married and living together. In this situation, I (TK) usually say that I want to contact the other parent directly. When I do contact the other parent, I say that I need his or her help to be able to help the child. I discuss that both parents know the child better than I can ever know the child because I spend less than 1 hour a week with the child. I also talk about needing as many possible points of view to truly know the child, I value both parents' perceptions equally, and that input from both parents is important to the child's growth. I also mention that I sometimes ask parents to do some things differently at home and I want both of them to hear my suggestions so that I can get feedback from all concerned parties. To honor their needs, I express a willingness to make reasonable accommodations and structure the parent consultation sessions according to their schedule and emphasize that they do not need to come to every single session. Few parents continue to resist some level of participation in response to a personal invitation from me in which I emphasize how important they are to the child and the child's progress.

If the child is in a stepfamily or joint custody situation, it is important for the counselor to at least meet any parents or stepparents who spend a significant amount of time with the child or have disciplinary power over the child. It is not usually productive to have repeated sessions with divorced parents who are still involved in custody battles or who are still conflictually enmeshed with one another. However, sometimes it is helpful to have one or two sessions that include all of the adults involved in the child's life to explain the process of play therapy and to stress the importance of consistency and communication for the sake of the child.

In many families, the problem really stems from family difficulties and not from the individual child who has been labeled as the "identified patient." When the family problems are minor, the parent consultation usually consists of encouraging the parents on the things they are doing well, making suggestions for minor adjustments in discipline and communication patterns, and helping parents learn to monitor changes in the child's behavior at home. With families in which there are more deep-seated problems affecting the child, the parent consultation is more complex. The counselor may choose to switch to family play therapy (Bowers, 2013; Gil & Selekman, 2015; Higgins-Klein, 2013), refer the family for family counseling, or help the family access other resources such as in-home family therapy.

Some children have problems that stem from difficulties within the marital dyad. It could be that they are acting out the conflict in their parents' relationship or serving as a scapegoat or distraction for their parents. If the marital problems are minor, the counselor can use parent consultation to work with the parents on better communication and cooperation within the marital dyad as well as within the parent–child system. When marital problems are moderate to severe, the counselor should probably refer the parents for marriage counseling outside the play therapy context whenever possible. (Neither of us do marriage counseling—we just don't like all that yelling.)

In many cases, the difficulty stems from the parents' lack of parenting skills. There is no owner's manual that comes with having children (believe us, if there were, we would have snatched one up). When children are born, parents have to learn how to discipline and provide the structure and routine necessary to young children. This is not an easy set of skills to learn. Parents may also lack communication skills and knowledge related to child development, both of which are very helpful in raising children. With families in which the parents are struggling with parenting, the parent consultation primarily consists of teaching the parents strategies such as listening skills, problem definition, goal recognition, solution generation, consequence setting, and encouragement. The extent of the parents' needs in this area will dictate the intensity and the content of the parent consultation.

Some parents have personal problems that prevent them from interacting in a nurturing way with their children. They may have emotional problems, residual problems from being sexually or physically abused, struggles with drug or alcohol abuse, or other difficulties that preclude appropriate relationships with their children. Parents sometimes have family-of-origin issues that interfere with their ability to parent. Adults who have not resolved critical issues with their own parents often have difficulty devoting the necessary energy to their children. With these parents, if the problems are relatively mild, the counselor can do some short-term personal counseling as a part of the ongoing parent consultations. However, some parents have such deep-seated difficulties that the time spent in parent consultation is simply not enough to have a discernible impact on the situation, and they need additional personal counseling. It is essential that counselors constantly monitor their own boundaries and work to keep the child and the child's issues separate from the parents' personal issues. This is a tricky situation and may be a time counselors wish to seek supervision.

Conceptualizing Parents' Lifestyles

Just as it is important to conceptualize children's lifestyles to optimize the play therapy process, understanding parents' lifestyles can help make parent consultation more effective (Kottman & Ashby, 1999). Your thoughts about parents' lifestyles will influence the content and the process of parent consultation. You will use your understanding of parents' Crucial Cs and personality priorities to guide you in tailoring your recommendations and teaching as a means of optimizing their cooperation and compliance. As parents describe their lives, their relationships with others, and the child's presenting problem, you will glean important clues about the parents' Crucial Cs and personality priorities from the parents' story and your own affective response to the telling of the story. This is a way to figure out how to "speak their language."

In this chapter, I (TK) describe my own affective reactions to illustrate how to use your affective response to help recognize parents' Crucial Cs and personality priorities. You may have totally different reactions to certain of these lifestyle elements. The goal is for you to begin to notice your reactions and use them in discerning the different groups of parents so that you can adapt your parent consultation in response to the lifestyle of the parents.

Crucial Cs

Although Lew and Bettner (1998, 2000) did not discuss the application of the Crucial Cs to adults, we have found that considering whether parents have mastered each of the Crucial Cs can be very helpful in our interactions with them. In the process of developing an understanding of parents, we consider whether parents have developed each of the Crucial Cs and how their own incorporation of each C (connection, capability, counting, and courage) into their lifestyle affects their relationship with their child and their child's lifestyle.

Parents who do not believe that they connect adequately or struggle with the skills necessary for making connections often complain about the quality of their relationships. They feel a distance in their interaction with their children and often mention that they do not know how to connect with others, including spouses or ex-spouses. They often have poor social skills, lack the ability to foster social interest in their children or have limited social interest, and struggle with ways to teach their children social skills. The children of parents who do not believe they can connect with others usually develop problems connecting because of these factors. Not having models for appropriate social skills or encouragement for the development of social interest, these children tend to struggle with making and maintaining relationships. Their presenting problems tend to cluster around friendship issues and getting along with others—both at home and at school. They often evidence attitudes and behaviors indicative of low social interest, manifested in their roles as social isolates, bullies, or social rejects with poorly developed positive social networks.

My (TK) usual affective response to these parents is a feeling of disconnection. I often feel sorry for them because they seem to struggle with connecting, but other than that I have a sense of being in the same room but not together with them. I do not feel drawn to building a relationship with them and really have to work on making connections. Depending on how much effort I have to put into the relationship, I may begin to resent their seeming lack of effort toward making a contribution to the interaction. It is essential to monitor my affective response to these parents so that I can stay positive about the relationship.

Parents who doubt that they are capable have strong feelings of inferiority, especially related to their parenting skills. These parents often report that they have consulted many professionals in search of a magical formula that will solve any problems experienced by the child. The complaints of this group of parents tend to fall into two dichotomous categories. They either express extreme self-doubt in the area of parenting and assume exclusive responsibility for their children's struggles or overcompensate and develop a sense of arrogance and challenge about their children's problems to protect themselves from their feelings of inadequacy. Those who blame themselves for their children's problems express concerns about their own parenting skills, attributing their children's problems to their own lack of ability. These parents often describe themselves as failures, in many different roles and situations (e.g., as parents, as employees, as partners). Parents who are overcompensating for their worries about whether they are capable tend to go toward the other extreme—blaming the child, their ex-wife, the child's teacher (etc.) for the problems the child is experiencing or complaining that they are parenting exactly the way they were parented, and "it worked for me, so it should work for my kid."

The children of parents who do not believe that they are capable usually struggle with similar issues as those of their parents. Their presenting problems often fall into the category of underachieving. They may not do well in school, have problems with motor skills, or feel generally inadequate. These behaviors stem from a lack of belief in their own abilities. Children who do not believe they are capable are not capable.

Parents who blame their own lack of skills for their children's struggles tend to evoke a protective sense in me—I want to help them to feel unashamed and adequate. I also want to jump in and teach them skills so that they will stop doubting that they are capable. Neither of these reactions is particularly helpful. I need to remember that it is disrespectful to try to take feelings (even those that are not constructive or useful) away from clients; it is much more helpful to acknowledge those feelings and help clients decide whether they wish to learn new attitudes toward themselves and their parenting abilities. I must also keep in mind that, no matter how many lessons I give in parenting skills, these parents will not successfully apply them until they have made some shifts in their willingness to believe that they can be capable as parents. Encouragement is a tool that will help to prepare the way for their learning and applying new parenting skills.

With parents who blame others as a way of compensating for feelings of inferiority, my usual response tends to be defensive. I want to defend the child, the spouse, the teacher, or myself—whoever is the focus of the parental wrath. It is often helpful to remind myself that these parents are doing the best that they can. I must avoid responding to their overcompensation as much as possible, because debating about who is to blame is seldom helpful. It is much more constructive to acknowledge the underlying feelings and encourage these parents for what they are doing well rather than pointing out that once again they have provided evidence that they are not capable.

Parents who do not accept that they count also fall into two separate camps: (a) those who present themselves as having little or no impact on their children, in their families, or on the school; and (b) those who try to make sure they count by overpowering everyone else. Those who have given up the possibility of being significant report that others do not take them seriously or hear what they have to say. In the initial interview, these parents frequently report that they do not know anything about their child and cannot answer questions about daily routine, friendships, and so forth.

These parents usually describe their reasons for bringing the child to therapy as being connected to the demands of others—the school recommended it, the child's grandmother insisted on it and she is paying, and so forth. They often decline to engage in the process of generating therapeutic goals for the child. Their belief that they have little or no significance undermines their ability to assume responsibility, so they abdicate the possibility of having power or influence in regard to their child.

Children of parents who do not believe they count may have similar issues—often these parents convey that all of the members of their family are not really important or valuable, which trickles down to the children. Other times, the parents take up so little space in the family that children develop a sense of entitlement. They may decide that they are the only people who count in the family and must be pampered or exalted in some way.

Especially because I struggle with the Crucial C of count, I usually have a strong emotional reaction to these parents, but my response can vary, depending on the parent and on how my own life is going. Sometimes I want to hop on a white horse and ride out to be their champion, making sure that everyone who comes into contact with them is forced to acknowledge that they are important, that they do count. Sometimes I get discouraged listening to how little influence and power they have, and I want to huddle in a corner and give up. Sometimes I get frustrated with their willingness to abdicate their right to be important in their child's life, and I want to do something to force them to give up their powerless stance. None of these initial responses is helpful for parents who do not believe that they count. Instead, I need to remember to encourage, encourage, encourage with my acknowledgment of their potential for making their child's life better.

Other parents overcompensate for their doubts about their own significance by demanding attention and trying to dominate others (their children, school personnel, the play therapist), presenting their viewpoints in an extremely forceful manner in an attempt to feel significant and ensure that they count. These parents always have extensive knowledge about what happens on a daily basis with their children, and they have heated opinions on therapeutic goals and how to achieve them.

Often my affective response to these parents is a feeling of being threatened in some way by them, compounded by a desire to show them that they are not quite as significant as they are pretending they are. This sense of challenge is an important cue for me—it means I must keep in mind that there are doubts underneath the overcompensation. It is impossible to be helpful to parents when I am feeling threatened by their desire to be significant in their child's life. I have to use self-management to stay empathic and respectful with these parents.

Parents who lack courage feel inadequate and unsure of themselves. They are extremely discouraged by the challenges of parenting. They describe their lives as bleak and defeating. They seldom take risks and tend to give up without trying. As they describe their struggles or the difficulties faced by their child, they may blame others, taking little or no responsibility for their part in the situation. When they are challenged or confronted with a situation they do not know how to handle, they usually shut down, refusing to attempt a solution. These parents often come to play therapy expecting the therapist to fix the problem with no input or effort from them. In discussing the presenting problem, parents who lack courage usually list behaviors that suggest their child lacks courage as well.

By modeling feelings of inferiority, hopelessness, and utter discouragement, these parents may be inadvertently teaching their children that there is no way to courageously cope with life's problems. Children of parents who lack courage often echo these issues in their lives—they tend to give up easily and refuse to try activities in which they are not guaranteed success. They are often labeled as underachievers at school.

It is very discouraging to listen to parents who lack courage. They seem to have an aura of hopelessness that is contagious. I often feel defeated and powerless as I listen to them, or I may have an urge to fix the problem for them so that they will feel better. Neither of these reactions is particularly helpful. It is important to remember that parents who lack courage can learn to take risks and learn to do things even though they are afraid. If I get so discouraged that I feel nothing will help their situation, then I will just add to their lack of courage. When I take on the responsibility for single-handedly making everything better for them, I do the same thing. I need to keep myself from catching their discouragement and remember that my most powerful tool with them is encouragement—acknowledging effort and small improvements.

Personality Priorities

Parents' personality priorities are a major influence on their style of parenting and their relationship with their children (Kottman & Ashby, 1999). As the therapist listens to parents describe their own lives and problems exhibited by their children, the parents' personality priorities are often evident, as there are patterns of complaints described by each of the personality priorities. Even when discussing appointment times and therapeutic goals, parental personality priorities are often clear to the play therapist. As with the Crucial Cs, the therapist can also use his or her affective response to parents as a guide for determining their personality priorities. We always consider the possibility that parents have a primary and a secondary priority, and we think about where on the range of constructive–healthy–functional to destructive–unhealthy–dysfunctional parents fall on the continuum of the manifestation of their personality priorities.

Parents with control as a personality priority tend to describe their world as "out of control." They often characterize their relationships in terms of making sure that they have control over others (e.g., children, spouse), control over situations (e.g., how things go for the child at school), or control over themselves. They frequently express feelings of anger and fear because it is impossible to achieve control over the various elements of their lives. Controlling parents use words like *disrespectful*, *disobedient*, *lazy*, *uncooperative*, *bad-tempered*, and *inappropriate* to describe their children. In discussing appointment times and goals for therapy, these parents are seldom willing to be flexible, demanding that schedules and therapeutic strategies accommodate their needs and desires.

Interacting with control-oriented parents, I (TK) often have the feeling of being powerless and "out of control" because of my reaction to their need to establish dominance. I frequently feel frustrated or annoyed by these parents' need to control all of their relationships and life circumstances. It is important for me to manage my own emotional reaction, avoid getting drawn into power struggles, and keep myself from feeling controlled by them.

Pleasing parents experience high levels of anxiety about their child's behavior and self-esteem. They also doubt their parenting skills. They may feel that they are not capable or that they do not count. Pleasing parents describe their lives in terms of their frustrated attempts to make sure that everyone else is happy. They often report that their spouse complains about their unwillingness to follow through with consequences or inability to be strict in their approach to discipline. Pleasers often get "constructive" feedback about their parenting or their child's behavior from friends, relatives, the child's teacher, and others. Because they work to avoid rejection or anger, this can result in a pampered child who has too much power. Pleasing parents often describe their child as being (a) demanding and overpowering; (b) overly aggressive and tyrannical; or (c) extremely anxious, easily overwhelmed, and lacking courage. They are always willing to work their schedule around the therapist's timetable, often offering to change other appointments to accommodate the therapist. In discussions about therapeutic goals for their children, pleasing parents are often very unsure of what they want. They tend to avoid committing themselves to a particular set of therapeutic goals or rely on others (a spouse, the play therapist, a grandparent) to determine the desired outcomes of the therapeutic process.

I really like pleasing parents—after all, their strongest desire when they are with me is to keep me happy. What is not to like about that? Because I am a pleaser, I am especially empathic as they are describing their constant struggle to please others. After a while, though, I get frustrated by these parents' unwillingness to take a stand with their child and with the other people in their lives. I believe that it is really important to follow through with consequences and to take responsibility for saying no when it will be in the best interests of the child (even though this is often difficult for me to do with my son Jacob, being a pleaser myself). It is essential when I work with pleasing parents to remember that these parents tend to believe that they count conditionally and need my unconditional acceptance. Having my support for taking a powerful stand with others without any disapproval from me if they do not always succeed can create a relationship in which pleasing parents can learn that they are capable and they do count.

Parents whose personality priority is superiority often struggle with the admission that they need to consult a counselor at all. Their description of their lives frequently sounds like a fantasy of perfection—except for this tiny fly in the ointment connected to their child. Superiority parents usually have very high standards for themselves and for their children. Their complaints related to the child often stem from the child's inability to live up to these standards in some way (e.g., failing or underachieving in school, being overly anxious socially, or not having enough friends).

These parents frequently believe that letting anyone else know there is a problem or asking for help is an acknowledgment of their own vulnerability or an admittance of the possibility that they really are inferior in some way to others. To compensate for their feelings of failure connected to the problem, these parents often gather information about the child's problem or diagnosis so that they can become experts in this area. Their reactions tend to be similar to those experienced by parents who struggle with being capable or significant. They either blame themselves, experiencing large doses of doubt and guilt, or blame someone else (e.g., their child, the teacher, their spouse), spreading large doses of recrimination. In some cases, these parents deemphasize the extent of the problem and discount the input from others about their child. Some superiority parents exaggerate or exacerbate the problem so that they can prove that their child is worse than all the other children. If they cannot guarantee that they will win the prize for "Best Child" or "Best Parent," they rig the deck so that they are a shoo-in for "Worst Child." The tendency of these parents is to establish their superiority over the therapist right from the start. They often spend the first phone call or the first session interrogating the therapist about his or her qualifications to work with their child, and they frequently want to dictate therapeutic goals with no input from the therapist.

I have to confess that my initial reaction to superiority parents is a sense of challenge. Because my secondary personality priority is superiority, I would like to prove to them that (even though they are pretty superior) I am even more superior than they are. I can also become intimidated because they really do know more than I do about their child's particular problem. These reactions are not helpful, however. Again, I must exercise self-management in my reaction to these parents. (Are you detecting a theme here?) It is not helpful to get into a contest about who is the biggest expert. Providing my credentials and a description of any areas of expertise I might have and admitting the areas in which I have no expertise in a matter-of-fact way is actually the best approach to questions about my qualifications. Reminding myself that these parents struggle with worries about their own competence and providing unconditional, empathic understanding and encouragement work much better than being defensive or overpowering, which might sometimes be my default response to them.

The primary complaint of comfort-oriented parents is that parenting is too much work. Being a parent takes time away from their ability to do what they want to do with their lives, which is usually to relax and have fun. These parents have a strong need to avoid tension and stress, and being a parent may be uncomfortable for them because it involves a certain amount of stress even with a child who is not experiencing difficulties. Having a child with problems increases stress levels exponentially. Comfort parents often report that raising a child takes much more energy than they anticipated, and they feel that they cannot comfortably invest the work that it would take to do a good job being a parent. They do not like setting limits or providing routine or structure, so they tend to parent from a laissez-faire perspective. This frequently causes problems because their child may be running wild or turning into a couch potato. The child may also be failing school, acting in hostile or overly aggressive ways with other children, refusing to do schoolwork, or rebelling against rules and structure. Comfort parents seldom recognize any of these conditions as a problem. They frequently see themselves as their child's buddy—someone who can share the fun aspects of childhood without the responsibilities of parenthood. The complaints of others (e.g., teachers, spouses, principals, mothers-in-law) sometimes become so stressful to them that they decide to take action and bring the child to play therapy. However, they often do this with the caveat, "fix my child, but do not expect me to make any changes." These parents have difficulty finding times that are convenient for bringing the child to therapy because therapy is uncomfortable and inconvenient. They seldom have concrete and specific therapeutic goals because they really want parenting to be easier, the child to not be so much trouble, and other people to leave them alone.

Comfort parents are usually delightful people. They are fun, spontaneous, and easygoing. My initial reaction to consulting with comfort parents is appreciation for their ability to go with the flow. I also like their honest enjoyment of the wonderful things about children and childhood. However, as the relationship progresses, I find myself feeling frustrated at what feels to me as comfort parents' unwillingness to do the work to become better parents. It is essential that I not get caught up in my need for them to make progress and make progress quickly. I also cannot take on the responsibility of providing the energy or impetus for change for them. I need to look at small efforts and evidence of small successes, and I need to have the patience to let them motivate themselves rather than trying to provide the motivation for them.

Stages of Parent Consultation

The Adlerian play therapist spends the first part of the consultation process building a relationship with parents, working to establish a cooperative partnership whose purpose is optimizing the atmosphere, attitudes, and interactions in the environments in which the child lives and learns. During the second phase of the consultation, the therapist uses questioning strategies, sand trays, and art techniques to gather information from parents about the child, family members, school personnel, and the child's world (e.g., neighborhood, friends, church).

As the therapist becomes familiar with the child's lifestyle and the lifestyle of the parents, he or she develops conceptualizations of the child and the parents that include information about Crucial Cs, goals of misbehavior, personality priorities, mistaken beliefs, private logic, and assets. On the basis of these conceptualizations, the next step is the design of a treatment plan for the play therapy process with the child and for the consultation with parents. (See Chapters 7 and 8 for a complete description of gathering information, developing conceptualizations, and designing treatment plans.) During the third phase of the consultation, the therapist uses various techniques (e.g., spitting in the soup, making guesses about lifestyle patterns, sand trays, art techniques , metacommunicating about underlying messages in their interactions with the child, and playful life-coaching strategies) to help parents gain insight into their own lifestyles and into the lifestyle of the child, with the intent of helping them make shifts in their attitudes toward themselves, the child, and their relationship. As the parents make transitions in perceptions and beliefs, the therapist moves into the fourth phase of the consultation, reorientation–reeducation, in which he or she uses role-playing, art techniques, sand trays, and playful life-coaching strategies to teach parenting skills (e.g., communication skills, problem-solving skills, and encouragement skills) and help the parents develop a sense of renewed confidence about their ability to parent the child.

During each of the four phases, the counselor may decide to adjust the approach to the parents on the basis of parental Crucial Cs and personality priorities (Kottman & Ashby, 1999). As the counselor builds the relationship, it is often useful to customize the explanation of the play therapy process and the benefits of play therapy. Taking the lifestyle of the parents into account in choosing strategies for building a relationship can also be helpful. By adapting the questioning strategies in the process of gathering data about the child's lifestyle and parents' lifestyles during the second phase, the counselor can often increase the depth and the amount of information available. Asking questions in a form designed to complement parents' style of communication, the counselor will be less likely to evoke a defensive reaction. The counselor can also use parents' Crucial Cs and personality priorities as the basis for his or her approach in the third phase of the consultation. It is possible to present inferences about lifestyle patterns in a way that enhances the probability of the parent hearing and accepting the feedback. During reorientation–reeducation, the counselor can keep elements of parents' lifestyles in mind when formulating recommendations about which parenting strategies would be helpful and what issues might be getting in the way of their parenting.

Building the Relationship With Parents

The Adlerian play therapist begins to involve parents during the initial telephone conversation. During this first interaction, the therapist asks for a brief description of the present difficulty and the history of the problem. This is also the time for discussing the practical aspect of the therapy process, such as how much it will cost and the time, day, and length of the play therapy sessions. The therapist also gives parents a brief explanation of the rationale and process of play therapy and answers any questions before setting up the first appointment, which is usually designed as a parent consultation without the presence of the child. The play therapist listens for clues about parental lifestyle factors that can affect the relationship between the parents and the child, the family atmosphere, discipline patterns, and so forth. It is important for the therapist to begin forming hypotheses about parents' Crucial Cs and personality priorities so that an understanding of these personality dynamics can inform the process of parent consultation.

During the first session with parents, the play therapist asks them to further elaborate about the presenting problem, describe any attempts the family or school has made to remedy the problem, and discuss possible goals for the therapeutic process. In this session, the therapist often explains the importance of the parents and other family members in the formation of the child's lifestyle, without implying blame.

It is important during the first session to explain the necessity of involvement by parents and other family members in the therapeutic process. If the problem seems to be home based, the therapist discusses that the solution will probably involve the entire family working together—changing the way they interact with one another and learning to support the identified-patient child. This will mean that some sessions of play therapy will just be for the child, but others will involve various family members—sometimes one parent, sometimes both parents, sometimes a sibling or two, sometimes the entire family. If the problem seems to be school based, the counselor discusses that the family will need to support changes that the child is making at home and the parents may have to act as child advocates with school personnel. Parents need to hear that their involvement and their willingness to change their own attitudes and behaviors send a key message to the child. They also need to understand how essential the role of encouraging the child's progress is and the importance of reinforcing the lessons taught by the play therapist for long-lasting changes to occur.

Many parents who bring their child to counseling feel that the very fact that their child needs help suggests that they have failed in their parenting. Sometimes these feelings of inadequacy can interfere with their willingness and ability to form a collaborative partnership with the therapist. With these parents, it is absolutely essential to establish rapport and a sense of shared responsibility before moving into making suggestions about parenting strategies or other interventions from the third and fourth phases of the consultation.

To ensure that the relationship with the parents develops in a positive direction, the counselor uses skills that are similar to the skills used in building a relationship in play therapy. (See Chapter 5 for skills for building the relationship with the child.) The counselor actively listens to parents, paraphrasing, summarizing, and reflecting feelings so that parents feel heard and understood. Often, having someone really listen to family members eases tensions in the family and relieves guilt or negative feelings about the necessity of consulting a helping professional. By asking questions and providing encouragement, the counselor conveys interest and caring to parents. With parents who are interested and willing, we often use some play therapy techniques with them as part of this phase. We may ask them to draw a picture of themselves as in their role as parent, make a sand tray containing figures that stand for each member of their family, bring in a song that represents each family member's strengths or struggles, demonstrate a movement or gesture to show how they feel when parenting is going well or badly, or some other creative way of establishing rapport.

Because it is really too early to give advice to parents (even if they solicit it, they are seldom really ready to make major changes in attitudes or behavior this early in the process), it is sometimes necessary to return the responsibility to the parent by asking, "What do you think you should do?" or saying, "I bet you could come up with some ideas you could try."

Encouragement is a key component in parent and teacher consultation in two different ways. It is essential that the play therapist (a) use encouragement as a tool to give parents and teachers feedback on their own improvements and efforts and (b) teach parents and teachers how to use encouraging techniques with children and other adults.

In describing the benefits of play therapy and parent consultation, the counselor can base his or her description on parents' personality priorities (Kottman & Ashby, 1999). With parents whose priority is control, it is often productive to explain that the process can help parents feel more in control of themselves and of their lives. This explanation is both accurate and reassuring to these parents. For parents whose primary priority is pleasing, the counselor can emphasize that the desired end result is a happier, more balanced child and a family whose members experience smoother communication, more cooperation, and reduced tension. In explaining the expected outcome to superiority-striving parents, the counselor can stress the previous accomplishments and expertise of the parents and suggest that play therapy and parent consultation can enable the parents to continue that trend and assist family members in enhancing their ability to meet parental standards. The description of the benefits for comfort parents should focus on the potential for life becoming less stressful and parenting becoming easier and more fun.

As the play therapist works to build the relationship with parents, it will also be useful to take the parents' Crucial Cs and personality priorities into account. With parents who do not easily connect, the play therapist must budget extra time for the first phase of the consultation, making sure that parents feel a sense of connection to the therapist before going any further in the process. With parents who do not feel capable or do not believe they count, it is important for the play therapist to use a lot of encouragement during this first phase, acknowledging the things that the parents do well and the places in which they have made a difference in the lives of their children. With parents who lack courage, the therapist would do well to remember to proceed slowly with the process of building the relationship. These parents often perceive relationships as risky. They do not make relationships easily or quickly, and the therapist will need to be patient with them.

Controlling parents are highly sensitive to the possibility that the therapist is trying to control them and that the consulting process might lead them to doing something that would be embarrassing or mistaken (Kottman & Ashby, 1999). They are distrustful of the therapy process, so it is imperative to go slowly to gain their trust. When they try to control you, it would be wise for you to remember that these parents are actually afraid of not being in control because they perceive that experience as being out of control. You will need to avoid telling these parents what to do, as they will react very poorly to advice or directives.

With pleasing parents, the best way to build the relationship is to serve as a source of encouragement (Kottman & Ashby, 1999). You can enter the relationship as a person who is positive, supportive, and relatively easy to please, someone who is not going to be angry or reject the pleasing parent no matter what. This will give you the leverage later in the consulting process to be able to serve as a counterbalance for any negative reactions these parents get from their child and other important people in their lives as they begin to believe that they can be more assertive and stand up to others.

The process of relationship building with parents who strive toward superiority will proceed more smoothly when you keep in mind that they are acting in ways designed to help them cope with strong feelings of inferiority (Kottman & Ashby, 1999). You must not let yourself feel threatened or challenged by these parents. For successful consultation, you must provide them with empathy, encouragement, and support rather than getting into a contest about who knows more or is more qualified. By acknowledging the expertise and assets of superiority parents, you can establish a very strong therapeutic alliance with these parents.

The key to a successful relationship with comfort parents is being relaxed and keeping interactions free of pressure (Kottman & Ashby, 1999). By interacting in a way that is gently positive and making sure to avoid overwhelming them by being too enthusiastic or energetic in the interaction, you will successfully connect with these parents. You can then use this relationship as a way to motivate comfort parents to make efforts that are not always comfortable for them.

Gathering Information From Parents

Although it is often necessary to allow parents to vent their feelings of frustration and helplessness about the presenting problem, after an outpouring in initial sessions, the focus should shift so that only a few minutes in each consultation are devoted to discussing the presenting problem and any developments related to it. You will want to avoid having the presenting problem as the primary focus of information gathering because you do not want to encourage family members to continue defining the child in terms of the presenting problem. This is important because it would be easy to get overwhelmed or discouraged if, every time you talked to parents, they spent the entire time complaining about their children and their lives. (We have been there, done that, have the T-shirt, and have learned our lessons—we want to save you this misery.)

During this phase of the consultation, the play therapist gathers information from parents about their perceptions of (a) the history of the child's development; (b) the child's lifestyle; (c) the parents' lifestyles; (d) the lifestyles of other important members of the family; (e) family values; (f) family atmosphere; (g) the child's interactions with family members, other children, and pertinent school personnel; (h) parenting attitudes and skills; and (i) any other information that the therapist would consider necessary to develop an understanding of the intrapersonal and interpersonal dynamics of the child, the parents, and other relevant individuals in the child's life. Appendix B has Children's Lifestyle Questions for Parents, which the play therapist can use to solicit information. Appendix B contains a list of questions that we use in gathering data about children and their parents. We do not use all of these questions with every parent. We pick and choose our questions to ensure that we gather the information we believe will assist us in understanding each particular family.

However, it is not helpful to sit and ask the parents questions and write the answers on this form, which might serve to undermine all the work you put into building the relationship in the first phase. There are many play therapy techniques you can use to gather information if you want to get imaginative and not just fall back on the old standard of asking questions. You can invite parents to do sand trays, adventure therapy techniques, life-coaching activities, expressive arts strategies (dance, movement, art, poetry, theatre), or any other creative method for gathering information. You will want to think about the modality that has the potential to be the best match with the parent—Is this a parent who feels comfortable simply talking? Is this a parent who would be more at ease doing a sand tray or an art process? Is this a parent who likes to move or listen to music? There are many different ways to frame asking a question—you can just ask it and expect a verbal answer, and you can ask it as a drawing stimulus, sand tray setup, or writing prompt.

For example, you could ask parents to do the following directive sand trays by picking figures that represent information about the following and arranging them in a sand tray:

- The people in our family . . . (Pick one to three figures to represent each of the people in your family).
- What bugs me about our family/what bugs me about being a parent . . .
- What I like about our family/what I like about being a parent . . .
- If there were family teams, who would be on each team? What would each of the teams stand for/be willing to fight for? Who would be in charge of each team?
- In family fights . . . (Who fights? Over what? How do fights get resolved?)
- What I am proud of about our family . . .
- What is important to this family (as a whole) is . . . To each of the members of the family?
- As a parent, I get angry at/about . . . As a parent, I get sad about . . .
- Three to five parenting mistakes I have made . . .
- When I make parenting mistakes, I feel . . .
- Three wishes I have for the family are . . .
- What are our family rules? Who is most likely to violate them? What happens when they do?
- What does the identified patient child do to get in trouble? How do I feel when this happens?

You could also use drawing techniques or collaging to ask these same questions if you have clients who would be more comfortable with using art to explore. With musical parents, you could ask them to bring in songs that represent each of the members of the family. With kinesthetic adults, you could ask them to show you how each member of the family moves.

Related to the child, the focus in the information-gathering process is on how parents perceive (a) the ways the child gains his or her significance in the family; (b) the patterns of interaction between the child and other family members; (c) the child's ideas about himself or herself, others, and the world; (d) the child's behaviors, attitudes, and motivations; (e) the child's assets; and (f) the child's methods of coping with problems. To figure out the themes woven into the fabric of the child's life, the counselor asks parents to describe the developmental history of the child or draw a timeline of the evolution of the family that includes the developmental history of the child. Information is also solicited (by asking questions, using sand tray, or using art techniques) on the birth-order position of each of the children in the family and the personalities of and relationships between the children. It is sometimes helpful to have parents rate the children in the family on such qualities as intelligence, helpfulness, materialism, and selfishness. This helps the counselor to begin to understand how the child's psychological position in the family affects the child.

Asking about the daily routine, the child's responsibilities, and how the child copes with difficult situations helps the counselor begin to understand possible goals of misbehavior, personality priorities, and Crucial Cs. Questions (or sand trays or art processes) about behaviors that annoy the parents, how they respond to those behaviors, how they feel when the behaviors persist, and how the child reacts when he or she receives reprimands for inappropriate behaviors help the counselor formulate hypotheses about the child's goals.

It is important to check with parents about any kind of event or circumstance that could have adversely affected the child. Most parents do not realize that events such as the death of a family member or pet, divorce, an earthquake, or circumstances such as having an alcoholic or mentally ill family member can have long-lasting consequences for children. The counselor may have to ask specific questions, giving many examples of the types of events or circumstances that could have an impact on children.

Related to the parents, the focus is on how the parents perceive (a) their marital relationship; (b) their own childhood and place in their own family of origin; (c) the patterns of interaction between the parents and other family members; (d) the ideas about themselves, others, and the world; (e) their attitudes toward each of the children; (f) their ability to parent; and (g) their views on and strategies for discipline. Again, you can use sand tray, art strategies, music, movement, and/or dance to solicit information in this area. The information elicited through these processes can give you a perspective on the family atmosphere and on the relationships within the family. Some examples of sand trays or drawings you could ask parents to do might be:

- I decided to be a parent because . . .
- My marriage is . . .
- As a kid, I was . . .
- What did I learn about being a parent from my parents?
- A self-portrait of me (as a person, as a parent, as a spouse . . .)
- The world is . . .
- What I love about being a parent is . . .
- The worst moment in my life was . . .
- The best time of my life was . . .

Another playful technique I (TK) use in this phase to discover what is really important to parents (as a way of exploring family values and goals for therapy) is the "stake in the ground" (K. Kimsey-House, personal communication, October 2001). I ask these adults to tell me–draw–do a sand tray about their primary "stake in the ground" (something so important that they are willing to fight for it) in their relationship with the child. I explain that, over the years of raising my son, I realized that many of the things I thought were important (him having a clean room, him doing well in school, him eating all of his vegetables) were not actually really important to me and many of them were not really in my power to control. What is important to me is that I have a positive relationship with him in which I convey my love and support to him—that is my primary stake in the ground—I am willing to fight for that, and, to a certain extent, I can control it. I do have some secondary stakes in the ground—I would like him to contribute to the family by being responsible with chores and to be mostly respectful and pleasant in his interactions with me. These are qualities I can model, encourage, and hope that he incorporates into his lifestyle, but I do not have the power to "make" this happen.

In thinking about adapting information-gathering strategies according to parental Crucial Cs and personality priorities, it has been our experience that it is often helpful to remember where the parents' emotional vulnerabilities and trigger points are. With parents who do not connect with others and parents who lack courage, we have found that it is actually better to be matter of fact and orderly about asking the questions. These parents actually seem to prefer the counselor to bring in a clipboard with questions and a pen to take notes. The routine of rather impersonal question-and-answer sessions seems reassuring to them because they do not have to take many personal risks in such an interaction. These parents often say that they do not know the answers to questions. With parents who struggle with connecting, this may be because of the tenuousness of their connection with the child; with parents who lack courage, this is usually because of their unwillingness to take a stand by asserting that they actually know things. Sometimes it takes the pressure off these parents if we ask them to take a guess about the answer or tell us what they think another person who was observing the family or a valued friend or relative would say in response to the question.

Parents who feel that they are not capable or that they do not count are often intimidated by the "just the facts" impersonal approach, so you will want to be conversational and casual with them, interspersing your questions with encouragement and letting them tell you stories about things that happen in their lives. They are often worried that you will discover their weaknesses as a parent, so they tend to equivocate when they answer. If you want more details, you have to be very careful to avoid sounding accusatory or too serious about needing specifics so that you can maintain the warmth and unconditional nature of the relationship. Taking notes is important with parents who believe that they do not count. This conveys that you value their input highly and believe that they are significant influences in the lives of their children. For parents who struggle with capable, count, or courage, they are often more willing to do creative arts processes, like drawing or sand tray, than answer questions because there is no "right" way to do a drawing or sand tray.

For parents whose primary priorities are either control or superiority, you will need to balance being organized and undemanding in the information-gathering process (Kottman & Ashby, 1999). There is a fine line between evoking their defensive posture if they think you are being too demanding or too controlling during the interviewing process and provoking their impatience if they think you are being too casual or not following some kind of procedure for structuring the interview and organizing the information you gather. They are often more comfortable with questioning rather than more playful approaches for gathering information because the loose nature of play is uncomfortable for them. Control and superiority parents will usually try controlling the focus and flow of the questioning and often have questions of their own to ensure that they get a chance to exhibit their extensive knowledge. You will want to ensure that you get all your questions answered without getting into a power struggle with them about how the interviews go, and it will be helpful to take notes to assure them that what they are saying is important. You will need to answer their questions without getting defensive, and you can model the courage to be imperfect by telling them, "I don't know" when you don't. (Something that is very difficult for both of us to do since we both have superiority as one of our personality priorities.) These parents prefer to protect their own vulnerabilities by focusing exclusively on information related to the child and the child's problem; therefore, it is sometimes difficult to get them to answer questions about themselves and their lifestyles. Patience, persistence, and the indirect approach are often necessary in this process.

When we work with parents whose primary priority is pleasing, we weave our questions into the conversation, emphasizing our gratitude for their cooperation (Kottman & Ashby, 1999). We may also try to get them to relax a bit by using sand tray, movement, drawing, music, or other play therapy techniques. These parents are hypersensitive to criticism; we are always careful to avoid communicating anything that would trigger a defensive reaction. Because they seldom get their own needs met, pleasing parents usually love this part of the consultation process because they get to have someone listen to their experiences with empathy and acceptance. (Because both of us also strive to be pleasing to people, we can empathize with their reactions, but we need to remember not to get hooked into their anxiety.)

For parents with comfort as their primary priority, we are always laidback, gathering information slowly in a low-key manner (Kottman & Ashby, 1999). These parents respond most readily to a relaxed atmosphere, telling their story in their own way, with occasional gentle nudging from us. We have to be especially patient when they complain about the child and about other people who have "pressured" them into coming to see a play therapist. They would often rather blame others than take a look at their role in problems and their responsibility for working to solve them. (After all, blaming others is more comfortable than looking at your own part in things.)

Helping Parents Gain Insight Into Lifestyles
The primary goal of the Adlerian play therapist in this phase of the consultation is to help parents gain a new understanding of themselves

and their child so that they can correct old self-defeating attitudes and exchange destructive patterns of thinking and behaving with constructive patterns. The therapist begins this process by stressing the assets of the child and of the parents, to start the parents thinking in more positive ways about their child and themselves.

The counselor has two paths during this phase of the consultation: (a) helping parents look at the child differently and (b) helping them look at themselves differently. Some of the time, the therapist simply talks to parents and other times it is more appropriate to use play therapy techniques. In working with parents on making shifts in their perceptions of and attitudes about their child, one of the first tools that we use is reframing behaviors that have been traditionally interpreted by family members as negative. We can explain how these behaviors express the child's creativity and uniqueness and how they sometimes make a contribution to the family (e.g., a child whose misbehavior keeps parents from recognizing problems in their relationship or the child whose clowning keeps a depressed parent from becoming so depressed that she needs to be hospitalized). In situations in which we want to use play therapy techniques, rather than conversation, we might use a sand tray that we would make for parents to reframe certain behaviors (e.g., putting a figure of a tornado hovering over a group of people huddled together in the corner of the sand tray to represent how they usually think about their child and his impact on the family, then substituting a figure of a bridge that makes a connection between several people). We model an empathic understanding of the child's motivation in an attempt to help parents see their child's behavior and motivation from the perspective of the child. We do this in a way that is matter of fact and nonjudgmental so that the parents do not feel as though we are criticizing their past behaviors and attitudes in any way.

During this process, we spend much of our time using myriad techniques to present parents with information about the child's Crucial Cs, goals of misbehavior, and personality priorities so they can begin to rethink the child and his or her behavior. We explain our understanding of the ways the child has decided that he or she gains significance in the family and in other relationships—how these methods of belonging are working for the child and how they are getting in the way of successful relationships and coping strategies. We also discuss the impact the child's birth-order position and any traumatic experiences may have had on the child and his or her lifestyle. In as nonjudgmental manner as possible, we make some guesses about how the child has interpreted the family atmosphere and what it means about himself or herself, others, and the world. Describing our hypotheses about the child's mistaken beliefs and private logic, we work to help parents develop an empathic understanding of their child's strengths and struggles.

Woven into these conversations with parents are our ideas about how their own lifestyles interact with the child's lifestyle, in both constructive and destructive patterns. We teach parents about their own Crucial Cs and personality priorities (sometimes in very direct, didactic ways and sometimes in more indirect, subtle ways). We discuss how these lifestyle elements can be complementary and conflictual in the relationship between the parents and the child. We suggest ways the assets of their Crucial Cs and personality priorities are helping in their parenting and how the drawbacks of these lifestyle components can get in the way in their interactions with their child. We might draw a diagram or do a sand tray for them to illustrate how the past interactions in their family of origin could be affecting their attitudes and behaviors in the present day. We want to help them examine the parenting they received and guide them to make conscious decisions about which attitudes, values, and discipline strategies from their family of origin they want to replicate and which ones they want to leave behind. We explore how other family dynamics (such as marital issues, drug or alcohol problems, in-law advice about parenting, sibling rivalry, etc.) are influencing their ability to parent effectively. It is helpful with some parents to explore their attitudes toward parenting, their self-images related to their ability to parent, their philosophy of discipline, conflicts between the parents about how to discipline, and their attitudes toward the various children in the family. As part of this process, we also like to discover what parenting strategies have worked in the past and what parenting strategies have not worked and the factors that have differentiated their application of the effective versus the ineffective strategies. The goal during this process is to help parents make shifts in their views of their child and themselves so that they are ready to learn and apply Adlerian principles in their parenting.

For instance, I (TK) might continue to use the stake-in-the-ground technique, working with a parent in this phase. When a parent has a stake in the ground about something he or she cannot control (like whether a child always makes positive choices or whether a child always does his or her school work), this is usually a setup for frustration on everyone's part, and it might be a helpful thing to investigate problem ownership at that point (Dinkmeyer et al., 2007). For instance, if the parent wants the child to have a clean room and the child does not care whether the room is clean or not, is this a problem owned by the child or the parent? In this case, the parent has a stake in the ground about the clean room, but the child does not. Although the parent can force the child to clean the room, this is really just an invitation for an ongoing power struggle. (I would know, as this was a huge continuing struggle between my son and my husband when Jacob was in elementary school.) I believe if a parent has a strong stake in the ground about something that is not within the parent's control and the child either does not have a stake in the ground about it or has a stake in the ground in the opposite direction, the parent needs to provide the energy to make it happen in a positive way. So in our scenario with the room cleaning, the parent could initiate the room cleaning, help with it, make parts of the process into a contest or game, transforming a power struggle into a fun and pleasant experience designed to contribute to a positive cooperative relationship builder.

This phase is probably the hardest and most threatening for the majority of parents because you are asking them to actually give up many of their old ideas, attitudes, and ways of interacting and adopt new (and frequently radically different) ways of interpreting relationships and situations. This is the crux of the consultation process, and it is pretty scary. To help parents feel more comfortable with this process and increase the likelihood that they make the cognitive and emotional shifts inherent in the process of gaining insight into lifestyle, you will need to keep their Crucial Cs and personality priorities in mind.

With parents who do not easily connect, it is helpful to continue to work strongly on the relationship, remembering to reconnect with them in every session. These parents seldom think about problems in terms of relationships, so you will have to be relatively concrete when describing the impact of their attitudes and behaviors on others. It is also extremely important to avoid any judgment or blame because they already tend to feel inadequate in the area of interacting with others, and if you are not careful, you can add to their perception that they are interpersonal failures.

With parents who struggle with feeling capable and parents who feel as though they do not count, you will want to use a great deal of empathy, encouragement, and humor—making connections between their current parenting and what they learned about parenting in their family of origin; pointing out patterns in the ways they have been thinking, feeling, and behaving—without attaching any blame to your observations. It is very helpful to talk to these parents about your belief that they can and will become more capable and that they can become powerful agents for positive change in the lives of their children. Your faith in their ability to grow in constructive ways can be a tremendous motivator.

For parents who lack courage, you will want to proceed very slowly with this phase of the consultation. It is necessary to keep the amount of insight-oriented information that you share with them small and manageable so that they do not feel overwhelmed by the changes you are suggesting that they make.

So that controlling parents do not feel as though you are trying to gain power over them, you should be relatively indirect and tentative in making your interpretations, explanations, and suggestions. It is often helpful to give them several different possible interpretations of lifestyle themes, purposes of behavior, Crucial Cs, and personality priorities and engage them in a dialogue about how each interpretation could apply to the current situation. Initially, keep the focus on the child and his or her lifestyle so that these parents do not feel threatened. As they seem more comfortable talking about lifestyle issues, you can shift the emphasis to the interaction between the child's lifestyle and their lifestyle, ultimately making guesses and interpretations designed to give them insight into their own issues.

With pleasing parents, it is essential to infuse encouragement into all of your interactions during this phase, making sure that you avoid criticism or judgment. If you can keep any negative nonverbal communication to a minimum, pleasing parents are usually very open to understanding how the patterns of interaction in their family of origin might be replicating themselves in their present family. As long as they believe that they can please you by incorporating new attitudes, beliefs, and behaviors into their repertoire, they are eager to reconsider their positions. However, they get very anxious about owning their own power, being assertive, and setting limits for their child, so it is necessary to work with them on ways in which they can feel more comfortable standing up to others and taking care of themselves.

What will work best with superiority parents is to present ideas and insights as a collaborative partnership—a meeting of two parties who have valuable information and expertise who are working as a team for the betterment of the child. You will have to represent yourself as a self-confident and knowledgeable expert in the field of play therapy who needs the parents' expertise on this particular family. The mutual respect engendered by this approach often circumvents any defensive reaction on the part of parents. You can start out this phase of the consultation concentrating on the child and his or her lifestyle to establish a pattern of collegiality before moving on to discuss the interaction between the child's lifestyle and the parents' lifestyle. When you are making interpretations and suggestions related to the parent, you will want to be extremely tentative, taking a similar approach to the way you would work with parents whose personality priority is control.

Parents whose primary priority is comfort need feedback presented in nonthreatening ways, with little pressure for them to move quickly to make changes. Humor is an invaluable tool with these parents because it lets them look at their own issues in a safe way. It is also helpful to keep your consultations brief and your input limited; working very slowly to help them gain insight increases the chances that these parents will hear you and make shifts in their attitudes and behaviors.

Reorienting–Reeducating Parents

The Adlerian play therapist spends the bulk of this phase building on the parents' new insights, helping them practice applying their altered attitudes and thinking patterns, and teaching them Adlerian parenting skills. It is important to tailor the format and the content of these sessions to the needs of parents and the child.

It is helpful to consider the parents' learning style and provide the teaching in a style that works for them. For instance, a few parents will just read and apply books on Adlerian methods of discipline. These parents prefer to acquire the ideas independently and then discuss their application with the therapist. Other parents need to have concrete verbal instructions, with numerous examples from their family interactions. With these parents, the play therapist will probably want to practice the skills with the parents in session and give a one-page written description of homework assignments so that they can practice the skills between sessions. Some parents learn better when they are in a group with other parents so that they can share their own stories, realize that other parents struggle with their own children, exchange ideas about how to cope, and get support and encouragement from parents who are in situations similar to theirs. Other parents will need to do sand trays about ways they could be encouraging, make Post-it Notes to pay attention to goals of misbehavior, use role-playing to experiment different ways to respond to their children, draw a poster of different ways they could foster the Crucial Cs at home, and other such activities as part of their learning process.

You would also be well advised to take the Crucial Cs and personality priorities of the parents into account when making suggestions for changing discipline strategies and teaching parenting skills. Many parents (especially those who do not feel capable, who do not believe that they count, who lack courage, and whose personality priority is comfort) often try a strategy several times or apply it inconsistently and then decide that it does not work for them. You will want to encourage these parents to give any new discipline procedure time to work. One way to do this is to point out that they used their old methods for a long period of time, and to be fair, they should give the new methods equal time. Although most parents are not really willing to go to this extreme, the humor inherent in the suggestion that they try the new skill for 5 or 6 years before giving up can help them gain a perspective on the situation. You can also encourage parents to be consistent in the application of any new strategies. Children learn more from what parents do than what they say. When parents are not reliable (a tendency in parents whose personality priorities are pleasing or comfort) in using the newly acquired skills, they send a message to children that they are not serious about pursuing a new style of communication and discipline.

We have found that parents who struggle with believing that they are capable and that they count and those who lack courage need to practice skills (using role-playing, drawing, or sand tray techniques) with us before they try to apply them with their children. I (KMW) frequently have these parents come into the play therapy session to watch me model the skills. I may ask them to practice the skills with their child in the play session and (privately) give them suggestions for modifications before assigning the skills as homework. When I ask them to use the skills at home, I make sure that I give them ample time during the subsequent parent consultation for giving me feedback on their application of the strategies. All parents need encouragement for trying the new skills, for improvements in their relationship with their child, and for not giving up easily if the skills do not have instant success.

Parenting recommendations should be delivered in a nonauthoritarian, tentative fashion to parents whose primary priority is control (Kottman & Ashby, 1999). You will find it useful to give them more than one option for dealing with problem behaviors because then they have a sense of being in control of how they respond in disciplinary situations. These parents want to learn tools for responding to misbehavior but have a tendency to overuse punishment and neglect the more democratic approach of consequences. Control parents do not like to adapt their responses to the child's lifestyle, preferring to demand that the child change instead of them. They will often want to get into a power struggle with you about the need for avoiding power struggles with the child. This gives you a great chance to model effective ways of staying out of power struggles. If you want to check up on the parent's follow through, do this in an oblique manner, making sure that you do not imply, either directly or indirectly, that the parent "should" do what you recommend. By presenting parenting suggestions in an indirect manner, through a metaphor or story about another family who struggled with a similar situation, you can avoid oftentimes potential defensive reactions from these parents.

With pleasing parents, we give specific directives about parenting strategies, complete with instructions to read parenting manuals and apply specific principles (Kottman & Ashby, 1999). We usually teach pleasing parents encouragement skills before asking them to set more limits because they are more comfortable with encouragement than setting consequences. Pleasers need to learn how to decide who owns particular problems because they assume responsibility for problems that they do not truly "own." We have noticed that pleasing parents are more likely to follow through with suggestions when they know that we are going to ask for feedback about their application of the skills they are learning. They are much more motivated to be strong parents (even in the face of anger or criticism from the child or other important people in their lives) when they think they can please us through the changes they are making in their parenting. In working with personal issues, it is very exciting to teach pleasing parents about their ability to assert their own power without being overpowering to others and to own the right to and responsibility for providing discipline and structure for their child. These parents are afraid of the reaction from others if they change the way they respond to problems, so we work with them on ways to cope with the fear of rejection.

Parents whose primary priority is superiority respond well to recommendations and teaching strategies that honor their sense of achievement (Kottman & Ashby, 1999). We often frame suggestions by acknowledging their abilities and challenging their competitive spirit (e.g., "I have only had a few parents who have consistently encouraged their child for every positive behavior, but I think you have the ability to do this"). We use their belief that they need to be superior for a constructive end. Because they often enjoy an intellectual puzzle, superiority parents usually like learning new concepts, particularly ones that have practical application, such as Crucial Cs, goals of misbehavior, and personality priorities. These parents take pride in reading materials and applying techniques at home and need a time to celebrate their successes, so we always ask about their efforts and, in the spirit of collegiality, give lots of encouragement.

Parents whose primary priority is comfort like parenting suggestions that are simple and concrete and can be applied with a modicum of effort (Kottman & Ashby, 1999). When we teach parenting skills to these parents and ask them to apply new techniques, we keep our request very small (e.g., "Make one encouraging comment to Salim today"). This increases the possibility that they will actually follow through. Because these parents have an aversion to discomfort, they resent it when we check up on them, so we might follow up with the child, asking if the parent has tried anything new.

Teaching Parenting Skills

As an Adlerian play therapist, you will need to assess parents' skills and decide which parenting strategies to teach. Frequently, required parenting skills include the following strategies: (a) listening reflectively, (b) defining problem ownership, (c) recognizing the goals of misbehavior, (d) setting logical consequences, and (e) encouraging. Some families will need to acquire additional skills (e.g., structuring, setting-up routines, and providing positive and constructive feedback to a child), and you must be willing to use didactic teaching and selected play therapy tools to help them explore many different democratic discipline strategies.

Listening Reflectively

One way to improve parent–child communication is for parents to reflect their children's feelings back to them (Faber & Mazlish, 2012). By using reflective listening, parents affirm their children and their experiences. When children feel heard and understood, this process can deepen the relationship with parents and their sense of security and self-esteem. You can teach parents simple reflecting skills, such as making open responses, attending to nonverbal messages, and using feeling words. The best way to teach parents to reflect feelings is to encourage them to ask themselves, "What is my child feeling?"; think of a word that describes that emotion; and put that emotion into a sentence. By giving parents this simple, concrete method for reflecting feelings, you will decrease the chances of them being overwhelmed by the prospect of changing their communication patterns. Some examples of reflective listening are

- "You sound excited because we're going to the ice-cream parlor."
- "It seems like you're kind of disappointed that you missed the bus."

Defining Problem Ownership

Many times the power struggles between a child and the parents stem from a lack of adequately defined problem ownership (Dinkmeyer et al., 2007; Gordon, 2000). The best way to decide who owns a problem is to ask, "Whose problem is it? Who is experiencing difficulty with whom? Whose purposes are not being met?" Gordon (2000) suggested that there are three possible answers to this question in the parent–child dyad.

1. The child's behavior is not bothering the parents, but the child's needs–purposes are not being met. For example, Kimana wants to go to a skating party but decides not to attend because she is angry with her mother. This does not interfere in any way with her mother's happiness, but Kimana misses a good time. In this type of situation, the child owns the problem, and it is not really a problem for parents as long as they can keep themselves from trying to protect the child from her or his own choices and behavior.
2. The child's behavior is not bothering the parents, and the child's needs–purposes are being met. For example, Kimana does not really want to go to the skating party, so she decides not to go. Her mother does not care whether Kimana attends the party or not. In this type of situation, there is no problem at all. Sometimes parents or children make a problem from a situation that is not really problematic.
3. The child's behavior is bothering the parents, but the child's needs–purposes are being met. For example, Kimana does not really want to go to the skating party, and she refuses to go, even though her mother had planned to go out and cannot find a babysitter for Kimana. If the child's needs–purposes are not thwarted, he or she will not have

very high motivation for engaging in problem-solving or cooperative behavior. In this situation, the parent owns the problem and must generate a solution that all parties can accept.

You can teach parents about these three possible configurations of problem ownership and encourage them to define ownership for each problem. This helps parents who are involved in power struggles with children over situations that are not really a problem for the parents. Defining problem ownership often prevents parents from rescuing children from the natural consequences attendant in situations that the children have created themselves. It also helps parents be realistic in defining their expectations for situations in which they own the problem and the child does not.

Recognizing Goals of Misbehavior
As indicated in Chapters 2 and 3, Adlerians believe that all behavior is purposive and that most misbehavior by children is directed toward achieving attention, power, revenge, or proving inadequacy. The Adlerian play therapist teaches parents how to recognize each of these goals and to tailor their response to the child depending on the purpose of his or her misbehavior. The best way to identify the child's goal is to examine the actual behavior, the adult's feeling when confronted by the behavior, and the child's response when disciplined (Dinkmeyer et al., 2007; Lew & Bettner, 2000; Nelson, 2011; Schafer, 2009). We have found it helpful to have parents practice identifying goals of behavior during parent consultations, with examples of situations they have encountered with their children. After the parents learn to identify goals, they must learn how to counter them. Several resources that are very helpful with this process are *Honey, I Wrecked the Kids: When Yelling, Screaming, Threats, Bribes, Time-Outs, Sticker Charts and Removing Privileges All Don't Work* (Schafer, 2009), *Positive Discipline A–Z* (Nelson et al., 2007), and *If I Have to Tell You One More Time. . . : The Revolutionary Program That Gets Your Kids to Listen Without Nagging, Reminding, or Yelling* (McCready, 2012).

With children whose goal is attention, the most appropriate parental response is to ignore them when they are asking for attention and to give them abundant attention when they are not asking for it. Parents of children whose goal is power must learn to set limits and establish logical consequences for inappropriate behavior while also allowing for age-appropriate power. One way for parents to achieve this is for them to learn to give children limited choices. Parents need to avoid getting into power struggles with these children—by strategically withdrawing from power struggles, parents can assert their own authority.

Children whose goal is revenge are especially difficult to parent because their behavior is frequently very hurtful. When interacting with these children, parents must not take the behavior personally and avoid showing hurt or frustration. They must be very nurturing, patient, and consistent with these children, engaging them in setting up the consequences for their misbehavior without showing anger or fear. In working with revenge-oriented children, it helps to remember that these children feel that they have been severely hurt themselves, and their behavior stems from these feelings.

With children whose goal is proving that they are inadequate, the most important components in parenting are encouragement (see Chapter 6) and perseverance. An invaluable resource for these children is *Encouraging Words for Kids: What to Say to Bring Out a Child's Confidence* (Bartlett, 2012). Parenting children who believe that they are inherently worthless can be extremely discouraging, so these parents need a great deal of encouragement and support from you and others in their lives to be able to continue trying to create situations and interactions in which their children can feel successful.

Setting Logical Consequences

An important component of Adlerian parenting skills is learning how to give choices and set up logical consequences in a way that engages parents and the child in a mutually respectful process designed to develop a sense of responsibility in the child (Dinkmeyer et al., 2007; Nelson, 2011; Popkin, 2014). In presenting choices, parents give the two alternatives: one being a way to correct the misbehavior and the other being a consequence for choosing not to correct the misbehavior. Examples of giving choices:

- "Jorge, you can choose to talk quietly when your sister is asleep, or you can choose to go to your room until she wakes up."
- "Leigh, you can choose to put your dirty clothes in the hamper, or you can choose to wear dirty clothes."

When giving choices, it is essential that parents use a tone of voice and choice of words that convey respect, kindness, and acceptance. Parents must never give a choice that they are unwilling to accept. If parents cannot tolerate the idea of having the child go to school wearing dirty clothes, they should not give that as a choice.

Consequences must be respectful, reasonable, and related to the transgression (Lew & Bettner, 2000; Nelson et al., 2007). Children will feel respected if it obvious to them that they have some control over what happens and that their parents are listening to their perspectives. Reasonable consequences should not be too lengthy or too painful for the children. Although sometimes it is difficult to generate a consequence that is related to the misbehavior, it is important that children can see some kind of logical connection between their behavior and the effect.

According to Dinkmeyer et al. (2007) in applying consequences, parents must adhere to the following basic principles:

1. Think about the child's behavior, feelings, and purposes.
2. Be kind and firm.
3. Avoid overprotecting the child. Let him or her experience the natural and logical consequences of his or her behavior.
4. Increase your level of consistency so that the child knows what to expect and can make decisions based on reasonable expectations.
5. Always convey respect to the child (verbally and nonverbally) even when you do not agree with or appreciate his or her behavior.
6. Encourage independence and responsibility.

7. Do not allow the opinions or disapproval of others to dictate your parenting behavior. Do what you think is right and respectful.
8. Consider who owns the problem and act accordingly.
9. Act more, threaten less.
10. Do not argue or give in to the child.

In setting up logical consequences, the parent should follow these steps:

1. State the limit in a nonjudgmental voice.
2. Reflect the child's feelings or make a guess about the child's goals and give an explanation of his or her position.
3. Invite the child to engage in generating alternative behaviors that are acceptable to both parent and child.
4. Engage the child in brainstorming consequences for transgressions at this point, or wait for the eventuality that the child decides not to abide by the agreement to engage in generating logical consequences. If the parent decides to brainstorm possible consequences, they enter into a negotiation process in which the purpose is to agree on a consequence that the child can enforce if transgressions occur.
5. Ask the child to comply with the agreed-on consequences or follow through on the consequences in a matter-of-fact manner, always conveying acceptance of the child and respect.

An example of the consequence-setting process:

1. I tell Jacob, my son (when he was a bit younger), that he must come home from his friend's house when he hears the church bells chiming five times: "You remember the rule that you need to come home for dinner when the church bell rings at 5 o'clock."
2. I reflect Jacob's reluctance to come home and give up having fun with his friend, and I explain my position: "I know you have a lot of fun with Thomas, and you feel sad that you have to stop playing and come home, but it is a pain for me to keep your dinner warm while everyone else in the family eats."
3. I invite Jacob to engage in generating mutually acceptable possibilities for solving the problem: "Can you think of some other way for you to remember to come home for dinner on time?" Jacob replies that he would like me to call him when it is time to eat. I agree to this: "OK, if you really want me to, I am willing to call you one time when it's time for dinner."
4. If Jacob does not abide by the agreement, I ask him to help decide on a consequence for the next time this happens: "Let's think of what can happen the next time you decide not to come home when I call you for dinner." Jacob suggests that he not get any dinner. I am reluctant to agree to this, so I counter with the suggestion that Jacob eat his dinner cold when he does get home. We agree on this consequence.
5. The next time Jacob comes home late, I remind him of our agreement and give Jacob the plate of dinner, unheated.

Although the parent can ask the child to generate the consequences before the actual transgression, this conveys a lack of faith in the child's ability to abide by their agreement. I prefer to wait to set up the consequence until after the child has chosen to violate the compact because I think this communicates my belief that the child will be responsible.

Encouraging

To be encouraging to their children, parents must learn to interact with their children without putting conditions on their acceptance (Bartlett, 2012). They must learn to give recognition for their children's abilities, strengths, and assets. In using encouragement with children, it is important for parents to give positive feedback for progress and effort, even when the final product is not perfect. It is helpful to engage with children in activities that are interesting to them, rather than always expecting them to show interest in adult pastimes. Parents can also demonstrate that they make mistakes themselves and do not expect their children to always be perfect.

Consulting With Teachers

Depending on the circumstances, the play therapist may also want to get parental consent to consult with another influential adult in the child's life: the teacher. This is especially important if the presenting problem relates to situations in school or if the problem is affecting the child's performance in school. The consultation with teachers goes through the same four phases: building the relationship, gathering lifestyle information, helping the teacher gain insight, and reorienting–reeducating the teacher (Kottman, 2009, 2013).

School counselors who are working with children using play as an intervention modality consult with teachers on a regular basis to determine how the child's difficulties are manifesting themselves in the classroom. Because they usually have insight about the child's behavior at school, school counselors are also excellent resources for outside therapists who work with children. They can also provide valuable information about the best ways to approach the child's teacher and help the therapist get an initial picture of the teacher's Crucial Cs and personality priorities.

Building the Relationship With the Teacher

If the child is experiencing a problem at school, many times the teacher is feeling defensive, so it is important for you to avoid seeming like a threat. The best way to approach the teacher is with a professional, collaborative manner based on your assessment of the teacher's Crucial Cs and personality priorities. It is helpful to lead with the fact that you need the teacher's help in understanding what is going on with the child because the child spends more time in the classroom than in the playroom. This statement will often help to disarm even the most defensive teachers and reassure them that you are not going to invade their classroom and try to tell them how they should be teaching.

Gathering Information About Lifestyles

Because the Adlerian play therapist needs to form a complete picture of a struggling child and his or her interactions at school, it is very important for you to gather information from teachers about the child's interactional patterns and attitudes toward self, others, and school. Many teachers seem to be more comfortable with answering questions or even filling out forms than they are doing sand trays or drawings. Depending on specific teachers' willingness to try more playful strategies for conveying information, you could integrate play therapy techniques into the information-gathering process. To form a holistic picture of the child and his or her lifestyle, you will want to know about (a) the child's attitude and behavior in different settings and with different individuals at school; (b) the child's conduct in various subjects, in the cafeteria, and on the playground; and (c) the child's interactions with peers, teachers, the principal, and other school personnel.

Sometimes it is helpful to solicit teachers' impressions about how the child's family could be contributing to the child's self-image or behavior. It is also useful to find out about the teacher's lifestyle, his or her teaching style, his or her attitudes toward the child, and usual methods of discipline. You will be looking for how the interface of the child's personality with the teacher's personality and teaching style might be contributing to the problem. Appendix C consists of inquiries the counselor can use to obtain most of this information. The counselor may also want to ask permission to observe the child at school, because witnessing can give the counselor a feel for the atmosphere in the classroom and for the child's relationships at school.

Sharing Insights With Teachers

One of the primary purposes of consulting with teachers is to share information and insight about the child with them. As the play therapy progresses, the counselor learns things about the child and the way he or she views himself or herself, others, and the world that can be helpful to the teacher. To protect the child's confidentiality, the counselor does not describe actual behaviors from play sessions, instead sharing inferences about the child's Crucial Cs, goals of misbehavior, personality priorities, self-image, psychological birth-order position, assets, attitudes toward authority figures, and any other data that might help the teacher to better understand the child. The counselor can also subtly make guesses about the interaction between the child's lifestyle and the teacher's lifestyle and between the child's learning style and the teacher's instructional style, especially when there seem to be mismatches that are interfering with the child's ability to be successful in school.

On the basis of the feedback from the counselor, teachers are often interested in learning more about Adlerian intervention strategies appropriate for overall classroom discipline or for working with this particular child. This provides a perfect segue to the reorientation–reeducation phase of the consultation.

Reorienting–Reeducating Teachers

The counselor often uses consultation sessions as an opportunity to impart information on Adlerian principles, such as the Crucial Cs, goals of misbehavior, personality priorities, logical consequences, problem ownership, encouragement, and classroom meetings that teachers can apply to classroom discipline. If the teacher is excited about implementing Adlerian discipline in her or his classroom, there are several resources that provide comprehensive plans for incorporating Adlerian ideas in schools: *Responsibility in the Classroom: A Teacher's Guide to Understanding and Motivating Students* (Lew & Bettner, 1998); *A Teacher's Guide to Cooperative Discipline: How to Manage Your Classroom and Promote Self-Esteem* (Albert, 2002); and *Positive Discipline in the Classroom: Developing Mutual Respect, Cooperation, and Responsibility in Your Classroom* (Nelson et al., 2013). These books contain concrete suggestions for using the goals of behavior, encouragement, communication skills, and classroom meetings as a means of understanding children and promoting responsibility and cooperation in the classroom.

Another model for training teachers in skills that could be helpful to the children in their classes is "Kinder Therapy" (Draper, White, O'Shaughnessy, Flynt, & Jones, 2001; Hess, Post, & Flowers, 2005; Solis, 2006; White, Flynt, & Draper, 1997; White, Flynt, & Jones, 1999; White & Wynne, 2009). In Kinder Training, the counselor trains teachers in the basic play therapy skills used in filial therapy and Adlerian constructs. The teachers initially practice these skills in a playroom, under the supervision of the counselor, and eventually apply the skills in their classrooms. The goals of Kinder Training include strengthening the teacher–child relationship, developing students' adaptive skills, increasing students' academic engagement, and enhancing teachers' classroom management skills. In a study designed to explore teachers' perceptions of Kinder Training, Edwards, Varjas, White, and Stokes (2009) found that elementary school teachers judged the Kinder Therapy model to be acceptable and effective, resulting in improved classroom management skills, improved student behavior, and enhanced teacher–child relationships.

Summary

One of the most important skills in successful implementation of Adlerian play therapy is consultation—with both parents and teachers. These adults can be excellent sources of information about children and of support for the changes children begin to make in play therapy. The play therapist uses both counseling and teaching strategies in engaging parents and teachers, matching the consultation to the needs of individual families and classrooms, and helping parents and teachers learn new ways of interacting with children.

Further Resources

Involving parents in play therapy:

https://a4pt.site-ym.com/?page=ParentsCornerHomePag
http://www.kathryndebruin.com/how-to-involve-parents-so-that-play-therapy-can-be-as-successful-as-possible-october-10-2009
http://www.play-therapy.com/professionals.html#design

Family play therapy:

http://www.lianalowenstein.com/articleFamilyTherapy.pdf

Parenting skills:

http://www.cdc.gov/parents/essentials/activities/index.html
http://childdevelopmentinfo.com/how-to-be-a-parent/parenting/
http://www.monkeysee.com/video_clips/14658-how-to-get-children-to-listen
http://www.parentencouragement.org/peppubs.html
http://www.positivediscipline.com/what-is-positive-discipline.html
http://www.positiveparentingsolutions.com/wp-content/ft/Ahh-Now-I-Get-It.pdf
http://thinkitthroughparenting.com/

Working with teachers:

http://digitalcommons.fairfield.edu/cgi/viewcontent.cgi?article=1055&context=education-facultypubs
http://www.goodtherapy.org/blog/play-therapy-gets-top-grades-from-preschool-teachers-1217122
http://incredibleyears.com/parents-teachers/articles-for-teachers/
http://www.lianalowenstein.com/articleClassroomManagement.pdf

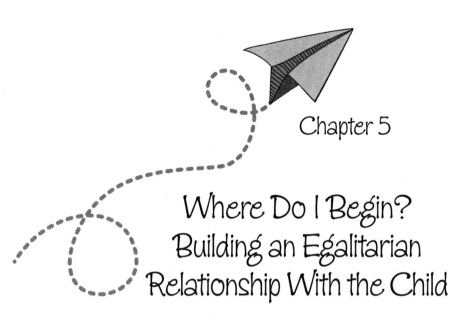

Chapter 5

Where Do I Begin?
Building an Egalitarian
Relationship With the Child

We want to build a relationship with you, and in doing so we start with a confession and a sort-of apology. This chapter was a difficult one to write. The egalitarian relationship is necessary for the counseling process, and it doesn't stop after the first phase has been established. We weren't sure how to emphasize this enough. Therefore, we are just going to lay it out—the relationship is necessary, and it manifests itself throughout the entire Adlerian play therapy process. Another challenge for us is that the relationship with the child is not the only relationship that needs to be fostered. Egalitarian relationships also need to be fostered between the counselor and parent and/or teacher. We devoted an entire chapter (Chapter 4) to working with parents and teachers so that we could avoid spending considerable amounts of time doing so in this chapter. The other difficulty we encountered was that there are so many skills used during the first phase we could go on forever, and we just couldn't leave any of them out. (You may have noticed this if you looked at the length of this chapter; sorry!) So, with that out of the way, we'll dive into strategies for building relationships with children in Adlerian play therapy.

The first thing the Adlerian play therapist must do is build an egalitarian relationship with the child. The counselor wants the child to know that the counseling relationship is a shared partnership between the two of them. The therapeutic relationship grows from mutual trust and respect. The main job of the play therapist during the first several sessions is to communicate respect for and trust in the child and his or her abilities. The therapist must earn the respect and trust of the child by being consistent, tolerant, and respectful.

Because the relationship is a democratic partnership, you and the child share the responsibility and the power in your sessions. Although you retain the right to make decisions about limits and other critical factors in the playroom, both you and the child have input into what happens in the playroom. It is important not to force the child to do or say anything in the playroom, except in cases in which the child would be endangering him- or herself or others. The child makes choices, and you must respect those decisions even when you do not particularly like them.

If we ask a question or make an interpretation and the child chooses not to answer, we convey our respect for the child by not insisting on an answer. If we ask a child to draw or tell a story and the child chooses not to do so, or does so in an unexpected way (paints instead of draws), we convey our respect by accepting that decision. As "they" say (whoever "they" are), "actions speak louder than words." To a child, what we do is much more important than what we say, so we must behave in a way that conveys a sense of shared power and responsibility instead of just talking about the egalitarian nature of the relationship. In our experience, if we want a child to perceive that we trust and respect him or her, we must always act in a way that allows the child to maintain a certain amount of power and control over what he or she is doing. We do not allow children to hurt themselves, other children, us, or the property in the playroom, but otherwise they can make many of the decisions about what happens in the playroom.

The play therapist works on building the relationship with the child from before the child comes to the first session until after the child has stopped coming to play therapy. The cornerstone of the egalitarian relationship is a philosophical belief that all people deserve respect and a degree of power in their lives. The Adlerian play therapist must believe in this tenet and use it as the foundation for the relationship with the child. Although building the relationship is the first phase of the counseling process, it is not a discrete phase that stops as soon as the play therapist establishes rapport with the child. The therapist continues to foster the relationship throughout the therapeutic process. Just as the gardener waters a plant even after it has begun to flourish in the garden, the Adlerian play therapist steadily continues to use relationship-building strategies to communicate this accepting and empowering philosophy to the child.

Meeting and Engaging the Child

Building the egalitarian relationship begins before the Adlerian play therapist meets the child. In service to this process, the therapist usually meets with the parents without the child in the first session. The purpose of doing this is to begin to establish a relationship with the parents so that the therapist can concentrate on connecting with the child in their first meeting with little pressure to pay attention to the parents.

As you enter the waiting room for your first session with a child, it is often helpful to nod an acknowledgment to the parents who brought the child but say very little or nothing to the adults. This helps to send the message to the child that you are not in some sort of "evil alliance" with the parents, and that the child is the most important person to you in the room at that moment. To begin building rapport immediately, you will want to go straight over to the child and get on eye level. This may involve kneeling, squatting, or sitting on a low chair or the floor. You want to make sure you are not looming over the child, looking big, powerful, or overwhelming (not too hard for us because we are both really short). You want to communicate that you and the child are partners in this world of play, and you do not want to look as though you are starting out with a size or power advantage.

When we greet a child, we always use his or her name. We introduce ourselves and tell the child how glad we are to see him or her. We tell the child that we are going to have a great time together. We want to convey a sense of excitement and fun about the play therapy session we are about to share. When we introduce ourselves, we tell the child our first names—not our last names or our titles. We are not planning on calling the child Miss or Mr. Jones, so why should he or she have to call us Dr. Kottman or Dr. Meany-Walen? I (TK) might say something like, "Hello, Isaac. I am Terry. I am very glad you are here today. We're going to have some fun!"

Going to the Playroom

After you spend a little time in getting to know a child, putting him or her at ease, and letting him or her get used to being with you, stand up and say something like, "It's time to go to the playroom now. Your mom (dad) will be waiting in the waiting room for us when we get back." As an important side note, be sure that during your initial meeting with parents you have clearly explained your expectations (or agency rules) that parents do not leave the building during the child's play therapy session. Avoid asking the child if he or she wants to go to the playroom or if he or she is ready to go to the playroom. Even in the first stages of the relationship, you do not want to ask the child a question or imply a choice that you are not willing to honor. By making the announcement that you are going to the playroom as a given, you are setting a precedent that says there are some things that you will control and some things that the child will control. By mentioning that the parents will be waiting in the waiting room for your return, you work to reassure the child that the parents are not going to abandon him or her and that the child will be safe and protected in the playroom. (Elementary school counselors usually already know most of the children in their schools, so this process does not have as many possible problems as it does for agency counselors and play therapists in private practice.)

Occasionally, a child is reluctant to go to a play therapy session. This does not happen very often if the therapist has presented the playroom as a positive and exciting place and himself or herself as a kind and fun person, and if the therapist is patient in timing the announcement—waiting for readiness on the part of the child. However, some children are more anxious and skeptical than others and may not want to go to the play session. It sometimes helps to tell the child that his or her parents can go to the playroom for the first 10 minutes and then the parents will return to the waiting room to wait. If this still does not reassure the child, the therapist can have the parent stay in the playroom and simply observe, or parents can sit in a chair in the hall outside the playroom with the door open so that the child can see that the parent has not abandoned him or her. I (KMW) have had children bring their parents' keys into the playroom with them. This helps to reassure the children that the parent cannot leave without them!

We do not believe in carrying or dragging a child to the playroom or having the parents do this for us. If we have a client who absolutely refuses to go to the playroom with us, we tend to work with parents in parent consultation without having play sessions with the child rather than forcing a child to come to the playroom. We believe that if we force a child to come to the playroom, we are violating the mutual respect necessary for an egalitarian relationship.

When we get to the playroom, we usually say something like, "This is our playroom. In here, you can do many of the things you want to do." We do not tell children they can do anything they want to do because there are things they cannot do in the playroom, such as hurting us, hurting themselves or other children, or destroying the material in the playroom. We also tell children that in the playroom we will share making decisions by explaining, "Sometimes I get to be the boss and decide what we are going to do, sometimes you get to be the boss and decide what we are going to do, and sometimes we figure this out together."

What Do You Think About Coming to Play Therapy?

Quite frequently, children enter the play therapy relationship with negative ideas about why they are coming to play therapy. Sometimes this is because of messages they get from their parents, and sometimes it is due to their own egocentric interpretation of events and interactions, their private logic, and their mistaken beliefs about themselves, others, and the world. To begin to counter any negative information or perceptions about the play therapy process, some play therapists keep a copy of *A Child's First Book About Play Therapy* (Nemiroff & Annunziata, 1990) in their waiting rooms or share this book with parents before the child's first session and ask them to read it to their child.

To explore children's understanding of the presenting problem, sometime during the first session with them, we ask them about their perception of the reason for coming to play therapy. We may ask them what they think we will do in the playroom or what their parents told them about coming to play therapy. We frequently ask them how they feel about coming and what they think they will get out of the process. If you work in a school, it is helpful to talk about what the child's teacher told him or her about coming to see you. This type of processing encourages children to explore their understanding of the reason for the referral to play therapy, understanding of the process of play therapy, and preconceived notions of what the relationship will be. It helps us begin to formulate an understanding of children's subjective interpretation of the presenting problem and their beliefs about what is going to happen in the play session.

When we think we understand the child's view of the presenting problem, of his or her therapeutic goals, and of the play therapy process, we try to reflect our understanding back to the child. We use restatement of content to capture the essence of his or her statements, so that we can see if we have understood his or her perceptions of the situation. We reflect the child's feelings about what has happened, what is happening, and what is going to happen. Our intent in both the restatement of content and the reflection of feelings is to communicate our respect for the child's position and perceptions and our desire to empathize—to see things from the child's perspective.

Just as with an adult client, we give the child some information on how we view the process of therapy and our role as therapists. To convey our convictions about play therapy, we give the child a very brief explanation that includes a description of the process, a comment about our experience, and a suggestion that the process of play therapy usually works to help children feel better about themselves and get along better with others. For instance, we might say,

> In play therapy, kids get a chance to play with the toys or talk about things that happen in their lives. I work with a lot of different kids in the playroom. After they have been with me in the playroom for a while, kids usually seem to feel better about themselves. Sometimes they also get along better with their families and their friends.

Sometime during the first session, we explain the nature of the egalitarian relationship we want to have with the child. Examples of statements describing the therapeutic partnership:

- "In our playroom, we will play and work together."
- "In here, we can do many of the things you would like to do together. Sometimes you will be in charge, and sometimes I will be in charge. We will take turns being the boss."
- "Sometimes you will play by yourself, and sometimes we will play together. Sometimes we can talk; sometimes we will be quiet. We will decide those things together."

We also want the child to know how we perceive the presenting problem. We may give the child a brief summary of what his or her parents or teacher told us. Examples of this technique would include the following:

- To Leonard, a second-grade boy whose mother reports that he is publicly masturbating and that other children are teasing him for this behavior, you might say, "Your mom says that sometimes you touch yourself on the privates and that the other kids at school tease you about this."
- To Juanita, a 5-year-old girl whose mother reports that she has low self-esteem and is constantly making negative comments about herself, you might say, "It seems that sometimes you say things about yourself that sound like you feel kind of sad and you don't like yourself very much."

- To James, a first-grade boy who has been acting out at home and at school, you might say, "Your dad says that sometimes you get into fights with him and your teacher."

In doing this, it is essential to keep the comments simple and on a vocabulary level that is similar to the vocabulary that the child uses. You must leave out any judgmental words or phrases, such as "bad," "good," "in trouble," or "you have a problem" and simply report your perception of the information in an objective fashion. It is essential in this process to avoid endorsing any negative perspective of the presenting problem provided by parents or teachers to prevent the child from identifying you with others in his or her life who are disapproving or critical. In this process, you are simply letting the child know what you have heard from parents or teachers so that you are not starting the relationship with any secrets or unspoken information interfering.

After we have conveyed the facts (and just the facts—reframed when possible), we wait and see how the child responds. If the child does not acknowledge or openly respond to our statements, we monitor his or her nonverbal responses closely—to look for recognition reflex (Griffith & Powers, 2007). The recognition reflex is an involuntary nonverbal reaction to a comment or interaction that reveals something about the way the person is feeling or thinking. It can be a smile, a flinch, a nod, a grimace, a shrug, or any other type of body language indicating an emotional or cognitive response to a situation. Sometimes the child totally disagrees with the adult version of the situation. Sometimes he or she clarifies details that do not jive with his or her perception of the situation. Sometimes the child ignores what we have said. It is not necessary for the child to acknowledge or understand the adult perspective. Whatever reaction we get gives us valuable information about the child, the child's lifestyle, and the lifestyles of the adults involved in the referral process. (We're getting ahead of ourselves—you'll find more about lifestyles and conceptualization in Chapters 7 and 8.)

An essential part of building an egalitarian relationship is to explore (as much as is developmentally possible) the child's goals for therapy. Many times a child is brought to the play therapist by his or her parents or sent to the school counselor by parents, teachers, or the principal, with therapeutic goals already determined by these adults. In these cases, the child seldom has any clearly defined goals for the therapy—at least in the initial sessions. However, usually even a reluctant child comes to play therapy with some things in his or her life that he or she wants to be different. The counselor can ask the child if there is anything he or she wants to change in his or her life, at home, or at school. When goals are evident—either conscious or out of the child's awareness—the counselor tries to accommodate the process to include these therapeutic goals.

Even when the child chooses not to discuss his or her goals, sometimes we detect behaviors or attitudes we think the child wants to change during the first several sessions. When this happens, depending on the maturity of the child and whether we think he or she is aware of these goals, we may ask the child about them. Frequently, a mature child who has given a great deal of thought to his or her presenting problem wants reassurance that we understand what is happening and that we are willing to help him or her work on that problem in the playroom. For instance, to Andrew, a child who has expressed conscious awareness of therapeutic issues and goals for therapy, I (TK) might say, "You mentioned that the other kids make fun of you on the bus. I wonder if dealing with that is something you might like to work on with me?"

It is also important for the counselor to clarify with the child the goals suggested by the adults in the child's life. With some children, especially older children and verbally sophisticated children, it is appropriate to discuss with the child ways to align all of the therapeutic goals—those of the child, parents, teachers, counselor, and any other interested parties.

Demystifying the Counseling Process

Just as with an adult client during the first session, the Adlerian play therapist talks to children about the nuts and bolts of the counseling process: logistics, parent consultation, and confidentiality. With most children, these explanations tend to be short and concrete. The play therapist can use puppets or dolls, do a sand tray, or draw pictures to convey this information if he or she believes that these strategies will increase the child's understanding and reduce any anxiety or apprehension on the child's part.

Logistics

It is important to let children know how often they will be coming to counseling, how long they will stay in the playroom, what day and time they will be coming, and how long children usually stay in play therapy. We invite children to ask questions about the playroom and what goes on there. We explain the details using language and concepts tailored to the child's development and verbal skills. For instance, to 3-year-old Charmayne, I (KMW) might say that we will be together every Monday (the same day they go to Mother's day out), that each week when she comes, we will play about as long as one of her Dora DVDs. To Justin, a very intelligent 8-year-old, I (TK) would tell him that he and his dad will come every Wednesday after school, he will play with me for 30 minutes, and that after we play I will meet with his dad for about 20 minutes while he waits in the waiting room. I might also mention that kids usually come to me once a week for about 6 to 9 months.

Consulting With Parents and Teachers

We explain to children that we will be consulting with their parents and perhaps their teachers. The way we explain this to children will of course depend on the arrangements we have made with parents and the children's maturity levels. For example, to Charmayne, I (KMW) would probably say, "I am going to talk to your mommy and daddy about new ways to play with you and talk to you so that everyone in the family is happy." To Justin, I (TK) might say,

I will meet with you and with your dad every week. You can decide whether I see you first or I see your dad first. I will talk to your dad to try to help him understand you and your behavior better. I will also make suggestions about ways that you and your dad can work on communicating in more positive ways and ways that you guys can get along better so that things will go more smoothly in the family.

If we were going to consult with Justin's teacher, we would explain that consultation in similar terms, saying something like,

I may be talking to your teacher about how things go for you at school. As time passes and we get to know one another better, you may have some ideas about how I can help Mr. Ray do some things differently in the classroom so that you have more fun and learn more at school.

Confidentiality

We want to communicate to the child that he or she has the right to privacy about the exact contents of play therapy sessions. However, many times information about the process in the playroom can help parents or teachers to better understand and interact with the child. To communicate this abstract concept in the child's vocabulary, we might say, "I will not tell your parents things that you say or do in the playroom. Sometimes I may share some of my guesses about why you do the things you do, or I may tell them some new ways to talk to you."

Without giving the specifics of individual sessions, we talk to parents and/or teachers about themes of play, goals of behavior, patterns of interacting, movement toward mastery of one or more of the Crucial Cs, increases in social interest or self-confidence, and assets or progress in positive behaviors with parents or teachers. We want to provide information and perspectives that will help these important adults improve their comprehension of the child's attitudes, emotions, thoughts, and actions and increase their support of positive changes the child is making. On the basis of our thoughts and feelings in our relationships with a particular child in the playroom, we may suggest ways for parents and/or teachers to change their own actions and reactions so that they can learn more appropriate ways to interact with the child.

There are several instances when the counselor cannot maintain the child's confidentiality about the contents of play therapy sessions. It is necessary to breach confidentiality of children when they have revealed information in the session that indicates that they are victims of abuse or suggests that they are potentially dangerous to themselves or others. Because the legal system does not provide children under the age of 12 with rights to confidentiality (Carmichael, 2006), there are times when the counselor feels an obligation to share information from the session with parents. Because of the legal limits to child confidentiality, it is appropriate to include in the initial statement explaining confidentiality to the child a comment such as,

If I think that someone is hurting you or you might hurt yourself or someone else, I will need to let your parents know about that. I want to try to make sure that you are safe. I would also have to tell your parents what happens in sessions if a judge tells me that I have to do so. I will always tell you in advance if I ever have to do this.

Giving the Child a Business Card

At the end of the first session with children, I (TK) give them my business card and tell them that if they ever need to talk to me, they should feel free to call me. This action lets children know that I consider them my primary clients and that my relationship with them is important and professional. By treating children as I do adults, I convey respect and further establish the egalitarian nature of the relationship. When I give children my card, most of them seem to feel special and important.

Adlerian Play Therapy Techniques for Building the Relationship

There are many strategies in Adlerian play therapy designed to help build the relationship between the counselor and the child. These include tracking behavior, restating content, metacommunicating, reflecting feelings, answering questions, asking questions, returning responsibility to the child, interacting actively with the child, and cleaning the room together. Each of these is discussed in the following sections.

Tracking, restating content, metacommunicating, reflecting feelings, answering questions, asking questions, and returning responsibility can be used directly or indirectly. With children who communicate directly about their lives, it is appropriate for the counselor to reciprocate and communicate directly with the child (e.g., tracking the child's behavior, paraphrasing what the child says, metacommunicating about the child's nonverbal reactions). With other children (and in some situations even with the children who usually communicate directly), it is more productive to use metaphors and communicate indirectly (e.g., tracking the doll's behavior, paraphrasing what a puppet said, metacommunicating about the nonverbal reaction of the toy soldier, asking the dinosaur questions about his family). When communicating indirectly, sometimes the counselor will talk about the puppets, dolls, or figures and sometimes he or she will talk to the toys, pretending that they can react and respond as if they were alive.

Tracking Behavior

One of the main tools of any play therapist in building a relationship, regardless of theory, is tracking behavior (Kottman, 2011; Ray, 2011). When the play therapist tracks behavior, he or she tells the child what the child is doing at that particular moment. The purpose of tracking behavior is to let the child know that the therapist is willing and able to communicate in the child's preferred mode of interaction: play. Tracking behavior is one way to let the child know that the therapist is with him or her, what he or she is doing is important, and he or she is the focus of attention. By tracking the child's behaviors in the playroom, the play therapist can convey an understanding that the child's play has meaning and significance. The following are examples of tracking behavior:

- Lien picks up a doll. You might say, "You're picking that up."
- Karl goes over to the mirror with the doll and pretends that the doll is looking at herself in the mirror. You would comment, "She is looking at herself."
- Maya paints a picture. You could say, "You're painting something."
- Oorjit uses one of the bigger dinosaurs to stomp on a smaller dinosaur. You might say to the bigger dinosaur, "You are jumping on that other one."

When tracking, it is important to limit labeling objects and actions. If you identify an object or action by a specific name, sometimes a child will feel bound by the label. (Initially, this can be more difficult than it seems—believe us, it takes a lot of practice to be this vague.) If you can avoid giving a specific name to an object or action, it can encourage the child's creativity and freedom of choice. By not calling an object that looks like a cabbage a cabbage, you grant the child the chance to decide that the cabbage is the head of a monster. By not saying that the child is jumping off the chair, you grant him the chance to fly around the room on a magic carpet.

We track quite a bit during the first several sessions with a child to establish a connection between us and the child. We do not track every time the child does something because this seems awkward and artificial. In the initial sessions, we probably track every second or third behavior. In later sessions, we track less and less frequently.

Restating Content

Another way to build the relationship with the child is to restate the content of the child's verbalizations. When you restate content, it is important to try and avoid simply parroting the child's exact words and intonations. The best restatements use your own words and inflections within the context of a vocabulary that the child can understand. Restatements of content should paraphrase the obvious message within the verbalization, and they should also acknowledge any nonverbal, covert messages within the verbalization. Examples of restating content:

- Roger says, "I am going to paint a picture." You might say, "So you decided that you want to paint."
- Tawana picks up a hammer and goes over to the log with the nails. She looks at you, seeming to ask permission, and says, "I am going to hammer these nails into the log." You could acknowledge both the verbal and nonverbal content by saying, "You look like you want to check with me to see if it's okay to hammer the nails into the log."
- Ang, a child who has been sexually abused, picks up an anatomically correct doll, moves the doll's hands so he is pointing to his genital

region and says in a squeaky voice, "The man at school touched my tootoo." A restatement of the content would be directed at the doll, "The man touched you there."

The counselor restates content to demonstrate to the child that what the child says and how he or she says it are important and worthy of an adult's attention. Restatement of content lets the child know that the counselor is paying attention and has heard what he or she was trying to communicate, on both a verbal and a nonverbal level.

Many people do not pay close attention to children and their words or their nonverbal communication. Listen with your ears and your eyes. By really listening to children and letting them know that we have heard, we demonstrate that we are different from many of the other adults they have encountered. This willingness to listen helps build the relationship with children.

As with tracking, we restate content more in the first four or five sessions than we do in subsequent sessions. As time passes and we believe that the child has internalized the importance of the relationship with us, we reduce the number of times we track and restate content in the session. The amount of time we spend tracking and restating content depends on the individual child. A child who has limited cognitive abilities or a child who thinks concretely may need continuing tangible demonstration that we believe he or she is important. A child who has strong cognitive abilities or a child who thinks on an abstract level may quickly process and internalize the message that the therapeutic relationship is special. A child who has been abused or neglected may be afraid to believe that we value our relationship with him or her and may need continuous evidence that this is so. Different children have different needs. We try to tailor our approach and the ways we use various intervention tools to the personality of each individual child we see in play therapy.

Metacommunicating

In metacommunication, the counselor *metacommunicates* (clever, huh?); that is, the counselor steps outside the interaction and communicates about the communication taking place in the relationship. This is like reading between (and sometimes perhaps even underneath) the lines. By metacommunicating, the counselor can help children begin to notice and understand their own patterns of communication. Often children are not aware that they are reacting or communicating in a certain way. Even those who are cognizant of their communication patterns usually lack the abstract verbal-reasoning ability to conceptualize what these patterns mean about them and their interactions. By commenting about what is going on (and frequently, what it means), the counselor can help children think more clearly about how and what they are communicating. Metacommunication is kind of an umbrella skill that incorporates a number of different techniques. It can involve reflection of feelings, questions, speculation about underlying messages, interpretation of the meaning of reactions or behaviors, and so forth. The focus of metacommunication can be on the following:

- Nonverbal communication on the part of the child (e.g., "You looked over here like you were checking whether it was okay with me if you played with the dolls").
- The child's reactions to the therapist's statements and questions (e.g., "You looked happy when I said we were going to do a puppet show. I am thinking that you really like doing puppet shows").
- Subtle reactions to or feelings about interactions between the therapist and the child (e.g., "I notice that you seem frustrated when I told you shooting darts at people is against the playroom rules").
- Subtle reactions to the relationship between the play therapist and the child or to the play therapy process (e.g., "I am thinking that you were not very happy to see me today").
- Nuances in the ways the child communicates (e.g., "I am noticing that when you feel frustrated your voice gets louder").
- The underlying message in the child's communication (e.g., as Mr. Fox tugs on my shirt but does not say anything, "Mr. Fox wants me to get down on the floor and play with him").
- The unstated purpose of the child's behavior (e.g., "It seems like you always ask questions about the time when we meet at 5 o'clock. I am thinking you want to make sure you get to your soccer match").

We conceptualize metacommunication as having four different levels, moving from very simple factual comments about the present to rather elaborate interpretations about patterns in the child's personality and overall style of relating to others and reaction to the world. The first level of metacommunication is when we simply point out that something is happening in the here and now (e.g., "You frowned when I mentioned your dad"). When we talk about patterns in the child's behaviors, reactions, or attitudes within a session or across several sessions (e.g., "You seem to get very sad whenever you mention your parents' divorce"), this is the second level of metacommunication. The third level of metacommunication involves commenting on patterns in the child's behaviors, reactions, or attitudes in the playroom that extend into other situations and relationships outside the playroom (e.g., "I have noticed that you like to be the boss in here with me. I am guessing that you also like to be the boss at home with your mom."). The fourth level of metacommunication includes pointing out patterns in the child's behaviors, reactions, or attitudes that typify his or her personality, coping strategies, interpersonal interactional style, approach to problem solving, approach to conflict resolution, self-image, and other aspect of his or her lifestyle (e.g., To a doll who is always yelling at the other dolls, "It seems as though you use yelling to get other people to do what you want, and I have noticed that you really like to get other people to follow your instructions").

Sometimes we simply describe the behavior or the pattern in a factual way, without adding any kind of speculation or guess about what the behavior or pattern means (e.g., "The rabbit hid under the pillow right after I said that about his mom"). Other times we use a more interpretive spin, focusing more on the meaning of the behavior or pattern, with little or no emphasis on the description of the behavior or pattern (e.g., "I am thinking when I say that your mom seems happy being married to your stepdad, you get kind of mad"). As time passes and we have more of a feel for what is going on with the child, we frequently combine a factual comment that describes the behavior or pattern with an interpretation about what it might mean (e.g., "You frowned right after I said that your mom seems happy being married to your stepdad. I am thinking you got kind of mad when I said that.").

When we describe the behavior or pattern using the "just the facts" method, we simply make a statement without qualifying it, but when we begin to interpret the meaning, we phrase the metacommunication in a tentative way. Because interpretation is always speculative, we want to be sure we convey to the child that this is what we think the meaning or underlying significance of the behavior or pattern is, making it clear we are not trying to force our interpretation on him or her. This also encourages the child to correct or clarify what the meaning or underlying significance is without feeling defensive. It can also ensure that we are not putting our ideas into the child's mind. When we are being tentative, we use conditional words and phrases like, "might be," "maybe," "I would guess," "I am thinking," "kind of," "seems as though," and so forth.

Reflecting Feelings

One of the primary reasons for doing play therapy with children is their developmentally based difficulty with verbally communicating their feelings. Therefore, it is the responsibility of the play therapist to monitor clients' expression of feelings and to reflect those feelings. Children constantly express emotions both verbally and nonverbally. However, they frequently lack awareness of their own feelings, and they may have a limited ability to understand or explain their feelings. Play therapy is a venue that gives children a way to express and understand their feelings.

Just as with the other skills, to be able to reflect the child's feelings, you will want to watch and listen. Posture, proximity, gestures, and facial expressions are all important components of the child's body language. The tone and pitch of the voice, the speed of the speech, and the inflection of the sentences all convey affective information. You must be aware of all of the elements of the child's communication to be able to accurately reflect emotions. Whether Seamus stands straight and proud or hunched and timid; whether Kate stands close to or far away from the counselor; whether Sayyid speaks in a timid, shaking voice or with a loud, clear timbre communicates many things about how the child is feeling and how he or she views himself or herself, the world, and others. (Likewise, remember that you communicate to the child with your verbal and nonverbal playroom behaviors. Pay attention to what you're "saying" to the child with your voice tone and pitch, inflections, body posture, dress, and physical proximity.)

Both play and verbalizations provide data about feelings. Choices about which toys, sand tray figures, or art materials to use can tell you much about what is happening in the child's life. The order with which the child plays with them can also be informative. How the child plays with toys and uses the sand tray figures and art materials can add more information about how the child is feeling. Does Fayola pick up the doll and then throw it on the floor and stomp on it? Does Felipe pick the doll up and rock it and sing to it? Does Melissa put one doll on top of another and move it up and down? Does Sekou use black paint to cover up his picture of his family?

You will also want to monitor the child's words. The child may express emotions verbally by talking directly to you about feelings, have puppets or dolls use words to express feelings, tell stories about the feelings or friends and relatives, or make random comments about feelings during the course of the play.

Although all of these factors are important components of children's affective expression, there is no set method for understanding the meaning of the various elements. All children have unique methods of expression. They often have different patterns of communication with the various people with whom they have relationships or within the various situations in which they find themselves.

Our goal is to learn how individual children are going to communicate with us. When we have figured this out, we adapt our own communication to theirs so that we can optimize our chances of conveying our ideas in a way that works for them. We spend the first several sessions observing and learning children's unique way of expressing feelings. We make a lot of guesses about feelings during the course of these initial sessions, and we watch how they react to each of our guesses. In this way, we determine how specific children are going to express their emotions.

Once you have gained an understanding of the child's unique method of expressing emotions, reflection of feelings is a very simple technique. All you have to do is to make a statement about what you think the child is feeling. Examples of reflections of feelings:

- "You look kind of angry when you hit that punching bag."
- "You sound very happy. It seems like you had a lot of fun at the zoo today."
- To a puppet whose dog died, "You feel really sad because your dog died."
- About a doll who is interacting with another doll, "When his brother said that to him, he felt really mad. He was so mad that he wanted to hit his brother."

When reflecting children's feelings, the counselor should keep statements simple and clear. It is not necessary to give children an elaborate analysis of why they are feeling those particular feelings or try to convince them that they should not be having those feelings. It is not usually helpful to ask children how they feel. They seldom have an answer to this question because they do not have that level of self-awareness or feeling vocabulary.

It is also not appropriate to use the phrase, "That makes you feel . . ." One of the basic premises of Adlerian theory is that a person's subjective interpretation of a situation will determine his or her reaction to the situation. Given this belief, no external force, person, or event can "make" a person feel an emotion. In play therapy, just as in counseling with adults, the counselor's job is to use language to help the client take responsibility for the client's emotions, attitudes, thoughts, and behaviors. The counselor can help the child to own his or her reactions and actions by carefully choosing the words used to reflect feelings.

Effective reflection of feelings requires using vocabulary that children can understand. Children who are 3, 4, 5, and 6 years old usually think in terms of sad, mad, glad, and scared. They tend to label all of their feelings with these words or with synonyms for these concepts. They seldom have the expressive vocabulary to label other, more subtle, emotions. They may not relate to abstract concepts or feeling words that represent "deeper" emotional nuances, such as humiliated, ashamed, content, or distraught. For instance, Santiago, a 4-year-old boy whose mother spanked him in front of the other members of his preschool class, may feel humiliated and ashamed, but he will not necessarily recognize these feelings if the counselor articulates them for him. He will recognize his feelings if the counselor says that he felt sad or angry. Sometimes the counselor will want to increase the child's feeling vocabulary by using words that are just a little bit beyond the child's expressive vocabulary (Kottman, 2011). The child can then choose to incorporate the concept in his or her receptive vocabulary and eventually use these newly acquired words and concepts expressively as well.

As children get older, they can understand more abstract feelings, and they are ready to increase their expressive vocabularies. With older children (7-, 8-, and 9-year-olds), if you use a word that the child might not comprehend, it is important to monitor his or her reaction to the comments closely. This way you can get an idea about whether the child understood the word. If the child does not comprehend the meaning of the feeling word, you can use a different, less abstract word to clarify the feeling reflection.

Usually the surface feelings expressed in the playroom are very obvious and simple. Deepak, a 7-year-old boy, comes into the playroom and says, "I got into a fight on the playground today. Billy beat me up. Now I'm going to beat him up in here." Deepak is obviously angry, and he wants to act out that anger in the playroom. Part of the responsibility of the play therapist is to reflect those simple, surface feelings. Sometimes the surface feelings are the only emotions present in the situation.

Other times the child may be experiencing underlying, deeper feelings. The counselor must reflect those feelings as well. Deepak may be feeling embarrassed that he got beaten up in front of the other children in his class. He may be feeling weak and afraid that this kind of thing will happen to him again. He could have a thousand subtle, less obvious feelings. We always consider what we know about the child and the way the child expresses feelings before we make a guess about the deeper emotions. It is not necessary or desirable to reflect a deeper emotion every time the child expresses a feeling. (That could be quite annoying or overwhelming to the child.) However, we want to be alert to the possibility that the child is experiencing underlying feelings and be ready to reflect them when they exist.

When the play therapist reflects a feeling, he or she must observe the child's reaction to the reflection. For example, if the child makes a verbal response, he or she may simply agree with the play therapist's comment. This usually means that the guess about the feeling was accurate but that it did not particularly affect the child emotionally. The child may disagree with the comment or correct the therapist's guess without a lot of emotion attached to the disagreement. This usually means the counselor's guess was off base. For example, you might say to Pepita, an 8-year-old girl, "Seems like you're kind of afraid of that rat." She could say, "No. I'm not afraid of him. I just don't want him here. My mom says rats are dirty, and I don't like dirty stuff." This type of disagreement is rather matter of fact and usually means that your guess was inaccurate but not particularly significant to the child. When this happens, you can try to use this as an opportunity to demonstrate the "courage to be imperfect" (Dreikurs & Soltz, 1964, p. 38). You could say something like, "Oh well. I made a mistake," or "Sorry I got that wrong. Thanks for helping me by telling me how you feel."

If the child disagrees with your guess in a vehement manner, it could mean that the reflection was accurate but that the child does not want to deal with those feelings at this time. For instance, when you make the guess that Pepita is afraid of the rat, she might say, "You're so stupid. Of course I'm not afraid of that rat. I'm not afraid of anything." In this case, Pepita seems to be overreacting to the comment. When this happens, you must use both your clinical judgment and your knowledge about this particular child to decide whether the child seems to be overly reactive to the comment. Whenever the child has this type of reaction to one of your reflections of feelings, you might want to make a guess about the feelings underneath the reaction and reflect them. You could say something like, "You seemed kind of angry when I said that you were afraid of the rat. You don't want me to think you're afraid of anything." To avoid getting into a power struggle over whether you are right, you could add, "Well, it's something to think about. Some people might be sort of afraid of rats."

A violent reaction could also mean that the play therapist's reflection was incorrect and that the child was hurt or angry about the inaccuracy. In that case, Pepita might say something like, "You never get anything right. You just don't understand me. I'm not afraid of the rat. I was just pretending, and you can't tell the difference." Again, you will want to avoid getting into a power struggle with her about your accuracy or your intentions. You can simply reflect the feelings inherent in the child's response by saying something like, "Seems like your feelings were hurt because I didn't understand that you were just pretending to be afraid. You're feeling kind of angry with me for not getting that, right?"

Even when the child remains silent, there is usually some type of bodily or play response. You must be alert to subtle, nonverbal cues to understand these reactions. (Sorry if we have been harping on this; we want to ensure you know Adlerian play therapists pay attention to all types of communication cues.) Never ask the child for a reaction or insist that the child confirm or deny your guesses. You will want to devote your attention to the child's body language and play patterns to try to discern his or her recognition reflex. For example, Sam is facing you when you make a reflection of his feelings, and as soon as you make the reflection, he turns his back toward you. You may have made an accurate reflection that has upset the child in some way, or you may have made an inaccurate reflection that the child is nonverbally rejecting. Sam may have also decided that he wanted something on the other side of the room and turned around to go and get it. It is important to avoid reading too much into every situation. As the story goes, "sometimes a cigar is just a cigar."

Answering Questions

Children in play therapy frequently ask the play therapist questions. Adlerians believe that children almost always have some purpose in asking each of the questions they ask. They may want to make contact with the counselor, test limits, explore the counselor's reactions, or have a hundred different goals. Before deciding how to answer children's questions, the counselor first needs to consider the purpose of the questions.

O'Connor (2000) listed three main categories of questions children ask in play therapy: practical, personal, and relationship. In a list of commonly asked questions, Landreth (2012) included several other types of questions that seem to fit into an additional category related to the ongoing process of play therapy.

Practical Questions

Practical questions ask for factual, commonsense information. They can include frequently asked questions such as the following:

- "Can I go the bathroom?"
- "Is it Friday or Saturday?"
- "How many more minutes do we have left?"
- "How do you open this jar?"
- "Do I come next week, or will we skip next week?"
- "How will I get back to my classroom?"
- "Is my mother still in the waiting room?"

Sometimes the child simply wants to know the answer to the question for the sake of the factual information. If this is the case, it is not really necessary for the counselor to make an elaborate guess or metacommunication about the underlying meaning of the question. Just answering the child's question with factual information is perfectly appropriate.

Oftentimes, even these apparently simple questions have an underlying message in them. When the Adlerian play therapist believes there is additional meaning, he or she should make a guess about the child's purpose in asking the question. For example, when Yamin asks, "Can I go to the bathroom?" he may just have to go to the bathroom. If you think this is the case, you can answer the question without further interaction. However, you may believe that Yamin is asking this question because he wants to know the rules in the playroom about leaving the room. Then you can make a guess about this curiosity with a comment like, "You're kind of wondering if it is okay to leave the playroom before our time is done." Depending on the child's response to this guess, you may either answer the original question or answer the underlying question the child is asking. If you believe that Yamin is unhappy in the playroom or resistant to some of your comments and that this question is motivated by his desire to leave and escape the therapeutic process, you could make a guess about his desire to leave or his feelings of unhappiness and resistance. The child's reaction to your metacommunication about his or her purpose in asking the question determines your next action. If Yamin agrees that his purpose is escape, you will probably not give him permission to leave. If he asserts that he just wants to go to the bathroom, you can choose to honor his request (and we imagine that you would certainly want to) as a means of continuing to establish the egalitarian nature of the relationship.

When Joo asks, "What time is it?" she could be worried that she is going to miss her soccer match. She could have six more things she has planned to do in the playroom and wants to know if she will have time to get to do all six of them. She could be bored or restless and want to leave, but she knows that you will not let her leave until the time is up. She could be thinking or feeling a thousand other things. We would make a guess about the underlying meaning of the question and then base any further interactions about this question on Joo's response.

Personal Questions
Sometimes a child in play therapy will ask personal questions. For example,

- "Are you married?"
- "Do you have any children?"
- "How old are you?"
- "Where do you live?"

Most of the time, the purpose in asking personal questions is to make some kind of connection with you and/or to help lower the child's anxiety. The most therapeutic course seems to be to metacommunicate about the child's purpose in asking the question and give a very brief, factual answer. Usually, when you answer the question in a straightforward manner, without appearing threatened in any way, the answer satisfies the child's curiosity and need for contact and reassurance. Sometimes, however, a child persistently continues to ask invasive personal questions. O'Connor (2000) suggested that this may be an attempt to gain control of the session. If you believe that the child's purpose in continuing to ask personal questions is to gain power, it is sometimes helpful to metacommunicate about his or her desire to control situations instead of directly dealing with his or her questions.

Relationship Questions
The third category is the relationship question. For example,

- "Do you like me?"
- "Do you play with other children like me?"
- "Can I come home to live with you?"
- "Do you like me better than the other kids who come here?"
- "If you could, would you adopt me?"
- "Do you wish I would come more often?"

These questions almost always have both an overt and a covert meaning. Children use relationship questions to determine the strength of the relationship and to protect themselves from investing more than you have. The most important response to this type of question is to reflect the feelings that motivate children to ask these questions and to metacommunicate about their purpose. When a child asks, "Do you like me?" you can respond with a comment such as, "I am guessing that you are not always sure if other people care about you, and you want me to let you know that I care for you."

Sometimes it seems important to reassure the child in response to relationship questions, but most of the time, we choose not to answer this type of question directly. They tend to grow from the child's insecurity and feelings of unworthiness, and nothing we say in answer to the child's question is going to counteract those feelings of inferiority. We hope that the growing relationship with the child and the child's increasing sense of competence and confidence will eventually fill that empty place within the child. Each counselor has to decide how to handle these questions on a case-by-case basis, depending on the child and the potential for the relationship. These types of questions can also trigger the counselor's own feelings of belonging and acceptance. If you find yourself feeling particularly moved in one way or another by these questions, you might consider exploring these feelings.

Ongoing Process Questions
Landreth (2012) provided a list of questions commonly asked by children in play therapy. Several seem to relate to the ongoing process of play therapy. For example,

- "What is this?" (pointing to some object in the playroom)
- "Do you know what I am going to do now?"
- "What should I do next?"
- "Can I throw this at the mirror?"
- "Why do you talk different than other people?"
- "Will you make it work for me?"
- "What is the right way to play with this toy?"
- "What do you think I'm going to color?"

Children's purpose in asking ongoing process questions is usually to help them define the parameters of the process of play therapy and the boundaries of the relationship between them and the play therapist. Children often use questions to solicit help, to try to please the therapist, or to get the therapist to make decisions for them. They may be afraid of displeasing the therapist or breaking the playroom rules. Because of these fears, their questions can be a strategy for keeping themselves safe. They may simply be afraid of taking risks and want the play therapist to eliminate the need for them to make choices or try new behaviors. They may also be trying to set up a game in which the therapist makes guesses about things that they are going to do or what they have on their mind. This can easily develop into a power struggle in which children constantly want to play some kind of never-ending guessing game, which is not therapeutic.

To avoid the possibility of dependency or game playing and to encourage the child's growth, we usually choose not to answer this type of
question. Instead of providing the answer to a process-oriented question,
we usually make a statement that gives the responsibility and control
back to the child (Kottman, 2011; Landreth, 2012; Ray, 2011). For example,
if Germaine asks, "What is this?" you might answer, "In here, you can
decide what that is" or "It's kind of tough for you to choose what things
are. It can be whatever you want it to be." If Tessa asks, "What do you
think I am going to paint?" you could answer, "Sometimes it's hard for
you to decide what to do, and in here that is your decision" or "You like
to know what you're going to do and try to get me to guess, and you're
the only one who knows what you're going to do."

Taking Time to Think
No matter what kind of question the child asks, you can give yourself time
to think before making any kind of a response. Whether you choose to
answer the question or not, the decision should be based on a conscious
consideration of the possible underlying meaning in the child's question.
Almost always, before you give any type of content-oriented answer to a
question, you will want to metacommunicate about the child's purpose in
asking the question or about the underlying meaning of the question. It
may also be appropriate to reflect the feelings that prompted the question.
The answer flows from your intuitive sense of how the child is feeling and
thinking. Whatever the response to the child's questions, your ultimate
goal is to build the relationship with the child and help foster the child's
self-understanding and self-esteem.

Asking the Child Questions

Sometimes asking questions is the best, most efficient way of getting the
information that the counselor needs to build a relationship with the
child and begin to understand the child's lifestyle. The questions should
not come out of the clear blue sky. They should flow naturally from the
conversation with the child or from the child's play. Any questions the
counselor asks should relate to what is happening in the session rather
than being artificially imposed on the basis of the counselor's curiosity. It
is important to remember that the counselor can ask the questions directly
(e.g., "Which of the kids in your family gets into the most trouble?") or
indirectly through a metaphor (e.g., "Which of the kids in that giraffe
family gets into the most trouble?"). Either way, the child's answer will
give the counselor valuable information about his or her lifestyle. It is
also important not to overwhelm the child with a series of questions that
resemble a police interrogation. To control my own natural curiosity, I
(TK) limit myself to four or five questions a session.

Types of Questions
Open-ended questions glean more information than closed-ended questions because they encourage the child to answer with more than just
yes or no. The therapist should begin questions with *how, what, when,*
and *where* and avoid questions that ask the child *why. Why* questions are

the most common type of questions adults ask children. Many adults seem to feel that problems can only be solved after the child answers the age-old question, "Why did you do that?" Most of the time, children do not know the answer to these questions, and even when they do, the answer does not particularly help the relationship grow or help the adult really understand the child's motivation. Why questions are past oriented. They delve into the historical antecedents of a particular event. The Adlerian play therapist is focused on the present and the future, only using information from the past to help build a picture of how the child functions in the present and make plans for helping the child move to a more constructive and happy future.

When the Child Does Not Answer a Question

Under many circumstances, when an adult asks a child a question, the child feels pressured to answer the question. If the child does not answer, the adult often tries to force an answer or punishes the child for not answering. In Adlerian play therapy, we want to "rise above" this traditional reaction. The child always has control over whether he or she chooses to answer your questions. The child may decide not to give a verbal answer to questions. This is the child's right. In an egalitarian relationship, either participant can choose whether to participate in the conversation or not. You will need to just accept the child's decision not to answer a question. It is also helpful to remember, though, that even if the child does not verbally answer the question, he or she will probably convey a certain amount of information related to the question through nonverbal communication or through play.

We usually make one of three different types of responses when a child chooses not to answer one of our questions. First, we may not say anything at all. This simply lets the child not answer without interpretation. Second, we may make a factual metacommunication, such as, "You decided not to answer that question." This type of reply conveys our respect and our belief in the child's right to make this type of decision. Third, we may venture an interpretive metacommunication about the child's purpose in not answering the question. Among possible purposes the child may have in ignoring the play therapist's questions are (a) the question may address a sensitive area that the child is not yet ready to explore with the play therapist, (b) the child may choose not to answer because she or he wants to demonstrate that the play therapist does not have the power to force an answer, or (c) the child may choose not to answer because he or she has learned in his or her family that ignoring adults is a reliable way of keeping them involved with him or her. (This is not to imply these are the only possibilities—just the ones that came to us as we were writing this section of the world's longest chapter.)

Nonverbal Responses

Regardless of the type of response you get to a question, you must always watch children's facial expressions, body language, and play behavior, noticing any nonverbal reaction to the question. (You've heard this before, right?) Even when children choose to ignore questions or give brief noncommittal answers, their behavior should communicate something about their reactions to the questions.

The child may make a face or flinch or have some other type of obvious recognition reflex. If this happens, we assume that we may have hit some kind of nerve, that this question has touched on a sensitive area in which the child may need some assistance eventually. If the child switches activities or accelerates the speed or level of behavior in the current activity, this may also indicate that the subject of our questions is an area that needs further exploration. If the child simply continues to play whatever he or she was playing when we asked the question, with minimal physical reaction, we usually believe that his or her ignoring of our question has little or no underlying significance. The child may be absorbed in the play or the question may involve some topic in which he or she is not particularly interested.

Adlerian Play Therapy Questioning Strategies

One strategy for building the relationship is using questioning strategies to get to know the child. Almost all of the questions in Adlerian play therapy fit into one of two distinct categories: (a) questions related to the presenting problem or ongoing events in the child's life and (b) questions related to the exploration of the child's lifestyle.

Sometimes we ask children questions about how they are currently handling some particular aspect of the presenting problem. Our purpose in asking this type of question is to let children know that what is happening in their lives is important to us, that we are concerned and involved in their lives both inside and outside the playroom. We are always sure to ask these questions in a nonjudgmental, supportive way so that children do not think that we are just checking up on them or urging them to make progress on the presenting problem.

There are two ways of asking this type of question. One way is to ask a general, "How is it going with . . .?" question. For example,

- If Lucinda has a history of talking back to her teacher and you have been talking about different ways of handling that situation, you might ask, "How is it going with your teacher?"
- If Jeremiah has a history of being teased on the bus, you could ask, "What's happening on the bus with the other kids lately?"
- If Yasmin reports feeling troubled about being adopted, you might ask, "What thoughts have you had lately about being adopted?"

The second way is to ask a specific, "How could you change one particular aspect of . . .?" question. For example,

- If David's presenting problem is public masturbation and you have talked about private places he could masturbate, you might say, "Where are some other places at home where no one would see you if you wanted to touch your privates?"
- If Catalina's presenting problem is inappropriate expression of feelings and you have been working on ways of appropriately expressing feelings, you might ask, "How could you tell your mom that you're angry about that without getting into trouble?"

- If Enrique's presenting problem is poor academic performance and Enrique has told you that he is particularly struggling in spelling, you could ask, "How did your spelling test go this week?"

Whether to ask this type of question depends on several factors, including children's ages, their cognitive abilities, and their openness to talking about the presenting problem and how it affects their lives. Children under the age of 7 or 8 and children with limited cognitive abilities may not understand why they are coming to play therapy. If this is the case, there is seldom reason to ask them questions about their progress outside the playroom or their application of new behaviors learned in the playroom to other situations. With these populations, it is usually best to rely on reports from parents, teachers, and other adults who come into contact with the children.

The other type of question Adlerian play therapists ask is designed to further establish the relationship by exploring the child's lifestyle. Dinkmeyer and Dinkmeyer (1977) adapted the work of Dreikurs (1967) and Mosak (1971) in developing the *Children's Lifestyle Guide*. I (TK) have further adapted this guide so that it is appropriate for use in play therapy. Lifestyle questions for children generally fit into four broad categories: family, school, social–friends, and general. A list of the kind of questions you can use in play therapy to build rapport and help you begin to understand the child and the child's lifestyle is in Appendix D.

Some of the family questions assume that the child has siblings. If the client is an only child, the counselor usually simply changes the comparative questions into straight information-seeking questions. This involves replacing questions such as, "Which of the kids is most like your dad?" with "How are you like your dad?"

It is important not to bring this long list of possible questions and ratings into the playroom. The counselor should become familiar with the list outside the playroom and be prepared to ask the questions that fit naturally into the flow of the interaction with the child.

Examples of how to blend questions into the normal communication patterns of the play therapy:

- As Florinda is playing with the dolls in the dollhouse, she tells you that the big male doll is the daddy. By adapting some of the family questions and asking her to tell you about the daddy, you can use the metaphor of the doll family to solicit her observations about her own father.
- Ichiro is playing in the kitchen area, and he tells you that he likes to help his mommy cook. You might explore his feelings about his mother by reflecting his feelings and saying, "Seems like you really like to do things with your mother." Then you could use this opportunity to ask a question, such as, "Which one of your parents are you most like—your mommy or your daddy?"
- Candace sets up the dolls so that they can be the students and she can be the teacher in some school play. You could use the metaphor to ask any of several questions about her attitude and behavior in school, such as "What do the kids in this class like best about school?"

or "As the teacher, what would you change about school since you are in charge?"

- Santiago is telling you about a video game he played during the week. You might use the following questions to explore: "What did you like about that video game?" "What is your favorite video game?" or "If you were the main character in that video game, what would you do to solve the problem?"

Asking a limited number of questions per session, it would take you many, many sessions to ask the child all of the questions in the list in Appendix D. It is not essential to ask every single question. You will want to select questions that help you to better understand children's perceptions of how they fit into their families and their peer groups. We always try to get a general idea about what the child sees as her or his assets and liabilities. We also ask questions that deepen our understanding of the child's perception of the problem and how he or she wants life to be different. This helps us formulate our goals for the play therapy relationship.

Returning Responsibility to the Child

It is really important, in most cases, to avoid doing things for children that they can do for themselves or making decisions for them. The primary method used in play therapy to make sure that this happens is to return responsibility to the child (Kottman, 2011; Landreth, 2012; Ray, 2011). By returning responsibility to the child, the play therapist directly or indirectly lets the child know that the child has the ability to take responsibility for himself or herself and be successful in his or her actions and choices. Many times the act of returning responsibility to the child gives the child who has little or no courage permission to take risks and try things that he or she would not ordinarily attempt to do. This technique can also be very helpful for children who do not believe that they are capable or that they count.

We return responsibility to children when they explicitly or implicitly ask for help and in some situations in which we feel a need to help them even though they have not indicated a desire for assistance. We almost always return responsibility to children when they ask us to do something for them that we believe that they can do for themselves. The following are examples of returning the responsibility to the child around behaviors:

- Sasha asks, "Can you zip my jacket for me?" You could say, "I bet you can do that for yourself."
- Phil asks, "Will you get that game for me?" You could say, "It's my guess that you can figure out how to get the game."
- Alberto says, "I can't tie my shoes." You could say, "You are wanting me to tie your shoes. You tied them last week, so I know that you can do it."
- Margarita says, "How do you make these handcuffs work?" You could say, "If you look at the way they fit together, I would say that you can figure it out."

There are times when we choose not to use this skill with children. We may believe that (a) the child is not capable of taking responsibility for the behavior; (b) the child is engaging in regressive behavior, and we believe that this behavior is appropriate for that particular child; (c) the child's history indicates that the child may need someone to take care of him or her in certain situations; and (d) the child's life is not going particularly well, and the child needs special nurturing. In these cases, we usually invite the child to collaborate with us on accomplishing the task by saying some variation of, "Let's work as a team and figure out how to do that." We may also metacommunicate about their desire for help by saying something like, "You know how to brush your own hair, and sometimes it feels good to have someone do it for you."

We never make decisions for children because we think they are always capable of making choices and we want to convey this faith in their decision-making power to them.

Some examples of returning the responsibility to the child around decisions:

- Dimitri says, "What color should I paint the rabbit?" You could say, "You can decide what color you would like the rabbit to be."
- Marta says, "What do you want me to do now?" You could say, "Right now you are in charge, so you can decide what you want to do next."
- Christopher says, "I wonder what baby's name is." You could say, "You can choose a name for him."
- Eva says, "What is this?" You could say, "In here, it can be whatever you want it to be."
- Nasir looks at a group of animal figures. Then he looks at you as if to say, "Which one should I choose?" You could say, "Looks like you want my help choosing what to play with, and I know that you can figure that out for yourself."

Interacting Actively With the Child

One of the ways that the Adlerian play therapist builds the relationship with children is to interact with them actively. Sometimes the therapist plays with children at their request. Other times, the therapist initiates playful interactions.

Children request that the therapist play with them for a variety of reasons— some of them positive and some of them not so positive. They could be (a) looking for a way to emotionally connect with the therapist, (b) inviting the therapist to use toys and play as a way of communicating, or (c) wanting a model for appropriate play behavior. Other times their motivation is not so constructive. At times, children ask the therapist to play because they believe that (a) they are expected to play with the therapist, (b) the therapist will be more inclined to like them if they ask the therapist to play with them, or (c) they cannot make good decisions and they want the therapist to determine the direction of the play (Landreth, 2012). They may also want to demonstrate some kind of power over the therapist or control over the session.

When a child requests that we play, we usually make a guess about the child's purpose in asking. Examples of metacommunications about the child's purpose in asking us to play:

- "It's hard for you to make up your mind what to do, so you think if you ask me to play with you that I will decide for you."
- "You'd really like to get to know me better, and if we play together we will learn more about each other."
- "If we play this game, then you think you can tell me what to do."
- "You seem kind of sad today, and you'd like to have me down on the floor and be closer to you."

Most of the time, if we think there is a chance that playing with the child will help to build the relationship in constructive ways, we metacommunicate about any underlying goal of the invitation to play and then we accept. However, when we believe that the child's purpose is manipulative or inappropriate, we make a guess about his or her goal and then decline the invitation. When we do this, we state our position in a nonjudgmental way, using a phrase like, "I choose not to play right now." It is important to watch for the child's reaction so we can also metacommunicate about the reaction.

Playing with the child gives you opportunities to model appropriate behaviors, reframe negative situations, teach skills, and examine goals of behavior. For example, Courtney, a child who thinks winning is so important that she is willing to cheat to guarantee her success, could benefit from the play situation therapeutically if you (a) reflect her feelings of frustration and fear of failure, (b) make guesses about her need to win and her need to control, (c) make guesses about her self-image and how that is affected by success and failure, (d) model socially acceptable sportsmanship and game-playing behavior, (e) encourage any appropriate behavior on her part, (f) reframe mistakes and failure in terms of opportunities for learning, and (g) teach her new interaction skills and alternative ways of playing the game without cheating.

When you choose to play with a child, it is essential that the interaction be a continuation of the therapeutic process. When you are playing, you need to retain your ability to make therapeutic comments, including tracking, reflection of feeling, metacommunication, and encouragement. You should not get so involved in the process of the play that you lose sight of your role as counselor.

It is helpful, whenever possible, to let children lead the play. You can ask children what they want you to do next to ensure that they feel that you are sharing the control of the interaction. If you forget to do this or the children do not like something you choose to do, children will almost always let you know that they wish for the interaction to move in a different direction or they wish that you would consult them more often or give them more control. When you think this course would be the most therapeutic one, you can try to accommodate their requests. However, with children who are trying to assert control over you, metacommunicate about the underlying purpose in their request and then inform them that you want to do things your way instead.

During role-playing or in a game such as hide-and-seek, the play therapist can let the child take the lead in the activity by using the "whisper technique" (Landreth, 2009; Kottman, 2011). In a role-playing situation, the therapist uses three separate and distinct voices: his or her own regular voice, the character voice, and a whisper. It is best for the therapist to use his or her regular voice to track, reflect feelings, metacommunicate, and generally make therapeutic comments about what is happening with the child. The therapist uses the character voice to say things in the character that the child has created for the role play. The therapist uses the whisper voice to ask the child what to do or say next, allowing the child to control the direction of the role play. Using the whisper voice to ask the child for directions seems to distinguish between the therapist and the character. The following is an example of using the whisper technique in a role play with a child:

Brian: "Let's play that the mommy gets mad and spanks all the kids."
Terry (regular voice): "You want to pretend that all the kids get spanked." (whisper): "Which one do you want me to be?"
Brian: "You be the mommy. I'm the kid, and I have the baby with me."
Terry (whisper): "What do I do now?"
Brian: "You say, 'You are in big trouble now!'"
Terry (whisper): "How should I look?"
Brian: "You look real mean, and you say it and you have the paddle."
Terry (in a mean character voice): "I'm going to spank you and the baby. I have the paddle."
Brian (running away from me, holding the baby away from me): "Ohh-hhhhh!"
Terry (regular voice): "You sound scared. Looks like you are going to protect yourself and the baby from me, make sure you're both safe."
Brian (still holding the baby away from me): "I won't let you hurt us."
Terry (regular voice): "It's important to you to keep yourself and the baby from getting hurt." (whisper voice): "What should I do now?"
Brian: "You chase me around the room and try to grab me and the baby."
Terry (whisper voice): "Should I say anything?"
Brian: "No, you just scream."
Terry (chasing the child around the room—character voice): "ARRRRRRGGGHHHH!"
Brian: "You can't get us!!!"
Terry (regular voice): "You know how to take care of yourself and your baby."
Brian: "Yup. You can't hurt us."
Terry (regular voice): "You sound pretty proud that you know how to keep safe." (whisper voice): "What should I do now?"
Brian: "You say, 'I can't get these kids. They keep getting away.'"
Terry (character voice): "I can't get that kid and the baby. They keep getting away. That kid knows how to keep them safe."

In this particular example, Brian ends the role play on a positive, encouraging note. He believes that he can protect himself and others. I (TK) added several encouraging editorial comments during the course of the role play, such as, "That kid knows how to keep them safe," to affirm his feeling of strength and his ability to take care of himself.

Often, however, children do not have such optimistic resolutions to their fantasies. This is perfectly natural. Most children who come to play therapy lack healthy self-concepts or accurate perceptions of their own assets. Role-playing with another person, regardless of whether children choose to play out an event with a positive or negative resolution, may help them gain a better understanding of themselves and others. As children direct role plays, they can explore different options and alternative behaviors for themselves. This is why many play therapists frequently encourage children to control the direction of the role play and the actions and words of the characters.

It is also possible to use the whisper technique to let the child be in control during interactive activities that do not involve role-playing, such as hide-and-seek and pitch-and-catch. When you use the whisper technique in these situations, the character voice gets omitted, leaving the whisper for asking for direction and your regular voice for making therapeutic comments. You would use the whisper to ask the child, "Where do you want me to hide?" or "How should I throw the ball?" or "How hard do you want me to hit it?"

Initially, especially with children from families in which they have too little power and children with chaotic families, children may not know how to handle being asked to take charge of the play. These children have yelled at us, refused to answer, and stopped playing. However, if we metacommunicate our ideas about what is going on with them and persist on asking them to direct the play, they usually overcome their distrust and get very excited about being in charge—sometimes to the point of becoming playroom tyrants and trying to boss us around even when we are not using the whisper technique.

There are times when we do not wish to let the child lead the direction of the play, such as when we want to teach the child a specific skill or when we believe the child is stuck during a fantasy play sequence and needs help moving forward in the play, which sometimes happens to children who have experienced traumatic events (Carey, 2006; Gil, 2010; Levine & Kline, 2007; Terr, 1990). In these situations, we simply decide what we want to do next (without consulting the child) and do it. Occasionally, if we have routinely used the whisper technique with a child and the child is used to being in charge of the play, there may be a strong reaction to this new way of doing things. However, most of the time the child simply goes along with the direction we have chosen.

Cleaning the Room Together

With most children, part of the process of establishing the egalitarian nature of the relationship in Adlerian play therapy is cleaning the room together. You want to let the child know that in the working partnership you are each responsible for your own actions, including cleaning up any mess at the end of the session. With children with whom you decide to have help clean up the room, you will work as a team to straighten the room together, in a collaboration that the child controls. The child is in charge of determining how the team goes about the task—who does what and the order in which you tackle each task. Your focus should be on the relationship-building process created by the collaborative tidying, rather than the product of a perfectly clean playroom. Although it is important to have the toys put away, being rigid about where things go is counterproductive.

How to Set Up the Cleaning Team

If the counselor decides that cleaning the room together is important, establishing the routine is very simple. Ten minutes before the end of the session, the counselor tells the child, "There are 5 more minutes before it's time for us to clean up together." Five minutes before the end of the session, the counselor stands up and says to the child, "OK. It's time for us to clean up the room together. What do you want me to do/put away? What are you going to do/put away?" These announcements and any discussion about the cleaning are articulated in the counselor's usual matter-of-fact voice, without any badgering or judgment in the tone of voice or body language. It must be clear that the cleaning is not a punishment or a reflection of the counselor's own need for neatness but rather an exercise in cooperation and shared responsibility. The reality is that many adults in the child's life will not let the child make a mess without cleaning up.

By putting the child in charge of the assignment of tasks and the pacing of the cleaning procedure, the counselor can usually engage his or her interest in the process. This avoids potential power struggles that might ensue if the counselor is more obviously directive and controlling. This technique communicates the counselor's interest in sharing the responsibility for the progress of the therapy and the growth of the relationship with the child. It also establishes that the child has a certain amount of power and control in this situation. I (KMW) often start by asking children which toys they want to put away. Rarely do children object when I present it this way although they may decide to pick up just one or two things. For me, this is fine. It's a place to start. For those rare children who say, "I don't want to put away toys," I might say, "You pick three toys to put away and I'll put away three toys." The small number usually satisfies these children.

If children get distracted, you can remind them that they chose to pick up the objects they are picking up. It is helpful to reflect their feelings and make a guess about their purposes in not following through with the task they assigned themselves. They may be trying to extend their time in the playroom; they may be trying to avoid doing their share of the cleaning and hoping that you will take over their responsibilities; they may be wanting you to take care of them. On the basis of children's behavior in the past, their present behaviors, and their nonverbal communication, you will probably have a good guess about their purposes. Then you can give them the opportunity to reconsider and reassign the tasks. Again, during this process, you need to be careful to avoid using a punitive or judgmental tone of voice or body language. You want to communicate the spirit of cooperation in both your verbal and nonverbal messages.

When we have a child who dawdles or gets easily distracted, we try to turn the cleaning up into a game. I (TK) may challenge the child to see whether he or she can pick up the assigned objects before I can pick up mine, or I may challenge him or her to pick the objects up faster this week than last week, offering to time us so we can see which time is faster. There are many creative ways of engaging the child in a positive manner, so that cleaning the room together does not become a power struggle or a disagreeable chore.

When a Child Refuses to Help Clean the Playroom
When you are not successful in avoiding a power struggle and a child absolutely refuses to collaborate on the room cleaning, you can give choices. Try the least restrictive choice first, by saying to the child, "You can choose for us to clean up the room together, or you can choose not to play with the (whatever object the child is not picking up at that point) next session." This is based on the premise that the child has not completely trashed the room and that it is possible to delete whatever objects he or she decides not to pick up from the repertoire of available options during the next session. If the child has taken most of the toys off the shelves or simply refuses to work with you at all on the clean-up process, then you can bring in the big-guns choice. You would say something like, "You can choose to help in the clean-up process, or you can choose to be in a different room without all the toys next week." When the child chooses this option, you reflect whatever feelings he or she is expressing and metacommunicate about the purpose of the behavior.

A child who chooses this option is usually testing the limits of the relationship and whether the play therapist will be consistent and calm. It is essential to maintain a pleasant, matter-of-fact demeanor and a non-judgmental, untroubled tone of voice when giving the child these choices. The play therapist must not have a vested interest in the child's choice. (As much as it might feel like it, it is not a competition between you and the child. We believe any time the adult joins into a power struggle just for the sake of the power struggle, the adult has lost.) To avoid getting drawn into power struggles and to convey the egalitarian spirit of the relationship, the play therapist must be perfectly amenable to either choice. If the child makes the decision not to clean up the room, the play therapist must not show that he or she takes this choice personally or negatively. If this is the case, the play therapist must not go back on his or her word by trying to coerce the child to make a different choice or by returning to the playroom in the next session. We are demonstrating trust in the child and respect for the child to make decisions that will be honored by us. (This is easier said than done—and it's really important!)

On the occasions when a client chooses the big-guns option, the counselor may wish to have the next session in an alternative, empty room or hang a sheet in front of the shelves. When this happens, I (TK) usually bring a game or some art materials into another location and tell the child, "You decided not to have all of the toys this week, so I chose which toys to use this week in our session." I seldom have a child who chooses this option more than once.

With children who choose this option repeatedly, the counselor should look very closely at the purpose of the child's behavior. Most of the time, these children have a massive need for power, or they exhibit many of the symptoms of ADHD. With the power-needy children, the counselor should reconsider using cleaning the room as a relationship-enhancing strategy. With the ADHD children, they may be indirectly trying to communicate that they are overwhelmed by a fully equipped playroom filled with toys. The counselor might want to think about moving the play sessions to a smaller room with less stimulation and fewer toys.

Exceptions to Cleaning the Room Together

Cleaning the playroom together is not an absolute rule in Adlerian play therapy. There are some children who come to play therapy exhibiting signs of rigidity and compulsive behavior. These children are "too tight" (Kissel, 1990) and need help feeling freer. Too-tight children often have control of self as their personality priority. In the playroom, they tend to automatically clean up after themselves and spend a great deal of their energy making sure that things do not get out of control. When we work with these children, we try to loosen them up. Too-tight children tend to believe they count conditionally and that they must continue to be too tight to be loved and accepted by others. This may truly be the message sent in their families, or it may be one of their mistaken beliefs. However, regardless of the origin of their tightness, we do not want to send them a message they can construe as recommending continued rigidity and compulsivity. Cleaning the room together could easily be sending a message that the children interpret as telling them that they need to persist in their pursuit of tightness. To loosen these children up, we reassure them that they do not have to tidy the room to gain our acceptance. However, to make up for the absence of this type of team-building experience, we usually have to work harder with too-tight children to establish a partnership in which we work together with them.

The counselor may also work with other types of children for whom collaboratively cleaning the room will not serve to deepen the relationship. For instance, I (KMW) would not ask Ajit, a child engaged in a perpetual power struggle with his parents about cleaning his room, to help pick up the room. Such a request will sabotage the relationship from the start. As an Adlerian play therapist, we always consider each child as an individual, with unique perceptions and problems. We try to tailor our intervention to each individual child based on our understanding of his or her particular lifestyle and needs.

Case Example

We are beginning a case example in this section that continues in Chapters 7, 9, and 10. In this chapter, the case example illustrates how an Adlerian play therapist can begin the therapeutic relationship with parents and use play therapy techniques to build an egalitarian relationship with a child during the first phase of therapy.

I (KMW) received a call from Mr. and Mrs. Simon who requested a play therapy appointment for their 6-year-old granddaughter, Phoebe. While scheduling the appointment, I inquired about proper documentation that gave permission for seeking counseling services for their granddaughter. They indicated that they had this documentation and would bring it to our first meeting. Because I wanted to meet with the adults before I meet with the child, and because they didn't have afterschool child care for their granddaughter, we scheduled a meeting during school hours, although that would not be our typical session time.

During our first session, I described my belief that children are not problems but that they have problems and that all members of the family are usually contributing to the problem (sometimes unconsciously). I asked about their willingness to be a part of the counseling process. They agreed without reservation and expressed a belief that Phoebe's father would be actively involved when he could.

Mr. and Mrs. Simon wanted counseling services because Phoebe had been acting out for the past 3 or 4 months, becoming increasingly argumentative and irritable. They reported that she had become demanding, talking back to adults, and refusing to follow directions at home and at school. In their last teacher conference, Phoebe's teacher reported that she was demanding of her peers, who did not like to play with her. Mr. and Mrs. Simon said that at home Phoebe often played alone, read a lot, and spent time with the family animals. They described where they lived as isolated, stating that "there's nothing for miles and miles." Although they started to notice Phoebe's behavior changes at home, they had thought it was a phase and had not decided to seek counseling services until they were informed of Phoebe's school behavior by her first-grade teacher.

Mr. and Mrs. Simon reported that Phoebe lived with them and with their son, Christopher, who is her biological father. Phoebe's father and grandparents are all European American. Phoebe is biracial (Latina and Caucasian). Her mother, Alicia, had emigrated from Mexico with her family when she was in junior high. She had been killed in a vehicle accident when Phoebe was 3 years old. They mentioned that Phoebe had very few explicit memories of her mother but held her in high regard and expressed missing her often.

Phoebe's parents had married when they were 18 years old. Soon after Alicia and Christopher were married, Alicia had become pregnant with Phoebe, and she was born before their first wedding anniversary. Alicia's parents had not approved of the relationship because of differences of religion between the two families. Alicia's family practiced Catholicism, and Christopher's family practiced Buddhism. When Alicia eloped with Christopher, her parents had disowned her, so Phoebe had never met her maternal grandparents. Mr. and Mrs. Simon were supportive of their son, his wife, and their grandchild. While Alicia was alive, they regularly took care of Phoebe when her parents were working or out with friends.

Following Alicia's death, Christopher and Phoebe stayed in the house where they had lived with Alicia for several years, but Christopher had difficulty making ends meet. His parents cared for Phoebe while he was at work, but this arrangement was not particularly convenient because his parents lived on an acreage outside of town, which involved a 30-minute commute. To alleviate these problems, Christopher had recently decided to change his work schedule to third shift so he could go back to school to get a college degree. To make things run more smoothly, Christopher and Phoebe moved in with his parents. Mr. and Mrs. Simon were retired and lived comfortably. Phoebe and Christopher did not create a financial burden for them. Mr. and Mrs. Simon enjoyed having Phoebe around and took great pride in tending to her. They admitted to being a bit indulgent at times, believing they were filling the void left by the death of her mother.

Moving in with her grandparents had necessitated a school change for Phoebe. She had switched schools approximately 4 months before our first appointment, during the middle of the school year. Because Phoebe had spent lots of time with Mr. and Mrs. Simon, the transition to living with them was not difficult. For years before they moved in with her grandparents, she had had her own room with furniture and toys at their home. However, the change of schools was difficult as there were no children living near their house and she did not know anyone at her new school.

In my first session with Phoebe, I started our session by telling her that in the playroom sometimes she could get to decide what to do and sometimes I would decide what to do. Because I knew that she frequently played independently or with animals, I didn't want to overwhelm her with big, excited gestures and ideas. I also knew that she was used to getting things to go her way. To create a sense of safety, I decided to give her two options. She could choose to play with the toys or she could choose to draw a picture. I wanted her to feel comfortable and in control (which I had already hypothesized was her personality priority based on her grandparents' description) to begin to build a relationship with her. Phoebe was hesitant about playing with the toys and quietly said she would like to draw a picture. Cautiously, she looked around the room, exploring the toys with her eyes, and moved to the child-size desk with art supplies. She seemed to be searching for direction from me, as if to evaluate my motivations for being with her. I metacommunicated to her about her curiosity, "You seem to be not quite sure about me and playing with me in this room." I also started to demystify the counseling process. "What did your grandma or grandpa say to you about coming to see me?" She indicated that she didn't know much about what people do in play therapy and wasn't sure why she was here, but thought she might be in trouble. I told her,

> Sometimes kids come to play with me because they are sad, angry, or confused. When kids feel these feelings, they sometimes do things like yell at adults, be mean to friends, or other stuff they normally wouldn't do. Do you ever feel sad or angry?

She nodded but didn't speak. I acknowledged that she might be feeling this way sometimes, but because this was our first session and we were still creating a relationship, I did not pursue this line of discussion further at that time.

Phoebe started to draw. She quietly drew a picture of her family. She took great care and time in making this picture. Following the energy of the session, I talked infrequently and made brief tracking statements such as, "You're using the brown color." I also metacommunicated about her intensity and focus on the drawing by saying, "You're really concentrating. I'm guessing that your family is really important to you." When she was done, she put down her crayons and described her picture. Phoebe included three people who she identified as mom, dad, and herself. She drew herself as a baby in the picture and talked about her mom loving her, holding her, and playing with her. There was a sun, clouds, and a tree in the picture. She said it was a "happy picture." Once she finished describing the picture, looking annoyed, she took the black paint and colored over the entire picture. I metacommunicated about this by saying, "You are covering everything in the picture up. I am guessing you really miss your mom." She continued to rhythmically black out the picture until our time was up without answering me. She did not want to take the picture with her.

As we walked to the playroom for our second session, I said, "Last time, I gave you two choices about what to do. This time, you get to decide how we spend our time." She started by playing with the kitchen toys. Phoebe played independently, whispering to herself. She appeared engrossed in her play but was cautious to not speak too loudly. I tracked her play: "You're making that." "You put that in the oven." "You're serving food." I also metacommunicated about her play, "You like to make sure things are just how you want them." "You play really quietly. I'm guessing that sometimes you don't want others to hear or notice you." I also made some disclosures about the play therapy process and my role as a play therapist. "In here, it's okay if you play quietly or loudly." "You can play by yourself or with me." "Sometimes I like to do fun things by myself, and sometimes I like to do fun things with friends and the kids who come and see me in here." After some time had passed, she brought me some food on a plate and we ate together. She began to interact more with me, instructing me to do particular things such as holding a bowl, stirring the food, or starting the microwave.

Throughout her play, she displayed a few instances of low frustration tolerance, becoming easily irritated or frustrated when things did not work out the way she wanted them to work out. For example, as she was playing with the food containers, the empty cereal boxes toppled over. One time, the pretend food fell off the plate she was carrying. In both instances, I could see her muscles tense and her jaw clench. She appeared as if she wanted to scream. I reflected her feelings and metacommunicated about her reactions. "You're mad those keep tipping over." "You don't like when things don't go the way you want them to." "Sometimes things just don't go your way, and you get frustrated when that happens." I knew I would remember this and look for evidence of this type of behavior and reaction in future sessions because part of the process in the first phase is beginning to assess the patterns in the child's lifestyle.

After I gave her the 5-minute warning, she asked if she would have to clean up the playroom. I told her that we could clean up together.

She seemed okay with my response. When it was time to start cleaning, Phoebe walked to the door stating it was time to go get her grandma and grandpa. I reminded her that the room needed to be straightened up before her time was over. She continued to stand by the door as if her feet were cemented to the ground. I started to set a limit about clean up. "It's a playroom rule that the toys are picked up before we leave. I know you'd like for me to pick up the mess by myself. I bet we could find a way for us to share picking up." She looked at me with uncertainty and suggested that she pick up the forks and spoons, and I pick up the bowls and plates. I agreed and together we cleaned up the room.

Throughout the two sessions she shared power with me, interacted with me, and started to share parts of her life with me. I knew we were on the path of the relationship and getting ready to move into Phase 2. I had some guesses about her Crucial Cs, goals of misbehavior, and personality priorities. I also knew that this relationship was fragile, and I had to move cautiously into the next phase.

Summary

The first phase of Adlerian play therapy, building an egalitarian relationship, begins when the counselor meets the child and continues throughout their interaction. In the initial sessions, the counselor begins to establish rapport by asking the child what he or she thinks about coming to play therapy and demystifying the process by explaining about logistics, parent and teacher consultation, and confidentiality. The counselor uses skills such as tracking, restating content, metacommunicating, reflecting feelings, answering questions, asking questions, returning responsibility to the child, interacting actively with the child, and cleaning the playroom together to continue to establish rapport and deepen the connection with the child. Encouraging, setting limits, and understanding Crucial Cs, mistaken goals, and personality priorities of discouraged children are also elements in the evolution of the relationship between the counselor and the child. These skills and concepts are discussed in Chapters 3, 6, and 7.

Chapter 6

Just Say "Yes!"
Just Say "No!"?
Encouraging and Limiting

Encouraging and limiting in the same chapter? You might be asking, "Why did they put these two skills together into a single chapter?" If we are trying to sound scholarly, we would tell you it is because these two skills are the core of what makes Adlerian play therapy Adlerian play therapy. (But that isn't really correct because really these two skills along with metacommunication, conceptualization, treatment planning, and a host of other things make Adlerian play therapy Adlerian play therapy.) If we were trying to sound metaphorical, we might say that encouraging and limiting are on the opposite ends of a spectrum of play therapist behaviors. Really, we just put them together because it seemed to make sense at the time. Anyway, this is the chapter about encouragement and limiting setting.

Encouraging

The Adlerian therapist consistently uses encouragement (Kottman, 2011; Sweeney, 2009; Yang, Milliren, & Blagen, 2010) throughout all four phases of the play therapy process. Encouragement is especially important in building the relationship with the child and in helping to reorient and reeducate the child. In thinking about using encouragement with children, the therapist should tailor the type and delivery of encouraging statements according to their Crucial Cs and personality priorities.

Convey Unconditional Acceptance

The therapist must value children as they are, right at that moment, without wanting, needing, or expecting any changes. If the therapist believes that children are good and worthwhile and conveys that faith to them, they are more likely to act as if they have all the attributes the counselor sees in them. Although unconditional acceptance is important for all human beings, it is absolutely essential for children who believe that they do not count or they "only count if . . ." and for children whose personality priority is pleasing.

Show Faith in Children's Abilities

The counselor must show faith in children's ability to cope with life. If the counselor conveys a belief that the children have the capacity to overcome challenges and solve problems, they are more likely to believe in themselves. The counselor's respect and belief help inspire the development of self-respect, self-confidence, and a sense of self-efficacy in children. The following are examples of encouragement designed to show faith in the child's abilities:

- "You figured that out for yourself."
- "Wow—you did it!! You look really proud of yourself."
- "You can decide how to do that."

When we encourage children to do a certain task, we want to be sure that they are capable of that particular accomplishment. Adults frequently insist that children can do something "if only they would try harder." If they are not capable in that particular area, this pressure to achieve is discouraging rather than encouraging to them, especially to children who do not believe they are capable to begin with. The play therapist should always look for improvement in children's abilities. Children need to hear encouraging words every time they make progress or try something they have been unwilling to attempt previously. It is important to watch carefully for signs of positive change and comment on them, no matter how small the improvement. This conveys the belief that children can grow and change. The following are examples of encouraging based on improvement:

- "You are learning how to get that holster buckled. Last week you had trouble getting it hooked, and this week you did it without any problem."
- "It looks like you're disappointed that the line isn't exactly straight, but you have that row a little straighter this time than you did the last time. You keep getting it closer and closer to the way you want it."

This method of encouragement is especially appropriate for children who struggle with believing that they are capable and for children whose personality priority is comfort. For children who do not have confidence in their own abilities, it is absolutely critical for some important adult to show faith in them. Because these children frequently want to argue about whether a show of faith in their abilities is justified, the play therapist must be prepared to give evidence to support this belief and to be steadfast despite negative feedback and doubt from the children. Because comfort children tend to avoid putting out the effort it would take to accomplish anything, they usually have very little evidence to support a sense of their own self-efficacy. When the play therapist expresses a belief that they can do whatever they set their minds to doing, it often motivates them to generate enough energy to change this pattern.

Give Recognition for Effort

Many times children only get noticed when they are totally successful in an endeavor. Sometimes children get so discouraged by this that they stop trying to do new things. In play therapy sessions, the counselor needs to make positive comments about children making an effort to do something. By noticing their efforts, the counselor acknowledges that making an attempt, especially when they are not guaranteed success, is important and worthy of respect. The following examples show giving recognition for effort:

- "Wow! You thought you couldn't do that, and you tried anyway."
- "You're really trying to fill that strainer with the sand. You're working hard on that."
- "You look a little disappointed that you didn't get the lines as straight as you wanted them to be. Sometimes things don't turn out exactly like you want them to and that's okay."

When acknowledging the child's effort, we usually reflect her or his feelings. It is important to point out any disappointment, anxiety, pride, or any other feeling we detect in the child. As we mention the child's behavior and feelings, we avoid using the word "but" in our comments. The word "but" in a sentence (e.g., "You didn't succeed, but you tried very hard") implies that an attempt does not quite measure up.

This method of encouragement is extremely appropriate with children who have limited courage and children whose personality priority is comfort or superiority. Children who lack courage have become so discouraged that they have given up trying. Even a tiny effort is a huge accomplishment for these children, so the play therapist must be constantly alert for opportunities to make positive comments about them being willing to take the risk of trying. Comfort children also tend to avoid putting out the energy to make an effort or take a risk, so they can use supportive feedback for any attempt at movement. Superiority children usually avoid doing things without a guarantee of success, so when they make an effort without this guarantee, it is a big deal.

Focus on Strengths and Assets

Part of the process of encouragement in Adlerian play therapy is focusing on strengths and assets. Many of the children referred for play therapy are not aware of their own assets. The counselor asks children during the first several sessions to talk about things that they do well and things that other people like about them. Many children say that they do not know of anything they do well and they do not know of anyone who likes them.

Even those who say that someone else likes them seldom know what that person likes about them.

We believe every child has something that he or she does well, something that he or she can contribute. When the child believes that there is nothing he or she does well and he or she does not have a positive contribution to make, it is often because he or she has not learned how to gain significance in constructive ways—in the family or at school. Sometimes the child's assets have gone unnoticed because of other factors (e.g., death in the family, divorce, multiple at-risk children, or a teacher who is personally struggling) that preclude the awareness or acknowledgment of the child's strengths. Other times, the child's assets have gone unnoticed in the family because the family values do not assign any particular merit to them. Sometimes the child's assets have gone unnoticed in school and in the family because the child has decided that she or he cannot gain significance by making a useful, positive contribution, and she or he creatively constructs a negative method of gaining significance. It's the play therapist's job to help the child become aware of assets by pointing them out to the child. Examples of encouraging the child to become aware of his or her own assets are the following:

- "You know how to figure out how to work things."
- "Once you decide you're going to do something, you sure don't give up very easily."
- "You look really proud of yourself for building that tower."
- "Wow! Seems like you know exactly what you want to do in the sandbox. You look pretty sure of yourself. I bet you usually know what you want to do when you decide to do something."

This is an essential strategy of encouragement for children who do not believe that they can connect, that they are capable, or that they count. With children who do not have faith in their ability to connect or the skills necessary to build and maintain relationships, it is a wonderful experience to have someone who notices their strengths. Because they have few close relationships with other people, they seldom are able to think of someone who likes them or believes that they have a contribution to make. The play therapist can make a great impact on these children by inundating them with positive feedback about their assets. It is also healing for children who do not believe that they are capable and children who do not believe that they count to hear someone else tell them that they are, indeed, capable and that they do count, which is what this method of encouragement provides.

We avoid using this approach to encouragement with superiority-oriented children, especially out-doers, because we have had it backfire on us several times. It seems that the more we notice their assets, the more they crave hearing about those assets, which can be counterproductive, because we do not really want them to overuse their accomplishments or strengths to counteract their feelings of inferiority. (After all, bragging about your accomplishments to establish you are better than others is pretty obnoxious.) These children often react to feedback about strengths by (a) demanding more and higher levels of positive feedback, (b) setting their standards even higher (e.g., "If you think that was impressive, wait until you see this"), or (c) escalating their tendency to compare themselves with others.

After you have formulated an idea about some of the child's strengths, you will want to extend the power of encouragement by sharing your discoveries with parents and teachers. Most of the time, a child who comes to play therapy has self-destructive, self-sabotaging elements in her or his lifestyle—private logic and mistaken beliefs about self, others, and the world. The box of her or his lifestyle is almost always causing a problem for the child, for other members of the family, or for teachers and other school personnel. One way you can help is to redefine the child for the important adults in the child's life. As you consult with parents and teachers, you can point out discrepancies between the child's behavior and the way the child, the family, and the school personnel have defined the child. This may involve pointing out unnoticed strengths of the child or reframing some of the child's behavior.

At first, parents (and teachers) may be resistant to this process. Family members and school personnel are usually convinced that the child belongs in the box and do not want to think of him or her in a different light. One of the primary reasons these important adults cling to the remnants of the box is that letting go of it will require that they change their own attitudes and behaviors. Another reason for resisting new ways of thinking about and interacting with the child is that if adults admit that this will be helpful and necessary to do, they will also have to admit that they have been in error in their relationship with the child. Getting around this resistance takes patience and the ability to remember that the adults have boxes of their own (as it turns out, they are people too) and may need help and encouragement to get out of them enough to let the child out of his or her box.

It is sometimes useful to begin the process of inviting parents and teachers to think about the child in different ways by acknowledging the parts of the box that are accurate. For example, Joan was an 8-year-old girl who always looked unkempt and refused to let anyone brush her hair. Joan's box was that she was a messy, uncontrollable child who refused to obey her parents and teachers. Joan's parents were both extremely tidy people who never had a hair out of place. Her behavior upset them considerably. I (TK) began by acknowledging that Joan was choosing to be kind of messy. Then I began to redefine her behavior as being creative and ingenious by talking about the interesting ways she chose to wear her hair and how intelligent and imaginative she was being to create some of the styles she wore. This method did not completely negate the box that Joan's parents saw around her, but it did add a new dimension to the way they viewed her.

Emphasize the Deed and the Joy of Doing, Not the Doer

Another technique for encouraging children in play therapy is to focus on the deed and the joy of doing rather than on the doer. This strategy allows the counselor to pay attention to positive actions and avoid making value judgments about children. Many people use phrases such as "What a good painter you are!" or "You're such a good little helper!" or "You're a real spoiled brat!" These comments imply that children have no inherent value apart from their behavior; that their value depends on what they do rather than on who they are. In play therapy, the therapist wants to convey caring to children, regardless of their behavior. One way to do this is to separate children from their behavior. The play therapist simply makes comments about children's feelings about their own behavior without making any kind of judgment or evaluation. By emphasizing children's sense of accomplishment and joy in doing things, the therapist can encourage them to continue to try useful behaviors. The following are examples of focusing on the deed and not the doer:

- "Wow! You painted a picture. That was fun for you."
- "You picked up all the soldiers and put them away. You look like you feel proud of yourself."
- "It seems as if you have fun pouring the water into the sand."
- "You really like shooting at me and at yourself in the mirror."

This is a very effective strategy for working with children who do not believe that they are capable or do not believe that they count. It is also helpful for children whose personality priority is pleasing or comfort. With children who do not accept their own competence and children with comfort as their personality priority, making sure that they hear feedback on their accomplishments can be really helpful. These children have always been so convinced that they do not accomplish anything that this process can be transformational. It is essential to watch their reactions to this kind of information, however, because many times they are so in the habit of not hearing or acknowledging positive feedback on their deeds that they will discount any encouragement that comes their way that is centered on their deeds.

Children who do not believe that they count or who believe that their significance is conditional and children whose personality priority is pleasing tend to spend a great deal of their energy looking for ways that feedback can be about them (in a negative sense). For instance, when someone says that they did a good job painting a picture, they immediately go to all the other pictures they painted and doubt whether those pictures were any good. When someone tells them they like the dress they are wearing or that they are pretty, they tend to think that this means their worth depends on their appearance. As the play therapist shifts the focus of the feedback to emphasizing the child's pride and sense of accomplishment and deemphasizing the connection between the child's behavior and the child's worth, this can help the child begin to believe that his or her worth is not dependent on pleasing others or on making sure that others notice or approve of him or her.

Focus on the Positives

When children's behavior has both positive and negative components (which it often does), it is much more helpful to them if the counselor can give them credit for the constructive aspects of their behavior and ignore the self-defeating, destructive aspects of their behavior. Many times, parents and teachers focus exclusively on the negative facets of children's activities without ever acknowledging the positive aspects. Parents and teachers make comments such as, "Only 97%? How did you mess that up?" or "You were fidgety the last 10 minutes of the movie. Why are you always so inconsiderate?" One way to encourage children in play therapy is to focus on the positive parts of their behavior, catching them when they are behaving appropriately or pointing out the appropriate parts of what they are doing. The following are examples of giving credit for the useful parts of children's behavior and ignoring the useless parts of the children's behavior:

- "You got a 97% on your homework? I bet you're pretty proud of such a high grade."
- "You were still for almost the whole movie. You really showed self-control."
- When the play therapist sets a limit on pouring water into the sand box, Bihn continues to pour some of the water, but pours the rest into the sink: "You decided that you could follow the playroom rules and not pour all of the water in the sand box."

Focusing on the positive has a similar effect to the encouragement tactic of emphasizing the deed on children whose personality priority is comfort and pleasing and children who are convinced that they are not capable and they do not count. It provides an experience in which they hear that others accept them—with no conditions. This method of encouragement is also helpful with children whose personality priority is superiority or control.

Because superiority children invest an inordinate amount of their energy on their feelings of inferiority and the ways that they are not living up to their own standards, they really pay attention to the negative aspects of their lives and the ways in which they are not measuring up. Children whose personality priority is control tend to focus on the things that they cannot control and waste their energies on trying to assert themselves over these out-of-control elements of their lives. By ignoring negatives and concentrating on positives, the play therapist models a more constructive way to approach self-evaluation and a more realistic way to allocate energy.

Show Involvement in the Person's Interests

Another way of encouraging a child is to show involvement in his or her concerns. The child may be interested in dragons, baseball, the circus, constellations, video games, or any number of topics. The child usually wants to discuss these interests with the important adults in his or her life. Many adults seem to be unwilling to take the time to listen to a child about the things he or she thinks are important, especially if the adult doesn't find them important or interesting. By conveying involvement in the child's excitement about his or her interests, you can encourage the child to feel good about self and the things he or she values. Examples of showing involvement in the child's interests:

- "How did your soccer game go last week?"
- "I see that you brought a picture of a dinosaur to the playroom. It seems like you know a lot about dinosaurs."
- "You got a new video game. You sound really excited. Tell me about how you play it."

This particular form of encouragement is easy to accomplish. All you have to do is to express a willingness to ask about certain topics, listen, and ask questions at appropriate intervals. Having the undivided attention of an adult about something that is important to them helps children gain confidence in themselves and their worth.

This encouragement strategy is especially helpful with children who do not feel significant and children who struggle with connecting with others. Having an adult concentrating on one (or more) of their interests can be incredibly encouraging to children who do not believe that they count because if they did not count, the adult would not bother to spend the time and energy to listen to them. Showing an interest in their interests is also very helpful to children who do not believe that they can make connections with others. (Remember, just like kids, you communicate your care for and interest in the child by what you say and what you do.) By engaging with the play therapist in this way, these children can experience what it feels like to have a reciprocal relationship with someone special. They can also learn, through the play therapist's modeling of this technique, an important social skill that they can use in other relationships.

Model the Courage to Be Imperfect

One of the most empowering encouraging remarks an adult can make to a child is an acknowledgment of a personal mistake. By modeling the "courage to be imperfect" (Dreikurs & Soltz, 1964, p. 38), the play therapist can send a powerful message that it is okay to make a mistake and not to be right all of the time. This is a very freeing experience for the child.

Examples of the courage to be imperfect as a tool for encouraging a child in the playroom:

- "I forgot to turn on the light. Thank you for turning it on for us."
- "Oops! I said something silly. That didn't make any sense."
- "I'm sorry. I goofed that up. I will do it differently the next time we play this game."
- "When we were playing catch, my throw went wild. I am really sorry the ball hit you."

Sometimes we purposely make mistakes so that we can model this behavior. We usually try to make our mistake something small and easily correctable, like the color of a crayon or using the wrong token if we are playing a game. (We say "purposely make mistakes" to protect our own ego. In reality, we often don't need to intentionally make mistakes because we both excel at spontaneously making mistakes.) We want to convey to the child that we can make mistakes, fix them, and learn from our mistake—that it is acceptable to be less than perfect. If we accidentally make a mistake that might hurt the child's feelings, we always apologize to the child. When this happens, the child is invariably shocked that an adult would apologize to him or her. As an Adlerian play therapist, it is essential to be willing to apologize as a way of showing respect and building an egalitarian relationship.

Obviously, this technique is great with children who lack courage. It is also powerful for children whose personality priority is control or superiority. When you show that you have the courage to be imperfect, you model to children that taking risks and making mistakes do not have to be devastating. Although these children usually have been told this many times before, having it demonstrated can sometimes make the idea more real to them. Actually seeing someone who they admire and respect (that would be you) make a mistake and cheerfully survive can help children believe that this is possible. This form of encouragement can move children to try new things, ask questions, and make mistakes. Making the abstract idea of "it's okay to make mistakes" into a concrete experience allows children to let themselves be a little out of control and gives them permission to be less than perfect.

Help the Person Realize Mistakes Are Opportunities for Learning

The play therapist can use children's own mistakes to encourage them. Many times children get very upset about making a mistake or accidentally breaking or spilling something in the playroom. The therapist can help them realize that it is often within their power to correct the mistake and help them determine ways of rectifying the situation. This process can help children learn from each mistake and decide if they want to act differently in the future. It can also help children learn to evaluate realistically any harm that could result from accidents. The following are examples of ways to use a child's error or accident to encourage and empower:

- "You look like you're really sad because you used blue paint when you really wanted to use red paint. How could you fix it so you feel okay about your picture?"
- "You sound angry because you lost the game when you put the X there."
- "You look kind of scared that something bad might happen to you because you spilled the paint. Accidents happen in the playroom sometimes. What is the worst thing that can happen if you spill some paint like that?"

When we are trying to help a child realize that he or she can learn from mistakes and recognize that errors in judgment or accidents do not have to be negative or devastating, we first focus on how the child is feeling about the mistake. It is helpful to use incidents in which the child seems to be feeling bad about the experience. The child may believe that there is nothing wrong with the current situation. In that case the old saying, "If it ain't broke, don't fix it," applies to working with children and play therapy. We do not intervene unless the child has a negative reaction. If the child does seem to feel badly, we reflect the feeling. Then we make a nonjudgmental observation about the facts of the mistake. In this process, we must be careful to avoid emotional language, negative labeling, and nonverbal expressions that might convey disapproval or anger. We sometimes make a comment that all human beings make mistakes at some point in our lives or lots of children frequently have accidents or make mistakes in play therapy.

This strategy for encouraging children works with the same populations as the technique of modeling the courage to be imperfect—children who lack courage and have superiority or control as their personality priority. By suggesting to these children that mistakes are not bad or fatal and reframing mistakes as potential learning experiences, you can help instill a belief that taking a risk and not succeeding is not the end of the world.

Make Sure the Person Discovers a Positive Way to Gain Belonging and Significance

Adlerians believe that all human beings have a need to belong. If they cannot find positive ways to gain significance, children will find negative ways to gain significance. A play therapist has several methods for helping children learn to belong in a useful way. One method to encourage children is to help them discover ways they can stand out in a positive way in their families or in school. The therapist can do this by focusing on assets observed in the playroom and suggesting ways that children can optimize those strengths at home and in their classrooms. Another method of encouraging children is to put them in the role of an expert about something that you want to learn. You can ask them for help or instructions on how to successfully execute some type of activity. You must, of course, choose an activity in which they feel they have some level of expertise and in which you feel that you lack expertise. (Because there are many things I [TK] know nothing about, this is not usually a problem for me! Jacob, my son, recently asked me, "Mom, what *do* you know about?") A key to this technique is to avoid faking ineptitude because children will recognize insincerity and this defeats the entire purpose. Only ask children for help when you genuinely want and need it. The following are examples of asking for help:

- "I don't understand the directions to this game. You say that you've played it before. Can you tell me how it is played?"
- "You know a lot about video games, and I don't usually play them. What is a good one you think I would like to learn to play?"
- "I can't get this cash register to work. Can you give me a hand?"

If you are working with a group in play therapy, it is sometimes helpful to structure some of the group activities to showcase each child's strengths and allow him or her to experience a positive way to gain significance in a group while the child also has continued therapeutic support and encouragement. Examples of ways to encourage a child to find positive ways of belonging to a group:

- "When we are in the playroom, I notice you always smile at me. I wonder what might happen if you picked out one person in your class who you wanted to be friends with and smiled at him."
- "You really know how to fix things in the playroom. I bet you could figure out something that you could fix like that at home."
- Talking to parents: "Heather has gotten a lot of practice at taking turns in the playroom. I would like you to play Old Maid or Go Fish with her every night this week. Let her go first and then take turns. Encourage her whenever she remembers to let you have your turn."
- Talking to a teacher: "Chang Zheng is feeling very proud of his drawings lately. The next several times he draws a picture, could you be sure to encourage this participation—and perhaps even hang his pictures on the bulletin board?"

Obviously, this encouragement strategy is especially effective for children who do not have connecting skills. These children constantly struggle with finding constructive ways to belong, and this technique provides them with a vehicle for learning connecting skills and gaining confidence in their ability to make and maintain relationships.

Setting Limits

We know that it is an "oldie," but we still love the quote from Bixler (1949), who said, "Limits are therapy" (p. 1). Setting limits is an essential component in establishing the relationship with children in play therapy (Bixler, 1949; Kottman, 2011; Landreth, 2012; Ray, 2011). By setting limits, the therapist creates a safe space in which he or she can establish and maintain an unconditional and accepting attitude toward clients, even if they are pushing the therapist's buttons. Limits also establish that the play therapy relationship is different from other relationships and is grounded in integrity and responsibility (Bixler, 1949).

In Adlerian play therapy, the therapist encourages children to express their emotions, wishes, thoughts, or fantasies—no matter the content. The therapist limits direct acting out of harmful behavior and helps children to generate socially appropriate methods of expression. Having clear and consistent limits in the play session helps the therapist to communicate a sense of safety and security to children. It also helps ground the therapy in reality. In real life, there are rules, boundaries, and limits. Admittedly, the situation in the play session will not always correspond directly to the real world. (Ogres and dragons and wizards, oh my!) However, the interpersonal relationship and a basic respect for the materials and the space in play therapy need to be grounded in reality so that children can generalize the insights and skills they acquire in the playroom to other settings and relationships. (In other words, kids aren't allowed to hurt you or themselves or deliberately damage the room or the toys.)

The aim of Adlerian limit setting is to enhance children's self-control and to teach them they have the ability to consider alternative behaviors and to redirect their own inappropriate behaviors. Because children actively participate in the process, they begin to develop a sense of responsibility for adhering to limits and consequences. In Adlerian play therapy, the counselor can use limit setting for the forces of good: to reduce the occurrence of power struggles and enhance the relationship with children.

What to Limit

The basic rules in Adlerian play therapy are as follows: (a) The time in the session has a limit; (b) toys stay in the playroom; (c) the child is not to damage the toys or other materials; and (d) the child is not to harm the therapist, himself or herself, or other children in the playroom. These limits are "absolute" limits (Bixler, 1949; Kottman, 2011). They are not negotiable because they protect people and property from harm and anchor the therapy to reality. The child does not have an active voice in deciding on these limits.

There are also some "relative" limits (Bixler, 1949; Kottman, 2011) in Adlerian play sessions. Activities such as pouring water in the sandbox, using the hammer, throwing objects, and finger painting are all behaviors that need to have parameters set, depending on the setting, the personality of the client, the personality of the therapist, the permissiveness of the child's parents, and the comfort level of the play therapist (Kottman, 2011). For example, you would probably be okay with a child putting two cups of water into the sand, but we bet you would not be okay with 12 cups of water dumped in there. You would probably not have a problem with the child shooting the dart gun (if you had a dart gun in your playroom), but most of us don't want to be hit by the darts, even when they are made of soft foam and don't really hurt. This type of limit provides room for allowing the children to participate actively in rule making and limit setting as well as in deciding on appropriate alternative behaviors and redirecting themselves.

When to Limit

If you can catch the child in the anticipation of the act, the best time to limit his or her behavior is immediately before the child does something that needs to be limited (Kottman, 2011; Landreth, 2012; Ray, 2011). There seems to be little practical or therapeutic benefit from confronting the child with a list of the limits and rules at the beginning of the play therapy. You could not possibly think of all of the behaviors that might need to be limited, and a partial list just serves to confuse (or challenge) the child. A list of prohibited behaviors can easily be a list outlining potential misbehavior in the playroom. A child with power as his or her goal of misbehavior or with a personality priority of control will use it as an invitation to try to engage you in a series of power struggles. Take it from us; children can generate enough inappropriate behaviors without getting any help from you.

The primary skill for the timing of limit setting is the ability to use children's nonverbal cues and behavior patterns to anticipate their limit-testing actions. Most of the time, if children are about to do something that they know might not be acceptable, they will nonverbally telegraph their intention. For example, Zack may look at you, look at the mirror, look at the dart gun, look at you, and point the dart gun at the mirror. About the time Zack begins to raise the dart gun, you should begin stating the limit. If you miss the prebehavior signals or are working with a child who does things impulsively or without warning, you need to be quick about limiting as near the beginning of the behavior as possible. If you miss the timing, you can always model the courage to be imperfect, by saying, "I didn't talk fast enough to tell you before you shot that time, and I want you to know that it's against the playroom rules to shoot the mirror."

How to Limit

In setting limits, it will be helpful if you can stay calm and matter of fact to convey that you believe the child is willing and able to abide by limits. To communicate that you believe that the child will follow the rules and demonstrate self-control, you should sit in the usual relaxed, comfortable posture—facing the child without frowning or grimacing. Your voice should remain at its normal pitch, speed, and intonation, not getting shriller, faster, or louder. (We say all this because as we watch recordings of our own sessions and as we observe our students, all of us tend to talk louder, faster, and/or shriller when we get anxious about setting limits or when we are worried that the child is not going to cooperate with the limits. Quite often, we lean forward in our chairs, tensed and ready to leap into action to prevent whatever we want to limit from happening.)

Steps in Setting Limits

Setting limits in Adlerian play therapy is a four-step process. First, the play therapist states the limit. Next, the therapist reflects the child's feelings or metacommunicates about the underlying message in or purpose of the limit-testing behavior. In the third step, the therapist engages the child in generating acceptable alternatives or developing solutions to a problematic situation in the playroom. If the child continues to break the limit, the therapist and the child collaborate in setting up logical consequences as the fourth step.

Stating the Limit

We use several different variations on our formula for stating limits. When we limit, we may say something like,

- "The rule in the playroom is . . ."
- ". . . is against the playroom rules."
- "It is against the playroom rules to . . ."

These phrases suggest that there are certain rules and limits that apply to all of the people who use the playroom. When limits are set in this way, children usually refrain from reacting as if the play therapist is the punitive authority figure imposing boundaries and preventing them from doing whatever they want. This formulation also tends to short circuit power struggles or adversarial negotiations about what children can and cannot do.

It is really important to avoid using phrases that make the play therapist into an authority figure, such as, "I don't want you to . . ." or "I won't let you . . ." or "You must not . . ." (I [TK] tried all of these when I was first experimenting with limiting in Adlerian play therapy. Take my word for it—all of these formulations made the limiting process personal, resulting in my clients taking the limit personally and engaging in power struggles with me about whether the rules applied to them and whether they had to comply with the rules. I developed the neutral way of stating the limiting through lots of trial and error—working out a way to have the setting of the limit delivered in the basic form of "Just the facts, ma'am; just the facts.")

Reflecting Feelings and/or Metacommunicating About Underlying Messages or Purpose

The second step in Adlerian limit setting is reflecting the child's feeling and/or metacommunicating about the underlying message in or purpose of the limit-testing behavior. Most of the time, when the child is about to do something that needs to be limited, his or her feelings are obvious. Examples of reflecting the child's feelings when limiting:

- "Seems as though you're feeling pretty angry at me right now."
- "You think it would be fun to climb on those shelves."
- "I can tell you're disappointed, and the sand needs to stay in the sandbox."

In some situations, the violation of the limit is not connected to a feeling. The child may be (a) testing you, (b) playing so intensely that he or she has not noticed the transgression, (c) trying to provoke a reaction from you, (d) trying to send a covert message to you, (e) trying to provoke another child in the playroom, or (f) trying to fulfill some other purpose unrelated to any kind of obvious feeling. In this case, it is probably more appropriate for you to metacommunicate about the underlying meaning in the message or metacommunicate about the purpose of the child's behavior. The following are examples of metacommunicating about the underlying meaning of the child's limit-testing behavior:

- "You wanted to let me know that I cannot control you."
- "You were wondering if I would do what I said I was going to do, so you are giving me a little test."
- "You are not sure that you can trust me to follow through, so you are shooting the dart gun to find out if you can trust me."
- "I am not sure that you heard me say that it is against the playroom rules to pour more water into the sand."

Examples of metacommunicating about the child's purpose during limit setting:

- "I can tell you're curious as to what I will do if you try to hit the mirror."
- "Seems almost like you wish I would get mad at you."

- "My guess is that you were paying so much attention to what you were doing that you didn't notice that you were hitting the mirror with the darts."
- "I kind of think you want Jamie to fight with you."

Many times, when the child does something that needs to be limited, he or she expresses emotions and has an underlying message or purpose behind his or her behavior as well. When this happens, you can reflect the child's feeling and metacommunicate about the message or the purpose. Examples of combining these two techniques:

- "It looks like you're feeling angry with me, and you want to show me that I can't tell you what to do."
- "You're disappointed because I said that it's time to go home. Seems like you're going to let me know you're disappointed by ignoring me when I tell you that it's time to clean up."
- "You are feeling really hurt by your dad not showing up when he was supposed to. My guess is that you'd like to hurt somebody else right now—kind of hurt them like you're hurting."

Generating Alternative Acceptable Behavior Options and Solutions
The third step in setting limits in Adlerian play therapy is helping the child generate appropriate choices for his or her behavior, coming to an agreement with the counselor about which of these behaviors are acceptable, and following through with this agreement by behaving in appropriate ways. One of the purposes of this collaborative process of limiting is the enhancement of the egalitarian nature of the relationship between the counselor and the child. Using this method to limit also helps reduce the child's tendency to ignore the redirection and continue to test the counselor's limits. It also teaches the child that he or she can generate appropriate behavior choices and substitute appropriate behavior for inappropriate behavior on his or her own—without the necessity of adult intervention. The child can apply these lessons about the power of self-monitoring and self-control in other relationships and situations outside the playroom. By practicing generating solutions to power struggles and difficult situations in the playroom, the child can learn the process of problem solving. (And, of course, that is ultimately what we want for children to be able to do.)

Most of the time, the main intervention in this step is to tell the child, "I bet you can think of something you can do that will be okay to do in the playroom." This encourages the child to begin a brainstorming process designed to generate some type of alternative acceptable behavior. You can use this step of limiting to work on the child's reality testing, awareness of rule-governed behavior, and creativity. You and the child can then negotiate and generate a list of behaviors that do not violate the playroom limits.

Sometimes the child either will not or cannot seem to think of socially acceptable behaviors or a solution. When this happens, you will often need to prime the pump by making suggestions for behaviors that will not violate the playroom limits. However, after you have one or two possibilities, you will want to refer the matter back to the child, by saying something like, "Those are some ideas. Let's think of another idea together," or "That is one idea. I bet you can think of another one like it." Don't tell the child what to do. (Sorry for telling you what to do here, but again, we are hoping you can learn from our mistakes and not do things that have backfired on us.) If you can engage the child in actively participating in coming up with possibilities for redirection, he or she is much more likely to follow through with the alternative behaviors.

For the absolute rules, such as not hurting the therapist or damaging the property, the actual boundary is not negotiable; but the alternative behaviors are negotiable. Examples of this process with the absolute limits:

- "The mirror is not for hitting, and I bet you can think of something that you can hit with the hammer that will be okay."
- "It's against the playroom rules to shoot me with the dart gun, and you can probably think of something in the playroom that you can shoot."
- "The baby doll needs to stay in the playroom, and you can figure out something you can make that you can take home."

Notice that we have used "and" instead of "but." One of the things we have learned over the years is that we are more likely to get compliance if we can avoid using "but." People tend to stop listening to you when you say "but." "And" just works better.

With the relative limits, you can negotiate the actual limit with the child as well as some possible alternative behaviors. Examples of this process with relative limits:

- "In the playroom, you cannot dump all the water you want into the sandbox. How many buckets of water would you like to dump? Well, 12 buckets is too many. What about two buckets? You'd like to dump eight buckets? That's still too many. What about three buckets? You would settle for four buckets? I think that's reasonable. What about you?"
- "I can tell you would like to use all of the pipe cleaners, and in the playroom we need to save some for the other children. I think six is a fair amount. How many do you think is good? You'd like to use 20? That's still too close to using them all. What about eight? You think that you need more than that. I can tell you're getting kind of angry, and you think that you should get to use all the pipe cleaners you want. Twenty is too many, and you think eight isn't enough. What do you think would work in between that? Twelve? I can agree to that. How about you?"

The definition of the acceptable behavior should be clear and measurable to avoid any misunderstanding on the part of either party. By adhering to this guideline, you can avoid getting into potential power struggles over the nature of the agreement. If the agreement is not concrete and measurable, the child may try to spend a great deal of time and energy quibbling over what the agreement meant. The following are examples of concrete versus vague wording for limits and alternate behaviors:

- *Behavior you want to limit:* Pointing the dart gun at a target that could potentially be harmed by a dart.
  Vague wording: "The gun is not for pointing in that direction."
  Concrete wording: "It's against the rules to aim the dart gun at the mirror, the lights, or me."
- *Behavior you want to limit:* Kicking a ball randomly around the play-room.
  Vague wording: "You can kick the ball softly."
  Concrete wording: "You can kick the ball, and it's against the rules to hit the mirror, the lights, or you."
- *Behavior you want to limit:* Pouring an unlimited amount of water into the sand.
  Vague wording: "You may not pour very much water into the sand."
  Concrete wording: "You may pour two cups of water into the sandbox."

Your aim for the end of the negotiation process is for the child to commit to a definition of what constitutes appropriate behavior in the playroom and agree to conform to this appropriate behavior. Most children do not initially know negotiation skills. Sometimes this is because they are used to getting their own way by engaging in power struggles or having temper tantrums. Other times it is because they have never had a voice in any decision-making process. No matter what the reason for lack of skill in this area, you may need to teach them how to state concretely what they want in a reasonable tone of voice and how to compromise. It is important for them to learn that just because they ask for what they want (even if they ask in a polite and respectful way) doesn't mean they will always get exactly what they want. (This is a useful tool for adults too—we have had a hard time learning it ourselves, but it does serve us well in the world. This knowledge can even keep us from throwing tantrums when we don't get our way.)

We usually keep the limits, agreements, and solutions we have generated with children in force from session to session. Most limits, agreements, and solutions are generalizable over time. There is no reason to reopen the discussion every time the child wants to do something that needs a limit if we have already reached an equitable solution. If we have decided that it is reasonable to be able to pour two cups of water into the sandbox, it makes sense that two cups of water will continue to be an acceptable amount of water to go into the sandbox. If we have decided that the dart gun can be shot at everything but the mirror, the lights, and counselor, it makes sense that these targets will continue to be proscribed.

However, sometimes the circumstances change. When this happens, the therapist may decide that this is the opportunity to model flexibility and reopen negotiations because the agreement needs some adjustment. For example, when a new child joins the play sessions, the therapist probably should decide to expand the list of prohibited targets to include other children. In certain situations, the therapist might decide that the agreement was not specific enough and that it needs some tightening. For example, if the agreement stated that the child would kick the ball softly and as time has passed, the therapist has discovered that he or she and the child have different definitions of "softly," the therapist might want to reopen the definition process. In other situations, the therapist and the child could decide that the agreement is not working out the way they thought it would and they want to rethink it. For example, Melissa and Gretchen, her play therapist, had agreed in a previous session that Melissa could use two buckets of water in the sandbox, but the consistency of the sand with only two buckets of water did not lend itself to Melissa's enterprise of sand castle construction. Gretchen could express a willingness to change the agreement for this particular venture.

With specific children, we opt to renegotiate every week, even when we always come to the same conclusion of what is acceptable behavior. Some children cannot remember and follow through on an agreement week after week and need a reminder of the rules and agreements that are in force in the playroom. With children who struggle with compromise and communication and children with poor impulse control, we sometimes set things up for them to practice these skills even if we have already negotiated a limit in a previous session.

Quite frequently, this third step is the last step you will need to use when setting limits. Most of the time, the child abides by the agreement he or she makes with very little fuss. You may have to remind the child of the agreement, but generally speaking, because the child was involved in the decision, he or she will have a vested interest in remembering the limit and complying with it.

Setting Up Logical Consequences

The fourth step in setting limits in Adlerian play therapy is imposing logical consequences when a child chooses to break a limit or not abide by an agreement. Logical consequences are an Adlerian method designed to encourage responsible behavior (Dinkmeyer et al., 2007; McCready, 2012; Nelson, 2011; Popkin, 2014). "If we allow a child to experience the consequences of his [or her] acts, we provide an honest and real learning situation" (Dreikurs & Soltz, 1964, p. 76). If the child chooses to break a limit or not abide by an agreement, the play therapist needs to discuss a logical consequence with him or her.

Logical consequences must be related to the misbehavior and be realistic, reasonable, and respectful (Nelson, 2011; Popkin, 2014). Logical consequences must be logically related to the limited behavior so that the child understands the connection between the transgression and the consequence. For example, a logical consequence related to breaking the limit of shooting the dart gun at the mirror might be that the child must put the dart gun away for the rest of the session. An illogical consequence or punishment for this behavior might be telling the child he or she has to sit in the corner for 5 minutes—because there is no connection between the child's behavior and the consequence.

Logical consequences must express the reality of the social order, not just the opinions and will of the person imposing them. For example, a realistic consequence for pouring sand onto the floor of the playroom might be for the child to have to sweep up the floor with a broom. An unrealistic consequence or punishment for this transgression might be for the child to have to copy "I am a messy child and will not spill sand on the floor any more" 20 times.

Logical consequences must be reasonable, and the consequence should be in direct proportion to the misbehavior. For example, a logical consequence for kicking a ball into the light fixture might be for the child to lose the privilege of playing with the ball for the rest of the session. An unreasonable consequence or punishment might be for the child to never get to play with the ball in the playroom again.

Logical consequences must be respectful to the child. The child should actively participate in both the decision-making process generating the logical consequence and the application of the consequence. To convey respect to the child, the therapist should always make sure that the child has a choice: to abide by the limit or agreement or to take the consequence. He or she should know and understand the consequences of any decisions before he or she makes them. Also important, the choices should be acceptable to the child and the counselor. This way, whether the child selects the limit or the consequence, the counselor is okay with the child's decision.

In the playroom, we have the child assume the responsibility for the follow-through of the consequence. We believe that this conveys respect to the child and communicates our belief in the child's self-control and ability to act responsibly. For example, a respectful logical consequence if Jahasanea purposely spilled paint on the floor might be the following: (a) ask Jahasanea what she thinks should happen as the result of this action and what she thinks should happen if she chooses to do this behavior again; (b) remind Jahasanea as she begins to spill the paint on the floor that the two of you had agreed that if she chose to do this again that she would be choosing not to get to use the paint for the rest of the session; (c) let Jahasanea make the choice without pressure from you; and (d) if she chooses to spill the paint on the floor, let Jahasanea be the one who cleans up the spilled paint and puts the paint away for the rest of the session. A disrespectful consequence or punishment would be yelling at Jahasanea for being "so messy" and telling her that she does not deserve to get to use paints anymore.

When you use logical consequences in the playroom, it is important to remember that the purpose of logical consequences is to help children learn to make responsible decisions and to let them experience the consequences of their choices. Consequences should not be a vehicle for you to impose your will on children or to win a power struggle or punish children for doing something that you do not like (regardless of how tempting that might be—and we know it is.) When you use logical consequences in the playroom, you must never convey a moral or value judgment about the child or the child's behavior.

The timing of the fourth step of limit setting depends on the child, the behavior, and the setting. Some children have poor skills in compromise and communication, so we use the limit-setting process to give them a chance to practice these skills in a safe environment. Other children have such poor impulse control that we use the limit-setting process to help them to learn to delay gratification and to communicate their needs and desires. The procedure we prefer is based on the assumption that the child is going to follow through with the acceptable behavior and not need a consequence. To convey this faith, we wait to discuss consequences until after the child has failed to follow through with our agreement and has violated the rule one time after the third step of the limiting. So, if the child breaks a rule, we set the limit and reflect the child's feelings or metacommunicate about the underlying message or purpose, we negotiate an agreement of what will be acceptable behavior, the child chooses to ignore or defy our agreement, and then we initiate a discussion about consequences for the next time the child does not abide by the agreement.

However, this sequence is not always possible or optimal. Sometimes the most appropriate time to discuss a consequence is during the negotiation for setting up the agreement in the third step. This linking of the third and fourth step is frequently necessary for (a) a child who has repeatedly demonstrated that he or she will not abide by agreements, (b) behaviors that are so totally unacceptable that they will have some type of adverse effect if allowed to happen even one time (e.g., punching the therapist or another child), (c) a therapist with a high level of anxiety about whether the child will follow through with the agreement, or (d) a setting that would preclude having the child act out some specific inappropriate behavior (e.g., a child who takes off his clothes and runs through the halls in an office building). There are other times in which there is no choice but for the therapist to go ahead and set a consequence even without the full cooperation of the child (e.g., the child is about to urinate on the floor). There may be other circumstances or relationships in which the therapist decides to accelerate the consequences to combine the third and fourth steps or to set a consequence without the participation of the child, but it is important for the therapist to seriously consider the message that this linkage is sending the child before making this decision.

We use the limiting process to convey our positive and supportive feelings for children. We wish to communicate that we want them to succeed and to learn to make responsible choices and that we will continue to care about them, no matter what the decision in any one specific interaction. As in all of our interactions with children, when we set up the logical consequences, we use a friendly, matter-of-fact voice, and make sure our body language does not telegraph anger or disapproval. Whenever the children choose a consequence, rather than abiding by the limit or agreement, we point out to them that they will have other chances to try again or make a new choice in another session. If they continue to choose the consequence, this usually means that we need to reevaluate their purpose and the effectiveness of the consequence.

Nelson (2011) suggested that, at times, it is better to generate solutions than consequences. She believes we should focus on "teaching children what to do because they have been invited to think through the situation and use some basic guidelines such as respect and helpfulness to find solutions" (p. 122). The third step of limit setting in Adlerian play therapy is designed to engage children in generating solutions so that it is unnecessary to resort to consequences. By working hard to help children learn to develop solutions that are related, respectful, reasonable, and helpful (Nelson, 2011), you can teach them a skill that will be invaluable in every aspect of their lives.

Putting It All Together

Although the individual steps sound pretty simple in isolation, putting them all together is a little trickier, especially because in the real world of the playroom the steps do not always progress as smoothly as they sound in a book. The following scenarios, predicated on the fact that each limiting-setting situation is going to be a little different from the others, are designed to illustrate how to integrate the steps of the limit-setting process.

Haq (age 5) aims the dart gun at Dennis, his play therapist.

Haq: "I am going to shoot you in the head."

Dennis: "It is against the playroom rules to shoot people with the gun."

Haq: "Well, I am going to do it anyway. You can't stop me."

Dennis: "You want to let me know that you don't care what the rule is. I am thinking that you are wondering what I will do if you don't do what I want you to do."

Haq: (Still aiming the gun, but not shooting it)

Dennis: "I bet you can find something in the room that is okay to shoot with darts or you could use something and pretend it is me."

Haq: "I would rather just shoot you, but I guess I could aim the gun at the big doll and pretend it is you."

Dennis: "Yes, you could. You could pretend you were shooting it at me when you are really shooting at the big doll."

Zorina (age 4) wants to pour a bucket of water into the sandbox. Star, her play therapist, thinks that this is a not such a good idea.

Star: "In here, the rule is that you can only put a small cup of water into the sand."

Zorina: "But then I won't be able to make mud. I want to make mud." (Starts crying and throwing sand out of the sandbox)

Star: "You are so angry about not getting to make mud that you are throwing sand. Throwing sand is also against the playroom rules. What is another way you can show me that you are mad without throwing sand?"

Zorina: "Stop talking!" (Continues to throw sand)

Star: "You don't like being told what to do. And, if you choose to throw another handful of sand, you will be choosing to lose playing in the sandbox for the rest of our time together."

Zorina: "All right. I will stop, but I still want to make mud."

Star: "Well, I might be okay with you putting more than just one small cup of water, and a whole bucket is still too much. How do you think you could make mud without dumping a lot of water into the sandbox?"

Zorina: "I don't know. How could we?"

Star: "Well, one idea would be to put some sand in the bucket and then pour some water in there and mix it."

Zorina: "I like that idea. Could we use this pan from the kitchen center instead?"

Star: "Sure."

Jacob (age 7) decides that he wants to leave the playroom halfway through the session to show his mother a picture that he has drawn. Jacob has a habit of leaving the playroom for protracted intervals, and Charlene, the play therapist, has decided that this behavior is his way of avoiding the work of the session.

Jacob (in an excited voice): "I have to go to the waiting room and show this to my mom."

Charlene (standing in front of the door): "Jacob, from now on the rule in the playroom is that we need to stay in the playroom until our time is over."

Jacob (in an irritated voice): "But I want to go show my mom this picture, and you always let me leave before this."

Charlene: "I can tell that you are excited about your picture and irritated that we have a new rule in the playroom."

Jacob (shouting): "Yeah and you are not the boss of me."

Charlene: "You want me to know that I am not in charge of you. Where do you think we can put the picture so we are sure to take it out and show it to your mom at the end of the session?"

Jacob (still angry): "Well, I want to take it now. If you don't let me, I am going to throw it away."

Charlene: "You could make that choice if you want to. Or you could put it right in front of the door so we don't forget to take it to show her when we are done. What else do you want to do for the rest of our time together?"

Hayley (age 8) has been sexually abused by several men in her life. She approaches her play therapist, Keshawn, with every intention of sitting on his lap facing him.

Keshawn: "Hayley, it is against the playroom rules to sit on folks' lap this way. I know that you would like to snuggle up and show me that you care about me, and we need to figure out another way for you to show me that you like me."

Hayley: "Why can't I sit like that? My mom's boyfriends always let me do it that way."

Keshawn: "Well, it sounds like it is confusing to you when I say you can't do something in here with me that your mom's boyfriends let you do with them."

Hayley: "So, does that mean that you don't like me?"

Keshawn: "No it doesn't. I like you very much, and I know that you like me. Let's figure out some way for you to let me know that you like me without sitting on my lap."

Hayley: "I could paint you a picture with hearts."

Keshawn: "Is that what you would like to do instead of sitting on my lap?"

Hayley: "No. I want to sit on your lap, but you won't let me, so I guess I will paint you a picture even though I don't want to." (Paints a picture, and comes over to give it to him, trying to sit on his lap)

Keshawn: "I know you want to sit on my lap, and it is against the playroom rules. How can we come up with a solution to this?"

Hayley: "You could remind me."

Keshawn: "That's one idea. Can you come up with something that you could use to remind yourself?"

Hayley: "Well, if I got close to your lap, you could stand up."

Keshawn: "I guess I am willing to do that, and I would like something that you could be responsible for doing too."

Hayley: "I can't think of anything."

Keshawn: "How about you paint a picture with a girl sitting on a man's lap with a line through it? We could put it on the floor by my chair."

Hayley: "I think it is kind of a dumb idea, but okay. We can try that."

Factors That Affect the Process of Limiting

As you begin to think about the limiting process, there are two different factors that should be included in the consideration. The first is your lifestyle—how your Crucial Cs and personality priorities affect the limit-setting process. The second is the lifestyle of the child—how his or her Crucial Cs, goals of misbehavior, and personality priorities influence the types of behaviors that must be limited and how he or she reacts to limits.

Therapist's Lifestyle

Many play therapists find limit setting to be personally stressful (Kottman, 2011). It is super important for you to be self-aware and intentional with your limit setting. An essential step in learning to limit effectively is to consider your own lifestyle, especially your personality priorities and your mastery of the Crucial Cs. By contemplating how these factors affect your willingness and ability to limit, you can enhance your limit-setting skills (which might even be up for consideration as superhero powers.)

Limiting is especially troublesome for play therapists whose personality priorities are control and pleasing, those who do not believe that they count, and those who doubt that they are capable. Therapists whose personality priority is control frequently believe that they must be in total control of themselves during the session, in control of how the session unfolds, in control of the child, in control of the process of play therapy, or some combination of these. When these therapists feel out of control, they tend to limit too many behaviors or use harsh language or angry nonverbal communication to try to reassert control. (Are you getting the idea that, if your personality priority is control, you like to be in control?)

Therapists with pleasing as their primary personality priority often worry—about whether the child will choose to abide by the rules, whether the child will adhere to consequences set, whether the child will be angry with them if they limit, whether dragons will land on the roof, whether the pink shirt they are wearing is too pink, and so forth and so on. (According to our husbands, children, friends, and neighbors, sometimes we pleasers seem to just worry for the sake of worrying.) This anxiety frequently results in pleasing therapists limiting in weak or singsong voices, limiting in such convoluted ways that the child does not realize that they have set a limit, or limiting little or nothing at all. (That's what we call "wimp limiting," and it doesn't work very well. We would know—we do it on a pretty regular basis, but it is often out of our awareness until we watch recordings of our play therapy sessions, when we force ourselves to de-wimp our limiting styles.)

Therapists who do not feel that they count are very invested in making a difference in people's lives. When they do not feel that they are making a difference, they can often take on too much responsibility for the lack or slowness of change or they may blame others for "just not trying hard enough." When a child is refusing to negotiate about acceptable behavior, breaking the agreement of acceptable behavior, or ignoring the consequences, these therapists tend to believe that this is because they are not important or valuable enough to the child to make a difference. Feeling discounted by the child's response to the limiting process, they often overreact, getting angry at the child and trying to overpower him or her to make sure that they have had an impact in the session. They sometimes go in the opposite direction and emotionally withdraw from the child to make sure that the child's behavior does not matter to them anymore.

Therapists who do not feel capable doubt their own skills when the limiting process does not go the way they anticipate. If their personality priority is comfort, they may simply give up, assuming that they will never be able to acquire the necessary skills. If their personality priority is control or superiority, they will often go out of their way to learn new skills or perfect the skills they already have, quite frequently ignoring the possibility that the difficulty in the limiting process may have nothing to do with their skills at all.

Regardless of the cause, many times this personal tension can result in unconsciously altering your voice and body language. This stress is manifested in various ways, such as frowning severely, talking in a stern voice, whining, assuming a submissive posture, and saying the child's name more often than normal.

To avoid this tendency, you must learn to monitor your own stress level, listen to your verbalizations, and become more consciously aware of your body language as you set limits. It will be important for you to examine what the tension is about and begin to work on resolving the cause of the stress that emerges during the limit-setting process or to plan more constructive ways of dealing with personal issues that might interfere with your ability to be therapeutic in the limit-setting process. Supervision or personal counseling can be a good strategy for gaining insight about personal triggers and skills for setting fair and objective limits and generating solutions to power struggles in the playroom.

Child Lifestyle Factors

The limit-setting process also depends on children and their lifestyles. Taking the child's Crucial Cs, goals of misbehavior, and personality priorities into account can be very helpful in successfully setting limits because the therapist can frame his or her communication about setting limits in ways that encourage specific clients and optimize the possibility of their participation in the process.

Crucial Cs

Children's willingness to participate interactively in the limit-setting process and their reaction to limit setting are influenced by the Crucial Cs they have mastered. Children who have courage and believe that they can connect, that they are capable, and that they count have no trouble in participating in their part of setting limits. They also tend to abide by the agreements set up in the third step and seldom need consequences. (Because they seldom need therapy, however, this is an unusual situation.)

Children who lack courage tend to do very little that gets limited, but when they do, they are very reluctant to engage in generating new behaviors or consequences. Their reaction to being limited usually involves being more overwhelmed by their own anxiety, with the result that they do very little in the playroom. It is always necessary to limit very gently and seldom with these children.

Children who do not believe that they connect with others also struggle with engaging in the limit-setting process and seem to withdraw more as the result of limits unless you are very careful to communicate that you and the child are still connected with one another. If you can convey this message, you can use the limit-setting process to build connecting skills with these children.

Children who do not think that they are capable interpret limiting as telling them that they have not mastered the skills needed to be play therapy clients. It is important that you set limits in such a way to affirm that these children are so capable that you are relying on them to decide which alternative behaviors are acceptable and to enforce their own compliance with any agreements or consequences they generate.

Children who do not feel that they count often take limits as additional evidence that they are not important and are often reluctant to engage in the generation of alternative behaviors, assuming that you do not really want input from them about alternative behaviors and consequences. If you do not take this discounting of your intentions personally, these children feel extremely encouraged by participating in the limiting process that really does convey that you respect their opinions and that they do count.

Goals of Misbehavior

The limits children break tend to be related to their goals of misbehavior. Just as other consequences for inappropriate behaviors evoke standard reactions, their response to limit setting can also be influenced by these goals.

Children whose goal is attention tend to do relatively mild forms of limit breaking, usually in the form of testing limits to see how you will react or to make sure that you are fully engaged with them. When they are limited, they seldom go on to break the same limit, so they practically never have to enter into the fourth step of limiting. They usually abide by the letter of their agreement but often try to determine how strictly they must abide by the spirit of the pact. They also love to negotiate—having that much solid attention is a very powerful experience for them, so they frequently break limits just to get to negotiate.

Children who are striving to assert their own power tend to break many rules in the playroom just to show that they are not under your control. They also frequently refuse to participate in generating alternative behaviors, choose to ignore their agreements, and decline to negotiate about consequences. You will need to remind yourself to stay disengaged from taking their behavior personally and to avoid getting into power struggles with them. When power-seeking children refuse to participate in the third and fourth steps of the process, you can often use limited choices to gain their cooperation. Metacommunicating about the purpose of their behavior during the limiting process can prove to be helpful, as often children feel a diminished need to prove that you cannot control them when you acknowledge this dynamic. It is occasionally necessary to evoke "the ultimate limit" (having to leave the playroom) with these children. However, try to avoid using this option with children who really do not want to be in the playroom because then they will simply escalate their negative behavior until they get to exit.

Children striving toward the goal of revenge are difficult to limit because they take limit setting personally and try to make the entire limit-setting process about you hurting them, not liking them, or not approving of them. They may also use limiting to be insulting or otherwise hurt your feelings. These children are very sensitive to nonverbal communication, so you must not show any personal reaction to provocation or arguments from them. It is absolutely imperative for you to avoid escalation that smacks of challenge or revenge. Limiting must go forth in a neutral fashion, with you keeping your cool and presenting the limit, the reflecting feelings, negotiating, generating solutions, and setting consequences in a matter-of-fact manner. You will want to know what your buttons are and have a firm grip on your ability to not let them be pushed by these children. Revenge-seeking children often take metacommunication about the underlying message as confirmation of their mistaken beliefs, so you will probably stick to reflecting relatively obvious feelings or making guesses about purposes.

Children who are trying to prove that they are inadequate seldom do anything that would involve setting limits. It is actually sort of exciting when these children are active enough to need limiting. Because they often interpret being limited as proof of their inadequacy, you may decide not to limit behavior that you would limit with other children.

Personality Priorities

Personality priorities can influence the behavior that gets limited, the children's involvement in the limiting process, and their reactions to limit setting. You can tailor the process to children's priorities.

Children whose personality priority is on the dysfunctional part of the control continuum manifest behaviors and reactions similar to children whose goal of misbehavior is power. Their behavior in the playroom often tests or defies limits, and they spend a great deal of time trying to show you that you cannot control their behavior. They tend to approach the cooperative aspect of limiting with distrust, but once they are engaged in it fully, they can become very vigilant in making sure that rules and agreements are followed by everyone in the playroom. Limited choices and metacommunicating about their purposes are strategies you can use to great effect with these children.

Children whose personality priority is pleasing seldom break rules. Those who are on the dysfunctional part of the pleasing continuum may continuously interpret your nonverbal behavior as being disapproving and may even attempt to limit themselves even when they have not broken any of the playroom rules. These children are hyperalert to nuances in communication, so you will want to sound almost cheerful in imposing limits on them. They are often reluctant to fully engage in the collaborative element of the process because they are afraid that whatever they suggest as acceptable behavior or appropriate consequences will not be acceptable in the playroom. You must be prepared to renegotiate consequences with these children because the consequences that they generate for themselves can be unreasonably harsh. Because pleasing children tend to be overly rule bound anyway, you can choose to ignore any minor league transgression, encouraging them to swing out and risk not always following all the rules.

Children with superiority as their personality priority do not break limits often, but when they do, they like to argue about exactly what the rule is and how they really were not violating it—that you are surely mistaken. Their attitude is designed to convey the message that they have a superior understanding of how negotiations should proceed and how consequences should be applied. It is helpful if you don't take this attitude personally and are prepared to calmly restate the limit or repeat the agreement without getting into a quibble about the exact interpretation of the wording. If you can do this, these children almost always cooperate eventually, even if only to prove that they do what they are supposed to do better than other children do. Sometimes it actually helps to short circuit the arguments these children are prone to start if the rules, agreements, and consequences are written down.

Children whose personality priority is comfort also do not break many rules, because breaking rules takes too much effort. When they do, they often are not very active in generating alternative behaviors for the same reason. You can wind up doing most of the work to generate several different sets of acceptable behaviors and asking the children to help narrow the field by making a choice of what would work for them. Comfort children almost always follow through with their agreement, so the fourth step seldom has to be evoked. Choosing not to abide by an agreement would just be too stressful for comfort children.

Summary

Encouragement and limit setting are an important part of building a relationship in Adlerian play therapy. To encourage children, the Adlerian play therapist conveys unconditional acceptance; shows faith in clients' abilities; gives recognition for effort; focuses on strengths and assets; emphasizes the deed and the joy of doing, not the doer; focuses on the positives; shows involvement in clients' interests; models the courage to be imperfect; helps clients realize they can learn from mistakes and that mistakes do not have to be negative or devastating; and makes sure clients discover a positive way to gain belonging and significance.

The therapist must make decisions about what to limit, when to limit, and how to limit before problems develop so that he or she can present limits in a reasonable, respectful way that avoids power struggles. In Adlerian play therapy, the therapist involves the child in the four steps of limiting: stating the limit, reflecting feelings or metacommunicating about the underlying message of the behavior or the child's purpose, generating alternative acceptable behaviors or solutions, and setting up logical consequences. The therapist's lifestyle and the child's lifestyle will both have an effect on the process of setting limits. The play therapist must keep these factors under consideration in deciding how and what to limit.

Further Resources

Encouragement:

http://www.centroadleriano.org/publicaciones/Beingenco.pdf
http://ct.counseling.org/2013/04/reflecting-as-if/
http://www.cyc-net.org/cyc-online/cycol-0205-encouragement.html
http://www.thekidcounselor.com/2006/10/encouragement-vs-praise

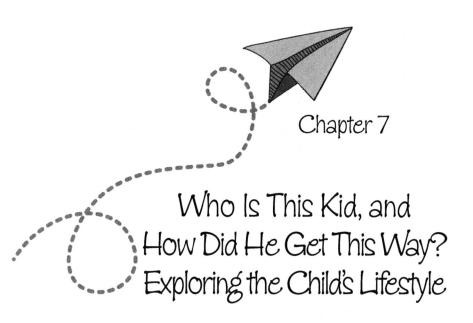

Chapter 7

Who Is This Kid, and How Did He Get This Way? Exploring the Child's Lifestyle

In the second phase of Adlerian play therapy, the counselor gathers information about the child's lifestyle to be able to help the child and the parents better understand the patterns of the child's thoughts, emotions, and actions. This process usually involves procedures designed to explore the family atmosphere, family constellation, early recollections, and functioning at life tasks to gather information about the child's assets, Crucial Cs, goals of misbehavior, personality priorities, mistaken beliefs, and private logic. When the counselor has accumulated enough information to be relatively confident of understanding the child's lifestyle, the process of formulating hypotheses about how the child views self, others, and the world and how his or her behavior reflects these perceptions begins. (This is the fun part—where you get to be a lifestyle detective—asking nosy questions, lurking in the waiting room and eavesdropping on family conversations, inviting the child to play out different scenarios, just like detectives on television.)

What Is Family Atmosphere?

Family atmosphere is the emotional "tone" of the family—the climate of relationships in which the children develop (Bitter, 2014; Maniacci et al., 2014; Sweeney, 2009). Family atmosphere is reflected in family values, family communication, and the affective tone of the interactions between family members. Understanding the family atmosphere is particularly important in Adlerian play therapy because it is continually influencing how children view themselves, others, and the world. People form their image of themselves and the way they can gain significance on the basis of their perceptions of how other people react to them. Their Crucial Cs, goals of misbehavior, and personality priorities are influenced by their interactions with their parents and the other members of their families. Children decide how other people are supposed to behave on the basis of their perceptions of how people act and interact in their families. Children's concepts about how the world works spring from their perceptions of the world in which they grow up—their homes and their families. They believe that the atmosphere of their family is representative of how relationships work and how life is supposed to be, and as they interact with the other members of their family and the rest of the world, they act as if this belief is a reality.

Here is something that scares us every time we think about it:

> The relationship between the parents is often the clearest indication of what will constitute the family's way of being and interacting. Parents are the models for how one gender relates to the other, how to work and participate in the world, how to get along with other people. Children may experience these models as joyful, angry, loving, frightening, strict, easygoing, involved, indulgent, protective or overprotective, hostile, nurturing, challenging, or respectful, to name a few. (Bitter, 2014, p. 133)

(Yikes! Wonder what that means for *our* children!?!)

Family atmosphere is based on a number of factors, including (a) parental attitudes toward the children; (b) parental discipline philosophies; (c) the parents' lifestyles; (d) the family values; (e) the family atmosphere of the parents' family of origin; (f) the marital relationship; (g) the parenting skills of parents; and (h) any personal problems that might interfere with parents' ability to provide warmth, respect, and structure for the children (Bitter, 2014; Dewey, 1971; Maniacci et al., 2014). Each family is unique, so there is no set formula for how these elements fit together or for the proportion of the different factors in the mix. However, there are certain typical patterns that frequently appear in families. Because children growing up in these typical families manifest certain common characteristics in their lifestyles (Adler, 1931/1958; Dewey, 1971), the play therapist may learn a lot about the child's lifestyle by studying them.

Types of Family Atmospheres

The most positive family atmosphere is democratic (Bettner & Lew, 1990; Dewey, 1971; Lew, 1999). The parents in democratic families exhibit strong parenting skills and provide consistent and reasonable limits and structure. These parents have positive attitudes toward their children and communicate love and respect in ways that instill all four of the Crucial Cs in their children. They usually have manageable personal problems, and any marital issues are under reasonable control. The children are active participants in the decision-making process of the family, and they have age-appropriate power and responsibilities, such as the ability to choose their own clothing and chores. Children who grow up in democratic families are self-confident, self-reliant, spontaneous, and articulate about their feelings and thoughts (Bettner & Lew, 1990). Most of the time, children from these families do not come to play therapy unless something traumatic such as sexual abuse or the death of someone close to them has occurred.

Many children in play therapy may come from families whose family atmospheres do not resemble this ideal climate. Unfortunately, the rest of the descriptions of family atmospheres are rather negative. Dewey (1971) developed a typology of family atmospheres that included rejecting, authoritarian, inconsistent, hopeless, suppressive, overprotective, pitying, high standards, materialistic, competitive, disparaging, and/or inharmonious. Family atmospheres are rarely pure and frequently overlap with one another so that a child could grow up in a family that has several different atmospheres, all of which contribute to the child's perceptions and ways of belonging. There are some family atmospheres that seem to naturally fit together, like a high-standards atmosphere and a competitive atmosphere or an authoritarian atmosphere and a suppressive atmosphere. When this happens, the child reacts creatively to the various elements of the atmosphere, which results in unique personalities for each of the children in a family. The reality is that, for every family atmosphere, there is a continuum ranging from a mild atmosphere that does not adversely affect the children to an extreme atmosphere that significantly and adversely affects the children. We tend to pay more attention to the affective tone of the family and the lifestyles of the parents and how they are having an impact on the child rather than focusing on the "type" in this system. We are going to use examples of families with parents who are controlling, overprotective, and chaotic–conflictual to give you a sense of how we think about how family atmospheres affect children.

Controlling, authoritarian parents often demand absolute obedience. They frequently believe that they must dominate to count, and they may have difficulty connecting with others in positive ways. Their discipline philosophy is based on the expectation that the children should have perfect behavior and adopt parental values without questions. They discourage discussion and expression of feelings. Often one parent dominates the other, with the family arranged in a hierarchical structure—the dominant adult at the top has the majority of the power, with the rest of the power in the family distributed among the other family members.

There are two different patterns of behavior in "typical" children who live in families with controlling, authoritarian family atmospheres. Children can become excessively conforming and compliant, or they become extremely rebellious. Conforming children are usually polite, timid, and anxious pleasers. They frequently lack courage, and they may develop nervous habits, tics, ulcers, and other physical evidence of stress and tension. Lacking spontaneity and initiative, they have difficulty solving their own problems and seek out authority figures to make decisions for them. They often feel that they only count when they are following the rules.

Most of the time, conforming children please adults, which reduces the chances of them getting sent to play therapy. If these children are referred to play therapy, it is usually for internalizing behaviors (e.g., nightmares, excessive anxiety, nail-biting). Teachers may notice the symptoms of anxiety and tension, a lack of childlike behavior, or limited resourcefulness and send them to the school counselor or an outside therapist. In the playroom, these children are hesitant to make choices for themselves, deferring to the therapist on the simplest decisions. They will struggle when you return responsibility to them because they have no experience making choices for themselves.

Rebellious children are often inconsiderate of others, argumentative, or sensitive to blame and praise. The children who take this route in response to authoritarian parents are usually striving toward power or revenge, with doubts about their ability to connect in positive ways and feeling unsure of their abilities. They frequently resort to evasive actions like lying and stealing in response to authority figures. Controlling, authoritarian parents usually bring rebellious children to play therapy to find ways of making them more compliant. In the playroom, these children look for evidence that you are going to turn out to be a closet authoritarian. They do not believe in the principle of an egalitarian relationship, testing the limits and your convictions and patience over and over again.

Controlling, authoritarian parents seldom agree with the democratic principles of Adlerian philosophy or parenting skills, so they may not keep their children in counseling with you. With these parents, you must be patient, reminding yourself that they are doing the best they know how to do, given their own lifestyles and fear of being out of control. The pace in parent consultation must be slow and steady so that the parents do not get too frightened of the eventual letting go of their illusion of total control.

Another example would be an overprotective atmosphere, in which indulgent or protective parents prevent children from learning by refusing to allow them to cope with difficult problems (Dewey, 1971). Sometimes these family atmospheres come about because of some difficulty children experience, such as chronic illness or learning disabilities, but more often they come about because of the personalities of the parents. Parents in these families protect their children from unpleasantness, sadness, and the reality of life, resulting in children who feel that they are not capable and, lacking courage, believe that they cannot deal with life's challenges on their own. Quite often, these parents gain their own sense of counting by taking care of every little problem for their children. Parental personality priorities are often pleasing or controlling, though occasionally a superiority parent will use overparenting as a way to demonstrate his or her superior ability to take care of the child. Many times, these parents grew up with difficult circumstances or in families with disparaging, competitive, high-standards atmospheres, in which they did not feel sufficiently nurtured, and they are trying to compensate for their own upbringing in their interactions with their children.

Overprotection often results in pampered children who never develop self-reliance. Children from these families usually lack self-confidence, have a strong need for approval, feel entitled, and exhibit a great deal of dependence on others. They develop an attitude that they do not have to be responsible for their own behavior because their parents have always prevented them from having to experience consequences for their actions. In their interactions with others, they may ask, "What's in it for me?" or "Who is going to take care of this for me?" They often work hard to prove that they are not capable and that they do not count unless others are taking care of them. They frequently lack courage, striving to prove that they are inadequate.

Most parents of pampered children do not see anything wrong with their children or their behavior and consequently seldom seek counseling for them unless forced to do so by an outside authority, such as the school. Teachers often have difficulty with these children in the classroom, either because of their arrogance or their helplessness, so school counselors frequently work with children from overprotective families.

In the playroom, these children will try to replicate their relationship with the parents with you. They act helpless, asking you to take care of all their needs and desires, or they are extremely bossy, working to dominate you and force you to comply with their wishes and serve them. These children tend to try to avoid taking any risks, so they play with toys that are similar to toys that they have at home, and they often express a desire to bring their own toys to the playroom.

Parents in families in which the atmosphere is chaotic–conflictual spend most of their time bickering and fighting. Dewey (1971) called these families inharmonious. They use the children as weapons in their ongoing discord. These parents are frequently so caught up in their marital struggles that they discipline in an inconsistent manner, depending on their mood and the status of the marital conflict. Even when these parents have adequate parenting skills and good connecting abilities, they do not apply them consistently, resulting in little structure or reliable parental support and nurturing. Constructively interacting with the children becomes less important than scoring points in the marital battle. These parents frequently come from families in which positive, proactive strategies for solving conflict were seldom modeled.

Children who grow up in this type of atmosphere often develop the idea that gaining power is the most important goal in interacting with others. Because they see their parents trying to gain control over one another, many times they decide that the best way to be safe and gain significance is to acquire power over others. Having witnessed verbal (and perhaps physical) abuse exchanged between their parents, children from chaotic–conflictual families usually believe that this pattern is the way relationships work. This perception can hamper their ability to connect with others, so they struggle with friendships and other social relationships. Their deficits in social interest and the elevated levels of tension they experience at home can lead them to break rules and put themselves and others in dangerous situations. They often believe that the only way that they can count is to show others how "bad" they can be.

These attitudes and behaviors frequently lead to referrals for play therapy. Oftentimes when the parents resolve their issues or they decide to divorce, they realize that the fallout from their lack of harmony has adversely affected their children, so they bring them to work with a play therapist.

Children from inharmonious families expect chaos and conflict, even when there is no reason for controversy. Because of this, they may be highly anxious in the playroom, or they may absolutely love being there. They tend to be hypervigilant about any kind of undercurrent that might lead to conflict, so they will monitor your verbal and nonverbal communication very closely, reacting to imagined anger and expecting to be reprimanded.

Investigating Family Atmosphere

Within the context of Adlerian play therapy, there are many different methods you can use to gather knowledge about the child's family atmosphere and how it affects him or her: (a) observing the child and parents; (b) asking questions; or (c) using expressive arts, sand tray, or movement activities. You can use any combination of these methods, depending on the child, the parents, and your own stylistic preferences—or you can bring in strategies of your own. Because Adlerian play therapy is "technically eclectic," other methods of exploring the family atmosphere are welcome. It is important to try to match the modality of your investigation with the child's usual way of communicating. For instance, with a child who has demonstrated an affinity to art, drawing and painting are usually the best ways to gather information; with a child who likes to do puppet shows or act things out, this approach will work best; and so forth. If the child has not shown a connection to a particular mode of expression, we usually start by asking for a drawing. If the child declines, we make a guess about the purpose of the refusal, and follow with a suggestion of alternative techniques designed to elicit similar information. With children who do not particularly like art, we often ask them to pick a toy, puppet, or sand tray figure as a symbol for each member of the family instead of drawing the person. After having them explain what each of the figures is and how they went about choosing that particular symbol for that person, we use common sense to make guesses about family dynamics. Some children feel threatened by depicting their family directly, so asking these children to do a collage with photographs of different animals that might go together to make a family can elicit information connected to family dynamics in their own families.

Observing the Child and Parents

Any time you can observe the child in the play session, parents in the parent consultation sessions, and the child and parents together in the waiting room (and, for those of you who are school counselors, at school events) and in family sessions, you should have your awareness tuned to the family atmosphere. Although this information cannot stand alone, observational data are sometimes more accurate than self-report from the child and parents (Duffy & Chenail, 2012). (You know—it is just hard for people to be objective about themselves and their own lives—and it might be that some clients are in denial or just trying to mislead you, so sometimes you have to take what they report with a grain of salt.)

In the play session, the child usually acts out family atmosphere situations with the dolls, animal families, puppets, and kitchenware. Playing with these toys, the child expresses thoughts and feelings about how his or her parents treat the children and each other, how family members interact, how family values are manifested or communicated in the family, and assorted other aspects of the family dynamics. The child's overall behavior will also give the therapist clues about the family atmosphere. For instance, a child who grows up in a family atmosphere in which the parents tend to be rejecting is often extremely needy, working hard to gain your approval; a child whose family atmosphere is characterized by violence may play out violent relationships in the dollhouse or in puppet shows. When you notice play patterns and themes that give you clues about family atmosphere, it is better to metacommunicate or reflect feelings connected with what is happening in the play in a metaphoric way, rather than directly asking the child to explain how the play relates to what is happening at home. Examples of metacommunicating about observations:

- Randy is playing with the puppets. One of the puppets keeps hitting the other puppet. The puppet being hit is making crying noises. You could say, "Sounds like that puppet is really getting hurt. I bet he wishes that other puppet would stop hitting him."
- Ho-Sook is playing with the dolls in the dollhouse. The mother doll hugs one of the doll children and ignores the other doll child. Ho-Sook, moving the mother doll, says, "I love my little baby." You could say, "The mother really cares about the baby. I wonder what kind of feelings the sister is having right now."
- Ringo aims the dart gun at you every time you reflect a feeling. You might say, "Seems like you want me to stop talking about feelings."

With two-parent families, the play therapist can observe the interactions between the parents during parent consultations or family sessions. It is helpful to get impressions of their relationship and the level of agreement and cooperation over parenting strategies. The therapist should observe nonverbal communication to see if it is congruent with the parents' words. The therapist can gather more information by pointing out any discrepancies and asking questions about the difference between verbal presentation and nonverbal reactions.

Observing the interactions between the child and the parents can provide you with additional important clues about family atmosphere. If the family waits together in a waiting room before sessions or you get a chance to see them at school events or in other settings, they often interact in more natural and realistic patterns than in your office. It can also be useful to have family play therapy sessions during the exploration stage (Kottman & Meany-Walen, in press). By watching family members interact in the session, you will be able to get clues about typical interactions, attitudes, and relationships—information that is invaluable in formulating lifestyle hypotheses.

Asking Questions

Another method of finding out about the parents' relationship, their discipline philosophies and practices, and other family atmosphere data is to ask questions about these family interactions. By asking some of the lifestyle questions found in Appendices B and D, you will be able to gather information about the family atmosphere.

It is essential to ask both the child and parents similar questions to get a multifaceted picture of how family members interact. This prevents just one person in the family from dominating your perception of the family situation and ensures that you have a rounded view representing both the child's and the parents' perspectives. In talking to parents, you will often start asking these questions during the first session. With the child, you will probably want to work on establishing a relationship for several sessions before asking family atmosphere questions. This depends on the child, however. There are many children who will just volunteer information related to family atmosphere in the first session. When this happens, we take this as permission to go ahead and start asking our questions. (Yes, both of us are super nosy . . .)

It is easy to turn into "the inquisition," so try not to overwhelm the child or parents with too many questions in a session. It seems to work best to ask three or four questions about the family atmosphere during each interaction. You will want to have several questions in mind that you could ask in the process of the session and as the session progresses try to weave the questions into the flow of the conversation in a natural fashion. Because so many adult–child interactions are filled with questions, we are always careful to monitor a child's nonverbal reaction so that we stop asking questions if the child is exhibiting a negative attitude toward our questioning.

It is also frequently helpful to use the child's play as a vehicle for asking questions indirectly. As the child is playing, you can ask family atmosphere questions metaphorically. The following are examples of using the child's metaphor for asking lifestyle questions:

- Jolene is playing with the doll family, and the doll father is yelling at the doll children to pick up their rooms. Instead of "breaking" the metaphor, you can use it to gather information by asking, "How do those doll kids feel when the father doll yells at them?" or "What happens if the doll children still don't pick up their rooms after the doll father yells at them?"
- Rocco is playing with the horse family. You could ask him to tell you about each of the members of the horse family. As you mentally decide which of the horses represents each member of Rocco's family, you might ask, "Which of those horse children is most different from the baby horse?" or "Which of those horse children does the mother horse like best? What does she like best about that one?"
- Letty is playing with the kitchenware and is throwing the dishes into the sandbox, looking angry. You could say, "Wow, looks like someone is mad and throwing dishes around." When Letty responds, "Yeah, the mom is mad again," you could ask, "They must be kind of scared. What do the children do when the mom is that mad?"

Using Expressive Arts, Sand Tray, and/or Movement Techniques

The Adlerian play therapist can also use expressive arts techniques or sand tray strategies to investigate clients' perceptions of the family atmosphere. Music, dance, puppet shows, and role-playing–acting are all appropriate forms of expressive arts in addition to art activities such as drawing, painting, and sculpture as ways for children to express themselves.

One approach is to ask a client to make a kinetic family drawing (KFD; Knoff & Prout, 1985; Nurse & Sperry, 2012), a drawing technique in which the client draws a picture of each member of the family involved in some activity. I (TK) do a variation on this technique with sand tray, called a kinetic family sand tray, in which I ask a client to choose one to three figures to represent each of the people in the family. You can also do variations on the KFD, like a kinetic family toothpick sculpture, a kinetic family collection of sock puppets, a kinetic family collage with actual photographs of family members or photos that represent family members cut from magazines.

When doing the more traditional version of the KFD, provide the client with several pieces of paper (a few more pieces than the number of members of the family) and a pencil, and tell the child to draw a picture of the family. Don't ask the child if he or she wants to do this because you want to avoid a refusal to draw the picture. Give the following instructions, adapted from the original 1970 version of the KFD to suit our purposes in Adlerian play therapy: "Draw a picture of everybody in your family. The picture should show everybody in the family doing something." It is often helpful to encourage the child not to draw stick figures, but don't prohibit this if it is the only way the child is going to draw the picture. (If you do this with parents too, it may even be more important to let them use stick figures because they tend to be more critical about their own art abilities than most children.) After the child finishes the drawing, you can ask some questions about the figures in the drawing and the family. (See Appendix E for questioning strategies to be used with the KFD to elicit information about the client's lifestyle.) To interpret the drawing, we use a commonsense approach, interpreting what the child has drawn each family member doing as representative of how the child perceives that person gaining significance in the family. We also look for interactional patterns and attitudes expressed in the drawing. Through the questions we ask about the family, we gather family atmosphere and family constellation data.

We might also ask children to do a Draw-A-Person (Nurse & Sperry, 2012; Oster & Crone, 2004), a Kinetic House–Tree–Person drawing (Buck, 1992; J. Rubin, 2011), a Family-Centered Circle drawing (R. Burns, 1990; Oster & Crone, 2004), a Rosebush drawing (Oaklander, 1978/1992), a Family Clay Sculpture (J. Rubin, 2011), or a musical activity with clients who don't like to draw to get more information about the family atmosphere. To do a Draw-A-Person, you give clients a piece of paper and tell them to draw a picture of a person (strangely enough—seems pretty simple, huh?). To do a House–Tree–Person drawing, you would give clients a single sheet of paper and ask them to draw a picture of a house, a tree, and a person. (The kinetic part is that, with only one sheet of paper, the house, tree, and person often interact.) For a Family-Centered Circle drawing, clients do three separate drawings—one of the mother, one of the father, and one of self. In each of the drawings, the person is drawn in the center of a circle, surrounded by symbols associated with that person. You could also do variations of each of these techniques using sand tray—a sand tray in which you have clients choose as many figures as they wish to represent themselves; a sand tray in which they choose a person, a tree, and a house and arrange them together in the sand; a sand tray in which they choose figures to represent each of the people in their family; or a sand tray in which they choose a figure to represent each person in the family surrounded by figures that are symbols associated with each person. In the Rosebush, you read a guided imagery to help clients visualize themselves as a rosebush and after they have completed the drawing, you would ask questions about what life is like for the rosebush. With children who do not like drawing, you could do the Rosebush as a theater activity, with them showing you how the rosebush might grow and move or what a person who is taking care of the rosebush might do to nurture it. The Family Clay Sculpture consists of giving clients clay and asking them to sculpt figures that represent each member of the family. (Bet you could have predicted that!)

You could also use music to facilitate exploration (Hadley & Steele, 2014). Several examples of using music to help children depict family atmosphere would be having them bring in a "theme song" for each member of the family or pick out a representative rhythm on a drum or play a representative tune on a flute. If you had a variety of instruments in your playroom, you could even ask them to use a different instrument to represent each family member and make a "symphony" of how it is to be in their family. If you have children who like to dance, asking them to do an interpretive dance to show how each of the family members moves and communicates feelings is often a great way to explore family dynamics (LeFeber, 2014). All of these techniques can give you information about how clients see self, others, and the world and about family interactions.

With children who are less inclined toward expressing themselves through traditional creative arts such as drawing, painting, music, and dance, you can use more active techniques to gather information. There are many different movement activities you could suggest—for instance, playing a "fake basketball game" with moves that represent different family members and how they interact, being a "robot" that walks and talks like family members, moving the way people interact in the family, and so forth can give you a great deal of information.

You can also ask parents and other family members to use expressive arts techniques to help you develop a "feel" for the individual members or the family as a whole. Comparing both the process and the product of the various members of the family is often very revealing.

Therapists must not feel limited to these particular applications of techniques. Creativity is (we believe) a hallmark of Adlerian play therapy, so we encourage play therapists to use their imaginations and knowledge of other methods of accumulating information in this phase of the process.

Family Constellation

Family constellation is the term coined by Adler and elaborated by Dreikurs to represent the operation of the family system, including parents, siblings, and other in the family of origin, together with any others living with them as members of the person's childhood household. It pictures the family by analogy to a constellation in astronomy, a group of bodies in motion, each of which has its place in relation to the places of the others. (Griffith & Powers, 2007, p. 37)

Family constellation is influenced by a plethora of factors: the personality traits of each member of the family, the emotional connections among various members, the dominance or submission of different members, the size of the family, age differences among the children, the gender of the children, sibling subsets, and the birth order of the children (Eckstein & Kern, 2009; Griffith & Powers, 2007; McKay, 2012; Sweeney, 2009). In Adlerian theory, the family constellation contributes greatly to the child's lifestyle because the family configuration during the child's formative years influences the child's fundamental attitudes and approach to life. Each birth-order position has certain traits that are typical of individuals who find themselves in that place in the family constellation. However, psychological position is more important than ordinal position. "Psychological birth order position is the vantage from which the child perceives and evaluates self, others, and the world, and from which the child forms convictions about what is required of—as well as open to—him or her" (Griffith & Powers, 2007, p. 84). There are many factors that influence psychological birth-order position. These factors include those that determine the entire complex of the family constellation, plus factors such as having a disabled child in the family, differential treatment based on gender, cultural background, family myths, educational experiences, physical development, and the time elapsed between the birth of children.

Psychological Birth-Order Positions

The purpose in gathering information about the child's family constellation is to determine how these various factors influence the child's perception of her or his place in the family and the methods he or she has chosen for gaining a sense of belonging and significance. Because each position has certain typical assets and challenges, the Adlerian play therapist gathers information about psychological birth-order position to find ways of encouraging the child by building on assets. The therapist can also use this knowledge as the basis for helping the child with challenges inherent in each of the birth-order positions.

Only Children

Because they spend much of their childhoods surrounded by people who are older and more proficient than they are, only children often develop skills that gain approval of adults, or they cultivate character traits such as shyness or helplessness that gain sympathy (Bitter, 2014; Leman, 2009). This can develop into personality priorities of pleasing or comfort. Only children usually enjoy their position as the center of attention but may also feel anxious because they are always under scrutiny. They are often sure that they count, though they may struggle to believe that they are capable. Because they do not automatically have playmates, only children may have difficulty learning to connect with other children, preferring the company of adults. Sometimes parents of only children pamper them, leading them to believe that they do not need to earn things by their own efforts and that they can have anything just because they want it. When this is the case, if others do not grant their requests, these children feel unfairly treated and refuse to cooperate. They like to be comfortable, avoiding tension and stress whenever possible. (Yikes—this sounds exactly like my [TK] only child, Jacob!)

Only children frequently have many assets, including independence, intelligence, well-developed verbal skills, spontaneity, a strong sense of fun, and creative imaginations. They can be highly self-entertaining and self-reliant. On the negative side, because only children do not have to share their parents' attention and their possessions with siblings, they may be only interested in themselves and their own interests, resulting in difficulties in connecting with others their own age.

In the playroom, typical only children usually fall into one of two categories of interaction. Either they will be highly independent and play by themselves without inviting you to play with them or they will be rather dependent and consistently try to engage you in interacting with them. Their play is always creative and imaginative. They often like to dress up as interesting characters or have the puppets, figures, and dolls acting out a variety of scenarios in which people or animals are having exciting adventures. When they play with the therapist, a parent, or another child in the playroom, they like to be in charge—telling play partners exactly what to do, where to stand, and what to say.

First-Born Children
First-born children have precarious positions in their families (Bitter, 2014; Leman, 2009; Sweeney, 2009). Being the oldest often entitles these children to special privileges and strong relationships with parents. ("And why would we not be entitled?" asks TK, an archetypal oldest child.) However, because this place is usually threatened with the birth of subsequent children, oldest children may feel dethroned. In terms of assets, first-born children are usually responsible, reliable, organized, achievement oriented, protective of others, nurturing, and helpful. Many times, they have strongly developed leadership skills and gain their significance in the family by coopting personality traits that are highly valued in the family. They tend to have strong social skills when interacting with adults because they have spent a lot of their time with older people.

The liabilities of typical oldest children usually involve taking these assets to the extreme. Oldest children can be overly responsible, excessively organized (making a sort of obsession with order), maladaptively perfectionistic, very competitive, overprotective, inordinately interested in pleasing others, controlling, and bossy. They often become so invested in achievement (staying ahead of the competition from the younger children to avoid being dethroned) that they neglect building relationships with other people. In many cases, their ability to connect with peers is weak because they are not always comfortable being equals with individuals their own age. They tend to believe that they only count if they are the smartest, most helpful, hardest working, and so forth. When oldest children feel threatened by younger children, they can become extremely discouraged, believing that they must be the first, the best, the most powerful, or they are worthless (just a bit of all-or-nothing thinking here).

In the playroom, oldest children are usually very neat, many times cleaning up after themselves even before you suggest that it is time to pick up the room. They are extremely responsible, wanting to know what the rules in the playroom are and what the consequences of not following the rules will be. Oldest children are likely to invite you to actively interact with them. When this happens, some oldest children are extremely bossy, dictating the details of the play and expressing irritation if you do not follow the letter of the law that they have set up. Other oldest children will want to wait until you decide what and how they are going to play to avoid the possibility that they might make a decision that you would not like. When they come in, many oldest children will want some time to just chat with you before they start playing. This gives them a chance to connect using their adult-like social skills, and it lets them make sure that you know that they are doing well at whatever activity in which they have decided they must excel. Every once in a while, an oldest child will come in and not act like an oldest—making a mess, being irresponsible, acting out of control. When that happens, you will want to put on your seatbelt and get ready for a wild ride.

Second-Born Children

Second-born children spend their entire lives striving to catch up to their older sibling, feeling a great deal of pressure and inferiority (Bitter, 2014; Leman, 2009; Sweeney, 2009). Quite frequently, especially if they are close in age, second-born children's personalities are exact opposites of the first-born children in their families. Because they never have undivided attention from parents, these children often develop the idea that they do not deserve attention—that they do not count as much as the first-born sibling or other children born after them. Because their older sibling usually develops motor and verbal skills before they do, second-born children often believe that they can never be as capable as the older sibling.

Most second-born children know that they can connect, and they usually have strong social skills because they learn early that they must get along with others. They usually put out a lot of effort because they have always felt a need to try harder because they are number two. Quite frequently, these children excel at athletics. Unfortunately, second-born children tend to be easily discouraged because they are afraid that they can never measure up to the older child. In families where the first-born children have adopted valued positive personality traits, second-born children sometimes adopt negative personality traits as a contrast to make a place of significance for themselves. They may also be hyperactive or anxious because they always feel as though they are in a race that they cannot win.

In the playroom, second-born children tend to be friendly and fun when they are at their best. They will use their connecting skills to build the relationship with you, and they use their willingness to try hard to figure out ways to have fun in the playroom. Quite often, second-born children are very physical, so they may do a lot of running, jumping, playing ball, setting up obstacle courses in the playroom. Because they are never sure that they are going to be able to catch up to the older child, they tend to keep score in everything they do—even in jumping or tossing a ball, they will know what constitutes a score and who is ahead.

Middle Children

If there is a third child in the family, the second child gets squeezed into the middle position (Bitter, 2014; Leman, 2009; Sweeney, 2009). Middle children do not have the rights of the oldest or the privileges of the youngest. These children often feel neglected and unloved—they are not sure how they count in the family.

Because they are in the middle of things, these children frequently become adept at mediating and peacemaking. They can see all the different sides of every situation. In some ways, this ability is an asset because it gives them a sense of objectivity that can be very valuable in understanding varied points of view. However, it can also be a liability because sometimes they have difficulty making decisions, and they can become overly worried about fairness. This capacity of looking at experiences and relationships from many vantage points enhances middle children's ability to be innovative and creative.

Not being the oldest or the youngest, middle children frequently struggle to find their places in their families. One place that they may find is that of the rebel child—the one who is different. This may be comfortable for a time, but they often also find it discouraging. In families in which this discouragement continues, middle children can drift toward the useless side of life and become problem children.

In the playroom, because middle children like things to be fair, they take turns really well and are usually willing to share power and responsibility. When they use imaginative, fantasy play, they frequently like to play more than one character, exercising their ability to see many points of view. These children occasionally have difficulty deciding how to occupy themselves in the playroom, spending an inordinate amount of time trying to determine what to do during their sessions. When there is more than one child in the playroom, middle children serve as conflict managers, working hard to make sure that everyone is treated fairly.

Youngest Children

Youngest children usually have few responsibilities and many privileges. They get attention for being babies without really having to do anything to earn the attention. Other people in the family wait on them, spoil them, and make decisions for them. Being the smallest and the weakest of the siblings (at least initially), youngest children often feel as though the other members of their families do not take them seriously. To compensate for this, there are three routes youngest children tend to take in life. They can become speeders, working hard to catch up and surpass their older siblings in the areas in which they excel. They can get discouraged and give in to their feelings of inferiority and decide that they might as well not even try to compete. They can choose to excel in areas that are completely different from those in which their older siblings excel. No matter what route they choose, youngest children are usually charismatic and entertaining. They have a strong sense of humor and the ability to manipulate people into giving them what they want. (We youngest children [i.e. KMW] may prefer to use the word "charm" in place of "manipulate.")

On the downside, youngest children frequently expect to get privileges without earning them and expect others to make decisions and take responsibility for them. They prefer not to lead, but sometimes have difficulty following if they do not see how the path can be to their advantage. Occasionally, their ability to get what they want may also get them into trouble because other people can begin to resent feeling manipulated.

Playing with you, their parents, or other children in the playroom, youngest children watch to see what the other people are going to do and then they decide if they want to do that or something else. They rarely initiate interactions, but once they notice something they want to do or get invited to join in the play, they are great at playing—it is, after all, their specialty. They tend to try to get out of cleaning the room, and they often resent it when you return responsibility to them, often attempting to manipulate you into doing things or making decisions for them.

Other Factors Involved in Family Constellation

If the family is large, there will frequently be several children who manifest the characteristics of each birth-order position. Whenever there is a gap of 4 or 5 years between children, a new sibling subset is formed. For example, in my family of origin, I (TK) was born first, and my brother Scott was born 2 years after me. Then my mother rested 4 years before my sister, Tracy, was born. Two years after Tracy, Brian was born, and 3 years later Tim was born. We have two distinct sibling subsets—called the Big Kids and the Little Kids. I am the typical oldest child, with all of the assets and liabilities. Scott is a relatively typical second child, although he also has some characteristics of the youngest child (very charming, highly competitive—always knows what the score is in every situation). Tracy is the oldest child in the Little Kids subset, but the middle child within the entire family. She has some of the traits of an oldest child and some of the traits of a middle child (kind of a bossy, really responsible peacemaker who dislikes conflict but loves to tell other people what to do). Brian is pretty consistently a middle child; he loves peace, comfort, and calm and wants everyone to be happy. He is often overlooked and does not seem to mind that. Tim, being the youngest of both subsets, is a superbaby. He is charming, manipulative, funny, a little narcissistic, and very creative.

In families in which there is no significant time span between children, the psychological components that affect the family constellation become even more important. Factors such as family values, family atmosphere, gender, and culture have a crucial impact on how the children perceive their roles in the family. For example, I (KMW) have four children—with a 13-year gap between the first and second. Of my three little ones, the middle is a girl. She is my only girl. Although she is the middle child of that subset, she is also the only girl, which gives her a special position within the family.

Investigating Family Constellation

To gather information about the family constellation and the child's psychological birth-order position, the Adlerian play therapist can use the same techniques as those used to investigate the family atmosphere. Observation; questioning strategies; and expressive arts, sand tray, or movement techniques are all useful methods of exploring the family constellation and psychological birth order. In this process, the therapist is looking for information that will help him or her understand the child's lifestyle, especially in the areas of assets and liabilities.

Many times, by observing the child in the playroom and with other family members, you can get a clear picture of how the child fits into the family. You will want to observe how the child interacts with siblings and parents and how siblings and parents treat the child. Observation of these relationships can give you a great deal of insight into the family dynamics. Asking parents questions about the various siblings and having them complete the Sibling Rating Scale (Appendix B) can help you form a picture of the family constellation and the psychological position of each child. You can also ask the child some of the questions from Appendix D in the process of play to ascertain how he or she sees each of the children fitting into the family. If the child seems reluctant to answer questions directly, you can use the metaphors presented in the play to ask questions about the family and the children.

Art techniques such as the kinetic family drawing, family symbol picture, and collages are excellent strategies for gathering information about family constellation and psychological birth order. You can ask the child to draw pictures, do puppet shows, make a sand tray, or find photographs to represent various family values. You can collaboratively draw a timeline with the child, with an emphasis on the birth order of the children. Collages, clay sculptures, music, dance, and/or puppets can be useful tools for helping the child to explore the cultural background of the family, different views of the relative value of males and females, or the effects of having a sibling with disabilities.

One of the ways that I (TK) explore family atmosphere and family constellation is The Garden, a variation I developed based on Violet Oaklander's (1992) Rosebush technique. First, I do a small progressive relaxation narrative, followed by a guided visualization that sounds something like this:

> Close your eyes. Now I'd like you to imagine that you are a plant in a garden. Become one of the plants in the garden and find out what it's like to be a plant. What kind of plant are you? Are you very small? Are you large? Are you wide? Are you tall? Do you have flowers? If so, what kind? They can be any kind you want them to be. Do you have leaves? What kind? What are your stems and branches like? Do you have any thorns? What are your roots like? Or maybe you don't have any—you get to decide. If you do, are they long and straight? Are they twisted? Are they deep? Look around you and see if there are any other plants in the garden [pause]. If there are other plants, what do they look like? Are there only a few of them or are there lots of them? Are the other plants the same as you or are they different?

Do the other plants have leaves . . . flowers . . . stems . . . roots . . . thorns? How close are the other plants to where you are? Are they the same size as you or bigger or smaller? Where is the garden? Is the garden in a pot or growing in the ground? Or through cement? Or even inside somewhere? Look around you . . . what else do you see? [pause] Are there statues in the garden? Animals? People? Birds? Is there anything around you like a fence? If there is, what does it look like? Does someone take care of you? If there is someone who takes care of you, what does he or she do to take care of you? Does that person also take care of the other plants? What's the weather like for you right now? What is your life like? How do you feel? What happens to you as the seasons change? Be aware of yourself as a plant in a garden . . . look carefully. Find out how you feel about your life in the garden and how you feel about the other plants and living things in the garden.

In a few minutes, I'll ask you to open your eyes and I want you to draw a picture [or make a sculpture or do a sand tray] of yourself as the plant and the rest of the garden. Then, later I'll ask you a few questions, and I will want you to talk about the picture as though you are the plant in the garden [longer pause] . . . When you are ready, open your eyes and draw [or make a sculpture or do a sand tray].

After I have guided a child through the visualization and he or she has completed an art project, I ask some questions, such as,

- What kind of plant are you, and what do you look like?
- Tell me about your flowers, leaves, stems, branches, roots, thorns, etc.
- Tell me about the other plants in the garden. Tell me about whether they are the same as you or different (bigger or smaller, same kind of plant, etc.).
- Tell me about where you are in the garden. Are you close to the other plants or far away? Where are you located inside the garden (i.e., middle, outside, edge)?
- Tell me about where the garden is. What kind of things do you see around you? How do you like living where you are? What else is in the garden with you?
- Who takes care of you? How do you feel about that? How do they look after you?
- Who takes care of the other plants? How do you feel about that? How do they look after the other plants?
- What's the weather like for you right now? What happens to you as the seasons change?
- How do you feel about living in this garden? If you could change the garden, what would you change?
- If you could move to a different garden, would you? What kind of a garden would be the perfect garden for you?

Crucial Cs

The same kinds of observation and questioning strategies can also be used to investigate the Crucial Cs. I (TK) developed several informal assessment tools that the play therapist can use in exploring the Crucial Cs—one is an instrument that parents or teachers can fill out, and the other is for children to fill out. These can be found in Appendix F. In addition to this, the play therapist can also use expressive arts, movement, adventure therapy activities, and sand tray to explore which of the Crucial Cs are strengths and which present difficulties for the child.

You could pretend to be a reporter and ask the child the following questions or you could ask them to answer using drawings or sand trays. You will want to pick and choose which setups you use, depending on what you already know about the child and on the child's developmental level. We usually use these questions with children ages 8 and older. Some of the concepts are too sophisticated for younger children, and some you might need to use different, more developmentally appropriate language in your set up of the activity.

Courage

In what situations are you the most courageous?
In what situations are you the least courageous?
In what relationships are you the most courageous?
In what relationships are you the least courageous?
How do you feel when you are being your most courageous?
What are the factors that interfere with you being courageous?
What do you find scary? Threatening? Too risky to try?
When do you like taking chances?
How do you decide whether to take a risk?
What happens for you when you don't succeed at something?

Connect

How do you connect with others?
How do you feel when you connect with others?
With whom are you most comfortable connecting?
What are situations in which you feel comfortable making connections?
What do you look for in potential friends?
What are some things that cause you to disconnect from others?
What happens when you disconnect from others?
How do you keep connection from happening with people with whom
    you don't want to connect?
What kind of friend are you?

Capable

What do you do well?
How do you feel when you are successful at doing something?
What is your proudest accomplishment?
What things are you willing to do that you cannot master?
What do you like doing?
How can you tell whether you are good at doing something?
What do you tell yourself about yourself when you don't master
    something?

Count

What do you contribute to your friends/family/community/work?

What do you feel you need to do to belong/fit in with a group?

If you were going to get an award for your contribution, what would it be for?

What makes you a valuable person?

What do you think you need to do to earn love?

What is your impact on others in your world?

What is your impact on the world?

One example of an adventure therapy activity you could use to explore the Crucial Cs of capable, courage, and connect might be, "I Can Do This" (Ashby et al., 2008). This is a game in which you and the child alternate demonstrating things you can do. You start off explaining that all of us have lots of talents and abilities, some rare and unique, some that others share, and that this activity is about discovering and trying those things out. You and the child will take turns showing something specific that you can do, and then the other person tries to duplicate it. It is often helpful if you go first to demonstrate—for instance, I (TK) can wiggle my nose. Most kids can also wiggle their noses, allowing them to feel courageous, capable, and more connected to me. If only one of you can do some of the things, that is okay too . . . just shows that everyone is unique and has special talents.

Goals of Misbehavior

As we described in Chapter 3, the usual method of investigating the goals of misbehavior is paying attention to the child's behavior and feelings when with a child or asking parents and teachers questions about the dynamics of their interactions. We ask about specific behaviors, the adults' observations of the underlying feelings experienced by the child, their reactions to the child's behavior, and the child's responses to correction. Another way of exploring the goals of misbehavior in the playroom is an adaptation of an inventory developed by Manly (1986).

Using puppets, dolls, or sand tray figures, the play therapist does a short show with one of the toys demonstrating a selected goal of misbehavior. The "misbehaving" toy would have "lines" that would be typical of children who manifest the particular patterns of thinking, feeling, and behaving usual in those who have that as their primary goal of misbehavior. This character could also narrate what he or she is feeling and thinking while he or she is saying the "lines" and acting out the negative behaviors. The play therapist could simply watch the child's reaction to the puppet play of each type of misbehavior to observe whether the child seems to have any kind of recognition reflex for a particular character. The play therapist could also ask the child what he or she thinks about that character or could ask the child to play out a character who did similar things. It might also be helpful to have other characters who would act out the typical responses of people (adults and other children) to a child who is manifesting that particular goal of misbehavior and observe the child's behavior to this (or engage the child in a conversation about the interaction between the characters).

Attention-seeking characters would do things to draw attention to themselves. They might bother others, brag, show off, act silly, be really loud, make messes, and the like. They could be mildly inappropriate and then when one of the other characters corrects them, they would stop for a little while, but later resume the inappropriate behavior. Other characters would express frustration and annoyance at this pattern. Attention-seeking characters would say things like:

- "I want others to notice me."
- "I want others to do more for me."
- "I want to be special."
- "I should get all the attention."
- "Why aren't others playing attention to me?"
- "I don't get enough attention."
- "I feel sad/mad/ disappointed when no one is noticing me."

Power-seeking characters would do things like having temper tantrums, arguing, lying, getting into power struggles with others, refusing to cooperate, and/or being disobedient or defiant. When one of the other characters corrects them, they would escalate their acting out, which would result in the other characters getting angry with them. Power-seeking characters would say things like:

- "I want to be in charge."
- "I want others to do what I want them to do."
- "I want/need to show others they cannot control me."
- "I want others to stop telling me what to do."
- "I want/need power."
- "I must have power/control to be safe/protect myself."

Revenge-seeking characters would do things like deliberately hurting others (either physically or emotionally), saying malicious or cruel things to others, being violent toward others, or threatening others. If one of the other characters asked them to stop or set some kind of consequence or punishment, these characters would become even more violent, aggressive, or vindictive. Revenge-seeking characters would say things like:

- "I believe I have been treated unfairly."
- "I want to get even with others."
- "I need to pay others back for hurting me/jerking me around."
- "I want others to feel what it is like to be hurt."
- "I want others to be sorry for what they have done to me."
- "I need to keep others at a distance so they can't hurt me."
- "I know that no one really cares for me."

Characters who are displaying or proving inadequacy would do things like—well, they wouldn't do much, actually. They would give up easily or not even make an attempt to do things. They might say they can't do things, they might be mute and refuse to answer others, they would be reluctant to try new things, or they would express extreme self-doubts. Essentially, they would be embodiment of discouragement. They might seek isolation from others. In extreme cases, they might be suicidal or self-destructive, but with younger children this would be an inappropriate subject for a puppet show. When other characters give them feedback or try to be encouraging, these characters would sink lower into their own self-doubts and discouragement. Characters whose goal is proving their own inadequacy would say things such as,

- "I want/need others to stop asking me to do things."
- "I want/need others to stop asking me to try harder."
- "I want people to feel sorry for me."
- "I want to be left alone."
- "I might as well not try because I wouldn't be successful anyway."
- "I can't do anything right."
- "I know I can't do it."
- "I'm a loser."
- "I am not important."

Because there is some overlap between the goals of misbehavior and the Crucial Cs (Lew & Bettner, 2000), this activity can also give you clues about which of the Crucial Cs need to be fostered as well.

Early Recollections

Each early recollection elicited by the counselor should be a single, specific incident preferably occurring before the age of 10. Early memories are not coincidences; they are often projections. In large measure, what we selectively attend to from the past is reflective of what we believe and how we behave in the present, and what we anticipate for the future. (Watts, 2013, p. 464)

Because people selectively remember events from their past, the situations and relationships they choose to recall usually have some type of significance for them. A client's early recollections can provide valuable clues about his or her lifestyle, mistaken beliefs, social interactions, and goals of behavior (Maniacci et al., 2014). Events that happened on a regular basis, such as going to Grandma's house every summer, do not qualify as early recollections. To count as an early recollection, the memory must be an event that happened just a single time. If the client cannot remember anything that happened, we usually ask him or her to tell us about something that someone told about a time when he or she was little—like a family story.

In Adlerian play therapy, gathering early recollections is one option for developing an understanding of a child's lifestyle. With children younger than 6 or 7, we sometimes have difficulty engaging them in the memory process necessary for success with this strategy, so we often do not try to gather them. This does not mean that you could not try to use this technique with younger children, but you will need to be especially patient and creative to interest younger children in remembering. Another option is to hope for spontaneous stories about "when I was little . . . ," which can be pretty funny coming from a 4-year-old. My (KMW) 4-year-old spontaneously tells me stories of when he was a baby. He insists that his sister taught him to walk and do many other things. His sister was not born when he learned to walk. He cares not about the pesky details that interfere with his portrayal of his past. Regardless, what it tells me is that he relies on his sister for support and encouragement. His existence is dependent on her existence, and he can't imagine a time without her. This is probably true given their 22-month difference in age.

Before asking the child for early memories, you will want to establish rapport, observe the child's usual behavior, and gather information about the child's family constellation. These preliminary procedures will give you a basis for deciding whether to ask the child to draw, tell, use a sand tray, or act out using puppets or dolls the early recollections. This should be based on the child's favored form of expression. The preliminary procedures also give you a context for understanding the meaning of the recollections and how they relate to the child's lifestyle. You will want to gather between five and seven early recollections. With a child, this should happen over the course of several sessions because the child may become bored and rebellious if the counselor expects him or her to spend an entire session just doing early recollections.

Depending on the chosen modality of expression, you can say something like,

- "Draw me a picture of something that happened when you were very little."
- "Tell me a story about something that happened when you were younger."
- "Use the dolls, puppets, or sand tray figures to show me a story about something you did when you were a little kid."

If the child uses drawing to capture the early recollection, you will want to ask him or her to tell about what is happening in the picture. No matter what form of expression the child uses, you should write down everything he or she says (during or immediately after the session). Detailed information will help you to interpret what the early memory means to the child. It is also important to ask the child to describe any feelings associated with the memory and to guess what age he or she was when the event occurred.

After the child has related several early recollections, the play therapist begins to look for the central theme of each memory and the overall pattern among the memories. By considering the following questions (Dewey, 1978; Eckstein & Kern, 2009), the therapist can begin to formulate ideas about the child's lifestyle:

- What is the feeling tone of each recollection? Is there a pattern in the feeling tones of the different recollections?
- What is the focus of each memory? What stands out as being the most important or vivid part of the memory? Is there a pattern in the foci of the different memories?
- Is the client part of each memory? If so, is the client an observer or a participant? Is there a pattern of being an observer or participant throughout the various memories?
- If the client is part of the recollection, is he or she alone or with others? Is there an intermemory pattern of being alone or with others?
- If the client is part of the memory, what is his or her relationship to the other people in the memory? Is there an intermemory pattern of relationships?
- If the client is part of the memory, does he or she give to or take from others? Is there a pattern?
- Is there a major concern with people or material possessions or the situation? Is there a pattern among memories?
- Does the client appear to feel or act superior to others or inferior to others in the memory? Is there a pattern?
- Is the client in control of the situation or is someone else in control? If the client is in control, how is she or he gaining the power? If someone else is in control, who is it, and how is he or she getting control? What are the patterns?
- Is the client taking care of others, or are others taking care of the client? If the client is taking care of others, how is this happening? If others are taking care of the client, how is this happening? What are they taking care of for the client? What are the patterns?
- What emotions does the client associate with the memory? How strong are those emotions? What does the client think the emotions are about? What are the patterns?
- Is the client conforming or rebelling? What are the patterns?

Children's early recollections can be distilled versions of their lifestyles. By examining these early memories and looking for patterns, the Adlerian play therapist begins to comprehend children's attitudes toward themselves, their relationships with other people, and their views about the world.

Functioning at Life Tasks

As defined in Adlerian theory, there are five tasks that must be mastered in our lives: *work, love, friendship, spirituality/existential,* and *self* (Maniacci et al., 2014; Sweeney, 2009). For children, we define the work life task as their functioning at school, the love life task as their relationships with other family members and their level of connectedness in their family, and the friendship tasks as their interactions with and attitudes about other children. Many children have not yet developed strong beliefs about the more abstract questions of how and why human beings exist, so for them the spirituality/existential life task can be defined as a sense

of purposiveness, optimism, values, and their beliefs about some kind of
higher being. Sweeney (2009) defined the task of self (or self-direction)
as including a sense of self-worth, a sense of control, realistic beliefs,
emotional awareness and coping, problem solving and creativity, sense of
humor, nutrition, exercise, self-care, stress management, gender identity,
and cultural identity. As we think about children and their functioning
at this life task, all of these elements can play a part in how well they are
doing at the task of self.

Observation of free play, interactions among family members, and
school behavior and information supplied by the child, the parents, other
family members, the child's teacher, and the school counselor can give
you a great deal of information about the child's functioning at life tasks.
It is also helpful to set up specific play situations, using school play, the
dollhouse, puppets, animal figures, and baby dolls, to investigate how
the child feels about, thinks about, and behaves in relation to each of
these tasks.

To explore the life task of friendship, you can ask the child questions
like: How do you get along with other kids? How would you describe your
best friend? What do you like about him or her? What does he or she like
about you? What kinds of things do you do together? Who are your other
friends? Where do you see them? What kinds of activities do you do with
them? Do you prefer to play with lots of kids all at once, just a few kids,
just one other kid, or by yourself? If you could change anything about
your relationships with other kids, what would you change? You could
also do art or sand tray activities about friendship, like asking the child
to use a body outline or body map (Santen, 2015) to design the perfect
friend, do a sand tray filled with figures that represent the qualities the
child is seeking in friends, or bring songs to sessions that express his or
her ideas about friendship. Asking the child to do a story or puppet show
about friendship is another way to explore this life task, as is reading
books about friends and having conversations with the child about what
happened in the books. With older children, having them write poems
(Kaufman, Chalmers, & Rosenberg, 2014) or making magnetic poetry
compositions about friendship is often fun and enlightening. You could
even do a variation of video play therapy (Frey, 2006; L. Rubin, 2008),
playing out (through puppetry or sand trays) the friendships in movies,
television shows, and video games that interest the child.

For assessing the child's functioning at the life task of work/school,
you can ask the following kinds of questions: How do things go for you
at school? What do you like best at school? What is your favorite subject?
What do you like least about school? What is your least favorite subject?
What would you be rather doing than going to school? What do you do
best at school? What does your teacher like about you? The principal?
The school counselor? The custodian? What would you like to change
about school? What do you get in trouble for at school? What happens
when you get in trouble at school? (What are the consequences, if any?)
Who disciplines you at school? How do you feel about that person? How
do you react when you get disciplined at school? You can also observe

the child in spontaneous school play or suggest that you play school together, either role-playing or with puppets or figures. It is also helpful to ask the child to do kinetic school drawing (KSD; Knoff & Prout, 1985) or some other variation of a kinetic school _____ (can be a sand tray, an interpretive dance, playing an instrument or some other expressive activity designed to explore the child's thoughts, feelings and perceptions of his or her experience at school). (See Appendix E for instructions on how to administer the KSD and questions to ask for further information on school interaction.)

For children, the love task is really about their connection to their family. The questions you would ask would be similar to lifestyle questions you would ask in exploring their family atmosphere and family constellation, such as: How would you describe each person in your family? Which of your brothers and sisters is most different from you? How is he or she different from you? (In a family of just two children, ask how the other sibling is different from the client.) Which of your brothers and sisters is most like you? How is he or she like you? (In a family of just two children, ask how the other sibling is like the client.) What kind of person is your dad? What kind of person is your mom? Which of your parents are you most like? How are you like him or her? What do you get in trouble for at home? What happens when you get into trouble at home? (What are the consequences, if any?) What do you do (how do you react) when you get into trouble at home? Which of your parents is stricter? What is he/she strict about? What happens when your parents disagree? What does your family do for fun together? If you could change anything about your family, what would you change? Obviously, you can also observe the child in family play or ask him or her to play with you in the doll house or the kitchen area. You can do a KFD or some other kinetic family activity (Dance! Art! Music!). With a child who does not like to draw, you could do an animal photograph collage of animals that represent each person in the family, a sticker collage with stickers symbolizing family members and their relationships, or a sand tray with figures representing each family member.

To explore the life task of self, you would ask lifestyle questions like: If you had three wishes, what would they be? If anything in your life could be different, what would you want to change? If you could be any toy in the playroom, what toy would you be? What do you like about that toy? What hurts your feelings? What is it about _____ that hurts your feelings? How do you act when your feelings are hurt? How do your parents and other people react when you feel hurt? What are you good at? What do you wish you were better at doing? What do you like about yourself? What do other people like about you? What do you wish you could change about yourself? You could also do art activities like a self-portrait in paint or clay (Sobol, 2010), the Rosebush, the Color-Your-Life technique (O'Connor & New, 2002), body outlines or body maps, and so forth. Asking a child who is interested in sports or video games to develop a story about a popular sports figure (Crenshaw & Barker, 2008) or a character in a video game (Enfield & Grosser, 2008; Riviere, 2008) may be another way to explore this life task.

For exploring the child's mastery of the spiritual/existential life task, you can ask the child's parents about spiritual issues related to the child and the family and you can ask the child questions like: What do you believe about God? Do you go to services? What do you do there? What do you like about it? What do you learn there? What do you think happens when people die? You can also initiate art activities such as drawing pictures of God, the Buddha, Allah, and other spiritual or religious figures or pictures of what happens when you die. Depending on the family's religious traditions, you could also read books to the child, such as *What Is God?* (Boritzer, 1990), *What Do You Believe? (Big Questions;* Star, 2011), *If I Could Ask God Anything: Awesome Bible Answers for Curious Kids* (Slattery, 2010), *Buddha at Bedtime* (Nagaraja, 2008), *Old Turtle* (D. Wood, 2007), or *A Solstice Tree for Jenny* (Shragg, 2001).

Lifestyle Conceptualization

It is essential to remember that the purpose of gathering all of this information is to help form a picture of the client and his or her world to be able to help the client gain insight into lifestyle and make changes in attitudes, perceptions, emotional responses, and behaviors. On the basis of the information gathered about the family atmosphere, the family constellation and psychological birth-order position, and the early recollections, a picture of the child's perceptions, basic convictions, private logic, ways of gaining significance, and goals of behavior emerges. Putting all of these data together, the Adlerian play therapist can start to formulate lifestyle hypotheses and the lifestyle conceptualization of the child, which are then used as the basis for planning the rest of the play therapy process.

Case Example

Continuing from Chapter 5, the case example in this section illustrates how an Adlerian play therapist can gather information about a child during the second phase of therapy and use this exploration to begin to formulate guesses about the child's lifestyle.

In my third through seventh play therapy sessions with Phoebe and in the parent consultation sessions with Mr. and Mrs. Simon, I gathered information about family atmosphere, family constellation, early recollections, and functioning at life tasks to form an understanding of Phoebe's assets, Crucial Cs, goals of misbehavior, personality priorities, mistaken beliefs, and private logic. Because I believed some of the dynamics of their own personalities were having an impact on Phoebe's behavior and attitudes, I also decided to do an informal conceptualization of both of her grandparents. Consequently, I gathered information from them about their families of origin. I chatted briefly with her teacher, who described Phoebe's in-class behaviors and her own skills and strategies for working with Phoebe. Both she and I felt comfortable with how she was handling Phoebe's behaviors. I decided it was not necessary to gather information for a lifestyle conceptualization of her.

In talking to Mr. and Mrs. Simon, I found that they had family backgrounds with many similarities. They had both grown up in working-class families, with single mothers, multiple children, and financial struggles. The atmospheres in both families were unpredictable and discouraged, characterized by inappropriate boundaries, erratic discipline, and worry about finances. Mr. Simon's mother was an alcoholic who was sometimes in recovery and sometimes using. She had difficulty maintaining a job because of her struggles with substances. She was involved in the Christian church when she was in phases of recovery, attending several different Protestant denominations, forcing her children to attend with her. Mr. Simon had never met his biological father. His mother had numerous boyfriends throughout his childhood but never moved in with any of them. The family moved around quite a bit because they could not consistently pay the rent on the apartments where they lived, but they were never homeless. Mr. Simon was the older of two children and felt responsible for taking care of his sibling and his mother.

Mrs. Simon's mother and father were married until her father died of cancer when she was 4 years old. Her mother never dated and immersed herself in the lives of her children. She worked at a low-paying job checking groceries in the local market. Mrs. Simon's entire family was heavily involved in the Catholic church. The interactions in her extended family of origin tend to be rather volatile and filled with conflict, sometimes about religion but also about finances, child rearing, and values. Mrs. Simon was the youngest of four children. She was usually doted on by her older siblings and her mother, but her mother used shaming and guilt as her primary parenting strategies. As a child, Mrs. Simon was quite adventurous and creative, and she tried to make the best out of most situations. For example, she made games out of odds and ends around the house, chased and caught bugs, and served as her mom's sidekick when she thought her mom felt lonely. Mrs. Simon's mother believed she was the last living part of her husband and gave her special attention and treatment.

As adults, Mr. and Mrs. Simon shared similar values of hard work, financial stability, and partnered relationships. Both of them had been raised by single mothers who had struggled, and they believed very strongly that children should grow up with both parents who worked at maintaining a strong marital relationship. They both also wanted to practice a faith that taught peacefulness, mindfulness, and harmony, which they believed they had found in Buddhism. Mrs. Simon was intent on sharing spirituality with her husband and extended family; Mr. Simon agreed to practice Buddhism with his wife but was a bit less invested. Although they had similar values and objectives, the methods that they used to operationalize them differed.

Mr. Simon had developed pleasing and comfort as his personality priorities. He reported that he didn't have many friends and found it hard to interact with others. He had the mistaken belief that he was not likable. I concluded that the Crucial C of connect was a challenge for him. Mr. Simon didn't like to take risks for fear of not succeeding or creating problems in his otherwise conflict-free life, which indicated that the

Crucial C of courage was also an area in which he struggled. Mrs. Simon had developed pleasing and achieving as her personality priorities. She believed that she needed to prove that she was worthy of being alive and needed a great deal of reassurance in her relationships with others, trying to make sure people would like her by not setting appropriate boundaries. She believed the only way she counted was by taking care of others. Both of them expressed that they felt great sadness and emptiness as a result of not having a father in their lives and wanted to make absolutely sure that their children and their granddaughter, Phoebe, felt loved and supported by as many people as possible. Mrs. Simon felt particularly sad and responsible for Phoebe's happiness because of her own loss of a parent when she was a child. In talking with them, I acknowledged that their own issues were getting in the way of their being as consistent and supportive of Phoebe as they wanted to be, which was contributing to the problems. I also tried to reassure them that the difficulties were not insurmountable. I suggested that their bringing their granddaughter to counseling affirmed their care and commitment to Phoebe and their son.

I had some information about Phoebe's perceptions about her family from the picture she drew and the kitchen play during the first two sessions. I wanted to gather more data about how she saw the family atmosphere and how she felt about the change of living arrangements. In the third session, I asked Phoebe to play in the doll house with me. She said she didn't want to play with dolls and wanted to play in the sandbox. Showing respect for her decisions, I suggested we play with the animals in the sandbox, and she agreed. Without further direction, she picked two giraffes and the two dolphins and placed them in one corner of a square sandbox. As she played with them, they appeared to interact kindly with one another. I asked her to tell me about the animals. She said, "The dolphins and giraffes live together. They make food, read books, watch TV, and play outside." I metacommunicated about her play and choice of animals. "They are getting along. I've never seen a giraffe and dolphin play together." She responded with, "They are not supposed to live together, but the dolphins had to move because the ocean was getting dangerous." (Although I didn't comment about this, I noticed that the animals she chose were typically docile creatures even though they lived in the wild.) There was a lot of space left in the sandbox, and I decided to ask what kinds of things happen in the other parts of the sandbox. She readily followed my lead and started to talk about other things that happen in the lives of these animals. She started by putting another dolphin in one corner of the sandbox and then buried it. To see where she would take it, I said, "You've buried that one." She said,

> This is the mother dolphin and was the best dolphin ever. She was like a princess dolphin who was loved by every other sea animal. She had lots of friends, was super smart, and was very pretty. She misses her baby dolphin.

As she said this, she looked back at the two dolphins and the giraffes. She looked thoughtful and I said, "I bet the baby dolphin misses her too."

With that, she went to the toy animals and picked a variety of animals such as tigers, lions, monkeys, gorillas, and zebras. She placed these in rows in a third corner of the sandbox. The animals were partnered with like animals (i.e., lions together, tigers together, and so on). I metacommunicated about the partnerships. She indicated that these animals were in school and said,

> The lions only like to play with other lions, and the zebras only like to play with other zebras. Zebras can't play with lions because they don't like each other. Animals don't like to play with animals that look different from them.

I pointed out her pattern of pairing animals that "look the same" and having distinct areas in the sand box. Lastly, she picked three toy dog figures and put them in the last corner of the sandbox. She looked briefly at that corner and then added a small dolphin to that corner. I said, "It seems like dolphins and dogs can play together even though they don't look alike." Without skipping a beat, she said, "Dogs are nicer than lions and tigers and other jungle animals. They will play with all other animals EVEN ocean animals. They aren't mean and bossy like tigers and lions."

Because Phoebe consistently discussed the animals within the metaphor, I decided to ask my questions indirectly, sticking to the metaphor rather than asking questions directly about her family. I asked her to tell me about the giraffe and dolphin family, what they liked to do together, what each one did well, what things they each got in trouble for doing, what contributed to their happiness, what they felt sad about, and what they would wish if they had three wishes. Phoebe asserted that the dolphin and giraffe family got along, the daddy dolphin (whom she identified as such) wasn't home much, and the baby dolphin was bored a lot. She said that the family liked to watch television, go for walks outside, and take care of the family animals. Phoebe told me, "The grandma giraffe is good at reading, cleaning, and snuggling. The grandpa giraffe is good at making pancakes and driving the car." She shared that, "The giraffes never get in trouble because they are big and get to make the rules. The baby dolphin gets in the most trouble because she doesn't like doing what the giraffes want to do." She said, "The giraffes never leave the dolphin alone. They want her to be a giraffe like them, but she can't be a giraffe. I think the giraffes are sad that the baby dolphin isn't a giraffe and they are happy when the dolphin does giraffe things. The baby dolphin is sad when she doesn't get to see her friends anymore and only gets to play with the giraffes." I pointed out that she didn't talk about the daddy dolphin and she said, "The daddy dolphin is always away. I don't really know much about him." By this time, it seemed that the baby dolphin was symbolic for how she saw herself (a fish out of water?), so I only asked about its three wishes. She told me that the baby dolphin wished "to go back to the ocean with her friends, her mommy, and her old home." She also wished others would stop telling her what to do and treating her like a baby. Phoebe was very cooperative in answering my questions, staying in the metaphor the entire time. Because our time was up, I did not ask about the other corners. I did ask her if I could take two photographs of the animals in the sandbox—one for her and one for me. She said that I could, and she was excited to show her grandparents the picture. I chose to not ask her to put the toys away, telling her that this week we would just leave things as they were but that the next week we would go back to picking up together.

As I thought about Phoebe's work with the animals and the sandbox, I recognized that she had revealed more information about the family atmosphere and how it was affecting her lifestyle. Phoebe seemed to perceive the family atmosphere as one in which she did not have a lot of power for decision making and yet was somewhat responsible for her grandparents' happiness. I think she also recognized, on some level, that her grandparents and father loved her and wanted her to be happy. On the basis of this interaction and my sessions with her grandparents, I believed that the Simon family manifested positive characteristics of love and support. However, at times Phoebe seemed to feel overly responsible for the happiness of her family members. She felt smothered and too protected with little opportunity to practice making decisions. Because she didn't live near other children and didn't have many friends yet at school, she didn't get to practice sharing power and negotiating relationships with people her own age either. Phoebe had learned that by taking a strong stand through being demanding or oppositional, she could get her own way and prove to herself that she was important and in control of herself.

Through her work in the sand, Phoebe had also told me great deal about her assets, her goals of misbehavior, her Crucial Cs, her personality priorities, and her functioning at the life tasks of family, friendships, and self. She seemed to feel rather suffocated or isolated in the family; she was either alone or being doted on in a way that protected her from making mistakes or trying new adventures. I thought this was partially because of her status as the only child and partially because of her grandmother having the similar experience of losing a parent at a young age. Mrs. Simon was trying to protect Phoebe from additional pain, which created frustration and feelings of being controlled from Phoebe. The distinct corners of the sandbox might be representative of feelings that the different areas of her life were not particularly well-integrated. In most of her interactions with adults, she was treated like a baby who needed to be constantly pampered and protected. In this way, she wasn't learning to cope with hardships or challenges. Both her grandparents and father cared deeply for her and wanted to make up for the death of her mother. Before moving in with her grandparents, she was used to always getting her way all the time. After she moved in with her grandparents, Mr. and Mrs. Simon attempted to take a bit more of a parental role and less of a grandparent role, which created confusion for Phoebe. She had to completely change schools, friends, and teachers. These changes created uncertainty, which fueled her desire for control. The more she felt out of control, the more she became demanding toward teachers and friends. Her behavior pushed away the other students, creating more distance and isolation between her and them. I believed that Phoebe was experimenting with how to find a place of significance in the family, one in which she felt like she contributed to the family and was free to make decisions. If she was not given the opportunity to make age-appropriate decisions and have developmentally appropriate responsibilities, she would "grab" power by being demanding and rude.

In our fourth session, I worked on gathering some more information about Phoebe's lifestyle, with a special interest in what she made of being biracial. First, I asked her to tell me some general early recollections. She declined to tell me any stories or act out any stories about when she was younger. I then tried to get a focused early recollection about a specific issue. I explained that sometimes when I was little, I felt kind of weird and different because I was poor and had ugly clothes, and I wondered if she remembered any times when she felt different from other kids or other people. Phoebe was very quiet for a long time, and I was beginning to worry that I had been too direct or that she had not really understood my question, but I just sat quietly waiting for her to respond. She finally told me a story about a time at her old school when the other kids asked why she didn't have a mom and why she didn't look like her dad. Phoebe related that she had tried to talk to her dad about this incident and her feelings, and her father had told her that the kids were just being mean and she shouldn't pay attention to them. He also told her stories about her mother being from Mexico, speaking Spanish, and knowing how to make lots of yummy food. She shared that he started to cry when they talked about her mom and she decided to never talk to him about her again. Phoebe commented that she wanted to talk about her mom because she didn't remember her, but was scared to talk to her dad because she didn't want her dad to be sad. After she mentioned this, we had a play disruption. She abruptly changed the subject and went to the doll house to play. Although I metacommunicated about my belief that she was un-comfortable about our conversation, she ignored me and stayed immersed in her play in the doll house the rest of the session.

I brought up the topic of Phoebe being biracial with her grandparents and got encouraging feedback. They worried about this, but thought that it wasn't a problem because she didn't talk about it at home. This also created an opportunity for me to express my belief that Phoebe was reluctant to share her feelings with others because she didn't want to up-set them. I told them that I believed Phoebe wanted to learn more about her mother and might feel more connected to her entire family if they could share warm and fun stories about Alicia. Mr. Simon was uncertain about this, but agreed to talk with Christopher about this possibility. Mrs. Simon agreed that this could be helpful and related it to her experiences of learning about her father.

In the fifth session, I decided to switch back to a less directive approach to see what information I could gather through Phoebe's free play. During this session, she played almost exclusively by herself, without asking me to play until the very end of the session. She painted pictures and played with the kitchen set. She cradled and fed the baby dolls. She played with some dinosaurs, having several of the bigger dinosaurs tell the smaller dinosaurs what to do and having the smaller dinosaurs argue with the bigger ones and just ignore them when they were being bossy.

I believed that the baby doll play was about her relationship with her mother and grandmother, she was feeling loved and cared for by her grandmother, and she was missing her mother. I also thought it might be connected to her feeling like a baby even though she was now a "big girl" who was capable of doing many things on her own. It seemed to me that the play with the dinosaurs was about the family constellation; her functioning at the life tasks of family and self and her goals of misbehavior, Crucial Cs, and personality priority. She felt that she had no power or control in her family or in her life and could act out getting control through the dinosaurs. She seemed to be developing the goal of power—trying to overpower others to make sure that she had some control over herself. This related to her personality priority, which seemed to be control. It was my interpretation that she felt pretty courageous but was struggling with the Crucial Cs of connect, capable, and count. She was not sure how she could connect, what she could do that demonstrated her competence, or whether she counted in the family.

Toward the end of the session, Phoebe took the lions, tigers, gorillas, and zebras from the earlier session and arranged them into groups. Then, she gave me the dolphin that she earlier identified as the "baby." She told me to move it from group to group, asking if they wanted to be friends. She spoke for the lions, tigers, and zebras, telling the dolphin to go away, that they did not want to be friends with her because she was different from them. She asked me to have the dolphin get mad and start jumping on the other animals to "try to make them be friends." I reflected the feelings of the various animals, especially the dolphin, who I believed represented Phoebe. As we played this, Phoebe seemed very sad, which I reflected and she acknowledged. Going back to the metaphor, I said, "I bet the dolphin is sad too. She wants to be friends with the other animals and doesn't know why they won't be her friends. She isn't sure how to make friends."

I wondered if this play was related to two different strands in Phoebe's lifestyle—one related to finding a place in the world and the other related to her feelings and evolving beliefs about being biracial or looking different from the other kids in her new school. (The children in the new school were predominantly Caucasian, with less than 3% of any other racial identity.) These play themes suggested that she was really struggling with understanding how she could fit with others and be accepted. She seemed to be struggling with the life tasks of friendship and love, unsure of how she could gain acceptance from her peers and from the other members of her family. Play from some of her previous sessions (the uncertainty in the first session, the compartmentalizing during her sand work) could easily have also been related to her wondering about how being biracial affected her ability to belong.

Phoebe came into the sixth session angry. Her grandmother reported that she had gotten into trouble at school for shoving another child, had thrown a tantrum because they were coming to therapy, and refused to come into my office. Mrs. Simon was unsure of what to do and bribed Phoebe with a trip to the toy store for coming into the session with me. Phoebe spent almost the entire session ignoring me and shooting the dart gun at the wall. I did not try to push her into interacting with me; I reflected her feelings of being angry and frustrated. I metacommunicated about getting in trouble at school and feeling like nobody understood her. I spent much of the session just watching her, trying to silently convey my unconditional regard for her. At the end of the session, she painted a picture of a face with tears running down the cheeks, tore it up, threw it into the trash can, and ran out of the room.

Phoebe came into our seventh session much happier than she had been in the previous session. She was very excited because she had made a new friend at school. I asked her to draw a picture of herself, her new friend, some other kids in her class, and her teacher. She consented to do this, and while she drew, I asked her some of the lifestyle questions from Appendix D about her friends and about how things went for her at school. She drew a picture of herself and two other figures. As she drew, she told me that she had a lot of friends at her last school and didn't have any friends at this school. She said that people were nice in the classroom but "nobody plays with me at recess or sits by me at lunch." When she was done drawing, I asked her a few questions from the list in Appendix E about the drawing. Phoebe believed that her new friend liked her because she had "been getting along better at school and with my teacher. The new girl didn't know I used to get in a lot of trouble so she was nice to me." When she had talked about the drawing for a short time, Phoebe decided to play with the cash register, assigning me to be the "checker-outer" and her to be the "shopper." As she shopped, she said that she was buying "gifts" for her friend, for herself, and her family members. She also was intentional about buying "Mexican food" and making sure that I knew she was buying such food. I found this interesting for a few reasons. For starters, typically when I play cashier with children, the cashier is the one in control. I metacommunicated about her sharing power, her desire to please her friend by buying her gifts, and fear of her friend deciding to not be friends with her. I also metacommunicated about her feeling connected to her mother and her desire to want to be like her mother.

Although I would continue to gather more information in subsequent sessions, I now believed that I had enough information to begin the process of conceptualizing Phoebe's lifestyle and making a treatment plan for working with her. I also thought that I could make a valid assessment of how her grandparents' lifestyles were having an impact on their interaction with her and develop a plan for helping them make some necessary changes in their parenting roles and the relationships within the family.

In the continuation of this case example in Chapters 8, 9, and 10, I outline my conceptualization and treatment plans for Phoebe, her grandparents, and her father. I describe some of the strategies I used to help Phoebe gain insight into her lifestyle, decide whether she wanted to make changes, and learn and practice some new skills and attitudes. I also discuss techniques I used in consulting with Phoebe's family to help them to better understand her and begin to make shifts in the family atmosphere and the parenting strategies to support the changes Phoebe decided to make.

Summary

In the second phase of Adlerian play therapy, the therapist uses specific strategies to explore the family atmosphere, family constellation, early recollections, and functioning at life tasks of the child and of the parents (and teachers when appropriate). The purpose of this process is to gather enough information about the child's assets, Crucial Cs, goals of misbehavior, personality priorities, mistaken beliefs, and private logic to be able to form a clear picture of the child and his or her social context. This picture will guide the therapist in helping the child and his or her family (and school personnel) make changes in attitudes, perceptions, thoughts, feelings, and behaviors during the third and fourth phases of the Adlerian play therapy process.

Further Resources

Family atmosphere:

> http://www.adlerian.us/atmosph.htm
> http://www.lifecourseinstitute.com/majorcon.htm

Birth order:

> http://www.adlerian.us/birthord.htm
> http://www.ncbi.nlm.nih.gov/pmc/articles/PMC3375868/
> https://www.psychologytoday.com/blog/fulfillment-any-age/201305/
> is-birth-order-destiny

Early recollections:

> https://ojs.lib.byu.edu/spc/index.php/IssuesInReligionAndPsychotherapy/
> article/viewFile/171/170

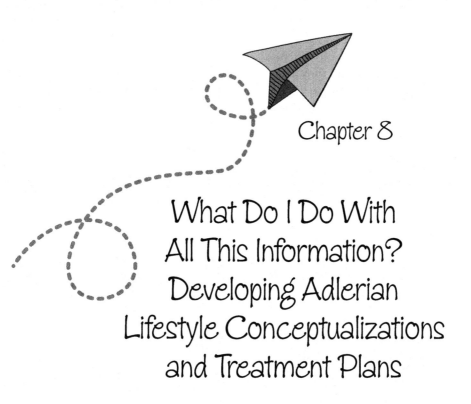

Chapter 8

What Do I Do With All This Information? Developing Adlerian Lifestyle Conceptualizations and Treatment Plans

Using the information gathered during the second phase of play therapy, the Adlerian play therapist formulates a conceptualization of the child that will help to guide the rest of the therapeutic process. This is that pivotal point when the therapist moves from understanding the client to helping the client to identify places where change is needed and initiate the processes of making changes. The therapist integrates information obtained through (a) observation of the child's play themes, the child's relationships with others, the child's artwork, and the child's behavior both in and out of the playroom; (b) the child's answers to the therapist's questions; and (c) interviews with parents (and sometimes with teachers). If the therapist believes that the adults in the child's life are significantly contributing to any problems experienced by the child, it is helpful to develop lifestyle conceptualizations for parents and teachers as well. Even when the adults are not contributing to the child's struggles, they can often help support the child in making changes, so conceptualizing parents or teachers can be useful. The play therapist conceptualizes the child and other people in the child's life and then devises a treatment plan for working with the child and anyone else that needs to make shifts in cognition, emotions, behavior, or attitudes to support the changes the child makes in the third and fourth phases of play therapy.

In Adlerian play therapy, you will not go into a session with a list of hypotheses about the client's lifestyle and explain them to the client. (Though it is kind of fun to picture the look on a child's face if you attempted this!)

It is important that you share the conceptualization with the client, but in a gradual, subtle way. In the third phase of Adlerian play therapy, helping the child gain insight into his or her lifestyle, you will metacommunicate and make guesses, use metaphors and art techniques, and offer interpretations of conversations and play to help the child gain a clearer and more objective sense of how he or she sees self, others, and the world and how she or he acts as if these perceptions are true. In consultation sessions, the therapist works to help parents (and teachers) cultivate a better understanding of the child's lifestyle, their own lifestyles, and how the interaction of the lifestyles of all concerned parties interact to affect the child.

Lifestyle Conceptualization

In developing the lifestyle conceptualization, the play therapist summarizes the critical elements of information gathered during the second phase of play therapy and generates a list of lifestyle convictions (the basic ideas on which clients base their behavior) and a list of behaviors that stem from these beliefs. (See Appendix G for a sample form to use for this process.) The play therapist can also examine clients' private logic as a further means of understanding their cognitions, attitudes, emotions, and behaviors. This process is designed to give the therapist a dynamic picture of clients, which methods they use to gain a sense of belonging, and the kinds of support they will need to help make shifts in their self-defeating patterns of thinking, feeling, and behaving.

Lifestyle Conceptualization of the Child

We know there are a lot of different things to consider when Adlerian play therapists conceptualize people, and we believe this is directly related to complexity and creativity of individuals. To aid in the conceptualization task (and because we believe it is necessary to effectively and efficiently work with clients and we want to make things as easy for you as we possibly can), we have provided a list of important areas to consider in conceptualizing lifestyle. The first step in developing the lifestyle conceptualization for a child is to summarize the following information and explore how the child's perceptions, attitudes, and behavior are affected by these elements of his or her lifestyle: (a) the child's assets; (b) the child's functioning at each of the five life tasks; (c) play themes; (d) the child's perceptions of his or her psychological birth order and how those perceptions affect the child's attitudes and behaviors; (e) the child's perceptions of the family atmosphere and how those perceptions affect the child's attitudes and functioning; (f) the themes in the child's early recollections that represent the child's view of self, others, and the world; (g) the child's goals of misbehavior; (h) the child's mastery of each of the Crucial Cs; and (i) the child's personality priorities and how they play out in interactions with others.

Assets
It is essential to develop a list of the child's assets, including positive personal traits, talents, skills, and attitudes. This list is the basis for most of the encouraging comments you will make throughout the relationship. It

is also invaluable in helping you reframe the child's behavior for parents and teachers. (It is much easier to counter negatives if you have a list of positives in your back pocket, so to speak.)

Take into account that sometimes what others perceive as a liability or problem for the child may contain the germ of an asset if the child is willing to make some shifts in the way he or she does things. You may have to look underneath destructive behaviors and attitudes to find potential assets. For instance, Bakr, who refuses to share toys with friends and makes up mean songs about others, has assets of assertiveness, creativity, and musical talent. In our case example, Phoebe does not have friends at school and often creates opportunities for other children to dislike her. Although her current use of this talent is concerning for teachers and gets in the way of her building relationships, she also has an asset of being determined and intentional.

Functioning at Life Tasks

In this part of our conceptualization, we frequently combine a quantitative and qualitative approach to assessing children's functioning at the life tasks. We use a 1-to-10 scaling system for each of the life tasks, with 1 indicating that the child is really struggling in this area and 10 indicating that the child is performing optimally in this area. We make qualitative observations about the child and how he or she is functioning in each of the five areas (work, love, friendship, spirituality/existential, and self). For instance, in assessing Lin-Joo's functioning on the life task of friendship, we might note that she seems to have many friends, but they are not the kind of friends her parents and teacher would choose for her. They are children who get into a lot of trouble at school. For Jorge's functioning at the life task of self, we might comment that he has a strong sense of self, demonstrated by spontaneity, creative problem-solving skills, and a witty sense of humor, but that he tends to use these skills in ways that demonstrate a lack of regard for others and their feelings. In describing Ingrid's functioning at the life task of school, we might note that overall her progress in school seems to be lagging behind those of the other children in her class but she excels in math and science.

You will need to consider information from the parents, teachers, and the child in deciding how the child is functioning at each life task. It is essential to consider that there may be differences between the child's perceptions and adults' perceptions of the child's functioning. If there are discrepancies, it is helpful to note these, perhaps even using two or more different sets of scaling and comments to represent the variety of opinions about the child's functioning.

Play Themes

In this section of the conceptualization, you will want to make a list of the important themes that are expressed in the child's play, metaphors, sand trays, and art making. Themes would include patterns in the way the characters in the child's play, art, sand trays, and stories interact with others, react to stressful situations, work to solve problems, deal with circumstances that are out of their control, talk about themselves and their capabilities, and so forth—whatever you believe will help in developing an understanding of the child's attitudes and behaviors.

You should also look for patterns in the child's relationship with the therapist. Does the child include you in the play? Does the child engage in solitary play? Does the child ignore you? Does the child act in a seductive manner toward you? Does the child seem to like and respect you? Is the child suspicious and distrustful of you? Does the child seem to find your attention soothing? Does the child try to engage you in arguing or power struggles? Any patterns in the interaction between the two of you can shed light on the child's usual patterns of relating to others.

Psychological Birth Order–Family Constellation

As noted in Chapter 7, the child's perception of his or her birth-order position and what it means are much more important than the actual ordinal sequencing of children in the family constellation. The goal in this section of the conceptualization is to examine any information that can give you clues about how the child perceives the practical implications of his or her birth-order position in this particular family. By considering whether the child is "typical" of his or her birth-order position, you can examine the dynamics of the family and explore messages communicated within the family about the role of each birth-order position. Because birth-order positions have specific assets and liabilities, you can use this process to organize your thoughts about ways to capitalize assets and remediate weaknesses. This exploration can also help you discover the child's basic convictions about self, others, and the world and his or her private logic around the rules inherent in that particular birth-order position.

Family Atmosphere

As with family constellation, the key to conceptualizing the family atmosphere is to consider the child's perception of the atmosphere and how his or her perception affects his or her lifestyle convictions and behavior. (You might be noticing that we care more about the child's perception about what happened than we do about what actually happened—it is kind of an Adlerian theme.) As you think about family atmosphere during the conceptualization process, you will need to integrate what the child has discussed and demonstrated about family dynamics during conversations, play, and art projects; what the therapist has observed during family interactions; and what the therapist has gathered in the way of information during interviews with parents (and teachers). With some families, the family atmosphere plays such a key role in the child's thinking about self, others, and the world that it is necessary for the therapist to develop a formal lifestyle conceptualization of the parents. For other families, it is not necessary to do a full analysis of the parents' lifestyles. Considering the impact of parental attitudes, personality priorities, Crucial Cs, and parenting skills on the family atmosphere will be sufficient. The interaction between the parents' lifestyles and the child's lifestyle is a critical factor that influences the messages the child incorporates into his or her views of self, others, and the world.

Early Recollections

If you have obtained early recollections from the child, you must analyze the themes in those memories for clues about the child's lifestyle. This section of the conceptualization is a summary of those themes and the implications for the child's current attitudes, cognitions, emotions, relationships, and behaviors. (See Chapter 7 for questions to consider in analyzing the early recollections for patterns.)

Goals of Misbehavior

This part of the conceptualization consists of a list of troublesome behaviors, adult reactions to those behaviors (including emotional responses and corrective action exhibited in response to the behaviors), and the child's reaction to adult responses to the behavior. You will look for patterns in these elements, hoping to find one or two typical goals of misbehavior for this child. It can be helpful to look for patterns across and differences between the child's goals of misbehavior in a variety of relationships and settings. For instance, Kent may be striving for power in his relationship with his mother but for attention in his class at school. It would also be helpful to note if certain reactions from adults are more or less successful in helping the child correct the misbehavior. This will help you generate solutions to problematic behaviors, which might include asking adults to shift their reactions and behavior in situations where the child's negative behaviors are working for the child.

Crucial Cs

Successful incorporation of all four of the Crucial Cs into the lifestyle is important to the emotional well-being of children, so this section of the conceptualization is devoted to tracking their acquisition of each of the Crucial Cs. You will want to make a global assessment of how the child is integrating ideas about each of the Crucial Cs into his or her perceptions about self, others, and the world.

As with the functioning at the life tasks, it is often helpful to use both quantitative and qualitative assessment of the Crucial Cs. We frequently use a 1-to-10 scaling system to record our perceptions of whether the child is incorporating positive beliefs about each of the Crucial Cs into his or her lifestyle. In this system, a 1 indicates that the child does not seem to have mastered the art of connection, doesn't believe he or she is capable or counts, or is not demonstrating courage; a 10 indicates that the child has absolute faith that he or she can connect, is capable, does count, or has courage; and the numbers between 1 and 10 indicate relative positions on this scale. For the area of connect, we make qualitative comments about the ways the child connects, the people with whom he or she connects, his or her level of social skills, and his or her attitude about connecting and level of social interest. In thinking about the Crucial C of capable, we make comments about areas in which the child believes that he or she is capable or not capable and areas in which he or she demonstrates competence or a lack of competence. When there is a discrepancy between the child's perceptions and our observations or the comments of other people in the child's life, we note this as well. For the area of count, we notice the relationships and situations in which the child believes he or she counts or does not count, relationships and situations in which the child actually does make a difference (in positive or negative ways), and circumstances in which the child feels that he or she counts conditionally. In considering the child's ability and willingness to exhibit courage, we make note of relationships and situations in which the child perceives he or she demonstrates courage or lack of courage and situations and relationships in which the child actually seems to demonstrate courage or lack of courage.

Personality Priorities

In thinking about the child's personality priority, you will need to consider how the child reacts to stressful situations and how the child tries to gain a sense of belonging and significance. In this section, it is important to list the one or two priorities that the child uses as coping strategies or patterns of interaction with others, along with the behaviors and attitudes that seem to support the priority. You will want to consider whether the child is functioning in the functional–positive range of his or her personality priorities or the dysfunctional–negative range. Additional comments about how the child's personality priority is affecting his or her functioning at life tasks, relationships with others, goals of misbehavior, and the Crucial Cs can enhance the usefulness of this section of the conceptualization.

Another helpful dynamic to consider here is the interaction between the child's personality priority and the personality priorities of the influential adults in the child's life. Some combinations of priorities seem to positively affect the child's relationships and functioning, whereas others seem to interfere with attitudes and interactions. For example, if Mr. Jackson's personality priority is control and his daughter Suzie's priority is also control, then this will generally lead to power struggles as being an inherent part of their relationship. If Mrs. Jackson's personality priority is pleasing, she may get along with Suzie better than her husband does.

Younger children may not have yet developed personality priorities. If this is the case, you can skip this section of the conceptualization or use it to discuss your assessment of the impact on the child of the personality priorities of parents and teachers.

Lifestyle Convictions

You will take all of this information and extrapolate statements that represent the child's lifestyle convictions and the child's belief about how his or her behavior must be if those convictions are true. In doing this, it is helpful to complete the following sentence stems (Maniacci, et al., 2014; Sweeney, 2009) as you believe the child would complete them:

I am . . .
I must be . . .
Others are . . .
Others must be . . .
My relationships with others are . . .

My relationships with others must be . . .
The world is . . .
The world should be . . .
Life is . . .
Life should be . . .
Based on these convictions, my behavior must be . . .

There are a plethora of responses each child could make to complete these sentences, so you will want to list as many different responses as possible for each stem. We sometimes have as many as 20 or 25 for each sentence stem for a child. (Yes, this can get tedious, but it will be so helpful in your efforts toward being intentional in your interactions with clients, it will be worth it.)

After generating these lifestyle conviction statements, it will be beneficial to go through and decide which of these beliefs are faulty or mistaken. By labeling specific convictions as self-defeating for the child, you can make a determination of which beliefs to target for intervention (with such techniques as spitting in the soup and therapeutic metaphors) during the third phase of play therapy. (Because you don't want to try to change convictions that are actually working for the child—you only want to try to change the ones that are self-defeating.)

Private Logic

An individual's "private logic" is premised on his or her unique evaluation of self, others, and the world, and what is required of him or her. In Adlerian therapy, we work with a client to uncover and explore the private logic by which the client has been answering such questions as (a) What kind of person am I? (b) What kind of a world is this? (c) What must a person such as I am do in a world such as this is to make a place for myself? In thinking about private logic, we ask, "What would have to be true to make an otherwise particular, peculiar, and socially senseless pattern of behavior, intelligible?" (Griffith & Powers, 2007, p. 81).

As part of the conceptualization process, you will look at the child's attitudes, cognitions, behaviors, feelings, and perceptions to find patterns that suggest that private logic is at work. Because private logic dictates that the child act as if his or her faulty convictions are true, discovering the child's private logic can give you a vehicle to facilitate change through communicating about basic mistakes, helping the child uncover hidden motivation, using paradox and humor to help the child look more closely at his or her behavior, and reframing the child's behavior (Sweeney, 2009). Whenever possible, you will want to help the child replace private logic with common sense—behavior that is logical to most people of a community and is in the interest of benefiting society (Griffith & Powers, 2007).

Lifestyle Conceptualization of Adults in the Child's Life
Parents
If you believe that parents are contributing to the difficulty experienced by the child, it is frequently helpful to do a thorough assessment of par-

ents' lifestyles. This gives you a basis for planning intervention with the parents during the third and fourth phases of the Adlerian play therapy process. You will want to do this from a place of compassion rather than blame, remembering that the parents are doing the best they can under the circumstances.

When you decide that this would be a useful procedure, you will take the information gathered through parent consultation interviews and organize it so as to provide a complete picture of parents' views of self, others, and the world; relationships; parenting; the children; and the spousal relationship. This strategy also allows you to consider parental assets and functioning in the role of parent. (See Appendix G for a format for organizing this information.)

Teachers

It would be relatively rare to consider a formal lifestyle conceptualization on a child's teacher necessary. However, if you feel that a teacher's issues are interfering with his or her ability to make the changes needed to support the child and his or her growth, it can be helpful to gather enough information to do a formal conceptualization. This process would involve a more extensive interview with the teacher than usually occurs, so the teacher would have to be a willing participant. If there is a teacher who seems to struggle with a certain "type" of child, sometimes a school counselor can put together a lifestyle conceptualization to share with the teacher to help him or her discover what about those particular children is "hooking" the teacher. (See Appendix G for a format to organize this information.)

Case Example

I (KMW) did the following conceptualizations for Phoebe and her grandparents to illustrate how to use this format as a method of organizing the information gathered in the second phase of Adlerian play therapy to generate a treatment plan for the third and fourth phases. I did not gather all of the information possible from Mr. and Mrs. Simon because I did not believe that it was necessary to do a complete lifestyle analysis on them. If I had been going to work individually with them on their own issues or on marital issues, I would have gathered more information from them, but I believed that they did not need extensive personal work to make a difference in helping to raise Phoebe. I included a bit of information on Phoebe's teacher but did not believe a complete conceptualization was necessary for her either.

Most of the time we do not work with managed care (TK is in private practice and KMW provides school-based services), and therefore we do these conceptualizations for our own personal use—to guide our thinking and planning. We tend to use lists and shorthand when we make notes on specific behaviors and attitudes rather than writing formal complete sentences. Play therapists who are including their conceptualization in records for managed care companies or agencies may have to conform to more formal writing rules and can use the following conceptualization outline as a guide to writing case notes.

Adlerian Play Therapy Lifestyle Conceptualization—
Phoebe Simon

Assets: Intelligent, creative, resourceful, engaging, insightful, desire for positive belonging, high standards for achievement, supportive family.

Functioning at life tasks:

School: 1   2   3   4   5   6   **7**   8   9   10

Academically above average; temper outbursts; talks back to teacher; occasionally refuses to do work.

Friendship: 1   2   **3**   4   5   6   7   8   9   10

Has no close friends and no specific enemies; usually plays independently; can be bossy and hostile when she doesn't get her way. Lives on acreage with no neighbors. Is not involved in activities that allow her to connect with peers outside of the school day.

Love/family: 1   2   3   **4**   5   6   7   8   9   10

Feels supported by her grandmother and grandfather; feels abandoned by her mother and father.

Self: 1   **2**   3   4   5   6   7   8   9   10

Believes she must be in control at all times; does not believe she is lovable or worthy of love; doubts her ability to do well; believes she must be perfect.

Spirituality/existential: 1   2   3   **4**   5   6   7   8   9   10

Sees spirituality/religion as a point of conflict; distrustful of a higher power because of her mother's death; uncertain and curious about death and afterlife.

Play themes:

Control—believes she must be in control at all times. Her primary aim is self-control, mostly becoming controlling of others when their behaviors interfere with her goals. She feels vulnerable when she is caught off guard or when things don't go as she had planned. When she is told what to do (and doesn't want to do it) or feels stuck, she responds with hostility or aggression.

Fitting in—believes she does not fit in with peers. She is biracial with no other biracial or Latino students in her classroom. She believes she fits in at home and does so by being the spoiled child. She gets attention by being demanding and her grandparents readily comply with her wishes.

Family constellation—psychological birth-order position: Only child and youngest child—in many ways seems to feel as though she has three parents (grandma, grandpa, father) who each swoon over her every move. She is intelligent, can get along well with adults, and can play well independently. She also feels like the youngest child, with her dad being an older sibling and sharing grandma and grandpa as parents. Much of her behavior fits the youngest pattern—charming (when she wants to be), creative, and spoiled (works really hard to get her own way and thinks that she should always be able to control situations). Overall, she is rather spoiled and expects others to accommodate to her needs and desires.

Family atmosphere: Mostly democratic, but with some pretty significant gaps and problems. She has too much control and decision-making power; her father has relinquished parenting responsibilities, creating confusion for Phoebe about roles and power. Grandparents try hard to be what they define as "good" grandparents. Adults in her life try to protect her from loss and hurt, and try to make up for the death of her mother by giving in to her wishes at the expense of her learning limits and boundaries. Grandparents and Dad are loving and warm. Dad is frequently gone because of work and school schedule.

Early recollections: One early recollection was given. It was about missing her mom, not understanding the loss of her mom, and being biracial and not fitting in.

Goals of misbehavior: Power—wants to be the decision maker and prove to others that they are not in control of her. She uses various strategies (e.g., "damsel in distress," aggression, oppositional behaviors) to gain and maintain power.

Crucial Cs:

Connect: 1   2   3   **4**   5   6   7   8   9   10

She has the skills to connect with peers and adults but uses these skills infrequently. She believes she has the capacity to connect but fears rejection and disappointment, creating a barrier to her motivation for connection with others. She mostly connects with animals and finds security with them.

Capable: 1   2   3   4   5   6   7   **8**   9   10

Believes she is capable and could succeed. She knows she is smart and skilled at a number of tasks. She questions her ability to maintain relationships.

Count: 1   **2**   3   4   5   6   7   8   9   10

Does not believe that she counts. Does not believe that others genuinely care about her. Does not believe that she makes a difference in the lives of others or in the world.

Courage: 1   **2**   3   4   5   6   7   8   9   10

Fears being imperfect and trying new things, for fear of failure. Believes she must be perfect and in control for bad things not to happen. Taking risks compromises her felt sense of safety and security.

Personality priorities:

Phoebe—control (of self; in the dysfunctional range on the continuum) and superiority (achieving type, which is in the positive–functional range).

Interaction between child's personality priorities and those of significant others in the child's life:

Phoebe and Mr. and Mrs. Simon—Phoebe's desire for and accumulation of power is not helped by Mr. and Mrs. Simon's difficulty with setting limits and boundaries.

Teacher and Phoebe—both parties desire control. Teacher requires compliance with classroom rules in order to teach and keep a safe learning environment for all students. Phoebe feels challenged and trapped when the teacher demonstrates her control, creating conflicts between them.

Lifestyle convictions: (We have marked mistaken beliefs–faulty convictions with an asterisk.)

I am . . . different than other people.
    . . . unsure of how I can fit in relationships.
    . . . bad.*
    . . . not as important as other people.*
    . . . destined to be lonely.*
    . . . not likable.*
    . . . smart.
    . . . loved by my grandparents and father.
    . . . good with animals.

I must be . . . in control.*
    . . . willing to overpower others to get what I want.*
    . . . charming to get what I want.*
    . . . independent so I don't have to rely on anyone else.*
    . . . mean to others to keep them away.*
    . . . willing to show other people that they can't boss me around.

Others are . . . not to be trusted.*
    . . . selfish.*
    . . . more powerful than I am.*
    . . . lucky.
    . . . loved and lovable.
    . . . different from me.
    . . . made to serve me.*
    . . . only in my life because they have to be (grandparents, teacher).*
    . . . not going to accept me because I am different from them.*
    . . . happy.
    . . . friendly to one another.

My relationships with others must be . . . guarded.*
    . . . tentative, always looking for a slight.*
    . . . showing them that they cannot control me.*
    . . . manipulative.*
    . . . purposeful and staged (e.g., teacher–student; group partners, parent–child).*

The world is . . . a place of uncertainty and confusion.
    . . . unpredictable.
    . . . lonely and sad.*
    . . . a place where no one protects me.*
    . . . filled with loss.*
    . . . a place where I have to work very hard to find a way to fit.*
    . . . a place filled with people who are different from me.

Life is . . . unfair and uncertain.*
    . . . lonely and scary.*

Life must be . . . predictable and safe.*

On the basis of these convictions/perceptions/beliefs/feelings, my behavior must be
    . . . controlling.*
    . . . manipulative.*

. . . kind.

. . . working hard to find a place.

. . . erratic—to keep everyone guessing.*

. . . hidden—to escape and retreat when I need.

Private logic: Phoebe's conclusions about herself, others, and the world are based on her mistaken belief that the world is dangerous, people leave her, and she is unloved–unlovable.

Adlerian Play Therapy Lifestyle Conceptualization— Abbreviated—Mr. and Mrs. Simon

Assets: Intelligent, hard-working, well-intentioned, loving to their son and granddaughter, strong sense of spirituality, willing to learn new skills.

Functioning at life tasks: All are fine, except they may struggle with self—too flexible and not creating boundaries or limits for their granddaughter. Their relationship with one another is strong and supportive. They create a good balance for one another. They are too lenient with Phoebe.

Functioning in role as caretaker: 1   2   3   4   **5**   6   7   8   9   10

They know they have some strengths and skills as caretakers. They feel challenged by Phoebe's recent home and school behaviors. They feel uncertain of how to help her. They are willing to succumb to Phoebe's every desire as compensation for her significant loss. They are connected and in communication with the school to support her and recognize that they need to make different caretaking responsibilities to help Phoebe practice cooperation and balance.

Family constellation—psychological birth-order position: Mr. Simon was the oldest child and Mrs. Simon was the youngest. In different ways, growing up, they both felt responsible for taking care of their mothers. They minimally recognize their struggle with treating Phoebe like the super baby, coddling her, protecting her, and not wanting to create strain or discomfort for her. However, they define these behaviors as encouraging love and support.

Family atmosphere: Their family-of-origin experiences were chaotic and unstable. As adults, they made the decision to maintain healthy relationships that valued the opinions of others. As caretakers, they strive for creating warm and supportive family atmospheres in which children felt safe, wanted, and loved. They both experienced distrust of Christian faith as children. They stated that they were intentional about making the practice of Buddhism a central part of their family life when they had Christopher and have since practiced peace and harmony in all of their relationships.

Early recollections: Not applicable (N/A)

Crucial Cs:

Connect: 1   2   3   4   5   6   **7**   8   9   10

They are strong in this area. They both connect easily with others. Although Mr. Simon stated he didn't have many friends, he also stated that he preferred fewer intimate friendships as compared with more superficial relationships.

Capable: 1 2 3 4 5 6 7 **8** 9 10

This is a moderate strength. They felt capable of raising their son and feel less capable of raising a granddaughter because of generational differences. They generally believe that they will succeed at challenges.

Count: 1 2 3 **4** 5 6 7 8 9 10

Mostly, they believe that they matter and count in the world. Their "count" with Phoebe feels conditional—they count if she is happy with them and is well behaved.

Courage: 1 2 3 **4** 5 6 7 8 9 10

They are willing to take chances in most areas of life. At this point, they are becoming increasingly leery of making mistakes with Phoebe. In some ways, they feel paralyzed with fear of making wrong decisions; thus, they follow her lead in most things.

Personality priorities:

Mr. Simon—pleasing and comfort, which works out well in their daily lives, but creates poor boundaries with Phoebe, which moves his pleasing into the dysfunctional range.

Mrs. Simon—pleasing and superiority; her desire to please Phoebe and be the very best at her relationship with her often creates poor boundaries and indulgence with Phoebe, which moves these into the dysfunctional range.

Lifestyle convictions: (We have marked mistaken beliefs–faulty convictions with an asterisk.) These are the lifestyle convictions they seemed to share that affected their relationship with Phoebe and the way they interacted with her.

We are/we must be . . . able to protect Phoebe from everything.*
   . . . warm and loving.
   . . . the stand-in for Phoebe's mother.
   . . . responsible to take away the pain for Phoebe.*
   . . . responsible for making other people (including Phoebe) happy.*
   . . . the best grandparents we can possibly be.
Others are . . . generally nice.
   . . . going to judge us if we are not perfect parents/grandparents.*
   . . . likely to believe we are bad people if we are not perfect parents/grandparents.*
   . . . not as spiritual/peaceful/mindful/harmonious as we are.*
   . . . selfish and demanding.*
   . . . good, kind, generous.
My relationships with others must be . . . peaceful and harmonious.
   . . . submissive.*
   . . . self-sacrificing.*
The world is/life is . . . uncertain and unpredictable.
   . . . not fair.*
   . . . filled with loss and pain.*
   . . . good and happy when things are peaceful and harmonious.

On the basis of these convictions/perceptions/beliefs/feelings, our behavior must be . . . designed in such a way that Phoebe feels safe and happy.*
   . . . designed so that we sacrifice for the sake of others.*
   . . . make sure that others can live happily and peacefully.*

Private logic: Seem to be overcompensating for the death of Phoebe's mother. Mr. and Mrs. Simon seem to believe, if they can make life easy and remove opportunities for hurt for Phoebe by giving in to her wishes and not setting boundaries for her, she will feel happy and not long for her mother.

Adlerian Play Therapy Lifestyle Conceptualization— Abbreviated—Christopher Simon

Christopher is not much involved in the treatment process because of his work and school schedule. His parents describe him as a good father who wants the best for his daughter. Because he isn't involved in the regular parenting routines, his lifestyle was not investigated (other than from brief reports from Mr. and Mrs. Simon). The parenting style change (from Christopher to Mr. and Mrs. Simon) and how it might affect the family atmosphere will be discussed. If I was going to continue to work with the family, I would request that Christopher be more involved in the process and explore his lifestyle more thoroughly.

Adlerian Play Therapy Lifestyle Conceptualization— Abbreviated—Teacher

Assets: Intelligent, caring, consistent, wants her students to succeed.

Functioning at life tasks: Love, friends, spirituality, and self are fine. Work—she reported losing motivation for working with young children. She prefers older elementary children or middle school children.

Functioning in role as teacher: 1   2   3   4   5   6   7   8   **9**   10

Is concerned about Phoebe's behavior in the classroom and her ability to build relationships with classmates. She enjoys teaching and feels a sense of value and pride in her career. She is losing interest in working with young children. She believes she would feel more satisfied working with students who are a bit older, perhaps in middle school. Recognizes her feelings of burnout and is attempting to not let that interfere with her ability to connect with Phoebe. She has strong relationships with other teachers that create support and encouragement for her. Gets along well with students' parents and regularly receives positive feedback from parents.

Family constellation—psychological birth-order position: N/A

Family atmosphere: N/A

Early recollections: N/A

Crucial Cs:

Connect: 1   2   3   4   5   6   7   **8**   9   10

Fairly strong—she generally connects with most people. She is feeling less connected with young children in the past year.

Capable: 1   2   3   4   5   6   7   8   9   **10**

Very strong—highly successful at work and personal life.

Count: 1 2 3 4 5 6 <u>7</u> 8 9 10

Believes she counts in most situations. She is starting to doubt her significance as a teacher.

Courage: 1 2 3 4 5 6 7 8 9 <u>**10**</u>

Willingly attempts challenges. Because she believes she is capable and will succeed, she isn't hesitant in taking risks.

Personality priorities: Control—her behavior seems to reflect that she is in the functional range of the continuum. She structures the classroom democratically, demonstrating respect and encouragement for her students. She holds high expectations (that are developmentally appropriate) for her students.

Lifestyle convictions: (We have marked mistaken beliefs/faulty convictions with an asterisk.)

I am . . . kind and generous.
    . . . hard working.
    . . . responsible, reliable.
    . . . unsure about my success as a teacher.*
I must be . . . able to maintain control of myself and my environment.*
    . . . able to trust others and myself.
    . . . structured to maintain and expect responsible behavior.
Others are . . . trustworthy.
    . . . trying their best.
    . . . not as competent as I am.*
    . . . sometimes out of control.*
    . . . good, kind, generous, lovable.
My relationships with others must be . . . structured.
    . . . one in which I can demonstrate my competency as a teacher and adult.*
    . . . democratic.
    . . . kind, considerate, helpful.
The world is/life is . . . full of opportunities.
    . . . sometimes unfair.*
    . . . sometimes dangerous.*
    . . . good/happy/fun.

Based on these convictions/perceptions/beliefs/feelings, my behavior must be . . . designed to guarantee that people are controlled.*
    . . . generous, helpful, and considerate. *
    . . . predictable and sometimes calculated.*

Private logic: She seems to be overcompensating slightly for her doubts about whether she counts as an early education teacher. She might believe that others must be controlled and organized for safety and positive outcomes.

Treatment Planning

The conceptualization of the clients sets the groundwork for the design of a treatment plan that outlines goals and intervention strategies for the third and fourth phases of Adlerian play therapy. The therapist can develop a treatment plan for the play therapy process, detailing a general guide for working with the child. It is often appropriate to make a plan for working with parents and teachers. Appendix G consists of forms for treatment planning for both children and adults.

I (TK) began developing this treatment plan format in response to requests from other play therapists for a more structured way of planning interventions for Adlerian play therapy and have received feedback that this plan helps counselors to understand their clients and create more efficient treatment goals and objectives. This structure should be customized to fit the needs of the therapist, the client, and the client's parents and/or teachers. Some play therapists work within settings that require many kinds of information not included in these forms or other formats for organizing their plan of action. When this is the case, they can integrate the Adlerian information into the treatment plan they are required to do.

Elements of the Adlerian Play Therapy Treatment Plan for the Child

The treatment plan for the child focuses on assets, life tasks, Crucial Cs, goals of misbehavior, mistaken beliefs, self-defeating behaviors, and skills. For each of these elements of the plan, you will want to determine (a) the focus of the intervention, (b) concrete goals for change on the part of the child, (c) play therapy strategies, and (d) the methods for measuring progress.

The specific goals for the treatment plan may be related to the presenting problem, specific objectives for the child's attitudes or behavior that have been suggested by parents and teachers, aspects of the child's life that he or she has expressed interest in changing, and changes assessed by the therapist as important for optimal well-being of the child. Some of these goals will have been discussed in the initial stages of the parent consultation (and teacher consultation). Some of them will evolve during the information-gathering process of the second phase of counseling and during the development of the conceptualization and the treatment plan. You should involve the child, parents, teachers, and other interested parties in generating the goals when appropriate.

When working to make changes suggested by the significant adults in the child's life, it is helpful to involve them in a reality-testing process designed to help them understand that play therapy is probably not going to eliminate all of the child's inappropriate or annoying behaviors and attitudes. We frequently ask the parents to give us a specific number of times (per hour, per day, per week, depending on what makes sense with the particular behavior) a behavior occurs or to rate their negative reaction to a specific behavior on a scale of 1 to 10. Then we tell them that we need to gauge how much improvement will be "enough." We ask them to specify how much reduction in the number of times the child does a certain behavior or the level of annoyance using the scaling would constitute sufficient improvement for them to be satisfied. We also ask them to define how important a change in a particular behavior is to them and their relationship with the child by asking, "How big is your stake in the ground about this behavior?" This process helps us focus on what needs to change and how much it needs to be different. Over the course of therapy, we can compare the child's behavior to the initial behavior. Many of the goals in Adlerian play therapy are concrete and observable, especially those connected with behaviors and skills. Other goals are more abstract because they have to do with changing beliefs, emotions, attitudes, and perceptions.

In this chapter, we will not provide an in-depth description of the strategies for working toward the goals, as intervention techniques are thoroughly covered in Chapters 4, 9, and 10. However, it is important to remember that helping children make changes in Adlerian play therapy and adults make changes through consultation is a multistep process. Adlerians believe that before clients actually give up their old self-defeating patterns, they must understand that those patterns are not working. (You may recall a famous TV personality saying, "How's that working for you?") To help them do this, in the third phase of counseling, you will use several different techniques to illuminate the clients' useless ways of thinking, feeling, and behaving by spitting in their soup, using humor, metacommunicating, and so forth. Finally, in the fourth phase, you work to set up ways to teach clients new patterns of thinking, feeling, and behaving; help them to practice these new patterns; and make suggestions for ways for them to apply their newly developed constructive thoughts, emotions, and actions in relationships and situations outside the therapy setting.

Defining the methods for measuring progress will depend on the counselor's setting. We usually use observation of playroom behavior, self-report, and reports from teachers and parents. If you need to use some more concrete objective measure to satisfy agency rules or funding sources, this is also perfectly acceptable.

Assets

In the treatment plan for the child, make a list of assets you believe will support the child's positive movement. The usual goal for this part of the plan is to increase the child's recognition of his or her assets and to encourage the child to capitalize on his or her assets. With assets that the child is currently using in self-defeating ways (e.g., Kumi is musical but makes up mean songs about peers), the goal will be to help the child make a shift to exhibiting the asset in positive, constructive ways.

With many children, it is necessary to start small in this area. For some children, it is huge progress for them to stop disputing every positive comment someone makes about them. For other children, the goal will be for them to "own" their positive attributes by acknowledging compliments or volunteering positive comments about themselves. As they feel more comfortable with their own assets, it will be important for children to constructively use their assets to make a contribution to the world in some way, so this might be the ultimate goal in this area. Some examples of goals for helping the child recognize and capitalize on assets:

- Tony will stop arguing with you when you point out his ability to fix things in the playroom.
- Shakeem will graciously accept compliments from his teacher about his academic accomplishments.

- Lucrecia will increase the number of times she verbally acknowledges her musical talent (in a play therapy session, at home, in music lessons).
- Daisy Mae will agree to tutor a first grader in math.
- Felicia will try out for a play.

Functioning at Life Tasks

In this section, if there is a particular life task the child does not seem to be mastering, consider what needs to happen in that area to help the child. The goals for changes in functioning at life tasks can be very general (e.g., learns skills for maintaining friendship) or very specific (e.g., does not hit or pinch his little sister). (I, KMW, need to work on that with my kids!)

Personality Priorities

Because each of the priorities has assets, liabilities, and a price to be paid, it is helpful to explore all of the facets of the child's personality priority. Quite often, it is possible to help the child recognize and capitalize on the positive qualities inherent in his or her personality priority (e.g., pleasers are kind people who are thoughtful and helpful, comfort-oriented individuals are fun and spontaneous, control kids are good leaders and organized, superiority kids accomplish big tasks and contribute to group projects). It is also helpful to explore the downside of the priority, especially those aspects of the priority that cause interpersonal problems (e.g., pleasers might not get their own needs met, comfort kids can become boring to other kids, controllers frequently refuse to take turns and cheat in games, superiority individuals tend to brag and put others down). Your goals in this section will involve helping children to learn how to take advantage of their assets and to reduce the negative effects of their attitudes and behaviors, moving them to the functional range of the continuum within their priorities.

Crucial Cs

If it is obvious that there is only one Crucial C in which the child is not grounded, assess whether the difficulty lies in limited belief in that area, a skill deficit, or both. Depending on which of these factors is contributing to the child's difficulty, plan ways to help the child enhance the belief, acquire more skills, or otherwise make shifts needed to ensure that the C gets incorporated into the child's lifestyle. With children who struggle with multiple deficits in the Crucial Cs, do some kind of triage, looking for the Crucial C that, if enhanced, will make the biggest difference in the child's life.

I (KMW) envision Crucial Cs as buckets. The fuller the bucket, the more "well" a child is in that Crucial C. My intention is to help the child to fill each of his or her buckets. When one bucket is overflowing, I tend to not continue to fill that bucket. Rather, I use my time and energy to fill an empty or less full bucket. For example, if, for Kate connect is overflowing and courage is nearly empty, I will focus on noticing ways she can fill courage by pointing out times when she is courageous (e.g., trying out for the play, asking a new kid at school to play at recess, removing an unsteady block from the Jenga® game, or doing a new task that she was earlier afraid of doing). The image helps me to concentrate on areas for growth as opposed to sticking mainly with areas in which the child is doing well.

Some examples of goals for helping children make shifts in their Crucial Cs:

- Tamera will tell one thing that she did to make a difference in her classroom. (Count)
- Josh will use basic friendship skills to make a connection with one child in the neighborhood. (Connect)
- Sinam will try something in the playroom that she has never done before. (Courage)
- Issac will tell his father two things he did well that day. (Capable)

Goals of Misbehavior

The ultimate goal in this area is to help children give up their misbehavior and learn to strive toward more positive goals (such as cooperation, making a contribution, and so forth). With some children, this actually happens, whereas other children do not completely give up misbehaving but can make shifts from a more destructive goal (like revenge) to a less destructive goal (such as attention). The first step in this process is helping them see what their goals of misbehavior are, followed by moving them toward insight that these goals are not serving their best interests. In some situations, the child is accomplishing exactly what he or she wants with misbehavior (e.g., Candace throws a tantrum in the grocery store and gets what she wants—power and a candy bar). When this is the case, you must work with the adults in the child's life to change the adults' reaction to the child's behavior and any other components of the child's ecosystem that support the child's misbehavior. Examples of objectives for working to change goals of misbehavior:

- Andrew will raise his hand and wait for the teacher to call on him. (Attention)
- Zaheer will let his mother have 15 minutes of uninterrupted time on the phone. (Attention)
- Sunny will say "yes" to three requests during the course of a week. (Control)
- Kyoko will take turns with you when playing a game. (Control)
- Denzell will play a game according to the rules written on the directions. (Control)
- Rosemary will not hit anyone at school (4 out of 5 days of the week). (Revenge)
- Travon will only say three disrespectful comments to his parents per day. (Revenge)
- Natalie will tell you one good thing that happened during the week. (Proving inadequacy)
- Jahasanea will make eye contact and smile at you when she comes into the session. (Proving inadequacy)

Mistaken Beliefs–Faulty Convictions

The goal in this part of the therapy is to help clients see that their mistaken beliefs are self-defeating and destructive. As you decide which of the client's convictions about self, others, and the world are getting in his or her way in coping with life's struggles, it is sometimes helpful to develop a hierarchy of beliefs—from the most self-defeating to the least because it is usually impossible to eliminate all of a client's faulty convictions at once. (But it would be nice, wouldn't it?) Before we think about asking a client to give up old patterns of thinking, we always have several other positive beliefs about self, others, and the world that we suggest to replace the negative ones. We use encouragement techniques (have we mentioned we use a lot of encouragement?) to introduce constructive statements about the client, other people in the client's family and school situations, relationships, life, and the world, hoping that he or she will begin to adopt these as lifestyle convictions. When working with clients on making changes in mistaken beliefs, it will often be necessary to explore their private logic and help them substitute common sense for the cognitive distortions and negative attributions inherent in private logic. Some examples of goals for substituting positive convictions for mistaken beliefs:

- Luke will shift from the belief that he is not as important as other people to the belief that he is just as important as others.
- Quintana will shift from the belief that she must always please others to knowing that she will still be likable and lovable even when others are angry with her.
- Jose will shift from the belief that he must not allow himself to get close to other people because he will always get hurt in relationships to a conviction that there are some relationships in which he will be able to trust others.
- Sherre will substitute the idea that the world is a place in which both good things and bad things happen to people for the idea that the world is a place in which nothing good ever happens to anyone.

Self-Defeating–Useless Behavior

In thinking about behaviors that need changing, consider short-term, immediate, and long-term needs of the child. Initially, it is essential to target behaviors that are getting the child in trouble, preventing positive interactions with others, and causing distress to others (e.g., picking fights on the playground, blatant disobedience of family rules). As these behaviors get under control, it may be useful to target other behaviors that are preventing the child from functioning optimally in the family and at school (e.g., ignoring overtures of friendship from other children, not doing chores). Rather than simply trying to eliminate negative behaviors, it is extremely important to help the child learn positive behaviors to take their place. Examples of goals for changing self-defeating behaviors:

- When Bobby gets angry, he will count to 10 and take 10 deep breaths (rather than punching the person who has aggravated him).
- Linnea will use "I messages" to tell her classmates when their behavior upsets her (rather than calling them names and yelling at them).
- Vijaya will ask other children to play on the playground (rather than spending recess sitting in the corner of the playground).
- Candi will comply when her mother asks her do one of her chores (rather than simply ignoring her or being defiant).

- Dexter will say, "May I please have that?" when he wants something that his sister has (rather than simply grabbing it).

Skills

There are many skills that children need in their lives—friendship skills, negotiation skills, problem-solving skills, self-regulation skills, and so forth. Part of the treatment-planning process is assessing skills that would enhance the child's functioning and developing strategies for teaching them these skills. Depending on the requirements of the therapy setting, you can break the skills down into their component parts or just make a general plan for skill training and practice. Examples of goals for skill development:

- Lynn will make eye contact and smile when she meets a new person.
- Fadil will demonstrate four friendship skills.
- Yasmine will be able to concretely state what she wants as the outcome of a negotiation.
- Song Bo will learn compromising skills.

Elements of the Adlerian Play Therapy Treatment Plan for Parents and Teachers

In developing a treatment plan for the adults in the child's life, the play therapist considers the adult's personality priority, assets, functioning at life tasks, lifestyle factors that might be interfering with the adult's ability to interact positively with the child, and parenting (or teaching) skills. Because the parent and teacher consultation process is always an adjunct to the work with the child, the treatment plan for these adults is frequently less detailed and specific than the treatment plan for the child.

Personality Priority and Crucial Cs

In this section, plan ways to custom design the interaction with the adult on the basis of the consultee's personality priorities and Crucial Cs. See Chapter 4 for more specific details on how to do this.

Assets

An essential part of the consultation process is recognizing and acknowledging the assets of the parents and teachers. By pointing out the positive qualities of these adults (attitudes, personal characteristics, and behaviors connected to their interaction with the child and those unrelated to parenting or teaching), you can plant seeds for further growth and strengthen the therapeutic alliance. As parents and teachers begin to feel better about who they are personally, they will likely become more self-confident and enjoy an increased sense of self-efficacy.

Functioning at Life Tasks

Some parents (and teachers) really struggle with balance in their lives. (Here, here. It takes one to know one! We also struggle with balance.) They may function well at work and experience major difficulties with their friendships; they may have a strong spiritual faith but a weak sense of self, and so forth. When this is the case, these adults often have difficulty coping with children who are experiencing difficulties. They just do not have the energy it takes to be fully present and supportive with others, including the children with whom they live (or work). When this is the case, the most helpful focus in consultation is working with them to achieve a better alignment in their functioning at the various life tasks. To make sure that you are respectful to these adults, it is essential to do this with their full awareness and consent. After all, parents and teachers don't want to feel manipulated into being counseled.

Lifestyle Factors

Many times, elements of the adults' lifestyle (personality priorities; values; Crucial Cs; basic convictions about self, others, and the world; and private logic) will interfere with their ability to successfully function in their role as a parent (or teacher). If these issues are relatively minor, it is appropriate to work with the adults on making changes so that their lifestyles do not keep them from parenting (or teaching) as well as they can. However, if these issues are moderate to severe, you might decide that the child and the adult will be better served by referring the adult for individual counseling of some kind.

Skills–Information Needed

There are many Adlerian skills that are appropriate for parents and teachers to learn (see Chapter 4 for examples of these). Choose the skills most likely to enhance the adult's ability to successfully interact with the child and devise a plan for teaching those skills to the adult. At times, there are other skills that the adults will need—skills that are not specifically Adlerian but that would be helpful in the interactions between child and adult (e.g., learning to set concrete limits or classroom management skills). With some adults, it will be more effective to actually teach the skills and provide a way for them to practice the skills and get feedback. Others will learn more efficiently through participating in a class or reading a book. (Sound familiar? We intentionally create interventions for parents and/or teachers that fit their personality priorities.) You must design the treatment plan with the learning style of the adult in mind. Sometimes there is just information that parents need, like education about child development or specific disorders (e.g., ADHD or depression). Your job would be to share relevant information with them in a way that feels useful to them.

Case Example

I (KMW) made a treatment plan for Phoebe with some concrete goals in mind for my play sessions with her and for her interactions with other members of her family. Because I felt that her grandparents were the primary providers of care, with the current absence of her father, and they needed to work together to develop some consistent guidelines, expectations, and consequences for responding to Phoebe, I did not devise separate treatment plans for them. Instead, I wrote a treatment plan that integrated goals and strategies for both parties into a single plan—they had complementary styles and strengths and this made the most sense to me as I thought about their family. Because Christopher (Phoebe's father) would presumably resume the parental role when he was done with school, I included a few goals and strategies for working with him. Adlerians believe that there is an internal consistency in an individual's personality; therefore, some of the goals and strategies overlap with one another—this is inevitable.

Adlerian Play Therapy Treatment Plan—Phoebe Simon

Assets **you want to encourage:** Creativity, engaging when she wants to be, insightful, wants to belong in positive ways.

Goals for change:
- Increase her ability to respond creatively in situations in which she is feeling stuck (instead of being tunnel visioned about solutions or resorting to aggression)
- Increase the frequency with which she exhibits engaging behaviors with peers
- Help her to recognize how insightful she is—about herself and about others
- Capitalize on her desire to belong in positive ways by enhancing her belief that she can belong in positive, rather than in negative, ways

Strategies:
Encouragement, metaphors (especially with animal figures and puppets), teaching adult members of her family to use encouragement, self-disclosure, brainstorming, discussions about problem situations experienced by her friends (and perhaps her own dilemmas). Family discussions about her mother, Mexican culture, and being biracial.

Progress measured by:
Observation of Phoebe in the play sessions, in the waiting room, and in family sessions; self-report by Phoebe; and reports from grandparents and school personnel.

Functioning at *life tasks* **that needs readjusting–balancing:** Work to help enhance her functioning in the areas of friendship, love–family, and self. School and spiritual–existential seem okay.

Goals for change:
- Increase self-efficacy about friendship
- Increase social skills, especially related to taking turns, following rules, sharing
- Increase her belief that she can gain significance in the family in positive ways
- Increase her belief that she can get her needs met without aggressive behaviors
- Increase positive feelings about her worth and whether she can make a contribution
- Increase her comfort with being biracial
- Increase her understanding of death and loss

Strategies:
Encouragement; discussion about being different, fitting in, ways to gain significance in positive ways (these may be direct but will prob-

ably use metaphors—that is, the dolphin–giraffe family metaphor); art techniques and stories related to being biracial (especially check out bibliotherapy resources in this area); using alien puppet to explore being different; drawings of ideal family; drawings of what the family would be like if her mom was alive; teaching social skills and negotiation skills; family session with grandparents, father, and Phoebe to clarify rules about boundaries, permissiveness, and discipline; arrange for Phoebe to participate in a friendship group with school counselor. Create a photo album–photo book about mom and mom's culture. Encourage family discussions and family photos to include mom.

Ways to optimize positive qualities and reduce negative aspects of personality priorities

Goals for change:
- Improve her ability to capitalize on the assets of her control priority
- Decrease the negative factors inherent in the priority of control

Strategies:
Power sharing, playing cooperative games, inviting her to organize and structure activities.

Crucial Cs **that need readjusting:** connect, count, and courage

Goals for change:
- Increase her ability to connect with others by improving social skills
- Enhance her belief that she counts
- Increase her belief that it's okay to not be perfect and that she can take risks and succeed

Strategies:
Encouragement; teaching other family members and teacher encouragement skills; metaphors (dolls, figures, puppets); homework of having her list something she did well or how she made a contribution; teach social skills and negotiation skills; arrange for her to participate in a friendship group with school counselor; arrange for her to join an extracurricular group such as dance, tumbling, soccer, theater, girls club, animal club, FFA, or tree growers.

Goals of misbehavior **that need readjusting:** Move from power to making a contribution and cooperation.

Goals for change:
- Increase her ability to share power with others
- Increase her willingness to risk making a positive contribution
- Increase her willingness to cooperate with others—both at home and at school
- Increase her trust in others to not overpower her if she does not have all the power

Strategies:
Sharing power with me in the playroom (sometimes I get to be the boss and sometimes she does—taking turns making the rules, deciding on

activities, etc.); encouragement of positive contributions and cooperation; cooperative games; working together as a team to clean up toys
in playroom; projects in which we must both cooperate to have successful completion (putting together puzzles in which we both have
required pieces; building tower with popsicle sticks, etc.); encouragement; teaching other family members encouragement skills; adventure
therapy trust activities (blindfolded walk, leaning, etc.); spitting in her
soup; humor.

Mistaken beliefs/faulty convictions **(self/others/the world/life) that need
readjusting:** Change convictions about self/others/the world/life
from negative self-concept, focused on differences being negative and
needing to overpower others, to more positive outlook.

Goals for change:
- "I am not as good/smart/powerful/accomplished/important as
others" to "I am as good/smart/powerful/accomplished/important
as others."
- "I am bad" to "Sometimes I do things that aren't kind or create
problems."
- "I must be in control" to "It is nice to be in control, but I will be safe
if I am not."
- "I must be willing to overpower others in order to get what I want"
to "I can cooperate with others to get what I want."
- "Others do not like me" to "People like me when I'm kind and not
bossy."
- "Others are not to be trusted" to "Others can usually be trusted."
- "Everyone who loves me leaves me" to "Sometimes people leave,
but it isn't because they didn't love me."
- "Others are more important/powerful/smarter/more accomplished
than I am" to "Others are just as important/powerful/smart/
accomplished as I am and that is OK."
- "People are not going to accept me because I am different" to "Everyone
is different in some way."
- "My relationships with others must be guarded/manipulative" to
"My relationships with others can be cooperative."
- "The world is a place of uncertainty and confusion" to "The world
is a safe place where I can count on my family and my friends."
- "The world is a place in which I do not have enough power" to "The
world is a place in which there is plenty of power for everyone."
- "Life must be fair" to "It would be nice if life was fair, and sometimes
it isn't."

Strategies:
Spitting in her soup, encouragement, metaphors and storytelling, art
techniques, mild disputing of mistaken beliefs and private logic (but
avoid getting into power struggles with her), encourage grandparents
and father to model positive self-talk.

Self-defeating–useless behavior **you want to change:** Reduce erratic
behavior, temper tantrums, and increase cooperative behavior.

Goals for change: (needed long range):
- Decrease temper tantrums
- Decrease other controlling behaviors
- Increase willingness to cooperate with others

Strategies:
Parent consultation stressing the importance of limits and consistent discipline procedures, problem ownership, logical consequences, and other factors; power sharing; cooperative activities in play sessions (playing games with rules, taking turns, etc.); spitting in soup about goals of misbehavior; family doll play; family play sessions in playroom; family sculpting; encouragement; metaphors. Discuss the benefit of structured group activities with peer such as sporting leagues, craft or reading clubs, or play dates that provide Phoebe with opportunities to practice cooperation. Consult with teacher and school counselor about social skills groups offered at school.

Skills **the child needs to learn:** Friendship skills, negotiation skills, power-sharing skills.

Goals for change:
- Increase friendship skills
- Enhance negotiation skills
- Increase willingness and ability to share power with others

Strategies:
Use dolls, figures, and puppets to teach skills; play cooperative games; bring in a second child or use other family members to practice friendship skills, negotiation skills, power-sharing skills; arrange for Phoebe to participate in a friendship group with school counselor.

Adlerian Play Therapy Treatment Plan— Consultation With Mr. and Mrs. Simon

Personality priorities **and** *Crucial Cs:* Mr. Simon's personality priorities are pleasing and comfort. He is capable and connects, although he believes that he doesn't count unconditionally and lacks courage to try new skills. Mrs. Simon's personality priorities are pleasing and superiority. She connects easily with most people and believes she is capable as a caretaker. Like Mr. Simon, she believes she only counts if Phoebe is doing well and lacks courage to take risks in changing her style of caretaking.

Strategies for consultation:
With both grandparents, stress assets and do lots of encouraging. Both of them are feeling at a loss about providing support and care for their grandchild. They are overcompensating for the death of Phoebe's mother, which interferes with their ability to set boundaries and rules for their granddaughter. Be sure to check for strengths in the relationships between grandparents and Phoebe before encouraging grown-ups to set limits because their pleasing personality priorities will get in the way of them following through with limit setting. Provide information about

typical child development and the grief and loss process so as to help Mrs. Simon understand what to expect and look for as Phoebe continues to mature. Emphasize Mr. and Mrs. Simon's relationship with Phoebe and their willingness to take on the responsibility for caring for Phoebe, encourage their belief that they count even when things don't go as well as they'd like with Phoebe. Create brief and specific strategies for Mr. Simon as complex and ongoing tasks might feel overwhelming for his comfort personality priority. Help Mr. and Mrs. Simon to understand the importance of positive social interactions for Phoebe and commit to helping her find one regularly scheduled group in which to participate (e.g., soccer team, reading club, yoga for kids, etc.).

Assets **you want to encourage:**

Mr. Simon—intelligent, patient, kind, dedicated to family.

Mrs. Simon—intelligent, loving, strong relationship skills, genuine concern for Phoebe and family.

Both have strong desire to be good caretakers.

Goals for change:

- Enhance their willingness set limits and boundaries
- Increase support systems for Mr. and Mrs. Simon
- Increase their understanding of child development, including psychosocial development typical of children
- Reassure them about their ability to care for Phoebe and capitalize on their desire to improve

Strategies:

Encouragement; teach about personality priorities and Crucial Cs in regards to their own dynamics and Phoebe's behaviors; teach about limit setting and choice giving; educate about child development; provide information about the grief-and-loss process; provide resources for and about grandparents raising grandchildren.

Progress measured by:

Observation and self-report.

Functioning at *life tasks* that needs readjusting/balancing: None needed.

Lifestyle elements **that may interfere with parenting success:** Personality priorities, family-of-origin issues, lifestyle convictions, Crucial Cs, Mrs. Simon's transference with Phoebe about loss of a parent during childhood.

Goals for change:

- Mr. Simon—increase willingness to engage in interactions such as limit setting and choice giving that will improve Phoebe's understanding of boundaries and increase her sense of safety. Decrease need for pleasing others.
- Mrs. Simon—increase understanding of self as competent and successful as a caretaker. Decrease need for pleasing others. Increase insight related to overcompensating with Phoebe for her own loss of a parent during childhood.
- Both—look at issues related to their beliefs about/attitudes toward raising children based on their roles in their families of origin.

- Both—provide information and education about grief processes (e.g., mother, moving schools)—Phoebe needs support but not overprotection.

Strategies:
Teaching about Crucial Cs and personality priorities, discussion about family-of-origin issues, discussion of values and beliefs related to raising children, work with Mr. Simon about comfort and pleasing issues; work with Mrs. Simon about superiority and pleasing issues; provide information and resources about grief and loss.

Parenting skills–information **needed:** Limited choice technique, reflecting feelings, encouraging, positive limit setting, logical consequences, and determination of problem ownership. Information about grief and loss in children; information about biracial children and how to help support them; information about child development.

Goals for change:
- Increase skills in all areas
- Decrease passive indulging application of child-rearing skills
- Increase confidence and sense of self-efficacy in child-rearing skills
- Give information about grief and loss in children, biracial children, and child development

Strategies:
Direct instruction, reading materials, practice in sessions with Phoebe, family play sessions, homework assignments for application of specific skills, encouragement.

Summary

The lifestyle conceptualization summarizes all of the information gathered during the second phase of the Adlerian play therapy and the parent (teacher) consultation. The therapist integrates the data about the child and the other members of the family into a format that crystallizes his or her understanding of intrapersonal and interpersonal dynamics. On the basis of this conceptualization, the therapist develops a treatment plan to guide the intervention stage of the therapeutic process with the child. Sometimes it is useful to develop conceptualizations and treatment plans for parents and teachers as well.

Further Resources

Parent consultation:

http://www.counseling.org/resources/library/vistas/vistas12/article_8.pdf

Adlerian counseling and lifestyle:

http://www.carterandevans.com/portal/index.php/adlerian-theory/172-life-style-identification-and-assessment
http://ct.counseling.org/2012/07/individual-psychology-relevant-techniques-for-todays-counselor/

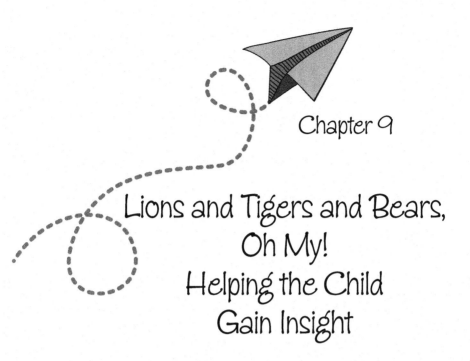

Chapter 9

Lions and Tigers and Bears, Oh My!
Helping the Child Gain Insight

During the third phase of Adlerian play therapy, the play therapist's goal is to help children better understand their assets; their Crucial Cs; the goals of their misbehavior; their personality priorities; their relationships; their basic convictions about themselves, others, and the world; and the behaviors they use to belong. As children gain insight into their lifestyles and a sense of clarity about how they use their behaviors to feel a sense of belonging and significance, they can reexamine their perceptions, attitudes, thoughts, feelings, and actions. In this reexamination process, children can decide whether they want to continue their lives just as they are or whether they want to make some changes. In conjunction with helping children to look more closely at their beliefs and their interactions with others, the therapist also works with parents to change any family dynamics or parenting strategies that might be supporting destructive behavior patterns. (See Chapter 4 for suggestions about how to help parents with this.)

Strategies for Helping the Child Gain Insight Into His or Her Lifestyle

During this phase of therapy, the Adlerian play therapist continues to use play as the primary basis for the interaction. (Does this sound redundant yet?) To help the child gain insight and by connecting what is happening in the play session to what happens in the rest of the child's life, the therapist makes interpretations in the form of tentative hypotheses and metacommunications about the various components of the child's lifestyle and helps the child generalize new ways of looking at the world. The therapist can also use metaphors, directed role-playing, art techniques, sand tray activities, dance and movement experiments, and adventure therapy techniques to help the child reexamine experiences and attitudes. Immediacy and confrontation are also useful counseling skills for helping a child gain insight.

Metacommunicating and Making Tentative Hypotheses

Because each of us operates out of our own unexamined assumptions and convictions, no one of us knows the Truth about another, and can only guess how the self, others, and the world looks to him or her; therefore, it is Adlerian practice to offer suggestions in the form of questions or qualified statements when interpreting another's world. (Griffith & Powers, 1984, p. 51)

Many of the interpretations in Adlerian play therapy take the form of tentative hypotheses, with you making guesses about the child's Crucial Cs; goals of misbehavior; personality priorities; private logic; and basic convictions about self, others, and the world. That you use qualified statements in this process invites children to participate in discovering themselves. Because the hypotheses are delivered in a tentative manner, children feel free to give you new information, correct erroneous assumptions that you have made, and protect themselves against insights that are still too painful to examine. The interactive, egalitarian nature of this process helps to reduce children's defensiveness and encourages two-way communication and the deepening of insight for both parties. We are not fortune tellers and are not spot on with each of our hypotheses every time. This works in our favor: We model the courage to be imperfect and as children correct our hypotheses, they provide us with information and often gain insight—a win-win situation.

The counselor often shares hypotheses about the connection between children's basic convictions and their acting as if those convictions are true. This technique is sometimes called "spitting in clients' soup." According to Maniacci et al. (2014), Adler (Ansbacher & Ansbacher, 1956) borrowed this unpleasant image but very helpful tactic from Charles Dickens's *Oliver Twist*. In that book, the children living in the orphanage were starving and when they got their main meal, it was meager bowls of thin soup. Because they were hungry, some of the children would run down the aisles of the room where they were eating and spit in the bowls of children who were not paying close attention to what was happening. Many of those children would be so disgusted they would give up the soup, and the spitting children would confiscate their portion, getting to eat double their usual amount of soup, even though it had spit in it. Other children would decide to go ahead and eat the soup even when it had someone else's saliva in it, but it would taste bad to them because of the spit. "Adler would use an interpretation to reframe the clients' symptoms in such a way that they would give them up—or if they still used them, they would be 'spoiled'" (Maniacci et al., 2014, p. 79). (I [TK] love this story—I was an English major as an undergraduate, and I was thrilled when I found out that Adler was basing part of his intervention on a Dickens book! Fan girl!) When the counselor accurately spits in clients' soup, clients may persist in the behavior, but once they gain an awareness of the underlying dynamics of what is going on, it becomes less likely to be something they want to continue.

Depending on the child's reactions, the child's style of play, and the particular situation, you may decide to communicate directly or indirectly. With a child who reacts favorably to direct interpretations, you will want to make guesses about the child's motivation and relationship patterns and talk about what the child's play and verbalizations might mean about the child. The following are examples of interpretation with direct tentative hypotheses and metacommunications:

- Riordan is kicking the punching bag and yelling, "I got you. You can't hurt me." You could say, "You seem to like being able to protect yourself. It looks like that is really important to you."
- Takiyah is painting a picture and asks you what color to paint a flower. you might say, "Sometimes you ask you what to do. I guess maybe you think if you do things that I want that I will like you better."
- Orlando is talking about how his brother always comes into his room and takes his toys. You might say, "Seems like it is hard for you when you feel like you don't have any privacy. I'm thinking that you don't like it when he doesn't do what you want him to do."

With a child who is resistant to or defensive about direct interpretations or who always brings the play back to a metaphoric level, you will usually want to focus on indirect interpretations, using the child's metaphor. This involves making tentative hypotheses and metacommunications about the actions and motivations of the toys—dolls, puppets, animals—or of characters in role-playing situations. Examples of interpretation with indirect tentative hypotheses and metacommunications:

- Harley is playing with the dolls in the dollhouse and has the littlest boy doll telling everyone else in the family what to do and getting angry because they are not doing it the way he wants them to do. You could say, "It seems like that little boy wants everybody to follow his directions and when they don't do it just right he gets kind of mad."
- In a role play, Violeta plays the mother and goes around making sure that everyone in the family has something to eat. The "mother" keeps complaining about needing to do stuff for other people. You could say, "Sounds like that mother might get tired of always taking care of everybody else. I think that maybe she wishes that she could just take care of herself and stop worrying about taking care of everybody else."
- Bakir is playing in the kitchen area, making a cake, and "feeding" the counselor. You might say, "When people take care of others, sometimes they feel pretty special and loving."

Using Metaphoric Techniques

Metaphor is a form of symbolic language that has been used for centuries as a method of teaching in many fields. The parables of the Old and New Testaments, the holy writing of the Kabbalah, the koans of Zen Buddhism, the allegories of literature, the images of poetry, and the fairy tales of storytellers—all make use of metaphor to convey an idea in an indirect yet paradoxically more meaningful way. This special power of metaphor has also been grasped by every parent and grandparent who, observing the forlorn features of the young child, seeks to bring consolation and nurturance by relating an experience to which the child can intuitively relate. (Mills & Crowley, 2014, p. 4)

In play therapy, the role plays, stories, puppet shows, sand trays, and artwork children create are all metaphoric ways for them to communicate about what is going on in their lives and an indirect way to process thoughts, feelings, attitudes, and experiences (G. Burns, 2005; Gil, 2014; Kottman & Ashby, 2002; Mills & Crowley, 2014; Perrow, 2008; Taylor de Faoite, 2014). You can use stories to (a) communicate messages to children; (b) teach them new ways of solving problems and interacting with others; (c) help them adjust their attitudes, perceptions, and outlooks; and (d) bypass their defensive reactions to more direct messages and teaching. The Adlerian play therapist can capitalize on the child's natural use of metaphors to help the child gain insight into his or her lifestyle. Five metaphoric techniques that lend themselves easily to play therapy application are (a) use of the child's own metaphor (see Chapter 5 for a description of how to do this), (b) custom-designed therapeutic metaphors, (c) Creative Characters (Brooks, 1981), (d) mutual storytelling, and (e) bibliotherapy. Unless we wanted this book to be WAY longer than it already is, we could not try to give you a complete understanding of the use of metaphoric techniques. If you are interested in learning more about this method of intervention, there are many books, articles, book chapters, and courses available on this subject.

Designing Therapeutic Metaphors for the Child
According to Taylor de Faoite (2014, p. 52),

As a therapeutic power of play, told and written stories are used to support the child's understanding of his or her feelings and experiences, their worries and anxieties . . . the specific power of stories and metaphors is that they provide a means of processing confusing feelings and experiences in the language of the imagination. The imagination is both the natural language of the child due to its concreteness and it prevents resistance associated with discussing issues directly with children.

In designing a therapeutic metaphor, the counselor develops a story that has some parallel to a situation in the child's life. Without pointing out the parallels, the counselor includes characters that represent selected people in the child's life and puts them into circumstances in which they experience problems that are similar to the problems the child is encountering. The characters express feelings that might echo the feelings of the child and other people who interact with the child. After some hardships, adventures, and attempts at solution, the characters usually solve the problem in a socially appropriate way. (Hopefully, because, really, what would be the point in the characters solving the problem in a socially inappropriate way? Most of the children we see already know how to do that.) This process is designed to give the child some ideas about new perspectives to take on his or her problem or potential solutions to deal with his or her own struggle.

There is some preparation you will need to do before you introduce any therapeutic metaphor. The process of therapeutic storytelling will work best in play therapy when you use toys as props, so you will want to watch which toys children like to use when they play and which toys seem to be a little scary to them. Spend time before you tell a story to children, listening to the kinds of stories they tell you and talking with them about books, movies, video games, and television shows they like. This will give you important information about what kinds of characters they like, what kinds of adventures appeal to them, and what kinds of emotional responses "hook" them. When you design your story with these factors in mind, it serves to increase their sense of involvement with the story, which can maximize the positive effects of the metaphor.

You will also want to consider how defensive the child is about certain situations and relationships so that you can determine how closely your story can parallel the child's real-life experiences. If the story is too close to the child's situation, he or she may shut down because it is too threatening. However, if the story does not have enough points of connection, it will not be interesting to the child. It is also important to consider the child's usual mode of communication to know how best to deliver the metaphor. If the child likes puppets, doing a puppet show will probably be the optimal way to deliver the metaphor. If the child likes movement and dancing, a story that incorporates music and movement will often appeal to him or her. If the child likes to draw, making a book with the words already in it that he or she can illustrate will probably be the best way to tell the story. (You get the idea—match what the child likes to do to how you deliver the story. The possibilities for the delivery system for the metaphor are endless, but they should be matched to the child's preferred format for play when possible.)

Many authors (e.g., G. Burns, 2005; Gil, 2014; Mills & Crowley, 2014; Perrow, 2008) have outlined their preferred procedures for designing therapeutic metaphors. We have taken their suggestions and combined them with our own experience and the experience of our students and supervisees to develop the following steps for devising therapeutic metaphors.

1. Before you begin to formulate your story, it is essential to decide your goal in telling the story. When you use stories in play therapy, you want to communicate or teach something to the child. During the third phase, you work to help the child gain insight into his or her lifestyle, so your

goal in this phase should be related to helping the child conceptualize self, others, or the world somewhat differently. When you use metaphors during the fourth phase, your goal will usually be related to teaching the child new behaviors. The goal for your telling the story should be relatively simple and concrete (e.g., wanting Felicity to acknowledge that being able to fix things is an asset; helping Felipe see that he is much more likely to connect with others if he does not hit them; helping Chandana recognize that she does not always have to control every interaction with her teacher). When you use a single story to try to work toward too many goals or when your goals are nebulous, your story will be diffused and ineffective.

2. On the basis of your previous interactions with the child, decide (a) which toys you want to use in your story, (b) whether you believe that the child will be more responsive to a story about animals or people or mythical creatures, (c) whether you believe that the child will be more interested in an event based in reality or a fantasy–fairy tale situation, (d) how close you can get to the actual situation in the child's life, and (e) how you want to deliver the metaphor.

3. Decide when and where you want the story to take place. It is best to dislocate the story in time, using either the past or the future as the time element of the story. Dislocating the story in space, using some other town, country, or world, is also helpful. Even if the story takes place last week or next month, in the next town or next door, by dislocating it in time and space, you create an emotional distance that allows the child to listen to the story without automatically having to think about the possibility that it might be about him or her. This sets the stage to bypass the child's defenses. If the story happens sometime in the past or in the future, some place other than here, it cannot be about his or her life (obviously, right?).

4. Describe the scene very clearly. It should not be completely the same as the child's situation, but it can have several parallels. The scene can be a natural setting ("in the jungle . . . "), a mythical setting ("in a place where all the animals could talk . . . "), or a realistic setting ("in my old neighborhood when I was a kid . . . ").

5. Describe the characters very clearly. Each character should have a name and physical and emotional traits as part of the introduction and description of the characters. The characters must include (a) the protagonist (an animal or person who represents the child) and (b) the antagonist (an animal, person, or situation that is creating problems for the protagonist). It is also helpful to have a resource person (someone who can provide advice or help for the protagonist—this character might represent the counselor, a parent, or teacher) and an ally or two (an animal or person who can provide support for the protagonist). Depending on the child and her or his level of imagination and maturity, these characters can be realistic or fantastic. Generally, the older the child, the bigger the cast of characters can be. With children under the age of 5, we frequently have either a resource person or an ally, but not both. Sometimes, depending on

the memory and verbal sophistication of the child, we leave these characters out, sticking to the good guy, the bad guy, and the plot.

6. Describe the problem encountered by the protagonist in concrete terms. This problem can be similar to the situation of the child, but the correlation should not be too obvious. You should not point out the parallel. It must be entirely up to the child to determine whether he or she wants to acknowledge the similarity. The problem can be related to a person and a relationship or to a situation that is causing the protagonist some kind of difficulty.

7. As the story proceeds, include different sensory information (visual, auditory, olfactory, kinesthetic, and tactile), so that the story becomes more "real" to the child. This will also help engage the child no matter what his or her primary information-processing modality is. Again, decide on how much detail to include on the basis of the developmental age of the child.

8. The protagonist should make progress toward overcoming the problem, but there should also be obstacles. The story needs to include a certain level of struggle so that the child feels that the protagonist has earned the final solution rather than simply having it happen. The resource person and the allies can help the protagonist when needed, but the protagonist should make the decisions and be responsible for the majority of the effort involved in overcoming obstacles and solving the problem. This conveys to the child that a person must be willing to work to bring about solutions to problems rather than having problems that just magically get solved.

9. Describe the resolution of the problem in concrete and clearly defined terms. The resolution does not have to completely eliminate the original situation, but it needs to demonstrate that the protagonist has made progress in learning to cope with the situation.

10. Remember your goal for the metaphor as you tell the metaphor—obstacles, the progress, and the resolution should all be related to the lesson you want to teach the child through the metaphor.

11. After the resolution, the characters should have some sort of celebration and affirmation of the changes in the protagonist. The focus of the celebration can be a party, with the allies and resource person congratulating the protagonist and the protagonist explaining to others what he or she has learned in the process of the adventure, or some other form of consolidation of the message of the metaphor. With younger children or older children who are very concrete, the resolution should blatantly state exactly what the protagonist has learned—how to see herself or himself and the situation differently; new attitudes toward self, others, and the world; new skills that will help him or her cope with similar situations in the future; or something similar to this. With children who are able to grasp more abstract lessons, the moral or learning does not have to be obviously stated but should be clearly illustrated in the story.

12. It is essential to watch the child's nonverbal reactions to the story as you tell it. Depending on the child's responses to the story (body language, eye movement and eye contact, activity and energy levels,

verbal comments, and level of participation), you may decide to make shifts in the story. For instance, if the child is extremely excited about a particular character, you might expand that character's role. If the child is getting restless or bored, you might wrap the story up more quickly than you had intended. If the child expresses interest in a more active role in the storytelling, you can either take turns or invite the child to take over the telling.

13. Decide if and how you want to process the story with the child (Gil, 2014; Kottman & Ashby, 2002). With some children, they want you to tell them the story and then let it go. When we work with these children, we find that it is usually best to honor their wishes. If and when they want to talk about the story, they will bring it up. Other children like to talk about the story without acknowledging that it has anything to do with them. With these children, we might ask them to talk about the feelings, behaviors, attitudes, decisions, consequences, relationships, and problem-solving strategies of the characters without mentioning that the story could be related to their situation. Other children actually bring up that the story has similarities to their own situation. We consider this an invitation to overtly process the connection between their lives and the story, inviting them to discuss the underlying messages and any lessons that they could apply in their relationship or with any struggles they might be experiencing. Gil (2014) suggested that you avoid asking closed or why questions and trying to get the child to explain the "real world" implications of the story.

The following is an example of a therapeutic metaphor I (TK) designed for Ramsey, a 7-year-old boy who lived with his aunt and uncle. Ramsey's mother and father had been killed in a car crash when he was 4, and he had generalized the anxiety from this experience into a reason to avoid taking any kind of risks, refusing to leave his aunt or try any new experiences. To help him explore the possibility of being a bit more courageous, I used a cheetah puppet to represent Ramsey and several other animal puppets to represent myself and his aunt and uncle. I used the fierce wind to represent Ramsey's anxiety and the stress related to his lack of courage. This is the metaphor:

One day a long time ago, Umi, a little cheetah cub whose name means Life, lived near a grove of banyan trees in the African plains with Jaha, a kindly lioness, and her husband, Badru. They lived next to a tree where a very smart vulture named Zahur lived. Umi lived with Jaha and Badru because his mother and father had disappeared when he was a very tiny cub. Umi always stayed very close to the trees because he was afraid that if he went very far from Jaha and Badru and the safety of the trees that he might disappear like his parents. He saw the other cheetah and lion cubs playing across a field, but he was too afraid to go over and play with them. He felt very lonely, but it was just too scary to think about leaving Jaha and Badru. Jaha and Badru were very concerned because they could not go and hunt together because one of them always needed to stay near the grove of trees with Umi so that he would feel safe. They were also worried because they knew that Umi would soon need to learn to hunt so that he could take care of himself, but he was so afraid that he was not learning to hunt. They did not know what to do to help Umi.

One day, when Umi was sitting around feeling lonely and sorry for himself, a fierce wind blew by, and Umi got swept up by the wind. Jaha and Badru came running out of the grove and shouted, "Umi, where are you going?" Umi cried out and waved at them, but he was holding on to a piece of wind and was afraid to let go.

The wind tossed him up and tossed him down. He was feeling very scared and a little sad and lonely. He missed Jaha and Badru already, and he was afraid that he would never see them again—that he was just going to disappear like his parents. Then he looked toward the ground, and there were Jaha and Badru running behind the wind. He heard them shout, "We are with you, and we will not let you be blown away. Try letting go, and fall down to us. We will catch you!" But Umi was too afraid to let go.

As the tornado went spinning over the plain, Umi saw some other little cheetahs playing and practicing their hunting skills. They looked like they were having a good time. Umi wished that he could let go and go down to see what they were doing and join in their games, but he was too afraid to let go.

Just then, the very smart vulture, Zahur, who was enjoying frolicking in the wind, noticed Umi riding along beside him. Zahur said to Umi, "Wow, isn't this fun? You look scared. Are you not having a good time?" Umi yelled, "No, I'm not!!! I don't like this at all, and I can't get out of here." Zahur shouted back, "Umi, can you scooch down to the end of the wind? I think you might be able to get away if you can do that." Umi replied, "No, I can't do that. I don't know how to scooch." Zahur shouted, "It couldn't hurt to try. Just let go of the piece of wind you're holding onto and slide!" Umi was very scared of letting go of the piece of wind because he didn't know what was going to happen, but he was even more scared of not ever seeing Jaha and Badru again and being lonely. He also thought that now would be a good time to get out of the wind so he could see what those cheetahs were playing. Umi closed his eyes, let go of the piece of wind, and scooched right down to the end of the piece of wind and popped out onto the ground right near the place in the plain where the little cheetahs were playing.

Up ran Jaha and Badru, who had been following the wind. They hugged Umi and told him how much they'd missed him and loved him. All the cheetah cubs roared and told him that popping off the tail of the wind was a very good trick. Umi thanked Zahur for his suggestion of letting go of the wind and scooching. He said, "You know, letting go of the wind was kind of scary, but falling wasn't nearly as scary as I thought it would be, and it was also kind of fun. Maybe I'll do that again sometime now that I know how to get out." Then he asked Jaha if it was OK if he ran over to play hunting with the other little cheetahs. Jaha smiled and nodded. Umi ran over to make some new friends and learn the ways of cheetahs in the hunt.

Creative Characters

Another storytelling technique that works very well with children age 8 years and older is Creative Characters (Brooks, 1981; Crenshaw, Brooks, & Goldstein, 2015). In Creative Characters, the play therapist uses several different characters to take turns telling a story with the child. The play therapist can record (either audio or video) the presentation of the story so that the child can listen to or watch it later, either in session or at home. Here is our adaptation of the technique:

1. Decide on the setting and the characters for the story.
   a. The setting can be either real or imaginary, but it should have some elements that are similar to the child's life. The more detailed description the beginning of the story is, the better chance that the child will get into the story.
   b. In designing the cast of the story, include a character who represents (a) the child; (b) the play therapist or another resource person with whom the child can consult about problem situations; (c) at least one ally for the character who represents the child; and (d) a reporter who asks the other characters for information, reactions, feelings, attitudes, plans, and so forth at various intervals throughout the story. You can also have a character to represent a problem situation or an antagonist in the child's life or you can have the main character encounter a dilemma that represents a difficult situation in the child's life.
   c. With the child's help, pick a puppet, doll, stuffed animal, or some other toy to represent each of these characters and give the characters names.
   d. Explain that each of the characters can talk and that you will tell the first part of the story, then the child will tell the next part of the story, you will tell the next part of the story, and so on. You can speak for all the characters at the beginning of the story, or you can assign certain characters to the child. However, it works best initially for you to speak for the reporter and the consultant, as the child may not understand how to interview the other characters or what kinds of advice a resource person would give to the other characters. Eventually, the child may also want to take over speaking for either the reporter or the consultant as well.
2. Tell the beginning of the story.
   a. Describe the setting and the characters in the story, emphasizing some of the physical characteristics of the toy or puppet that represents that character.
   b. In the beginning of the story, have the character representing the child face a dilemma or problem. The dilemma can resemble the child's presenting problem or another challenge facing the child. Be sure to make the connection relatively subtle and oblique, not emphasizing the parallels to the child's life.
   c. Have the main character work to solve the problem or change his or her relationship with the character or situation that represents the difficulty in the child's life, with the help of the ally characters.

d. The reporter intermittently interviews the other characters to find out how they are feeling and what they are thinking as the action of the story progresses.

e. The wise consultant–resource person provides advice, different perspectives, and information to the other characters as the story progresses.

3. Let the child take over the telling until he or she wants to hand it back.
4. Take turns with the child, telling the story, being the various characters.
5. End the story with some socially appropriate resolution of the dilemma or challenge facing the protagonist and a celebration of the positive attitudes and behaviors demonstrated by the protagonist and his or her allies. Usually, the reporter makes some kind of a summary statement at the end, congratulating the various characters on their efforts and progress and underlining the lessons you want the child to learn from the story.

Mutual Storytelling

Mutual storytelling is a metaphoric counseling technique developed by Richard Gardner (1993, 2004) that is particularly suited to Adlerian play therapy (Kottman, 2003, 2011). The basic strategy in mutual storytelling is for the counselor to ask the child to tell a story. Using the same characters, setting, and dilemma as the child's story, the counselor then retells the story with a different, more constructive middle and ending.

I (TK) have adapted the basic design of Gardner's technique to fit into the process of Adlerian play therapy. With younger children (up to about 7 or 8 years of age), I usually set the stage by asking the child to choose a set of puppets or animals, pretend they can talk, and tell a story with them. With older children (8 or 9 years and older), I often set the stage by telling the child that she or he is the guest of honor on a television or radio show (Gardner, 2004). I frequently make a recording of the child's story as if she or he is telling the story as a part of the show. Sometimes I ask the child to draw a picture and tell me a story about what is happening in the story, and sometimes I just ask the child to tell me a story with a beginning, middle, and end without any other setup.

It is helpful to suggest that the child invent a story that has not happened in real life or been the plot of a television show, movie, video game, or book. This keeps the story in the "made-up" realm, which lets children process their experiences without evoking their defenses and encourages children to use their creative imaginations. One problem that I have encountered using this technique is that many children appear to prefer to have their fantasies created for them by others rather than create their own fantasies. I have had quite a few clients who reported that they could not think of an original plot. When this happens, I just let the child tell me the story of a book, movie, video game, or television show. I do this because I have observed that even if the children do not have confidence in their own imaginations or are accustomed to using the creative products of someone else, they often impose their versions of reality on the plot they use. Their choice of a particular storyline and the way they tell the story reveal much about their lifestyles, and I can still use the story as a springboard for making suggestions for different interpretations of life situations or for possible solutions to problems.

The story needs to have a plot of some kind. The way I explain this to children is that the story needs characters and something needs to happen to those characters—they need to have some kind of problem to solve or adventure to experience. The story also needs a beginning, middle, and end. Sometimes children have difficulty with plot development, but I am willing to prompt them when this happens. If they are telling a story and it suddenly peters out, I often ask questions about what happens next, what the characters say in that situation, how the characters feel about the experience, and so forth.

As the child tells the story, I listen carefully to determine how the story metaphorically represents what is happening in the child's life. The story often has elements that illustrate the child's intrapersonal dynamics, specific situations or problems that are bothering the child, the child's typical mode of solving problems, and the child's relationships with significant others. I put my understanding in the context of what I already know about the child's lifestyle and look for ways to use my retelling of the story to help the child gain insight into his or her lifestyle. In this process, I ask myself the following questions, some of which were adapted from Gardner (1993, 2004) and some of which are designed to organize my thinking about the lifestyle themes and patterns embedded in the child's story:

- What is the overall affective tone of the story? What does the affective tone of the story tell me about the client's life?
- How do the actions of the characters in the story fit with what I already know about the client and the important people in his or her life?
- How do the situations or problems in the story resemble situations or problems encountered by the client in his or her life?
- Which characters represent the client?
- What are the (mis)behaviors of the characters that represent the client?
- How do those (mis)behaviors fit with my conceptualization of the client's goals of misbehavior? For example, does the character get into power struggles or try to prove that he or she cannot be controlled by others as would a person whose goal is power?
- How does the character who represents the client feel in the story? For example, has the character been hurt badly by others, and does he or she feel a need for revenge as would a person whose goal is revenge?
- How do the other characters in the story feel or respond to the (mis)behaviors of the character that represents the client? For example, are the other characters annoyed by the client–character, which would indicate that the goal of misbehavior is attention, or are they angry, which would suggest the goal is power?
- How would I feel or react if I had a similar interaction with someone like the character who represents the child? How would most adults feel or react to the character's behavior?

- If there is some kind of correction or consequences for negative behavior in the story, how does the character that represents the child react? For instance, does the character just give up as a person whose goal is proving inadequacy would?
- What does the story tell me about the client's Crucial Cs? How do the characters in the story connect with one another? Which of the characters are capable and in what ways? How do I know which characters feel that they count in the story? In what ways do characters manifest courage or lack of it?
- What does the story tell me about the client's personality priority? What does it tell me about the personality priorities of the other people in the child's life? Which characters seek to be comfortable, be in control, please others, or be superior to others? How do the characters go about doing this?
- What does the story tell me about how the client views himself or herself?
- What does the story tell me about the client's views about and attitudes toward other people?
- What does the story tell me about the client's usual approach to relationships?
- What does the story tell me about the client's attitude toward life?
- What does the story tell me about the client's usual approach to problem solving?
- What does the story tell me about the client's level of social interest?

After listening to the child's story, you will want to tell the child that you would like to tell another story about those same characters. This avoids the negative connotation of telling the child that you want to retell the story, which could easily imply that the original version was not good enough. Then you tell the story, using the same characters, same setting, and the same beginning as that of the child's story. The retelling should have a different middle and ending of the story, illustrating (a) more socially appropriate methods of problem solving; (b) more positive ways of viewing self, others, and life; (c) different ways of acting on personality priorities; (d) positive ways of building relationships and interacting with others; (e) strategies for feeling more connected, capable, significant, and courageous; (f) methods of gaining and manifesting courage; (g) alternative interpretations of personal issues that seem to be interfering with the child's ability to gain significance in appropriate ways; and (h) behaviors motivated more by striving toward cooperation and contribution than striving for attention, power, revenge, or proving inadequacy.

It is not necessary to retell the story immediately. Sometimes we might wait until later in the session to retell the story, and sometimes we might wait until a subsequent session. As we prepare to retell the story, we consider the following questions. We do not include elements related to all of these questions in the retelling. Instead, we tailor the retelling to the needs of the specific client who told the original story. You will need to consider the following:

- What is your goal in retelling the story? What do you want to teach the client with your narrative?
- What positive characteristics/traits/skills do you want to encourage in your client through this story?
- Which characters will you leave in? What will you try to accomplish with these characters? Do you want to add any characters? What traits will you incorporate in any added characters? Why would those characters be important with this client?
- How can you emphasize the strengths of the client's personality priority? How can you make clear the disadvantages of or price paid by having this personality priority? How can you suggest ways to capitalize on the strengths of this personality priority and minimize the price paid?
- Which of the Crucial Cs do you want to stress in the story? How can you illustrate strategies for connecting with others, becoming and feeling capable, gaining confidence in being significant, and having courage?
- Are you going to incorporate some kind of consequences for the (mis)behaviors in the story? What kind of consequence would be realistic, related, and respectful?
- Are you going to incorporate some kind of positive consequences for positive behaviors in the story? What kind of consequence would illustrate the importance of positive behaviors?
- How could you redirect any characters who are striving toward goals of misbehavior?
- How can the characters model more positive attitudes toward solving problems?
- What method of conflict resolution or problem-solving strategy do you want to illustrate in the retelling? How can you resolve the conflict in an appropriate and realistic way in the retelling?
- How can you incorporate more positive ways for the characters in the story to view themselves, the world, and others in the retelling? How can you incorporate more positive attitudes in the characters?
- How can you illustrate more appropriate ways of building relationships and getting along with others in the retelling?
- How can you illustrate alternative interpretations of personal issues that may be interfering with the child's ability to function?
- What social skills or other skills do you want to illustrate?
- What can you do in the story retelling to enhance the child's social interest?

The following is an example of mutual storytelling I (TK) cocreated with Keesha. I asked her to tell me a story with a beginning, middle, and end. She told me the following story:

There once was an elephant who lived in the jungle. The elephant liked to eat the leaves at the top of some tall trees. One day, all the leaves in his neighborhood were gone, so he decided to go to a different area in the jungle to get some leaves. He walked and walked until he found just the right tree with the leaves that he liked to eat. The only problem was that there was a family of monkeys who lived in the tree, and they didn't want him to eat all the leaves from their tree. They told him to go away, but he wouldn't. He wrapped his trunk around the tree and shook it until the monkeys fell out. They were really mad, and they tried to get back up into the tree. The elephant kept shaking the tree, but they still tried to climb it. The monkeys decided that they might be willing to share the leaves, but the elephant didn't want to share. The elephant told the monkeys if they didn't get away from the tree that he would stomp on them. They gave him the tree and went away.

Listening to this story, I believed that the elephant represented Keesha and the monkeys represented the other members of her family and her classmates. The overall affective tone seemed to be kind of bleak to me: The elephant got what he wanted, but there was no joy or celebration involved in the process. The story seemed to illustrate Keesha's lifestyle, exemplified by her view that she had to be powerful and in control, that others should be doing what she told them to do, and that if they did not she just needed to escalate her threats and she would get what she wanted. She seemed to feel that to count, she needed to overpower others. This was her usual manner of relating to others and of solving problems.

My goal for the retelling was to introduce the idea that Keesha did not have to overpower others to get her needs met. I wanted to suggest more constructive ways of solving difficulties, including negotiation skills. I thought it helpful to suggest that she could be significant without being overwhelming, with the goal of increasing her social interest. The following was my retelling:

There once was an elephant who lived in the jungle. The elephant liked to eat the leaves at the top of some tall trees. One day, all the leaves in his neighborhood were gone, so he decided to go to a different area in the jungle to see if he could get some leaves because he was very hungry. He walked and walked until he was really tired and feeling a bit crabby. Finally, he found a tree with the leaves that he liked to eat. The only problem was that there was a family of monkeys who lived in the tree, and they didn't want him to eat all the leaves from their tree. They told him to go away, but he didn't want to go away. He was hungry and crabby, and he wanted to eat those leaves. The elephant told the monkeys, "I am going to shake your tree and make you fall out if you don't let me have the leaves." The monkeys said, "Hey, wait a minute. Maybe we can work something out. We don't mind sharing some leaves with you today, but we live in this tree, and we don't want to lose all our leaves." The elephant said, "But I am tired, and I don't want to walk any farther to find more leaves for myself." The monkeys told him, "We will share some of our leaves with you today, and you can sleep here tonight. Tomorrow we will help you find some more trees with this kind of leaves. We can jump from tree to tree to help you." The elephant said, "Why would you help me to find some leaves?" The monkeys said, "You seem like a friendly animal, just a little tired and grumpy today. We would like to help you and be your friends." The elephant smiled. He hadn't had very many friends so far, but he would like to try to make some. Making friends with the monkeys seemed like it would be a good start.

With the retelling of a story, you can help the child gain insight into his or her lifestyle and examine whether he or she wants to make any changes in the box in which she or he is living. You can use bibliotherapy to do the same things.

Bibliotherapy

Another metaphoric intervention frequently used in Adlerian play therapy is bibliotherapy (Karges-Bone, 2015; Malchiodi & Ginns-Gruenberg, 2008; Recob, 2008; Shechtman, 2009). Bibliotherapy is a strategy in which books are used as a vehicle to help the child gain insight, consider a different perspective, or learn alternative ways of interacting with others. Bibliotherapy can communicate information, stimulate discussion, provide solutions to problems, and create awareness that others have dealt with similar problems.

To use bibliotherapy in play therapy, you would bring in a specific book designed to help the child gain insight or make behavior or attitude changes. You could read the book to the child, the child could read the book to him- or herself, or you and the child could read the book together. You can discuss what happened in the book and how it relates to the child and the child's lifestyle and situation, or you can just go on with the session without discussing anything.

With a child who prefers direct communication, it is usually appropriate to ask the child if he or she wants to talk about any thoughts, feelings, and reactions to the book and how it relates to his or her life situation. A child who would rather communicate indirectly through metaphor may not wish to discuss how the book relates to his or her life. This should not prevent you from using bibliotherapy with such a child. Many times, the child will learn things from the book without any verbal processing or will learn things from reading and discussing what happened in the book without actually mentioning any real-life situations. In choosing a specific bibliotherapy book for a child, it is essential to consider the following factors:

- The book must relate to the unique situation and issues of that child in some way.
- The book should be suitable for the child's developmental level and vocabulary. In deciding who should read the book, you must also be aware of the child's reading ability.
- The book must be well written, exciting, and involving. The perfect book involves all of the child's senses, evokes emotional and cognitive responses, and engages the child's imagination.

We have found (over a lot of years of experience) that children's literature books seem to work better than "therapeutic" books most of the time. We believe this is because they are better written, better illustrated, and make their points a bit more subtly than books that are designed to target a therapy goal. This doesn't mean that there are not good "therapeutic" books—it just means you should be discerning in choosing the books you use in your sessions.

To find appropriate books, you can consult a children's librarian (they are amazingly good sources of suggestions for great books for kids) or obtain an annotated guide to children's literature, such as *The Read Aloud Handbook* (Trelease, 2013), *Best Books for Children: Preschool Through Grade 6* (Barr & Gillespie, 2010), or *Best Books for Children, Supplement to the 9th Edition: Preschool Through Grade 6* (Barr, 2013). Guides such as these are usually organized by topic and contain plot summaries as well as reading and developmental levels.

You can choose books to help children with specific elements of their lifestyles. For instance, to help foster the Crucial Cs of courage, you might read a child any of the following books:

- *Beautiful Oops* (Saltzberg, 2010)
- *You've Got Dragons* (Cave, 2003)
- *One* (Otoshi, 2008)
- *The Pout-Pout Fish and the Big-Big Dark* (Diesen, 2010)
- *Courage* (Waber, 2002)
- *Scaredy Squirrel* (Watt, 2006)
- *Bravery Soup* (Cocca-Leffler, 2002)
- *The Worrywarts* (P. Edwards, 2003)
- *Wemberly Worried* (Henkes, 2000)
- *Wilma Jean, the Worry Machine* (Cook, 2012)
- *Orion and the Dark* (Yarlett, 2014)

To help instill a sense of being capable in a child who was struggling with that Crucial C, you might use books such as the following:

- *Sky Color* (Reynolds, 2012)
- *The Pout-Pout Fish Goes to School* (Diesen, 2014)
- *I Want Your Moo* (Weiner & Neimark, 2009)
- *The Little Engine That Could* (Piper, 2005)
- *Most Magnificent Thing* (Spires, 2014)
- *If I Could Keep You Little* (Richmond, 2010)
- *Elephants Can't Jump* (Willis & Reynolds, 2015)
- *How to Catch a Star* (Jeffers, 2004)
- *A Perfectly Messed-Up Story* (McDonnell, 2014)

With children who are having difficulty believing they count or are stuck thinking they count conditionally, the following books would be great resources:

- *Zero* (Otoshi, 2010)
- *Chrysanthemum* (Henkes, 1991)
- *Unique Monique* (Rousaki, 2003)
- *Lilly's Purple Plastic Purse* (Henkes, 1996)

- *The Invisible Boy* (Ludwig, 2013)
- *Red: A Crayon's Story* (Hall, 2015)
- *You Are Special* (Lucado, 1997)
- *I Believe in You* (Richmond, 2011)

Children who have difficulty connecting with others might benefit from books like these:

- *Don't Need Friends* (Crimi, 1999)
- *Recess Queen* (O'Neill & Huliska-Beith, 2002)
- *Zero* (Otoshi, 2010)
- *Two* (Otoshi, 2014)
- *Scaredy Squirrel Makes a Friend* (Watt, 2007)
- *Chester's Way* (Henkes, 1997)
- *Hygiene . . . You Stink* (Cook, 2014)
- *Stick and Stone* (Ferry, 2015)

If you are working with a child whose goal of misbehavior is attention, the following books are examples of bibliotherapy interventions you could use:

- *The Day Leo Said I Hate You!* (Harris, 2008)
- *Noisy Nora* (Wells, 1997)
- *Llama Llama Red Pajamas* (Dewdney, 2005)
- *I Need My Monster* (Noll, 2009)

With children whose goal of misbehavior is power, the following books might be helpful:

- *Recess Queen* (O'Neill & Huliska-Beith, 2002)
- *Zach Gets Frustrated* (Mulcahy, 2012)
- *I Just Don't Like the Sound of No!* (Cook, 2011)
- *All for Me and None for All* (H. Lester, 2012)
- *Bad Kitty* (Bruel, 2015)

For children striving toward revenge, the following book titles are examples that could help them explore the underlying dynamics of their interactions with others:

- *The Grouchies* (Wagenbach, 2009)
- *Horrid Henry's Revenge* (Simon, 2001)
- *Blossom's Revenge* (Geras, 2002)
- *Llama Llama Time to Share* (Dewdney, 2012)

The following books are examples of resources you could use with children whose goal of misbehavior is proving their inadequacy:

- *Pete the Cat and His Magic Sunglasses* (Dean & Dean, 2013)
- *The Pout-Pout Fish Goes to School* (Diesen, 2014)

- *The Pout-Pout Fish* (Diesen, 2008)
- *Shy Charles* (Wells, 1988)
- *The Invisible Boy* (Ludwig, 2013)
- *The Boy Who Didn't Want To Be Sad* (Goldblatt, 2004)

If you wanted to use books to help shift children from the destructive manifestation of their personality priorities toward the constructive manifestation, the following books would be examples of possible bibliotherapy tools.

For children whose personality priority is comfort:

- *Score One for the Sloths* (H. Lester, 1987)
- *The Pout-Pout Fish* (Diesen, 2008)
- *The Pink Refrigerator* (Egan, 2007)
- *Sparky!* (Offill, 2014)

For children whose personality priority is control:

- *Recess Queen* (O'Neill & Huliska-Beith, 2002)
- *One* (Otoshi, 2008)
- *Wallace's Lists* (Bottner & Kruglik, 2004)
- *Chester's Way* (Henkes, 1997)
- *Princess Penelope's Parrot* (H. Lester, 2001)
- *You Get What You Get* (Gassman, 2013)

For children with pleasing personality priorities:

- *Zero* (Otoshi, 2010)
- *Giraffes Can't Dance* (Andreae, 1999)
- *A Color of His Own* (Lionni, 1997)
- *A Bad Case of Stripes* (Shannon, 2004)
- *Ruby, the Copycat* (Rathmann, 2006)

For children whose personality priority is superiority:

- *The Other Dog* (L'Engle, 2001)
- *The Girl Who Never Made Mistakes* (Pett, 2011)
- *Unique Monique* (Rousaki, 2003)
- *Better Than You* (Ludwig, 2011)
- *I Am Cow, Hear Me Moo!* (Esbaum, 2014)
- *I Don't Want to Be a Frog* (D. Petty, 2015)

You might have noticed that several of these books are on more than one list (and others could be put on several of the lists, we just didn't want to take up that much space in the book). That is because you can use them for more than one targeted intervention. Depending how you set it up and how you process it with the child, a book could help with a variety of issues. Plus (as you have probably noticed by now), there are many overlapping issues—like children who are on the maladaptive side of the control personality priority often have power as their goal of misbehavior and may be struggling with the Crucial C of connect or be overcompensating for believing they are not capable or they don't count. This list is totally not exclusive. Now that we have planted the seed that you can use children's literature to help children gain insight (and, in many cases with reorientation and reeducation by teaching them specific skills or instilling more positive attitudes or outlooks), you will begin to have brainstorms about which books you can use with which children to accomplish your therapeutic goals. For instance, you could use *Katie's Babbling Brother* (Hutchins, 1996) with a child who is struggling with a younger sibling getting a lion's share of the attention in the family; *Ish* (Reynolds, 2004) with a child who is too tight and you are working to provide some loosening; *This Is Not My Hat* (Klassen, 2012) with a child who is stealing; *The Adventures of Beekle: The Unimaginary Friend* (Santat, 2014) with a child who is being teased about having an imaginary friend; *A Handful of Quiet: Happiness in Four Pebbles* (Hanh, 2012) for teaching a child to self-regulate using meditation and mindfulness. Yikes—okay, we could get very carried away with this line of thinking—maybe we should write a book about books you could use in therapy! You get the idea. Be prepared to find books that you loved when you were a child and raid the books on your own children's or grandchildren's bookshelves for using in your sessions from now on.

Directing Role Plays

During the third phase of Adlerian play therapy, the counselor can use directed role play to help children get insight into their patterns of thoughts, feelings, and behaviors and begin to consider new ways of thinking, feeling, and behaving. This is especially effective with children who are stuck in a particular negative fantasy or who are replaying a traumatic event. These children repeatedly play through a scene with a discouraging ending—session after session, without ever changing the progression or the outcome of the drama.

In situations in which the counselor believes this repetition is allowing for catharsis or abreaction, it is appropriate to use the whisper technique to let children control the course of the role play until they decide they are ready to change it. Other times, the counselor's clinical judgment suggests that children are perseverating on the negative outcome because they do not know how to change the scenario (Kottman, 2011). These children may not have enough data to generate other possibilities or enough insight to be able to see alternative paths for resolution. After six to eight repetitions with these children, we try to change the course of the role play by adding a different character or taking the narrative in another direction without using the whisper technique to get instructions from the child. In situations like these, we do not want the child to be in charge of the direction of the play because he or she does not seem to be able to use the play in a therapeutic way.

In some cases, children may be exhibiting posttraumatic play (Gil, 2006, 2010; Malchiodi, 2014; Terr, 1990). In posttraumatic play, children seem to be almost retraumatizing themselves with the play, which is neither cathartic nor therapeutic. If the counselor suspects this is the case and is feeling unsure about what to do, it is helpful to reexamine the course of the therapy, consult with colleagues about the best course of action with this child, or seek supervision. One possible intervention strategy with these children is to suggest that the play or role play go in a different direction. When we decide to change the course of the role play, we usually use the character voice rather than the whisper voice or our regular voices. This way, we can keep the suggestions and redirections we want to make framed in the metaphor of the child's role play.

The following is an example of a role play with a child who needs help to get out of a stuck position. Cassandra (age 6) had been sexually abused by her stepfather. She acted out a scenario in which a monster was coming to hurt her and she wanted to hide but could not move. She repeated this for 10 sessions in a row. I (TK) believed that Cassandra felt stuck in this scenario, and even though she knew her stepfather was in jail and we had discussed good touch and bad touch and how to protect herself, she continued to feel helpless and unable to protect herself from a personal violation in any way. Initially, I let Cassandra control the scenario without my influencing the course of the role play. It always played out something like the following:

> *Cassandra* (in a loud, deep voice): "I am the bad monster, and I am going to come into your room and hurt you."
> *Terry* (whisper voice): "What do you want me to do?"
> *Cassandra*: "You say, 'I'm scared and I can't keep him out of my room. He's going to hurt me, and I can't stop him. I can't even move.'"
> *Terry* (character voice): "I'm scared, and I can't keep him away from me. I can't even move. He's going to hurt me, and I can't stop him." (regular voice): "Sounds like this is a scary monster, and I can't stop him from hurting me." (whisper voice): "What should I do now?"
> *Cassandra*: "You look scared and hide under the covers." (her character voice): "You know you can't hide from me. I can hurt you any time I want to, and you can't stop me."
> *Terry* (hiding; whisper voice): "What should I do now?"
> *Cassandra*: "Say, 'No, no, no, no!!! Go away and leave me alone.'"
> *Terry* (character voice): "No, no, no, no!!! Go away and leave me alone!" (regular voice): "Sounds like I'm really scared of this monster and wish I could make him stop hurting me. I feel like I just can't though. I can't get him to leave me alone. I can't even move."

Sometimes Cassandra played the frightened child, and sometimes she played the monster. The basic sequence stayed the same, with the child having no power and the monster having all the power. After the 10th repetition, I decided to try to help Cassandra gain insight by changing some of the representations of the child as helpless and model some appropriate boundary setting and ways of handling boundary violations. I still used the whisper technique, but when I was the child in the role play,

I changed some of my comments to more empowered language, and I made some suggestions of alternative solutions to the problem.

> *Cassandra:* "I am the bad monster, and I am going to come and hurt you."
>
> *Terry* (regular voice): "That monster says he's going hurt me." (whisper voice): "What should I do?"
>
> *Cassandra:* "You say, 'I'm really scared of that bad monster. He can do whatever he wants to me, and I can't stop him.'"
>
> *Terry* (character voice): "I'm really scared of that bad monster. He thinks he can do whatever he wants to me, and he believes that I can't stop him. I wonder what he would do if I locked the door to my room and didn't let him set foot in this room." (whisper voice): "What should I do now?"
>
> *Cassandra:* "You look scared and hide under the covers." (In her character voice): "You can't hide from me. I can always get you. So what if you lock the door? I will just break the lock."
>
> *Terry* (character voice): "You think you can break the lock, but if you do, I can tell my mom."
>
> *Cassandra* (character voice): "You can't tell your mom. If you do, I will just tell her that you broke the lock yourself. Then you will really be in trouble."
>
> *Terry* (whisper voice): "What shall I do now?"
>
> *Cassandra:* "Tell the monster that my mom won't believe him. She knows I never lie."
>
> *Terry* (character voice): "Ha!! My mom won't believe you. She knows that I never lie. She will believe me, and you won't ever be able to come to my house again. You might even have to go to jail."

I did two basic things in my altered version of this role play. I used language to reframe the situation, and I suggested some alternative ways of handling the situation. I changed the child's words slightly, from "He can do whatever he wants to me, and I can't stop him" to "He thinks he can do whatever he wants to me, and he believes that I can't stop him." This small change in the language took some of the monster's power away from him and gave that power to the child. By introducing the idea that the child might be able to gain some control over the interaction by locking the door and talking to her mother, I attempted to communicate to the child that there are other ways of perceiving and reacting to the situation, that there are ways for her to gain more power in this interaction and perhaps other interactions. This was not a permanent solution to the child's difficulties, but it helped her gain some insight and gradually ease past the stuck place represented by her perseveration on the role play.

Using Art Techniques

The Adlerian play therapist can expand the art techniques used in the exploration phase to help the child gain insight into her or his lifestyle. Extending kinetic art experiences, creating cartoon helpers (Mills & Crowley, 2014), drawing body outlines or body maps (Santen, 2015; Steinhardt, 1985), making puppets and masks (Buchalter, 2009), and crafting symbolic representations of the child and significant people and important situations in the child's life (Lombardi, 2014; Oaklander, 1978/1992; Ray, Perkins, & Oden, 2004; Segel, 1991; Wolf, 2014) are some art techniques the therapist can use in this stage of therapy or in any of the other three stages. If you are comfortable with art interventions, you will want to explore other resources for creative possibilities to include in the play therapy process.

Extending Kinetic Art Activities
By bringing kinetic family drawings and kinetic school drawings from the second phase into later sessions, the play therapist can use them to help children reevaluate their perceptions of themselves, others, and the world. The therapist can also ask children to draw different pictures with the family or school theme. Children can draw pictures of the ideal family or ideal classroom, visualizing changes that they would like to have happen. They can draw pictures of different people in their lives and how they would like to change their relationships with them. They can pretend that they have a magic wand that could make all the problems of the family go away and draw a picture of what the family would look like if this happened. In all of these activities, the emphasis would be on the relationships between the various people in the lives of the children.

It is important to remember that this strategy can be tailored to the individual child and his or her art talents and preferences. If a child feels more comfortable painting or using clay, stickers, pipe cleaners, collage, dance, music, or any other form of artistic expression to represent what is happening in his or her life, you should use that medium for encouraging insight. By responding creatively to the child, you can design nonverbal techniques that will encourage self-expression and psychological awareness.

Creating Cartoon Helpers
In cartoon interventions, children create cartoon helpers who can help them with their problems (Mills & Crowley, 2014). You can use the cartoon helpers as a vehicle for making suggestions for new ways to look at self, others, and the world. Children can use the cartoon helpers as a vehicle for finding their own inner strengths and resources for coping with difficulties. Drawing cartoon helpers can provide ways for children to express and cope with fears and anxieties and ways for exploring alternative methods of solving problem situations and relationships. Older children (age 8 and above) seem really to like these strategies. There are an infinite number of ways you could use cartoon helpers, limited only by your imagination. One example of this type of intervention involves three steps. The child:

1. draws a fear, worry, or hurtful situation;
2. draws a cartoon helper who can help deal with the problem; and
3. draws how the fear, worry, or hurtful situation will look when it is resolved.

In this strategy, the child generates the solution to the problem. The cartoon helper serves as a metaphoric bridge from the problem to the solution.

Another example of a cartoon intervention involves the child drawing a problem situation. You could make several different copies of the cartoon and invite the child to develop multiple different cartoon helpers with different strengths to help solve the situation. This encourages the child to consider the possibility that there are multiple solutions to any problem.

A third example of using cartoon helpers would be for you (if you can draw—neither of us can, but we have some amazing students who have used this technique) to draw a cartoon hero who had positive things to say to the child that the child seems to be reluctant to hear directly from you. The cartoon hero can serve as an indirect vehicle for pointing out strengths and assets.

Drawing Body Outlines

Another art activity that can help children gain insight into their lifestyle involves the child lying on the floor on a large sheet of paper while you trace around his or her body. You can use these body outlines in a number of different ways. Santen (2015) used body outlines to help children who are dissociating by visualizing "their subconscious strategy after a traumatic experience, by picturing the inner landscape that emerged as a way to cope" (p. 126). Steinhardt (1985) described a procedure for using body outlines in which the counselor engages the child in dialogue about the identity of the figure. After the child has identified the figure, he or she fills in the details of the drawing. Steinhardt suggested that the child frequently makes the outline a self-portrait. By asking questions and making guesses about the child, his or her perceptions of self, and his or her relationships with others, you can use this drawing in the process of helping the child gain insight into his or her lifestyle. If the child chooses to make the outline a portrait of someone else, you can use the identity of the drawing and the completion of the portrait to further explore the child's perceptions of others and the world.

We have found this technique to be useful with children who need to change the strength of their personal boundaries. With children who have weak personal boundaries (quite frequently children who have overprotective and suppressive families or who have experienced sexual or physical abuse), we draw the outline very faintly. We use the body outline drawings to help them become aware of times when their boundaries are inappropriately weak. With children who have impermeable boundaries (usually children who feel rejected by their families or who have been significantly hurt by others and seek to protect themselves), we draw the outline with heavily reinforced lines. We use the drawings to help these children consider the possibility of opening their boundaries to let others approach them in friendship and support. Adopted children or children in foster care can also benefit from this intervention strategy. We use the body outline to help these children differentiate the physical, mental, and emotional traits that come from their biological and environmental influences. If you happen to be working with children who are not comfortable with your tracing around their bodies, you can also teach them to make very large "gingerbread people" on the paper and use them the same way.

Making Puppets and Masks

Many children love puppets, and the ones who also like art really love making puppets. You can make puppets out of just about any material—flowerpots, fly swatters, wooden spoons, feather dusters, old gloves, cardboard rolls (yes, toilet paper or paper towel rolls), popsicle sticks, and anything else you can imagine (Buchalter, 2009). One of our favorites is using old gloves to make puppets representing the child and a friend, sibling, or parent and then asking the child to put them on and have a conversation between their hands. You can use this to facilitate the child developing insight into the usual kinds of conversations he or she tends to have with others and even move into the fourth phase and have them practice more socially appropriate conversations. Sometimes kids will even invite you to put on a glove and join in the conversation.

I (TK) developed a Popsicle stick puppet technique I called Pocket Pals for one of my clients who was having difficulty making friends, partly because she was trying to be friends with the most popular kids in the third grade. (And, I hate to say this, but she was not the kind of person most popular 8-year-olds would want to befriend—short, chubby, nerdy, with multiple learning disabilities and ADHD). I wanted her to get insight into the kinds of people she wanted as friends and the kinds of people who would want her for a friend. I had her list the things she wanted in a friend and had her draw symbols (like a heart for caring and ears for being a good listener) on a Popsicle stick. I had her make a list of the positive attributes she brought to a friendship and make another Popsicle stick person to represent herself. She decided the two Popsicle sticks would be friends and they could and hang out whenever they wanted (in her pocket mostly, but sometimes she took them out and played with them). The other children in her class were actually curious about the Pocket Pals, and (for a short time) she was quite popular because she was willing to take Popsicle sticks her mother bought for her and make friends for the other kids in her class.

Children also love masks—masks made from paper plates, tin foil, paper mâché, purchased plastic or cloth, cut-out felt. You can use them to help children gain insight into their thinking and feelings. For example, they can use masks to illustrate the face they show the world and the face they hide from everyone else, what they know about themselves and what other people know about them, the negative things they tell themselves and the positive things they could tell themselves, the feelings they experience when they are alone and the feelings they experience when they are with others.

Using Symbolic Representations

There are many other ways to use symbolic representations of the situations and relationships in children's lives so that they can begin to make shifts in their attitudes, perceptions, thoughts, feelings, and behaviors. For instance, Oaklander (1978/1992) described "The Rosebush" in which children draw rosebushes (which usually stand for themselves and their life situations). After they have finished making the drawing, the counselor engages the rosebush in a metaphoric dialogue about its life. Children also can draw all of the members of their families symbolically—designing a special symbol for each person in the family (Oaklander, 1978/1992). The counselor can use this information to help children understand their thoughts, feelings, and reactions to the other members of their families. It is also appropriate to use this technique to help children who are struggling in school to express their impressions of their teachers and classmates (Ray et al., 2004).

Another method of helping children gain insight uses animal photographs selected from magazines (Segel, 1991). Animal phototherapy interventions can be used with individual clients, with groups, and in family sessions. In the original version of this activity (Segel, 1991), the counselor gives the client a selection of photographs gathered from magazines depicting a variety of animals. In the assortment of photographs, the counselor includes many different "types" of animals—wild, domestic, aggressive, "sweet," and so on. The client chooses an animal that has some kind of appeal for him or her, and the counselor asks the client to describe the animal. The counselor then asks the client to respond to the following questions:

- What drew you to pick this animal? (With younger children, we ask some form of the question, "What do you like about this animal?")
- What positive qualities do you share with this animal? (With younger children, we ask, "How are you like this animal?" or "How do you act like this animal?")
- What positive qualities does this animal have that you wish you shared, but don't? (With younger children, we ask, "What are the things this animal does that you wish you could do?")
- How would your life be different if you did have those positive qualities? (With younger children, "How would you be happier if you did those things?")
- What keeps you from having those positive qualities? (With younger children, "How come you don't do those things?")
- What changes are you willing to make in your life to acquire those positive qualities? (With younger children, "What are you going to do differently so you can be more like that animal that you like?")

I (TK) have adapted the original activity to give children two different ways to explore the dynamics in their family (or classroom). In the first version, I give clients a selection of photographs gathered from magazines depicting groups of animals; some of the photographs are of obvious families, some of them contain a gathering of animals from the same species, and others contain a gathering of animals from a variety of species. I ask the client to choose "a family" or "a class," depending on whether I want to explore issues related to home or school. After the client makes a choice, I ask for a description of the gathering. Then I ask the following questions, using the metaphor of the photographs as a way of allowing to the child to explore these issues indirectly:

1. What are the strengths and weaknesses of this family (class)?
2. What does this family (class) do well? What does this family (class) do poorly?
3. What would the members of this family (class) like to change about the family (class)?
4. What is the main difficulty encountering this family (class)?
5. How would the lives of the family (class) members be different if this difficulty was eliminated?
6. How do you think the family (class) could go about eliminating this difficulty?

With some children, I may move to less metaphorical questions:

1. How does this family (class) resemble your own family (class)?
2. What strengths does your family (class) share with this family (class)?
3. What weaknesses does your family (class) share with this family (class)?
4. What would you like to change about your family (class)?
5. What is the main difficulty in your family (class)? How does it resemble the difficulty of the family (class) in the picture?
6. How would the lives of the members of your family (class) be different if this difficulty was eliminated or reduced?
7. How would the lives of the members of your family (class) be the same if this difficulty was eliminated or reduced?
8. What part do you play in creating or maintaining this difficulty?
9. What are you willing to do differently to help eliminate or reduce this difficulty?
10. What do you think other members of your family (class) need to do differently to eliminate or reduce this difficulty?
11. How can you communicate with other members of your family (class) about this?

In a second adaptation of the animal photograph activity, I give the client a selection of photographs gathered from magazines depicting individual animals. I ask the client to choose an animal to represent himself or herself and an animal to represent each of the members of his or her family and arrange them on a large piece of poster board. I then ask the client to describe (a) each animal, including assets and liabilities; (b) how the family member resembles the animal, stressing assets and liabilities; and (c) how each of these animals relates to the animal that represents the client. After we have established these relationships, I often ask the child to have the animals "talk" to one another, move them around on the paper, and see how the animals react. I may also ask other questions or metacommunicate in an effort to help the client gain new perspectives on the relationships in the family and how he or she interacts with others. This is a fascinating exercise to do with multiple family members because it can help them gain insight into how they are perceived by one another.

Other art activities you could do would be to have children make pets, draw bridges, build bird's nests, create timelines, paint dragons or monsters, make collages, make a worry tree, or construct a volcano (Buchalter, 2009; Joiner, 2012). For instance, if you were working with children who believe they are unlovable or who feel untrustworthy, making a pet is a wonderful thing to do. You would first have them make a list of things they need to feel loved or trusted and then have them create a pet with various materials, like Styrofoam balls, yarn, pipe cleaners, and glitter. The idea is that the pet would have the qualities or skills needed to convey love or trust (kind of like having an invisible friend who cares for you and believes in you). When working with children who need to move from one place to another (either literally or figuratively), you can have them draw a bridge or cut construction paper and make one. The bridge can represent how they can move from one place to another (not speaking to a younger sister to having a positive relationship with her, failing every spelling test to passing them, etc.). If you have children on your caseload who have difficulty asking for or accepting nurturing, making bird's nests out of cut-up cardboard or yarn or pipe cleaners with them is an activity you can use to help them explore how they could learn to do this. You can help children make timelines to explore the events in their lives that have had an impact on the way they see themselves, others, and the world. After reading *You've Got Dragons* (Cave, 2003), you can have them paint or draw their dragons and then help them figure out how to conquer them (or make friends with them if that seems to work better). Making collages with pictures and words cut out of magazines is another art tool for helping children gain insight into their lifestyles. You could have them make a collage about the things they like about themselves, ways to make friends, things that bug them, ways they could be more courageous, activities they could do that would be a contribution to their family or class, and a thousand other topics. They could draw, paint, or use construction paper and glue to make a mosaic worry tree that would give their anxiety a physical expression. You could then have them add elements to the creation that would show ways they could self-sooth so that they were not so bothered by their worries. With children who have anger issues (that phase totally cracks us up—lately we have had 4- and 5-year-olds telling us that they have "anger management problems"—argh!), you could help them make a paper mâché volcano and use baking soda and vinegar to make it explode, then discuss ways to keep the explosion from making a huge mess. Again, the possibilities are endless—just use your imagination.

Sand Tray Activities

During this phase of play therapy, sometimes the Adlerian play therapist asks the child to create sand trays and sometimes he or she creates a sand tray for the child (or parents in some cases). Most the time, the trays the child does are directed trays—with instructions from the play therapist designed to help foster insight.

The following are examples of trays you could suggest during this phase:

- a Wonderful, Fantastic Day or a Horrible, No Good Day
- three wishes

- favorite book, fairytale, movie, TV show, video game
- a dream the child has had
- things that bug the child and what could be done to make them better
- a time when the child felt successful solving a problem
- a time when the child felt discouraged trying to solve a problem
- timeline tray (my life, my week, my year, etc.)
- the kingdom of the Prince (King, Princess, Queen) of Quite a Lot
- a place where everything is easy, comfortable, successful
- a life in which the child is guaranteed success at everything
- meeting a character who breathes fire (or other traits that symbolically represent something that the child must encounter in another person or situation in his or her life)—the question is, "What will you need to take to be able to deal with this character?"
- going to a new world (a place the child has never been before—you would describes it—it can be a dinosaur world, a new planet, outer space, etc.)—the child picks a character that represents him or her and a character who knows something about this world and is going with him or her and can give advice—the tray is planning the trip and what the characters need to take with them
- a situation in which someone who has a problem similar to the child's problem enters a maze (or obstacle course), using objects in the tray as obstacles—the child names the destination, chooses a character to traverse the maze, finding solutions for dealing with the obstacles along the way

You can also create trays for the child as a way to help him or her gain insight. The following are some examples of trays you could make for the child, like a sand tray that shows:

- your understanding of how the child sees self, others, and the world;
- your understanding of child's private logic;
- your understanding of the parent–child relationship;
- how the family atmosphere or family constellation is affecting the child;
- your perception of the child's Crucial Cs/personality priorities/goals of misbehavior and how they are being played out in the child's relationships with others; and
- figures that represent the child's mistaken beliefs who interact with a "wise" character who is there to reframe the mistaken beliefs or spit in the child's soup.

At times, you might decide to do an interactive tray, in which both you and the child take turns putting figures in the tray. One example would be a tray in which you and the child use figures to depict a problem and then you would take turns adding things to the tray or take things out of the tray to show potential solutions. Another would be to set up a tray as a mutual storytelling experience, in which the child tells a story in the sand tray and then you retell the story or you co-tell a story like the ones in Creative Characters.

Dance and Movement Experiences

With children who are tactile–kinesthetic learners or children who just like to move or express themselves physically, there are many dance and movement activities that can help them gain insight. One of these that both of us use is to have children show us how they move in certain specific circumstances—for instance, when they feel shy, feel confident, have just passed (or failed a test), are around someone they like (or dislike), have had a fight on the playground or at home before school, and so forth. We tend to have them move in a positive way, in a less positive way, and then back to the positive way. This gives them a chance to "lock in" the positive bodily experience. When we are working with children on particular relationships, we might have them coach us about how the other person in the relationship might move, show us how they move when they are interacting with that person, and then we perform a "dance" together about that relationship. Sometimes we help these children design a new, more constructive dance they could invite the other person to perform with them as a way of moving toward a more positive place within the relationship. We also might give children a homework assignment connected to movement—we might ask them to watch the popular children in their class, watch people they know are confident or successful, or watch children they know have a lot of friends to see how these other people move through the world. (Foreshadowing: in the fourth phase, we will ask them to see if they can move in those same ways, often resulting in their moving through the world in more constructive ways.) Again, just as with all of the other strategies in this phase, the only limits to what you can do to help children gain insight into their lifestyles are your own imagination and your willingness to experiment and take risks in trying new things.

Adventure Therapy Techniques

There are many adventure therapy techniques that would be helpful in this phase. There are a plethora of these techniques described in a variety of books, so we are only going to give you the directions for a couple we often use: Safety Cars (Kottman et al., 2001) and Circles of Comfort (Ashby et al., 2008). If you get into adventure therapy, you can always go out and get more resources (especially those two we just referenced—I (TK) need to plan for my retirement . . .).

Safety Cars is a great game to help a child who might have had issues with trusting or being trusted to get to experience a safe way of taking a risk. This activity is also a great way for a child to practice asking to have his or her needs met or to learn to give and take feedback and encouragement. Here is how you would play:

1. Stand in front of the child, with both of you facing the same way. Hold your hands out in front of your chest in a protective position. You are the "car."
2. Have the child stand behind you with his or her hands on your shoulders, back, or hips (depending on your relative heights). The child is the "driver."

3. Remind the driver that it is his or her job to keep you safe and to help you feel as safe and comfortable as possible. It is his or her job to make sure that you come to no harm.
4. As the car, explain that it is your job to give the driver feedback, suggestions, and other input to make sure that you feel safe. You can explain that you might ask for the driver to slow down, speed up, give you more encouraging comments, and so forth.
5. Tell the driver that you trust him or her so much you are willing to move around the room with his or her guidance with your eyes closed.
6. Proceed to have the driver drive you around the room for 2–5 minutes.
7. If the child is comfortable after being the driver, you can switch and have the child be the car and you the driver. You can give an option of having his or her eyes open or closed, depending on how comfortable and trusting the child is feeling at the time.
8. You can process how each role felt and what the child might need to feel more confident as the driver and comfortable as the car the next time you play this game.

Here's how you would play Circles of Comfort as a way to help a child (usually one older than 7) explore his or her level of comfort with specific situations or relationships:

1. Use masking tape or rope to form a larger circle and a smaller circle inside of it (sort of resembling a target).
2. Explain to the child that the areas inside and outside of the circles represent different degrees of "comfort."
3. Tell the child that the area inside the smaller circle in the middle is the "comfort zone." In this area, the child would feel relaxed and comfortable, not anxious or stressed at all.
4. Explain that the area between the smaller circle and the larger circle is the "challenge zone." In this area he or she might feel challenged; it will be a little more stressful or anxiety-provoking than in the comfort zone, but should not feel awful or terribly unpleasant, just uncomfortable.
5. Finally, explain that the area outside the larger circle is the "chaos" or "crazy" zone. In this area, the child might feel out of control and very stressed and anxious.
6. Next, you will ask the child to move to a different area (i.e., comfort, challenge, or chaos–crazy) based on his or her reaction to a particular situation or relationship. Some examples would be speaking to a group of 100 other kids, singing a solo in music class, taking a math pop quiz, flying on an airplane, having the principal come on the loud speaker and tell the whole school that he or she would like to have you come to the office, making a speech to your class, having a new baby brother or sister, moving to a new school. (You will want to tailor the list you use to things you know are going on in the child's life. The list is only limited by your own imaginations—go wild!)
7. We don't ask kids to tell us why they are comfortable or uncomfortable; we just watch for patterns—remembering that why questions are kind of a "no-no."

Immediacy and Confrontation

Immediacy, confrontation, and humor are all action-oriented techniques that the Adlerian play therapist can use to help the child better understand her or his lifestyle. They can lead to new ways of looking at self, others, and the world and to changes in behavior. (Humor comes easily to us because we think we are hil-ar-ious!)

Immediacy

When using immediacy as a counseling technique, you would metacommunicate or ask a question about what is happening in the here and now of the relationship with the client. Immediacy can involve communicating about a reaction on the part of the counselor or about a nonverbal response on the part of the client. The purpose of immediacy is to use what happens in the safe counseling relationship to help the client become more aware of his or her own reactions and of how other people respond to him or her.

With children, you have to use immediacy with caution. You will want to be very careful not to sound accusing when using immediacy because adults often ask children questions about what is happening with them in an accusing way and children often assume that you are doing the same thing. Your words, tone of voice, and nonverbal communication must always be nurturing and supportive when using immediacy in play therapy.

You must also consider the developmental level of the child before using immediacy. Younger children (up to 7 or 8 years old) will have very little awareness of their own reactions and frequently cannot recognize them when you comment on them. Older children may not be aware of their own reactions, but they are frequently able to respond to questions or comments if you use immediacy with them. Examples of immediacy:

- "I noticed that you looked kind of scared when I moved my chair closer to you. What was going on with you at that moment?"
- "I feel like you're kind of mad at me right now."
- "We both had a really good time playing catch with each other."
- "When you yell at me, I feel kind of scared, and I wish that you would ask for what you want without yelling."

Confrontation

Confrontation as a counseling tool involves pointing out discrepancies in the client's communication. These discrepancies can occur between (a) the client's verbal and nonverbal communication, (b) what the client is saying and what the client is doing, (c) what the client is reporting in the present session and what the client reported in past sessions, or (d) what the client is reporting and what the counselor has observed. In play therapy, the counselor can also mention discrepancies between what the child is reporting and what parents or the teacher reports or between the message contained in the child's play in the current session and the message of the play in previous sessions.

The purpose of confrontation is to help the child become more aware of inconsistencies in his or her thinking, feeling, and behaving. Many times, the discrepancies in the child's interactions result from private logic and mistaken convictions that would not necessarily make sense to others. By pointing out discrepancies, you can help the child gain an understanding of the misperceptions or distortions in his or her assumptions.

With children, we use confrontation very sparingly and gently. It is not our job to catch the child in discrepancies, but when they occur we sometimes choose to use confrontation to highlight them so that the child can begin to catch himself or herself in mistaken convictions and perceptions. We try to do this in a nonthreatening way, with a gentle, questioning tone of voice and supportive demeanor. Just as with immediacy, it is essential to avoid sounding accusing to the child, so we confine our confrontations to a mention of the facts and just the facts. (You do not want to jump up and yell, "You lying little . . . I've got you now." That would be a bad technique.) Examples of confrontation:

- "I've noticed that you say you're not scared of that spider, but when you picked it up you looked like you were kind of scared."
- "You said that you weren't getting in fights with your brother anymore, but last week while I was talking to your mom you two got into a fight in the waiting room."
- "When we were talking last time, you said that you got all As on your report card. When I talked to Mr. Hayes, he said that you had one A and the rest Cs."

Making Connections Between the Play Session and the Real World

By making connections between the child's thoughts, emotions, reactions, and behaviors in the play session and the child's thoughts, emotions, reactions, and behaviors outside the play session, the Adlerian play therapist can help the child generalize insights gained in the third phase of counseling. The therapist points out (a) instances in which the child is acting as if his or her private logic and basic convictions are true in situations in the playroom and in relationships and situations outside the playroom; (b) inappropriate strategies for problem solving in the playroom that could be getting in the way for the child outside the playroom; and (c) times in which the child is demonstrating changes in attitudes or behaviors that could be generalized to other situations in the child's life. Any time the therapist notices thought patterns, attitudes, or behaviors that occur in the playroom that could be transferred to situations and relationships in the child's life, he or she must communicate about this to the child, with suggestions for application in "the real world." Examples of making connections include:

- When Hijiri orders you around during the session, you could say, "It seems like you really like being the boss in here. I'm guessing that you also like to be the boss at home."
- With Krista, whose presenting problem is anxiety and an inability to develop relationships with others, you might say, "I've noticed that you and I have gotten to be friends with one another. I wonder

what would happen if you decided you wanted to make friends with someone in your class in school."

- To Lorenzo, a maladaptive perfectionist, when he makes a mistake painting a picture but decides not to destroy the picture, you could say, "So you decided it was a mistake to have a blue sun instead of a yellow sun like you wanted, and you are going to leave it that way anyway. I'm thinking that it would be really cool if you decided it would be okay if you made a mistake on a math paper or spelling test too."

This connection process can help make the transition into the fourth stage of Adlerian play therapy: reorientation and reeducation. As children begin to understand the connection between how they think, feel, and act in the playroom and how they think, feel, and act in the real world, you can help them examine their behavior and begin to transform insight into action.

Case Example

The case example in this section is a continuation of the case example from Chapters 5, 7, and 8. It is designed to illustrate how the play therapist can use the tactics outlined in this chapter to help children gain insight into their lifestyles and decide if they want to make any changes in their perceptions of and attitudes toward self, others, and the world and in their behavior.

My (KMW) overall goal in the third phase of the Adlerian play therapy process with Phoebe was to help her gain an understanding of how she saw herself, others, and the world and how she acted on the basis of these perceptions. Specifically, I wanted to help Phoebe:

1. Make shifts in her attitudes about the life tasks of friendship, love–family, and self.
2. Learn to catch herself when she acted as if she needed to overpower others or as if she was insignificant, inadequate, or incapable.
3. See herself in more positive ways—without the negative box in which she had been living—to be able to recognize and capitalize on her assets.
4. Incorporate positive attitudes into her lifestyle about her ability to connect, be capable, and be significant.
5. Recognize that her striving toward the goal of power was not getting her what she wanted or serving her best interests.
6. See herself as unique, special, and wonderful rather than alien or bad.
7. Have an experience in which she was able to trust another person and not feel the need to overpower or please.
8. Explore the possibility of interacting with others in cooperative ways rather than feeling the need to be in charge.
9. Feel more comfortable with being biracial.
10. Contemplate the possibility that the world is a safe place rather than a place of uncertainty and confusion.

To increase Phoebe's insight into her interpersonal and intrapersonal dynamics in Sessions 8 through 17, I used encouragement, returning responsibility to the child, power sharing, limit setting, tentative hypotheses, metacommunication, spitting in her soup, role-playing, her metaphors, mutual storytelling, bibliotherapy, art techniques, immediacy, and humor. I worked with Phoebe's grandparents, to help them change their patterns of interacting with Phoebe and create developmentally appropriate boundaries and limits. As a way of moving from the third phase of therapy to the reorientation–reeducation phase, I pointed out parallels between Phoebe's attitudes and behaviors in the playroom and her attitude and behaviors in the real world to help her generalize changes she was making in our sessions.

Phoebe needed a great deal of encouragement. (After all, her current behavior strategies created safety and predictability for her. However, they were not particularly useful in building relationships and acting in a socially useful way.) Although she was not so discouraged that she had become depressed or begun to strive to prove that she was inadequate, she had incorporated many negative beliefs about herself and her ability to belong in positive ways into her lifestyle. To counterbalance these convictions, I stressed her assets, returned responsibility to her when she was demanding that I make decisions or do particular tasks for her in the playroom, and pointed out progress and effort. I began to reframe being "different" as being unique, exploring various perspectives on ways for her to attain a sense of belonging and significance.

Because Phoebe's personality priority was control and the primary goal of her misbehavior was power, I set up many circumstances in which we could share power. These situations included alternating who decided what we were going to do in a session and playing games (e.g., tossing a ball back and forth, Jenga®, cashier/store) in which we took turns and I limited the number of times she could change the rules to give herself the advantage. Sometimes during our play, I used the whisper technique to let her direct the play, and other times I did not let her control the play, acting and speaking independently without consulting her. I also metacommunicated about the purposes of her behaviors, such as, "I'm guessing you wanted to change the rules so that you could win" or "You don't like to lose and change the rules of the game to guarantee that you win." I made guesses about what other people thought about her game play behaviors, such as "I'd bet that kids at school get mad and don't want to play with kids who change the rules." We also played some cooperative games (e.g., Sleeping Grump, Snail Race, and Max) and did several cooperative art projects (e.g., making a rocket ship out of random materials using a hot glue gun; creating a joint collage) to allow her to experience what it was like to trust others to do their part and share ideas and power. When she reacted negatively to these opportunities to collaborate, I spit in her soup about her perceived need to always be in charge and her lack of trust in the positive power of cooperation.

Throughout the earlier phases and in the third phase, Phoebe tested the rules of the playroom (e.g., threatening to pour cups upon cups of water in the sandbox, insisting she take home toys, aiming the dart gun at me). Challenging playroom rules is typical of children in the dysfunctional range of the control personality priority. The primary purpose of these behaviors was to show me that I could not control her and that she would make her own choices. I did not take these feints personally as I knew they were about her need for safety and predictability. I took the opportunities to metacommunicate about the purpose of her behavior and engaged her in generating alternative, appropriate behaviors. Several times, she chose to violate the agreements we negotiated (pouring sand on the carpet, throwing some blocks at the one-way mirror), which necessitated our setting up consequences for future transgressions. I spit in her soup about when she did this kind of behavior, she seldom got her way, as the consequences frequently prevented her from using her favorite toys. I never had to invoke the consequences we set up because she always abided by the agreements after those first violations. Her willingness to abide by the rules when she chose proved her ability to abide by expectations that were meaningful to her. As time passed and she became less invested in being in control of everything and everyone and moved more toward cooperation, she stopped testing the limits—though at times she still wanted to renegotiate the rules of the playroom.

I used tentative hypotheses, metacommunication, and spitting in her soup to help Phoebe begin to recognize her goals of misbehavior, Crucial Cs, and mistaken beliefs. I metacommunicated about her perceived need to be in control all the time; about her struggles with feeling capable, significant, and connected to others; and about her mistaken beliefs that she was less powerful and not as valuable as others and destined to be lonely. I also used these techniques to challenge Phoebe's perception that she had to always be in control or she would not get what she wanted and needed.

During this phase of the play therapy, I metacommunicated with Phoebe about the patterns in our relationship, her nonverbal communication, and her reactions to my statements and questions. I pointed out when she asked me to make decisions and do things for her in an effort to get me to try to control her so she could overpower these efforts. When she was being nice to me because she wanted something and thought that she could get it by "buttering me up," I metacommunicated about this pattern and connected it to her mistaken belief that she needed to manipulate and control others. I reflected that she looked sad and forlorn when she was talking about her mother and her old school. I spit in her soup about her belief that she only knew people cared about her when they did things for her and that people always left her.

Throughout the relationship, I watched for recognition reflexes when I metacommunicated and made tentative hypotheses to see how these interpretations landed with Phoebe. At first, she was so oppositional that she reacted in a visibly negative way—arguing, sneering, calling me names, and so forth. As time passed, she began to react to my interpretations more positively. She smiled and nodded; she shrugged, frowned, and shook her head. I metacommunicated about the various reactions and made guesses about what they meant. Sometimes she confirmed my guesses, and sometimes she ignored me.

Many times in our sessions during the third phase of therapy, we role played, did puppet shows, and created kinetic sand trays about school and family situations, using Phoebe's metaphors for various situations and relationships. We played school, with the teacher (sometimes played by me and sometimes played by Phoebe) initially being "mean," getting into power struggles, and harshly punishing the children. As time passed, the teacher gradually became less of a tyrant and the children grew more cooperative. We also played house—mother and child, with themes of nurturing relationships and loss; father and child, with themes of nurture, lack of encouragement, and uncertainty; and grandparents and child, with themes of overindulging relationships, lack of encouragement, and disappointment. The mother–child relationship appeared to improve in that the child appeared more comfortable and confident over time as compared with initially appearing clingy, sad, and desperate. The father–child relationship appeared to improve a little. The child became less critical and angry with father and more understanding and accepting; the father became more attentive. The grandparents–child relationship showed the greatest changes, with the child being able to ask for what she needed rather than demanding it.

The families of land and sea animals also had repeated reappearances, with some positive evolution in their relationships over time. These dolphin characters seemed to always represent Phoebe and her perception of herself as being different from others and not fitting in the world where others belong and thrive. I used these interactions to ask questions, metacommunicate, spit in her soup, reframe behavior, suggest alternative perspectives, and other strategies for helping her gain insight into her lifestyle patterns, especially those related to her loss of her mother and change in homes and schools and her Crucial Cs. I had several conversations with the dolphin toy about what it was like to be different and about what it was getting from persisting in thinking being different was negative. I applied the mutual storytelling and Creative Characters interventions about Godzilla, who seemed to like to overpower others but who was really trying to protect himself and help other people. Phoebe concluded that she was misunderstood, sad, lonely, and unsure of how to make friends.

Phoebe really liked reading, and bibliotherapy was especially successful with helping her to see herself, others, and the world in different ways. Here are some books that seemed to have a powerful impact on her:

- *Hope* (Monk, 1999; a book about a biracial little girl)
- *The Pout-Pout Fish* (Diesen, 2008), *Two* (Otoshi, 2014), *Scaredy Squirrel Makes a Friend* (Watt, 2007), *How Do Dinosaurs Play With Their Friends?* (Yolen, 2006), *When a Dragon Moves In* (Moore, 2011; books about making connections)
- *The Girl Who Never Made a Mistake* (Pett, 2011) and *A Perfectly Messed Up Story* (McDonnell, 2014; books about trying to be perfect)
- *Millie Fierce* (Manning, 2012; a book about being assertive, not aggressive)

- *Alexis and Ralph the Dragon* (Kowalski, 2009), *The Name Jar* (Choi, 2003), and *Giraffes Can't Dance* (Andreae, 1999; books about being different/unique from others)
- *Have You Filled A Bucket Today?* (McCloud, 2006); *Zero* (Otoshi, 2010; books about count, connect, and social interest)

I encouraged the family to have reading festivals in which family members read stories out loud to one another and have conversations about the stories. Their favorites were *Families, Families, Families* (Lang & Lang, 2015), *A Handful of Quiet: Happiness in Four Pebbles* (Hanh, 2012), and *My Grandma's A Ninja* (Tarpley, 2015). The family also watched movies. They watched *The Little Mermaid*, and I gave Phoebe's grandparents some suggestions about how to talk about Ariel's (the main character—for the one or two people who haven't seen the movie) transformation and getting accustomed to living in a new place. As an added benefit, Ariel's mother is not a part of the movie (she passed away prior to the start of the movie). Ariel lives with her father and her ocean friends. After the family watched this movie, Phoebe and I talked about how she and Ariel were similar and different. Phoebe was quick to note that Ariel's mother had died.

We did several art activities (e.g., collages, Rosebush, making pictures together) and construction projects (e.g., making a tower, designing bracelets, creating masks) to give Phoebe the experience of cooperating. She made a collage of the "perfect family" of pictures of animals, in which she used a combination of water and land animals. She represented herself with a starfish (which was much bigger than the other animals), her father as a pony, her mother as a dolphin (she later added details of flowers and a crown on her mother), her grandma as a rhino, and her grandfather as a sea turtle (a medium-sized animal that was cartoonish instead of real looking, like the other pictures). I explained that I knew a little about starfish; I knew that starfish were really unique and special because they could grow back their arms if something happened to them. She smiled ear to ear and said, "Hey, that's kinda like me! Bad things happen to me and then I get better." I also pointed out that the starfish was the biggest animal in the picture. She explained it was because she is in charge of the family and everyone is always worried about her. She said that her mom was really special and beautiful just like a dolphin, and she wished she could see her again. She wished her father would be around a little more, and she liked to ride horses with him. She liked that her grandmother was a little wrinkly like the rhino and wished that her grandmother would relax a little instead of being so "worried and antsy all the time." She said that her grandfather was already perfect—funny and playful. After she described each of these animals, she found a variety of pictures of baby animals, and she frantically pasted them on the paper. She said that even though these were not in her family, she did wish that she had friends and kids to play with at home.

Phoebe took this collage home with her, and I talked with Mr. and Mrs. Simon about the collage and possible meanings behind her animal choices. Together, we decided that Mr. and Mrs. Simon, Christopher, and

Phoebe would create a collage about Phoebe's mother. This was to include parts of her cultural identity. Phoebe could add pictures of things that she remembered or thought about her mother, and the others could fill in some gaps of information such as the day Alicia found out she was pregnant or special songs that Alicia sang for Phoebe.

Phoebe seemed to really like doing this activity and responded positively when I asked her in a later session to make a collage of "all the animals inside you." We first traced her body and then she put pictures, words, and clippings from magazines onto her traced body. I wanted her to get the idea that her personality was multifaceted—that she had positive qualities as well as the qualities that she perceived as "bad." When she was finished gluing and drawing, she grinned and said, "Wow! I am like a zoo. Look at all the parts of me. Sometimes I can show people I'm a tiger, like when I am bossy and other times I can show people I'm a kangaroo, like when I want to have fun and be silly." I metacommunicated about her ability to decide when she wanted to show people different parts of her. She said, "I know that. I get to choose when I am a tiger, a kangaroo, or any other animal." This seemed amazingly insightful to me.

Throughout our relationship, I used immediacy and humor with Phoebe. Because she was always looking for critical feedback, I had to be careful to make comments that involved immediacy or humor in a cheerful, friendly voice, otherwise she would get defensive. Several times, I could tell from her nonverbal reaction that she was interpreting something I said as criticism, so I metacommunicated about her reaction and used encouragement and confrontation to point out that my comments were meant positively rather than negatively.

Throughout this phase in the play therapy, I worked with Mr. and Mrs. Simon on their own lifestyle issues, their perceptions of Phoebe, and their parenting (grandparenting?) skills. I used humor, metacommunication, spitting in the soup, and encouragement to help them learn more about their own lifestyles and to make shifts in their perceptions of Phoebe. We had discussions about how their personality priorities, Crucial Cs, mistaken beliefs, and private logic were creating difficulties in their interactions with Phoebe. I supported them in their efforts to learn to be more consistent and in setting up ways for Phoebe to feel more important and powerful in the family.

By Session 18, Phoebe had moved from a relatively discouraged lifestyle position and her attempts to constantly maintain control over everything and everyone. She had made significant progress in her willingness to share power with others. She seemed to have some insight that being cooperative, rather than controlling, was more likely to result in positive interactions with others. Phoebe had made progress from thinking of herself as someone who was different from others in negative ways to thinking of herself as someone who had strong potential as a friend. She had started acknowledging her strengths and recognizing areas in which she was capable. She had also shifted her stance on whether or not she counted—she had begun to believe that she could make constructive contributions. In my assessment, Phoebe was ready to move into the reorientation–reeducation phase of play therapy, so I increased the number of times per session that I pointed out connections between her attitudes and behavior in the playroom and her attitudes and behavior with her family and in school.

In the continuation of the case example in Chapter 10, I describe intervention strategies I used to help Phoebe learn and practice new attitudes and behaviors for implementation at home and school. I also discuss the methods I used to consult with her grandparents to help them support these changes and for ways to prepare Phoebe and her grandparents for termination of the play therapy process.

Summary

In the third phase of Adlerian play therapy, the primary goal is to help the child gain insight into his or her lifestyle. The therapist uses active and interpretive techniques (tentative hypotheses, metacommunication, metaphors, directed role-playing, art techniques, sand tray techniques, adventure therapy activities, immediacy, confrontation, connections between play session behavior and real world) to accomplish this objective. In working with parents and teachers, the play therapist attempts to help them gain insight into the child's lifestyle at the same time they gain insight into their own patterns of thinking, feeling, and behaving. New understanding of themselves and of the child allows the significant adults in the child's life to make changes in attitudes, thought processes, and behaviors.

Further Resources

Metaphors in therapy:

http://www.counseling.org/knowledge-center/vistas/by-year2/
vistas-2005/docs/default-source/vistas/vistas_2005_vistas05-art12
http://www.lianalowenstein.com/articlesMovingStories.pdf
http://www.playtherapyseminars.com/Articles/Details/10003
http://www.researchgate.net/profile/Onno_Hart/
publication/253853518_The_use_of_metaphors_in_psychotherapy/
links/00b7d5210a9dd817e5000000.pdf

Drawing and art:

http://www.creativecounseling101.com/art-therapy-counseling-
techniques.html
http://www.creativecounseling101.com/the-mandala.html
http://files.eric.ed.gov/fulltext/EJ875395.pdf
http://intuitivecreativity.typepad.com/expressiveartinspirations/
top-50-art-therapy-blogs.html

Sand tray and miniatures:

http://www.creativecounseling101.com/play-therapy-activity-
miniature-work.html

http://www.creativecounseling101.com/sand-tray-therapy.html
http://www.goodtherapy.org/sand-tray-sand-play-therapy.html
http://www.counseling.org/knowledge-center/vistas/by-year2/
   vistas-2008/docs/default-source/vistas/vistas_2008_webber
https://www.txca.org/images/Conference/SCC/12/25Armstrong.pdf

Other techniques:

http://www.mddcapt.org/Liana_Lowenstein_Article.pdf
http://pegasus.cc.ucf.edu/~drbryce/Narrative%20and%20Play%20
   Therapy.pdf
http://pegasus.cc.ucf.edu/~drbryce/Play%20Therapy%20Techniques.
   pdf

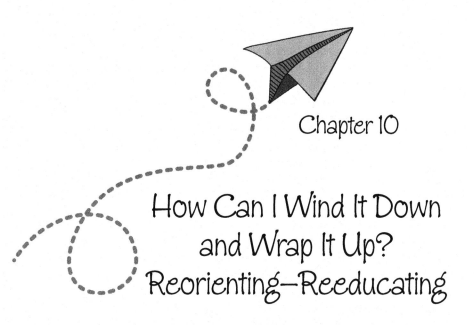

Chapter 10

How Can I Wind It Down and Wrap It Up? Reorienting–Reeducating

During this fourth and final phase of therapy (the home stretch, so to speak), the play therapist shifts roles slightly, moving to a more directive, teaching-oriented function than in the earlier phases of therapy. The primary goals of therapy during the reorientation–reeducation phase of Adlerian play therapy is for children to learn positive ways of (a) viewing themselves, others, and the world; (b) expressing feelings and behaving in various situations; (c) building relationships with other people; (d) solving problems; (e) optimizing their assets; (f) mastering the Crucial Cs; (g) functioning at life tasks; (h) manifesting the constructive aspects of their personality priorities; and (i) getting their needs met. To meet these goals, the Adlerian play therapist uses toys, art materials, sand trays, and other tools in the playroom, along with role plays, therapeutic metaphors and bibliotherapy, and movement and adventure activities to facilitate the reorientation–reeducation of child clients and the significant people in their lives.

To help children consolidate the new perspectives on their lifestyles, private logic, and basic convictions they gained during the insight phase (if things went the way we want them to go), the Adlerian play therapist continues to metacommunicate about patterns in their attitudes, feelings, thoughts, and behaviors. (We know you might be getting tired of us saying you should be metacommunicating; it is, however, one of the core skills of Adlerian play therapy. As we often say to our students, "Metacommunicate, metacommunicate, metacommunicate . . . ")

In this phase, the play therapist also works with children to consider and choose more constructive behavior and interactional patterns and develop better ways to solve problems and get their needs met. As children begin to explore new perceptions, behaviors, and skills, the counselor provides situations in which they can practice applying what they have learned in play sessions during the third phase of therapy. The therapist also helps children learn to recognize and generate opportunities to practice applying what they have learned outside the play session. It is important to give children chances to report back to the therapist about what is happening in the process of generalizing the new learning to other situations and relationships. Many children referred for play therapy have deficits in social skills, negotiation skills, strategies for sharing power, methods for managing feelings, strategies for making and maintaining friends, and so forth. One of the primary tasks of the play therapist during this phase is to offer opportunities for them to learn and practice those skills. An essential component of the play therapist's job during this phase of counseling is to encourage children and parents about the growth they have made and help them get ready for terminating the play therapy relationship. ("Yikes!" you say. We know this is a lot, and remember, you already know many wonderful techniques for teaching children new skills and behaviors. You will just be expanding the focus of your teaching to include thoughts, emotions, behaviors, and attitudes and working toward being more systematic, playful, and creative about delivering your teaching. Let's substitute a "Wee ha!" for that "Yikes!")

During this phase of play therapy, you get to give yourself permission to be as imaginative as possible. There are limitless creative methods for generating alternatives, teaching skills, practicing alternatives and skills, and encouraging. We describe several different ways to approach each of these tasks, but we hope that you do not limit yourself to our suggestions. The more creative you are during this process, the more effectively you can tailor interventions to the needs and talents of the children and families with whom you work, inviting children and their families (and teachers) to cocreate the process of Adlerian play therapy.

Using Brainstorming–Problem Solving to Help Children Generate Alternative Constructive Thoughts, Feelings, Actions, and Attitudes

As children's perceptions of themselves and how they can gain a sense of belonging and significance change, their patterns of thinking, feeling, and behaving also change. As we mentioned in earlier chapters, people act as if what they believe about themselves, others, and the world is true. Because of this as children change their beliefs about self, others, and the world, they will begin to make shifts in the way they act and react. However, having spent their lives proving what they used to believe about themselves and not having any experience behaving as if their changed perceptions are true, they often need some help in making this shift. One of the most important things we have learned from working with people is that we must not ask clients to give up their old ways of acting and interacting with others until we have helped them acquire new ways of acting and interacting.

Children are frequently wiser than most adults realize. (And they are often wiser than the adults in their lives—at least we have often noticed our own children are wiser than we are—and the older ones don't hesitate to point that out.) Many times, children know what they are supposed to do, but they have chosen not to use appropriate, constructive behaviors because the "acceptable" behaviors do not fit into their perceptions of themselves. For instance, if 9-year-old LaDonna believes she is a "bad seed," she is going to act in ways that reinforce that belief. With other children, "acceptable" behavior may not serve the goals of children's behavior, their private logic, their mastery of the Crucial Cs, or their personality priorities. Children often choose behaviors that seem to get their needs met, even if those behaviors also get them into trouble. For example, since 5-year-old Fayyad's mother gave birth to twins, he has been acting out—having tantrums and being uncooperative and argumentative. Fayyad's parents have tried lecturing, giving him time-outs, and spanking him, but none of these things seem to be working. Looking at this situation, we would guess that Fayyad feels left out and somewhat powerless given the current circumstances in this family and the goal of his misbehavior is attention and power. Because he is getting his need for attention and power partially (though clearly inadequately) met by behaving in ways that require his parents to interact with him and try to get him to stop his inappropriate behaviors, he will continue these behaviors unless his parents figure out other ways to give him attention and help him feel more in control.

Hopefully, during the third phase of play therapy, you will have helped children gain insight into their patterns and mistaken beliefs, so that they are ready to learn new, more constructive ways of living. One way to move children forward is to help them examine their thoughts, feelings, behavior, and attitudes related to specific situations in which they would like to act more constructively. Through this process, children can explore thoughts, feelings, behaviors, and attitudes that might be more useful and constructive than those they have traditionally manifested in those situations.

This process can be done directly or indirectly, just as in the earlier phases of play therapy. On the basis of what you already know about the child, you will choose a way of interacting that has worked during the previous phases. With a child who prefers to process verbally, you could just have a conversation. You could talk about what the child has thought, felt, or done in certain specific situations and help him or her to generate a list of possible alternative ways to think, feel, and behave in future situations. You could design a therapeutic metaphor, read a bibliotherapy book, or use mutual storytelling with the child to explore alternative thoughts, feelings, behaviors, and attitudes through metaphor. You could suggest a role play or use the puppets, dolls, or a sand tray to reenact a specific situation, with part of the reenactment featuring you or the child doing a color commentary on thoughts, feelings, behaviors, and attitudes—both those from the past and those the child could use in the future. With a child who readily uses art for self-expression, developing an art activity in which the child uses thought bubbles over characters drawn, painted, or stamped to express thoughts, feelings, and attitudes could be effective. You could also use music, dance, and movement to give the child a platform for creative expression and for generating different ways to think, feel, and behave. It is often helpful to use playing a game or doing an adventure therapy activity with a child who is more comfortable with those modes of interaction.

Many times, children suggest different possibilities for acting and reacting without your supplying any ideas for them. It is important to invite them to participate in generating alternatives for themselves. They are much more likely to follow through consistently with alternatives they have proposed themselves than they are to follow through with options others have proposed for them.

With children who initially say they cannot think of any possibilities, you can try brainstorming and problem-solving tactics to help generate some alternatives. Either directly or through a metaphor, you would ask children to list (without considering practicality or possibility) all of the ideas that occur to them. You would make a list of the ideas they suggest, perhaps even adding an idea or two. Next, you go through each of the possibilities, considering the advantages and disadvantages of each idea and whether the children (or the characters in a metaphoric intervention) could actually carry through with it in real life. You can use this process to eliminate any ideas that are too far-fetched, narrowing down the possibilities to several choices. You would then collaboratively consider the remaining possibilities to explore potential outcomes and consequences of each. On the basis of this deliberation, children choose one or two of the possibilities to try (or have the characters of the metaphor try).

If you are working with a child who prefers direct communication over metaphoric communication, you would invite the child to practice using the alternatives in the play session. Having practiced in session, you would then suggest making a plan for how the child can practice using the alternatives in a specific situation at home or school. You would want to help the child come up with situations at home or school that would be safe for practicing, ones that would optimize the chances that the child will receive positive feedback from the other people involved. At times, you might even want to warn parents and teachers that the child is going to be experimenting with new thoughts, feelings, behavior, or attitudes to be sure they are able to support the practicing, even when it doesn't go perfectly. After the outside-the-session practice, the child can then report back to you about what happened when the child tried the new thoughts, feelings, actions, or attitudes. This allows you to provide the child with encouragement and support. The following is an example of using the direct approach to help the child generate alternatives.

Ms. Jacobsen, Kyle's school counselor, established a relationship with him, explored his lifestyle, and helped him reexamine his perceptions that he must always be in charge and the best way to be safe was to intimidate others. Kyle was feeling safer and less angry in the play sessions and in his classroom, but he was not sure how to interact with others without being aggressive. Ms. Jacobsen wanted to help Kyle learn to feel more secure and confident in his relationships with others, appropriately express his feelings of anger and resentment, and interact with others without trying to overpower them. She chose to work with him first on his behavior related to interacting with others. She pointed out that he had shared control with her in their play sessions and made a connection between his ability to do this with her and his ability to do this with his teacher. They brainstormed a list of possible ways that Kyle could share control with his teacher without getting into power struggles with her. The list included choosing not to respond to his teacher; telling his teacher how he felt in a quiet, but assertive voice; using a puppet to talk to his teacher when he was upset with her; and giving his teacher choices about what he was willing to do in the classroom. Although they decided several of the ideas (using a puppet in the classroom, ignoring his teacher when she talked) might not go over very well with Kyle's teacher, they decided that several of the ideas he had generated might work. Although Ms. Jacobsen suggested he try just one of the ideas, he insisted on trying telling his teacher how he felt in a quiet but assertive voice and giving his teacher choices about what he was willing to do in the classroom during the next week. They used role-playing to practice how he could follow through with these behaviors in interactions his teacher.

Kyle tried both of the new behaviors during the week. One of them worked very well, and the other did not work all that well for him. (Guess which one . . . telling his teacher he was willing to either stay in his seat or stop blurting out, but not both did NOT go over well, but communicating about his feelings in an appropriate voice worked very well.) When he met with Ms. Jacobsen the next week, they evaluated his progress, and she provided lots of encouragement for his efforts and the changes that he had made. They made plans and practiced more behavioral changes for the next week and discussed ways that Kyle could use the effective technique in other situations, such as in his interactions with his mother. As he was consolidating these behavioral changes, they also worked on making changes in his thoughts, feelings, and attitudes in a similar fashion.

Some children are not willing or able to engage in such a direct approach to generating alternatives. When this is the case, the play therapist needs to exercise creativity and use the play media, art techniques, role-playing, metaphors, bibliotherapy, or other possible tools in the process. Children who are not comfortable with the direct approach are frequently willing to do the same brainstorming or problem-solving process through storytelling or other indirect means. You could ask them to generate new ideas for a puppet or doll, a character in a story or book, or a person they have drawn or sculpted with pipe cleaners or clay—their symbolic representative. The process continues as the children help decide which course of action is the best for the symbolic representative and how he or she can follow through with the changes. The children can even act as coaches so that the doll or puppet (or other symbolic representative) can practice the alternative thoughts, feelings, or behaviors. The following is an example of the indirect approach to helping children generate alternatives.

Masika, a second-grade girl, always cried whenever she got less than 100% correct on assignments. Her counselor, Pablo, investigated Masika's lifestyle and discovered that her need to be perfect was related to her psychological birth-order position, her family atmosphere, her personality priority, and her Crucial Cs. Masika was the oldest child in a family that valued education and had very high standards. She had a need to outdo others to feel that she was valuable and important. She struggled with some of the negative aspects of superiority as her personality priority, and she did not believe that she counted unless her academic performance was perfect. In parent consultations, Pablo discovered that Masika's parents both had superiority as their personality priorities, tending to judge their adequacy as parents by their children's performance in school. Pablo worked with Masika's parents on recognizing that they were very good parents, regardless of the grades attained by their children. He also worked with them on ways to let Masika know that she was valuable and important no matter what her grades were. When Pablo made guesses to Masika about her belief that she would not be significant or lovable unless she was perfect, Masika denied this. Because Pablo recognized that Masika was feeling defensive about this major part of her lifestyle and Masika had traditionally used metaphors to communicate about feelings with which she was uncomfortable, he decided to use an indirect approach to communicate with her about this pattern. He used metaphors, artwork, and sand trays to help Masika gain insight into her lifestyle, which seemed to work well. Masika began loosening up a bit and developing a strong sense of self-acceptance, but she continued to have impossibly high standards for herself.

Pablo decided to use the puppets to tell Masika a story and engage her in brainstorming some alternative thoughts for a puppet representing her. He told her a story about Green Frog, a puppet who thought that he had to be the highest jumper in the pond. Green Frog told himself that if he couldn't outjump all the other frogs in the pond, they wouldn't like him anymore, and he would have to go live somewhere else. One day, the frogs on the pond had a jumping contest. Even though Green Frog tried his best, he didn't jump the highest. He was really embarrassed and mad at himself. He even decided that he needed to move to a different pond because now the other frogs wouldn't like him. Green Frog had started packing his suitcase to move when along came his friend, Yellow Frog. Yellow Frog couldn't believe that Green Frog thought he had to move just because he didn't jump higher than all of the other frogs. Pablo then asked Masika to help him think of some other things that Yellow Frog could tell Green Frog about not being the best jumper and some other positive ways that Green Frog could get noticed in the pond. After Green Frog heard all of the things that Yellow Frog and the other frogs liked about him, he decided that maybe the other frogs would like him even if he didn't jump the highest. Pablo, knowing that Masika liked music, suggested that they write a song for Green Frog to remind him that he was "just good enough." Pablo ended the story with Green Frog developing a willingness to consider that perhaps the other frogs liked him just because he was himself and feeling happier about himself and his place in the pond. This story seemed to help Masika shift her thinking about herself and her high standards. After the story, she seemed more willing to accept that, although she would not always be able to be perfect, she was "just good enough."

How elaborate the process of generating alternatives is depends on the children's developmental level and reasoning ability. With younger (up to about 7 years old) children or children who do not have highly developed abstract reasoning ability, we tend to keep the process very simple. We usually target behaviors (rather than thoughts, feelings, or attitudes) with this population because they are not always aware of being able to control or change their thoughts or feelings. As the children change their perceptions of themselves and their behaviors and as other people react differently to them, their thoughts, feelings, and attitudes frequently shift without conscious effort on their parts. We also restrict the plan to changing one behavior at a time, and we enlist the help of parents and teachers to support any kind of behavior change.

With older children and young children who have highly developed abstract reasoning skills, we find that they often like the idea of having power over their thoughts, feelings, and attitudes as well as their behaviors. They frequently want to dive into this process and change everything all at once. Working with this population, our goal is to develop a reasonable plan that the children can actually accomplish. We usually ask them to concentrate on a single area—thoughts, feelings, behaviors, attitudes—at a time, focusing on changing two or three reactions in specified situations. This keeps the plan from becoming overwhelming. Gradually, we introduce the idea of integrating the alternative thoughts, feelings, behaviors, and attitudes and generalizing the new methods of acting and reacting to other situations.

Teaching New Skills and Behaviors

Even when the brainstorming or problem-solving strategy works and children integrate new constructive thinking, feeling, and behavior, many children remain challenged by deficits in specific skill areas. When this happens, the play therapist needs to teach the children new skills, behaviors, or both. The therapist determines, on the basis of observation of the children's actions and interactions in the playroom and consultation with parents and teachers, which skills and behaviors they need to acquire. As with the other strategies in play therapy, the therapist should be as creative as possible in this process, using a direct or indirect approach to teaching skills depending on the most efficacious method of communicating with particular children.

In our experience, the most frequently needed skills are social skills, negotiation skills, direction-following skills, and emotional self-regulation skills. In many situations, children also need to learn behaviors inherent in sharing power with others. These are certainly not the only skill sets you will want to teach children. Individual clients may need to learn how to decide who owns a problem, ask for more or less responsibility in their families, ask for what they need, be assertive without being aggressive, make appropriate decisions, communicate appropriately about thoughts and feelings clearly, calm anxiety, stop obsessive thoughts, and a million other skills. To teach skills to clients, you must decide what you want the desired outcome to be. On the basis of your own observation of the children's actions and reactions, plus reports from parents and teachers, you will define how you will know when they have successfully acquired the skills they need. It will also be helpful for you to break down complex tasks and skill sets into their component parts, to make the teaching manageable. Although I (KMW) would like to say I am going to teach Grant communication skills, I must first determine which communication skills he has and which ones he needs to acquire. Only then can I teach him to deliver "I" messages and reflect feelings to others.

Children who have trouble with the Crucial C of connect struggle with knowing how to appropriately interact with others. Many children who have ADHD or learning disabilities and children who are on the higher functioning section of the autism spectrum also benefit from training about how to get along. Although we should be careful communicating with parents that we are not going to miraculously transform these children, it is often helpful for them to learn and practice social skills. Thinking about teaching social skills can be a little overwhelming because there are a million skills that help people get along with one another. If you are not familiar with the individual components that make up a repertoire of social skills that can help children successfully build and keep relationships, it might be useful to consult a social skills curriculum such as *Teaching Social Skills to Youth* (Dowd & Tierney, 2005) or *Skillstreaming the Elementary School Child: A Guide for Teaching Prosocial Skills* (McGinnis, 2011). When we teach social skills, we include behaviors such as making eye contact, smiling, sharing, taking turns, giving appropriate feedback, asking appropriately to get needs met, following rules, and playing cooperatively.

You can teach all of these things through playing simple games like rolling a ball back and forth, taking turns, making eye contact, and saying please and thank you. Another method of working on these skills is to play card games, like UNO, Go Fish, or Blink, or board games, like Sorry, Chutes and Ladders, Trouble, Don't Let the Pigeon Drive the Bus, or Connect 4. When you want to teach behaviors necessary for making and keeping friends, you can use body outlines to design the perfect friend, role plays to practice how to set boundaries and appropriately express feelings, or puppet shows to demonstrate how to ask someone to play.

You can also teach friendship skills using sand trays, art activities, and adventure therapy techniques. If you want to do a directed sand tray with the child, you could suggest a tray about a figure that is looking for friends, having the child bring in several other figures and figure out how to be friends with each of them. One of my (TK) favorite art activities is to have children trace their hands. On their left hand, I have them showcase a quality they bring to the relationship on each finger. They can make a list, draw things, or use stickers or stamps to show the things they bring to a friendship. On the tracing to their left hand, I have them use the same materials to explore what qualities they want in a friend.

An adventure therapy strategy we often use is Mirror Mirror (Ashby et al., 2008). In this activity, you and the child face one another and determine who will "go first." That person is the initial "leader" in the activity. Explain that the leader in each pair will engage in some physical movement (model something fun like waving one hand or turning to the side), and the other participant in the pair is to mimic that movement so that it looks like the mirror image of the leader's actions. After a brief time, stop and switch roles. If you are working with a child who enjoys verbally processing your activities, you can have a brief conversation about whether the child liked to lead or follow better. This can be extended to how it applies in relationships with friends if you think it would be useful for the child.

You might also want to teach children skills for appropriately interacting with adults. Many children need to learn to use polite language to express their feelings and get their needs met in their relationships with authority figures. You could role play being the principal and have a conversation with the student practicing being respectful, play school alternating you being the teacher and the student, or invite a parent or teacher into the session to play.

Teaching negotiation skills can be very important if you work with children whose personality priority is control, who need to learn to interact with others without trying to overwhelm them. This work begins with helping children learn to assess realistically what they really need (or want) and what they are willing to give up to get what they need (or want). As children engage in negotiations, they will have to state clearly and concretely what they need (or want), keeping in mind an idea of what they are willing to take based on a compromise. They have to learn to take turns, stating their position and listening to the position of the person with whom they are negotiating.

Children also need to learn that the end result of negotiating may be a compromise in which they do not always get the result they desire or expect. You can certainly do this teaching through role-playing, puppet shows, and bibliotherapy. Cooperative board games, like Hoot Owl Hoot!, Stone Soup, Say the Word, and Max, are wonderful resources to help teach negotiation skills. You can also play games originally designed to be competitive and change the rules a bit to make them more collaborative. I (TK) developed a version of Apples to Apples to play with a group of children, and we simply decide who wins each round by consensus. (Let me tell you, this involves a LOT of negotiating.) We often teach negotiation skills through playing games we coinvent with kids—in designing the game, we have a conversation about rules we want to have. Actually, occasionally even if we are playing a board game or card game, we negotiate about the rules we want to have. For instance, while UNO is usually played with seven cards each, I (TK) often play it with three cards or 10 cards each. Even though I learned the game as having you draw from the pile until you get a card you can use, sometimes I play just drawing a single card if I don't have anything in my hand that will work.

Often a part of this work is teaching assertiveness skills to children, especially children whose personality priorities are pleasing or comfort. If you are working with children who appreciate bibliotherapy, a really good book designed to teach assertiveness is *The Mouse, the Monster, and Me: Assertiveness for Young People* (Palmer, 2009). If you want help with activities you could use to teach assertiveness, *Cool, Calm, and Confident: A Workbook to Help Kids Learn Assertiveness Skills* (Schab, 2009) contains a plethora of interesting exercises. Not all of them involve play, but remember you can always take an activity from a workbook and make it into a play activity by using toys, puppets, art, or sand tray figures.

Many of my play therapy clients have had difficulty following directions and must learn how to do this. They need help breaking down three- and four-step directions into their component parts, remembering subsequent steps while executing the first step, and then executing the rest of the steps one at a time. We teach them to think about each component part of the directions and to do things one step at a time. Although this seems simplistic, this idea is very helpful to children who struggle with multistep instructions. You can do this by playing hide-and-seek with toys or sand tray figures, Mother May I?, and Simon Says. We have also been known to play robots—with one person being the "controller" and the other person being the robot who has to follow the directions given by the "controller." Sometimes we take turns giving instructions while the other person draws a picture, makes an origami figure, or sculpts something in Model Magic or Play-Doh following the instructions. It is also fun to have one person make a drawing and then describe the drawing to the other person who is making a drawing or a sand tray based on the instructions. When you check to see how close you got to recreating the original drawing, laughter ensues. (This even helps kids learn to use a sense of humor as a coping strategy when things don't turn out the way they wanted, which is a really good skill for maladaptively perfectionistic children and children manifesting a not-so-adaptive version of the control personality priority.)

An important skill for children whose primary goal of misbehavior is power is learning how to share control of situations without trying to grab the power from others. We want these children to learn that they can occasionally let someone else be in charge. One way to teach them this is simply letting them experience having someone else control the situation while they wait for their turn to be in charge. In our play sessions, we set up situations in which we are in charge so they can experience what it feels like to be safe in a relationship but not be in control. As part of this process, we practice taking turns and sharing. One way to do that is to tell a shared story in the sand tray. You would start the story, putting a figure into the tray and giving a two- or three-sentence introduction. Then the child puts an object in the tray, adding several sentences that explain what is happening, followed by you choosing an object and adding several sentences designed to help move the story along. Alternately, you and the child choose objects and add several sentences moving the story forward, ending with the child placing the last object and finishing the story.

After children get accustomed to sharing power with us, we often ask the parents, a sibling, or another child into the playroom so that the children get an opportunity to experience having someone else share the power. We then give the family homework assignments to practice this at home, and we often ask teachers to make sure that the children have opportunities to experience sharing power at school too. Many of the activities described as vehicles for teaching negotiation skills and direction-following skills will also work for helping children learn to share power.

Children who tend toward the maladaptive expression of their personality priorities often need to learn emotional regulation skills. Pleasers are often anxious, comfort children often struggle with knowing how they feel, superiority children tend to be easily overwhelmed by stress, and controllers often have "anger management issues." Traumatized children, children with ADHD, and aggressive children can also have difficulties with emotional regulation. With these children, it is essential to begin by helping them learn to recognize and appropriately express their feelings. With some children who lack the expressive vocabulary to label emotions, it is useful to develop activities designed to expand their feeling vocabulary. We often do this by reading books about different feelings. Some books you can use for this would include:

The Way I Feel (Cain, 2000)
Today I Feel Silly and Other Moods That Make My Day (Curtis, 1998)
Sometimes I'm Bombaloo (Vail, 2002)
The Feelings Book (Parr, 2000)
The Monster in the Bubble (A. Green, 2012)
In My Heart (Witek, 2014)

Some children, especially those who have experienced trauma, need to learn to check in with their bodies, learn where certain emotions manifest in them, and evaluate how they physically feel when they are experiencing them. Oftentimes, it helps to do a visualization or body scan to help them just learn to tune in to their bodies and recognize physical sensations. After doing a body scan, many children respond positively to drawing what they feel and assigning emotional labels to the sensation. Other children like to do sand trays, movement activities, or body outlines to express what they have discovered in their bodies. As they learn to recognize their emotions and where and how they are manifested in their bodies, it is often helpful to explore their triggers. Sometimes we play a guessing game with them, trying to narrow down the situations and relationships that seem to evoke specific emotional reactions. Other times we collaboratively draw or paint pictures or do sand trays to explore triggers. As they learn about how certain emotions feel and explore what evokes those emotions, it becomes time for children to learn to express those emotions in appropriate ways. There are many resources for working with children who struggle with specific emotions, especially anger. If you do not have experience developing interventions for children who find anger a challenging emotion, *Seeing Red: An Anger Management and Anti-Bullying Curriculum for Kids* (Simmons, 2014) contains helpful suggestions, many of which you will have to adapt to a play therapy setting. Some bibliotherapy resources you can use with this population include:

When I Feel Angry (Spelman, 2000)
When Sophie Gets Angry—Really, Really Angry (Bang, 1999)
I Was So Mad (Mayer, 2000)
Anh's Anger (Silver, 2009)
Llama Llama Mad at Mama (Dewdney, 2007)

You can also teach children who are often triggered by events in their lives strategies for activating their parasympathetic nervous systems as a way to calm themselves. Some techniques adapted from Levine and Kline (2007) and Hansen and Medius (2009) for doing this would include guiding children in the following:

1. Relaxation—teach them to relax their tongue, eyes, and jaw muscles; help them feel tension draining from their bodies and going into the earth; ask them to run warm water over their hands.
2. Progressive relaxation—walk them through their bodies looking for tense places they can release.
3. Exhalations—use big exhalations as a way to bring calm and peace.
4. Imagery—teach them to imagine a safe place, imagine themselves as being able to calm themselves down, imagine themselves as super heroes, imagine their fairy godmother/father or guardian angel coming to help them, and so forth.
5. Balance their heartbeat—teach them to (a) breathe so that exhalation and inhalation are the same duration, (b) imagine they are breathing in and out through their heart areas, and (c) think about a pleasant warm emotion moving through their hearts as part of their breath.
6. Focused breathing—teach them to inhale, pause, exhale, pause, and note any physiological changes that occur.
7. Talking funny—teach them to press the tip of their tongue against their lower teeth, relax their tongue, and try to talk. This relaxes the tongue, pumps and relaxes the brain, causing flow of cerebrospinal fluid, which helps them feel more relaxed. (The kids we work with LOVE this one.)
8. Tongue stretch—teach them to stick out their tongue and, with clean fingers, pull on it gently. This relaxes the root of tongue and brain stem.
9. Yawn on purpose—this one is self-explanatory. It helps them "come down out of your head," increases production of serotonin, balances flow of cerebrospinal fluid—all good things for calming us down.
10. Jiggling—just get them to shake their bodies. This boosts the rhythms of pulsation, which supports life, liveliness, and well-being; it also loosens us up when we feel stiff or rigid.

Providing Practice of New Skills and Behaviors

As children learn new skills and behaviors, they need a chance to practice in the secure atmosphere of the play therapy relationship before they attempt integrating their new skills and behaviors in other relationships. You can choose to have the child practice exclusively with you in the playroom, or you can ask someone else to join you and the child.

Practicing With the Play Therapist

Usually, the initial step in this process is for children to practice the alternative behaviors in the playroom, indirectly, through storytelling or through role play, which can be with puppets, dolls, sand tray figures, or other toys. This involves a rehearsal of what children will say, do, think, and feel and what the other people they encounter will say, do, think, and feel. You can also use a more direct approach and ask children to role play various scenarios to give them a chance to hone new skills and gain self-confidence. By exploring future situations through play, children can gain a concrete idea of how to apply newly acquired behaviors outside the playroom. They can also explore possible reactions of other people and possible obstacles in particular situations and consider how they will want to deal with difficulties.

Practicing With Another Person in the Playroom

As the child's comfort level with new behaviors, thoughts, attitudes, and feelings grows, you can invite the parents, a sibling or two, one of the child's friends, or another child client into play sessions. This allows the child an opportunity to continue to practice with someone who is important to him or her in an environment that is supportive and safe. For instance, the child can practice social skills, negotiating skills, emotional expression, self-regulation, and ways to share power with "real" members of his or her life. The child also gets experience in sharing your attention and affection in a setting in which he or she can explore emotions such as jealousy and pain.

If we bring one of our other clients or one of the client's friends in for a small-group, play therapy experience, we look for certain qualities in the second child. We try to consider where potential group members fall on the continuum from (a) aggressive to submissive, (b) active to passive, (c) outgoing to withdrawn, and (d) hyperactive to depressed and choose a child (or children) who can balance out our client child. We do not want two very controlling children in the same session because, faced with another controlling child, even a child who has learned to feel safer when he or she is not in control will fight for power. We also try to avoid mixing a controlling child with a pleasing child because a pleasing child just lets the controlling child have his or her way, and they never have to compromise.

When you bring in another child, as always, the key to doing play therapy with a small group (even if the group is just two people plus you) is being present with the children—all else should be secondary. You will have to really focus on not getting too caught up in the "action" of the session so that you can be fully present and connected to each of the children. You will want to relax and pay attention to your own reactions and to the flow of the session and the interactions. It is important to re-

member that you don't have to pressure yourself to answer too quickly or
too often. There is a lot more action in group sessions than in individual
sessions, so it is important to take time to think. You won't get to talk
as much as you usually do in an individual session (there is just less air
time), so make your comments count. Your primary focus will be on the
client, with less attention on the other children. You will need to look for
patterns in the following dynamics:

1. *Interaction between the children, relationship between the children, patterns
   of communication between the children, and methods of gaining significance–belonging.* You can ask yourself: "Where is/who has the power
   in the relationship, and how do they interact around the power?"
   "Are there patterns of pleasing in the relationship?" "How do they
   connect with one another?" "How do they demonstrate courage in
   the relationship?" "How do they demonstrate to one another that
   they are capable? Is this an important part of their relationship?"
   "How do they establish that they count in the relationship? How
   do the children demonstrate that they believe that the other person
   counts?" "Who plays what with whom?" "What did they talk about?"
2. *Interaction between the children in relationship to you.* You can ask yourself questions like these: "Are they jealous of any attention I give
   to the other one(s)?" "Do they feel a need to jockey for position in
   terms of power or attention they get from me?" "Is connecting with
   me more important to them when they have other children in the
   session?" "How do they go about connecting with me in the context
   of having another child in the room?" "Who tries to join with me in
   order to gain power or control over the other child?" "Who tries to
   make sure they get my attention in order to affirm that they count
   more than the other child?"
3. *Individual interactions among each of the children and you.* Ask yourself the
   usual questions you would ask in a play session, such as, "What is the
   goal of this child's behavior?" "What is this child's personality priority,
   and how does he or she go about behaving related to that priority?"
   "Which of the Crucial Cs does this child seem to have incorporated
   into his or her views of self, others, and the world?" "What are this
   child's mistaken beliefs?" "What are this child's assets?" "How does
   this child's private logic get in his or her way?" "What is this child
   re-proving about himself or herself?" "How can I react differently
   than the child expects so that I don't reinforce these ideas?"
4. *The affective tone and flow of the group in this session.* Ask yourself
   questions like these: "What is the affective tone of the session?"
   "How has each person in the session contributed to the tone of the
   session?" "Who has had a big impact on the group today, and how
   has that impact played out?" "What has been the interactional flow
   between group members?" "Who has controlled the session? What
   have they done to get control of the session? What have they done
   with the control they have had of the session?" "Were there themes
   in the content of the session?"

5. *The tone and flow of the group over time.* Look for patterns and themes over time. A group (even of two children and you) is really a micro-cosm of society—you can find out how the children act in the real world, what their lives are like, how others react to them, how they interact with others by just observing the tone and flow in the group. Ask yourself questions like these: "What are the patterns in the af-fective tone of the group?" "What are the patterns of who controls the group?" "What are the patterns in the interactional flow of the group?" "How can I use the strengths of each child to help the other children in the group?" "How does what the children do in the group reflect their thoughts, feelings, and behaviors in the rest of their lives?" "How can I use what happens in the group to teach them new ways of interacting and reacting in the rest of their lives?"

To avoid chaos, you will probably want to create more structure than you do if you are just working with one child. You may even want to set up the "schedule" for the session in the initial interaction of the session. How many minutes will you be doing some kind of planned activity and how many minutes will the kids be allowed to have for spontaneous play? What order will these be in? (It is best to have any planned structured activities before you let them have free play.) Every once in a while, you may just want to see how the kids play together without any structure.

When we introduce the idea to our clients, we tell them that we think it might be fun to have another child (or two or three) join us in the playroom. We may make some suggestions about activities we could do with additional people to share the fun. Usually children are excited about the idea of adding someone else to the play therapy process. They are frequently getting rather bored by the time we do this and are close to being ready to terminate their therapy.

If the child has a violent negative reaction to this suggestion, it usually means that we have moved too quickly and the child is not as close to termination as we had assumed. When this happens, we reevaluate the progress of the child by talking to the child about his or her purpose in not wanting another child in the play sessions and consulting with parents (or teachers when we are working in a school) about their impressions of what is happening with the child. After this reevaluation, we discuss the situation with the child, and we decide how to proceed. Most of the time, the child needs to continue individual work for a time, and he or she will eventually bring up the idea of having another child join us when he or she is ready for this step.

Before we introduce the second child into the playroom, we talk to the client about confidentiality and about the playroom rules, especially those related to safety. We also talk about how often the second child will join us in the playroom. Many times, we decide to have the additional child come to every other session for about 4 to 6 weeks. We frequently ask parents and other family members to come to play therapy sessions, par-ticularly during the fourth phase. Sometimes we even switch into family play therapy sessions (Kottman & Meany Walen, in press). This gives the

other members of the family a chance to try out more appropriate interactional patterns and parenting skills. The playroom can be a laboratory
for family members to experience new ways of relating to one another
in a safe environment in which they can get supportive suggestions and
encouragement for the effort they expend and the progress they make.

Termination

When considering termination, you will want to look for positive movement
in the presenting problem and positive changes in the child's behavior in the
play therapy sessions (Kottman, 2011). Related to the presenting problem,
you can ask, "Have the child's attitudes, relationships, and behaviors at
home or school that were creating difficulties changed in a positive direction?" By discussing this question with family members, teachers, and the
child and by observing the child's behavior with family members in the
waiting room or in family sessions in the playroom (and/or with teachers
and classmates), you can gather information about progress related to the
presenting problem. Because play therapy is seldom a "miracle cure," it
is really important to compare the child's initial functioning with his or
her current functioning rather than considering current functioning in
the abstract. It helps to make this more concrete if you have asked the
adults with whom children interact to use scaling or tabulating to get a
numerical estimate of occurrences of annoying behaviors. It is also helpful to ask parents and teachers to quantify their appraisal of children's
general affect and happiness by using a scale of 1 to 10. It is important to
look for improvement rather than a complete transformation.

In Adlerian play therapy, you will look for evidence in your sessions
that children have altered their basic convictions and their lifestyles. It
should be obvious that their goals of behavior have moved from the
negative goals of destructive attention, power, revenge, or proving inadequacy to more positive goals. They should have acquired many of the
positive characteristics of a child who has courage, believes that he or
she can connect, is capable, and does count. Children should be making
shifts in the ways that they act on their personality priorities—moving
away from the limiting aspects and moving toward the strengths. Their
interactions with others should show evidence of increased social interest and awareness of the rights of others. Their behavior should be more
constructive and appropriate.

So that children are not surprised by the move toward termination,
about three or four sessions before the last session, we like to let them
know that we are thinking that we will stop meeting together. We summarize the progress we have observed in the playroom and the progress
noted by the children, parents, and school personnel. We solicit their
perspective on changes they have experienced in thoughts, feelings, behaviors, and relationships with the important people in their lives. After
this discussion, we bring up the idea that they have improved so much
that we no longer think that they need help like the help they have been

getting in the playroom. We watch closely for negative reactions to see if children are feeling normal sadness at the idea that an important supportive relationship will be changed or other emotional reactions that could indicate that we were wrong about readiness for termination. We reflect feelings, make interpretations, and use encouragement to help them explore thoughts and feelings. We also tell them that this does not mean that we will no longer have a relationship. I (TK) give children my card again and let them know that any time they feel a need to come back or to talk to me, they should feel free to do so.

During the remaining sessions, you can have a "countdown" so that children know how many sessions are left. During these last sessions before terminating, children will often quickly go back through many of the behaviors, attitudes, and play experiences that they experienced during the entire course of the play therapy. They are experiencing a fast-forward recapitulation of what they have learned and how they have changed through the play therapy process. It is essential to warn parents and teachers that a parallel situation may occur at home and school. Frequently, behaviors and attitudes that have long since disappeared suddenly surface, which can be frightening for concerned adults. If you explain in advance that this is a normal process, it is usually possible to prevent parents and teachers from reverting to their old patterns in response to this recapitulation.

Case Example

This case example is a continuation of the case example in Chapters 5, 7, 8, and 9. The narrative in this chapter is designed to illustrate how the counselor can reorient and reeducate the child, helping the child generate more positive thoughts, feelings, and actions; learn new behaviors and skills; practice these new behaviors and skills; and get ready to terminate the play therapy. In the case study, I (TK) have also demonstrated ways for the counselor to implement practical changes through parent consultation during the fourth phase of Adlerian play therapy.

My primary goal with Phoebe in the reorientation–reeducation phase of play therapy was to help her to build a constructive behavioral repertoire based on her increasingly positive thoughts and feelings about herself, others, and the world. I wanted to increase her capacity to solve problems in socially appropriate ways and to enhance her social skills and negotiating skills so that she could contribute to society without demanding that her own needs be met immediately. This involved her practicing taking turns, following rules, letting others decide on activities, and so forth. I also thought that it was important for her to practice sharing power with the other important people in her life, especially with her grandparents, father, and potential friends at school. I believed that Phoebe would benefit from participating in activities that included other children her age, such as soccer, scouts, or drama. I thought an important task for Phoebe was to celebrate her cultural heritage and describe ways in which she was similar and different from her other family members. I also wanted her to be able to clearly evaluate and articulate her own strengths to others without being arrogant or judgmental.

I simultaneously worked with Mr. and Mrs. Simon to help them practice the new skills they had learned. We specifically focused on using encouragement, deciding problem ownership, giving choices, allowing for natural consequences, and using logical consequences. During the few times that I worked with Christopher, I emphasized the importance of spending time with Phoebe. He committed to creating even small opportunities to spend time with his daughter. A few of the things he did to reach out to Phoebe included calling her during his breaks at college and leaving silly notes and surprises for her on days that he worked long hours.

Following her lead, I decided to combine direct and indirect communication with Phoebe. We had honest discussions about topics she was willing to explore directly, we did some brainstorming about real situations in her life, and we role played some situations using actual relationships and circumstances and other situations using animal figures to represent various people in her life. In several instances, we used metaphoric stories, bibliotherapy, and art projects for our reorientation work.

Because Phoebe showed strong verbal skills and abstract reasoning abilities, it was possible to verbally process several issues directly. We had conversations about how she could get her needs met in the family without using her temper, being manipulative, or demanding things be her way. We talked about her mother, how much she missed her, and how she felt lonely at times. We discussed her desire for more friends and brainstormed ways for her to make and keep peer relationships. In another interaction, we processed her belief that others would leave her and that she was destined to be alone. Initially, she was reluctant to talk about race and being biracial. She had a longing to feel more connected to her mother, and she was willing to talk about race when we related her Latina heritage to her mother's cultural roots.

Phoebe enjoyed reading and engaged in bibliotherapy during Phase 3, so I used several books with Phoebe to help her better understand her mother's death, living with grandparents, and being biracial. Some books that I used with Phoebe about death were *Gentle Willow* (Mills, 2003) and *What Is Death?* (Boritzer, 2000), books about coping with death and loss. Parts of the book, *Is Nothing Something? Kids Questions and Zen Answers About Life, Death, Family, Friendship, and Everything in Between* (Hanh, 2014), were used in different ways to help Phoebe understand death, the importance of friends, and family. This book was consistent with the Simons's spiritual beliefs, and her grandparents asked to borrow it to read with her. We read *The Family Book* (Parr, 2003) to help Phoebe see different combinations of families and give her a platform for talking about race and differences. *Let's Talk About Race* (J. Lester, 2006), *Shades of People* (Rotner, 2010), *The Colors of Us* (Katz, 2002), and *Whoever You Are* (Fox, 2001) were also used to stimulate conversations about race and identity. Her grandparents asked to borrow several of these books too.

We used puppets and dolls to practice friendship skills and work on sharing ideas, toys, and power. I arranged with Phoebe's school counselor to include Phoebe in a friendship group with some other kids from her grade. Phoebe also began taking soccer lessons. It turned out that Phoebe had a natural knack for soccer. She couldn't wait for practice to play with her new "friends," and she practiced at home with her grandparents and dad. She became quite good at soccer and was well liked by her teammates. As an added bonus, Phoebe learned that her mother loved to watch soccer, and the whole family rooted for the Mexican team when they played on television.

We continued our story of Godzilla and ended up rewriting the plot. As Phoebe would now have it, Godzilla was no longer smashing buildings and cars. She said, "He learned how to be nice and tell people how he was feeling instead of yelling, screaming, and pounding." The people of the town decided that he should be mayor. They threw him a big party and everyone attended, "because they loved him so much." As Godzilla, the mayor, directed the town and made rules for the people, he often took into account other people's ideas. It appeared to me that sharing power became a more integrated and consistent part of her lifestyle. Occasionally, I would throw in an obstacle over which she had no control, such as an earthquake, traffic jam, new people moving to the town, or a new town rule. She took the interruption in stride and even had a town vote on the new rule, making sure to say that "It's only fair for everyone to get to decide." Throughout this play, I continued to metacommunicate about her goals of behavior and her budding social skills. I'd say things like, "Godzilla is really learning to be a leader because he listens to the townspeople's ideas" and "Hey! Godzilla is kind of like you. You used to get mad and bossy, but now you've found other ways to tell people how you feel."

I felt that it was important to include other members of the Simon family in many of our interactions during this phase of therapy. We did several sessions in which we worked on trust issues, playing small-group adventure–challenge games (Ashby et al., 2008). In one session, we conducted a round-robin strength bombardment, in which all of the family members listed the positive attributes of the other members. We also used family sculpting with Phoebe as the sculptor to demonstrate how she felt in her family. In a session with Christopher present, they did a kinetic family sand tray. Phoebe used her zebra and dolphin animals. By the end of the session, Mr. and Mrs. Simon each had a zebra miniature, and Christopher and Phoebe had the dolphin miniatures. They spontaneously developed a story about a loving family where everyone belonged and felt valued.

Phoebe had stopped having temper tantrums by the time we got to Session 20. Her friendship skills had blossomed and she had even had one sleepover with a girl from school by Session 22. She had a developing sense of who she was in terms of race and connection with her mother. The family went from avoiding discussions about Alicia to regularly and joyously talking about her. This seemed to help each of the family members in various ways.

Despite these wonderful accomplishments, Phoebe still needed to work on being less demanding with her grandmother; Mrs. Simon also needed to work on her boundaries and willingness to give in to all of Phoebe's requests. During Session 23, I reminded Mrs. Simon about natural and logical consequences and provided examples of and role played ways she could use these with Phoebe. I asked Mrs. Simon to read *Positive Discipline* (Nelson, 2011). We discussed this book and strategies that she would use with Phoebe. I checked in with Mrs. Simon during the next 2 weeks. She said the ideas she took from the book were helpful—she had started to hold family meetings—and she had noticed a positive change in the way Phoebe and she interacted with one another.

Mr. Simon had shown great improvement in his willingness to set boundaries. Even with her newly acquired parenting skills, sometimes Mrs. Simon still struggled with a tendency to overprotect and pamper Phoebe. Neither of them was consistent in setting limits, although they were improving significantly. I decided to introduce the idea that perhaps their own lifestyles were interfering with their relationships and boundaries with Phoebe. I drew a chart to illustrate my "mental picture" about some of their relationship patterns, personality priorities, and Crucial Cs that developed from their own family of origin. (I'm a visual person and believe I communicate more clearly when I can draw pictures or charts.) This graphic illustration seemed to help them both make several small shifts in their private logic, which resulted in more consistent application of boundaries and consequences. I also encouraged them to be supportive of one another.

Although it was certainly not a "miracle cure," by Session 30, it was obvious that Phoebe had made good progress toward her goals. She was more cooperative, she felt more capable, she could articulate and "own" many of her positive attributes, she had more confidence about belonging at home and school, and she had begun to recognize that she could make a significant contribution to others and the world. She also felt more connected with her mother and her cultural heritage. Although Phoebe was more at ease with being biracial, she still felt a bit uncomfortable with this at school. She teetered between showing off her Mexican culture like a badge of honor and trying to hide it to feel more like the other kids. On the occasion that she did get into trouble at home and school, it was because she was trying to let others know that they could not control her. However, the intensity and frequency of these incidents were significantly reduced. Phoebe still did not like to lose at games, but she was much more willing (and able) to take turns, negotiate, and compromise. Mr. and Mrs. Simon felt more confident about themselves in their grandparent role and more comfortable in helping Phoebe understand the death of her mother and her cultural connection to her mother. They were willing to make sure Phoebe had opportunities to play with other children in organized groups (e.g., soccer) and unorganized group (e.g., birthday parties, play dates).

At the time of termination Christopher was finishing up his degree and was looking for first-shift, full-time employment. His initial plans were to continue living with his parents so as to not disrupt Phoebe's stable home. He acknowledged the importance of spending quality time with Phoebe and maintaining the connection between Phoebe and his parents if and when he and Phoebe moved into a house of their own. The entire family seemed happier and more balanced.

In Session 30, we (Phoebe, myself, Mr. and Mrs. Simon, and Christopher) decided to have two more individual sessions with just Phoebe and myself to consolidate what she had learned and to process the ending of our relationship. She followed the typical pattern of going through the playroom and playing with just about every toy she had used since the beginning of our sessions. On the last day, she took one of my business cards, gave me a hug, and said, "Gracias." I said, "De nada." She said, "Can I come back if I need you again?" I said, "Of course!" She said, "Can we all come back if we need you?" I said, "Of course!" She looked at her grandparents and her dad, who were all sitting and waiting for her, smiled at them, smiled at me, and said, "I don't think we will need to, but you never know."

Summary

The reorientation–reeducation phase of Adlerian play therapy is the most directive phase of the process. In this phase, the play therapist uses the play process to help children operationalize and apply all of the shifts in feelings, thinking, and behaving they made in the previous phases. They master new ways to express their feelings and behave in different settings, they work on skills for making and maintaining relationships with other people, they experiment with methods for dealing with problems. They learn and practice tools for recognizing and "owning" their assets, mastering the Crucial Cs, optimally functioning at life tasks, manifesting the positive elements of their personality priorities, and getting their needs met in appropriate ways.

Further Resources

Bibliotherapy:

http://www.ala.org/tools/bibliotherapy
http://www.best-childrens-books.com/bibliotherapy.html
http://www.carnegielibrary.org/research/parentseducators/parents/bibliotherapy/
http://www.medscape.com/viewarticle/734236

Role-playing:

http://www.nadta.org/assets/documents/adolescent-fact-sheet.pdf
http://www.playtherapyseminars.com/articles/details/10007

Termination:

http://www.counseling.org/resources/library/Selected%20Topics/Play%20Therapy/voluntary%20play%20guidelines.pdf

http://creativityintherapy.blogspot.com/2012/09/memory-book-termination-activity.html

http://eric.ed.gov/?id=EJ200434

http://www.prolibraries.com/apt/?select=session&sessionID=53

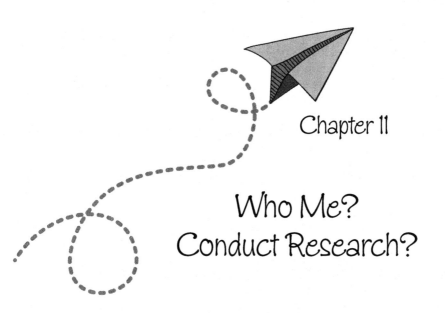

Chapter 11

Who Me?
Conduct Research?

We get it. You may not care much about research, or perhaps the thought of reading a description of previous research is on your to-do list right next to digging a big hole to the other side of the world. Please, bear with us. We think this information is useful in a number of ways:

- You can share with parents, teachers, administrators, agency supervisors, insurance companies, and others information about presenting issues, client demographics, and settings in which there is empirical support for the efficacy of play therapy.
- You can track down the research articles and book chapters we have cited for suggestions about treatment planning or specific interventions to use with different children in your clinical practice.
- You might find that there are a number of different ways to conduct interesting and useful research.
- You might be surprised to learn research can be fun! (We know—not likely, but we are giving it a shot anyway.)

Support for Play Therapy

Play therapy has become a well-researched, empirically supported method of working with children within diverse populations, settings, and presenting issues (Bratton & Ray, 2000; Bratton, Ray, Rhine, & Jones, 2005; LeBlanc & Ritchie, 2001; Lin & Bratton, 2015; Ray, 2006, 2011, 2015; Stewart & Green, 2015). The most commonly researched approach to play therapy is child-centered play therapy. Child-centered play therapy has been shown to be effective at reducing a variety of presenting issues, including problem classroom behaviors; low academic achievement; self-concept; anxiety; and more specific diagnoses such as management of somatoform disorders, ADHD, intermittent explosive disorder, and autism. Child-centered play therapy has also been found to be effective with people of various cultures, such as Ugandan orphans, children who are homeless, and children who have intellectual disabilities. (See Appendix H for citations.)

Other authors have published case studies or suggested strategies from a variety of approaches to play therapy for working with children of various cultures and presenting concerns. Some represented cultures include Muslims, Koreans, and child refugees. Authors have also included play therapy strategies or modifications for work with children with autism, anger and aggression, bullying issues, selective mutism, externalizing behaviors, attachment disorders, grief and loss issues, sexual abuse, children in foster care, children whose parents are separated or getting divorced, chronically ill children, and those who have experienced natural disasters. (See Appendix H for citations.)

Adlerian Play Therapy Research

Only recently has Adlerian play therapy made the research scene. Together with a colleague, Sue Bratton, we created a means to develop and execute a rigorous randomized control trial research design to evaluate the effectiveness of Adlerian play therapy. Kottman (2009) created a treatment manual and provided advanced Adlerian play therapy training and ongoing supervision to multiple treatment providers. Meany-Walen oversaw the project in which 58 children, who qualified for inclusion in the study based on borderline or clinical levels of disruptive classroom behavior, completed the study. Results were significant, with effective to very effective treatment effects. The results demonstrated that children who received Adlerian play therapy reduced problem behaviors and increased on-task behavior, and their teachers experienced a lower level of teaching-related stress (Meany-Walen, Bratton, & Kottman, 2014). Subsequent research articles also demonstrated Adlerian play therapy as effective at reducing children's problem behaviors (Meany-Walen, Kottman, Bullis, & Dillman Taylor, 2015) and increasing children's on-task behaviors (Dillman Taylor & Meany-Walen, 2015; Meany-Walen, Bullis, Kottman, & Dillman Taylor, 2015; Meany-Walen, Kottman, et al., 2015).

Considerations for Research

You may be interested in conducting your own Adlerian play therapy research, and we want to encourage you to do so. The current climate of the helping professions is moving us toward requiring treatments to have evidence that support their effectiveness to be used or for counselors to be reimbursed. Therefore, more research is needed to support the effectiveness of Adlerian play therapy with children from various cultures; with a range of presenting concerns; and in different settings such as schools, private practices, or hospitals. The aim of this chapter is to provide you with information and tools to help you conduct and publish your own research.

Warning: You will need information about research design and analysis that goes well beyond what we provide in this chapter. The information that follows is meant to assist you in your research, and we provide what we believe can be valuable resources for conducting Adlerian play therapy research.

So Many Methods, So Little Time

Quantitative, qualitative, mixed . . . oh my! You may be thinking to yourself: Which one matters? Which one is easiest? Which one can I do? No definitive answer exists. Despite what people will tell you, no single research method is more important than another. Each of the methods adds valuable information to the play therapy literature and helps to guide clinical practice. To help you figure this out, consider the following questions.

1. *What do you want to know?*
   You'll make decisions on which method to use based on what you want to know. For example, if you are wondering whether Adlerian play therapy is effective at reducing depression symptoms and to what degree, you might use a randomized control trial, which is a quantitative method. If you are interested in learning what parents think about the play therapy process, you will probably use one of the many qualitative measures. For researchers interested in the process of Adlerian play therapy and what happens over the course of time, a single-case research design might be used to see how a child's ADHD behaviors change before, during, and after the Adlerian play therapy intervention.

2. *What or who are your supports?*
   What support do you have for conducting research? On the basis of the method you use, there will be particular things to consider as you develop your research plan. If you work in community settings or private practice, you might consider partnering with a nearby university counseling, social work, or psychology professor. Many professors are obligated to do (and hopefully are interested in) research. Universities also tend to have resources such as statisticians and students who are eager to help. The university employee or student can complete the institutional review board application that is necessary to ensure ethical research of human participants. As an assistant professor, I (KMW) often conduct research and would be thrilled if a counselor in the community asked to partner with me on research. Don't be shy. Often times you can contribute as much or as little as you want and still be involved in research.

3. *What are your financial needs?*
   Research costs money. If you are working with participants who are not your regular clients, you may or may not be charging for your services. You'll have to supply arts-and-crafts materials, toys, or other playroom materials if you don't see research participants in

your office. You may need to purchase psychological or behavioral assessments or scoring software for your computer. These assessments tend to be kind of expensive. Recording equipment for fidelity checks or qualitative interviews may be a necessary part of your research. If you are doing interviews with participants or asking participants to complete assessments, you may offer them a stipend for their time, such as a $10 gift card to your local coffee shop.

One way to handle the financial cost of doing research is to search your community for foundation grants. We have received grants from local, state, and national organizations to help support our research costs. Sometimes the grants are a few hundred dollars, which can pay for assessments. Other times, grants can be thousands or millions of dollars. We have frequently used the help of our friends and family to cut down on costs. Terry's husband has helped set up and wire recording equipment, saving money on electrician and maintenance costs. Kristin's husband and son built dollhouses and puppet theaters to reduce the cost of additional playroom materials.

4. *What are your personnel needs?*

Your personnel needs depend on (you guessed it) what you want to know and the type of research you're conducting. If you are doing an intervention research design (mixed or quantitative), you will have to consider the number of participants and treatment providers you will need to complete your study. In one study that I (KMW) conducted, I had nearly 100 participants and 25 treatment providers. In another study, I had five participants and one treatment provider (me). Before you start, you need to determine how many people you need and how many you can access.

5. *How do you get started?*

If you consider yourself a research newbie, start by connecting with someone who has research experience (a colleague, a previous professor, a member of a professional organization). This will help to keep you encouraged and on the right track. We'd hate for you to get started conducting research only to find that you can't use your data because you didn't start with a clear plan. You may also begin your research by familiarizing yourself with current literature. What have other researchers done? What kinds of articles do you find most interesting? You might look more into those types of research designs for ideas on how to guide your project.

We want to reiterate that this is far from a complete list of things to consider. This is merely a way to get your wheels turning so that you can be set up for success.

Points to Ponder

Although it would be lovely, the likelihood of us getting the opportunity to sit and chat with everyone who wants to do Adlerian play therapy is unlikely. However, when we do have the chance to talk with Adlerian play therapists about conducting research, we find that we run into a few of the same questions. These concepts are relevant to research because to say that the researcher is doing Adlerian play therapy, he or she must, in fact, do Adlerian play therapy. This means, that the play therapist engages the child in interventions tailored to address the client's lifestyle and needs.

- *I conceptualize from an Adlerian perspective, but I am exclusively nondirective in the playroom. Is that still Adlerian play therapy?*
  Here's the skinny—no, if you are never directive in the playroom, you are not doing Adlerian play therapy. Adlerian therapy is built on the expectation that the counselor will challenge, educate, or reorient clients to new ways of finding belonging and significance. Adlerian play therapists might not be terribly directive during Phase 1 (except every once in a while to show that sometimes the child gets to be the boss and sometimes the therapist gets to be the boss), but they will always be directive sometime during Phases 2, 3, and 4. They won't be continuously directive, but at some point they will direct the child in play, conversation, or activity. If you are super uncomfortable with being directive, Adlerian play therapy almost certainly isn't for you, and you probably won't want to be doing research into this approach anyway.
- *What decides how directive I am?*
  The answer, of course, is "It depends." (This is almost always our answer to practically everything.) The phase of therapy, your own personality, and what you know about the child will guide how and when you are directive. We know this is a bit redundant, but (just as a reminder) you might not be directive a lot during Phase 1, but you will be more directive during Phase 2 (e.g., asking the child questions, requesting that the child does a puppet show, asking the child to draw a picture of a family, etc.), Phase 3 (e.g., asking the child to tell you a story so you can do mutual storytelling, inviting the child to do a sand tray with you, offering to do a puppet show for the child), and Phase 4 (e.g., teaching the child how to "walk like an Egyptian," inviting the child to role play asking another child to play, giving the child a choice between playing Don't Break the Ice or making rows of dominos and knocking them down).
  If you are a pretty assertive (bossy) person, you will be more likely to be directive; if you are more reserved (not bossy) person, you will be less likely to be directive. Terry is MUCH more directive than Kristin, and, yet, we are both Adlerian play therapists. (But even Kristin gets into being officious sometimes—ask her husband and children!)
  The child's presenting problem and the family dynamics will probably also have an impact on how directive you are. If a child has been engaged in power struggles with the adults in his or her life, you will want to look at the way the family handles things. You will handle a child who has too much power differently than a child who has too little power. (If this does not sound familiar, check out the section in Chapter 3 on goals of misbehavior.)

The child's lifestyle is also going to influence how directive you are. A child who has a personality priority of control might be more comfortable being in the lead. He or she might not trust you to make decisions. Similarly, a child who has proving inadequacy as a goal of misbehavior might be more than happy to let you be in the lead. During Phases 3 and 4, we engage these children in sharing power, but we do it in different ways because the children are different. For example, a client of mine (KMW) with a personality priority of control routinely wanted to play store. She was always the cashier, and I was instructed to purchase items and bring them through her checkout lane. During Phase 3, I told her that I would like to be the cashier and she could purchase things from me. Although initially hesitant, she shared these roles with me. Ultimately, she became more willing to share power and had less of a need to be in control in the playroom and when she was with her teacher, friends, and mother.

- *How much planning needs to go into being directive?*
  Directive activities can be planned ahead of time or might spontaneously develop through the course of play. I (KMW) work at a local elementary school with groups of children who have a hard time getting along with others. I usually have them do some activity such as a puppet show, game, or collaborative craft that requires preplanning from me and interaction and negotiation from them. These activities might take the entire session or they could take 5 minutes. Either way, I have learned something about my clients, and I have created opportunities to provide feedback to them and encourage them to try different prosocial behaviors. Other times I have spontaneously directed the play. When this same group of children got too loud for the school setting, I engaged them in brainstorming ways that would remind them that they were getting too loud. The group members decided (on their own) that they would hop on one foot and flail their arms in the air (a little dance of sorts) to get the others' attention that the group was getting too rowdy. This method created opportunities for the children to negotiate and problem solve. I could not have planned this prior to our session, and I could not have allowed the noise to continue at that level. This group used their created reminder dance for the remainder of our sessions together.

- *Wait! The treatment manual doesn't tell me exactly when and how to do things. What should I do?*
  Treatment manuals are designed for a number of purposes, not limited to (a) guiding providers such as counselors, play therapists, and social workers through the treatment process; (b) outlining a treatment that has some suggestion of effectiveness; (c) creating a way to evaluate treatment fidelity—that is, making sure that the treatment provider is doing the intervention as it is designed; and (d) facilitating training and supervision of treatment providers. Treatment manuals, or treatment protocols, come in a variety of designs ranging from very structured to a more fluid and negotiable plan. The treatment determines the design.

The nature of Adlerian play therapy lends itself to a more fluid style of treatment protocol. Here's what we mean. Remember that Phase 1 (building the relationship) must be accomplished before you start Phase 2. However, you'll never stop working at maintaining or strengthening the collaborative relationship. Therefore, you cannot simply check Phase 1 off the to-do list. In Phase 2, your mission is to investigate and understand the lifestyle. You can do this in a number of ways (see Chapter 3 for examples) and over a period of time. Phase 3 is designed to help the child gain insight into his or her lifestyle. You will create custom-designed interventions that respond to the client's needs and lifestyle. Because the interventions will be uniquely tailored to the individual, we could not possibly demand that you adhere to a particular set of techniques. Rather, you will have to use your clinical judgment, experience, and trial and error to decide what to use and how to evaluate its effectiveness. That said, initially, we worked long and hard to make an Adlerian play therapy protocol that was linear and concrete in an effort to make research easier and more systematic. What we noticed was that as we focused on manualizing the process in a rigid, cook-bookish way, we lost sight of the uniqueness of the child and the essence of Adlerian theory.

Sure, this poses a potential obstacle for the Adlerian play therapy researcher. But wait—we created an outline and some tools that can assist you in applying the manual, assessing treatment fidelity, and evaluating client progress. We believe the following information and resources will be useful to you with your clients, during supervision, and for research purposes. If you are interested in doing research into Adlerian play therapy, the treatment manual (Kottman, 2009) is available to use. Just contact me (Terry), and I will send it to you.

Doing Adlerian Play Therapy Research

Therapist Training

To gain proficiency in Adlerian play therapy, the therapist must meet the minimal standards of a master's degree in a mental health field, the equivalent of an introductory-level course in play therapy, 40 hours of training in the specifics of Adlerian play therapy that include the principles of Individual Psychology, and supervised practice using Adlerian play therapy with children. Ideally, the supervisor would be an Adlerian play therapist, but we know this may be hard to find in some communities; the supervisor must be trained in Individual Psychology and play therapy. The therapist should have at least 10 hours of supervision that includes the supervisor observing the therapist using Adlerian play therapy with children. This training would meet the minimal requirement for facilitation of Adlerian play therapy research.

Logistics of Sessions

Adlerian play therapy sessions often range from 30 to 50 minutes. The timing and frequency of sessions will be based on the setting, development and presenting concerns of the child, or other important factors determined by the principal investigator. Regardless of the time and frequency, there should be consistency and predictability to replicate or adjust the treatment design. This also provides structure and planning for the children and the adults who might be coordinating care for the child. Most of the time, the therapist will conduct a parent or teacher consultation. These sessions last approximately 20 to 30 minutes and might be at different intervals than the play therapy sessions. Adlerian play therapy does not define a required number of sessions for success of the process. Professional judgment, or treatment design in some cases, is used to assess progress and the child's movement through the four phases of Adlerian play therapy.

Therapist's Visual Attitude

With all children, the therapist should be actively involved in the process of play therapy, expressing interest in what the child is doing and saying. The therapist should be relaxed and comfortable in the session with the child and the play. It is important for the tone and affect of the therapist to be congruent with the child's tone and affect, and the tone and affect of the therapist's responses should be congruent with what the therapist is saying.

What Do You Do, and When Do You Do It?

The following is a list of skills that Adlerian play therapists use in each of the four phases of Adlerian play therapy. This is a list; it is only a list. You will find descriptions of each of the skills and concepts within the chapters of the book that correspond with the phases. Because we don't want to create strenuous work for you, we have provided chapter references for your convenience.

Phase 1—Building an Egalitarian Relationship

In the first phase of Adlerian play therapy, the counselor's goal is to create a welcoming, inviting, and encouraging environment. The counselor wants the child to feel safe enough to share or not to share personal information. The relationship creates a foundation for the remainder of the counseling process. Because it is essential that a collaborative relationship is established and children will have different levels of willingness to engage and partner with the play therapist, this phase will take different lengths of time with different children. For example, Phase 1 might be established in half of the first session with one child, and it might take at least three sessions with a different child.

This list of skills is used with *all* children (see Chapter 5 and 6):

- Meeting the child
- Asking the child, "What did your parent(s) (and/or teacher) tell you about coming here?"
- Demystifying the play therapy process for the child
- Tracking behavior
- Restating content

- Metacommunicating
- Reflecting feelings
- Answering questions
- Asking questions
- Encouraging
- Interacting actively with the child

The following are strategies that the Adlerian play therapist uses with *some* children.

- Returning responsibility to the child
- Using the child's metaphor
- Cleaning the room together
- Setting limits in a four-step Adlerian process (see Chapter 6)

Phase 2—Exploring the Child's Lifestyle

In the second phase of Adlerian play therapy, the therapist continues to use many of the skills from the first phase and adds the following skills with every child. On the basis of the information gathered during this phase, the Adlerian play therapist completes the Lifestyle Conceptualization and Treatment Plan–Child Form (see Appendix G). Completion of this form is evidence that the counselor has satisfied Phase 2 of Adlerian play therapy. The treatment plan and goal setting will be dependent upon this information.

- Exploring the child's family atmosphere (Chapters 7 and 8)
- Exploring the child's family constellation (Chapters 7 and 8)
- Exploring the child's functioning at life tasks (Chapters 7 and 8)
- Exploring the child's assets (Chapters 5 and 8)
- Examining the child's goals of misbehavior (Chapters 3 and 8)
- Exploring the child's Crucial Cs (Chapters 3 and 8)
- Exploring the child's personality priorities (Chapters 3 and 8)
- Exploring the child's lifestyle convictions and private logic (Chapter 8)

With some children the therapist will use the following skills:

- Returning responsibility to the child (Chapter 5)
- Using the child's metaphor (Chapters 5 and 9)
- Cleaning the room together (Chapter 5)
- Setting limits in a four-step Adlerian process (Chapter 6)
- Soliciting early recollections (Chapters 7 and 8)

Phase 3—Helping the Child Gain Insight

In the third phase, the Adlerian play therapist continues to use skills from Phase 1. A list of techniques designed to bring about opportunities for the play therapist to help the child gain insight are provided in Chapter 9. These are suggestions and techniques that we have found helpful. Customized interventions and other activities might be helpful to the Adlerian play therapist and client as well. The therapist's responses during this phase will consist of the following skills:

- Metacommunicating about:
  – A single event, behavior, or interaction and/or the meaning of a specific event, behavior, or interaction
  – A pattern within a session
  – A pattern across sessions
  – A pattern in the playroom that extends to other situations or relationships outside the playroom
  – A lifestyle theme or conviction, mistaken beliefs, or private logic
- Spitting in the client's soup about mistaken beliefs, private logic, or self-defeating behaviors
- Using one of the metaphoric techniques
- Using sand tray, art activities, movement exercises, and/or adventure therapy activities

Phase 4—Reorienting and Reeducating the Child

In Phase 4, the Adlerian play therapist continues to use many of the skills from previous phases while adding strategies designed to teach the child the new patterns of thinking, feeling, and behaving that will help with the reorientation–reeducation process (Chapter 10).

- Helping the child generate ideas for the following, as appropriate:
  – Capitalizing on assets
  – Improving functioning at one or more of the life tasks
  – Fostering improvement in Crucial Cs
  – Moving toward healthy functioning in personality priorities
  – Shifting from goals of misbehavior to more positive goals
  – Substituting positive convictions for mistaken beliefs and common sense for private logic
  – Reducing self-defeating behaviors and learning positive behaviors
  – Increasing abilities in needed skills (e.g., social skills, negotiation skills, communication skills, assertiveness, taking appropriate responsibility for behavior, etc.)
- Providing the child the opportunity to practice the above skills as appropriate, both in the play sessions and in situations and relationships outside the play sessions

Parent and Teacher Consultation

In Adlerian play therapy, consultation with parents and/or teachers is usually an integral part of the process with children who are struggling with issues connected to family, home, school, and everyday social functioning. If the investigator wishes to extend the research to include work with parents, guardians, or school personnel, he or she would use the following description of parent–teacher consultation.

The following lists of phases and skills that are used with the parent/teacher parallel those that the Adlerian play therapist uses with the child. The underlying principles of Adlerian theory do not change. Rather, the ways in which the researcher engages the adult and moves through the four phases shifts.

Phase 1—Building an Egalitarian Relationship With the Parent/Teacher

This list of skills is used with parents/teachers. (Chapter 4):

- Meet the parent/teacher
- Describe the practical aspects of play therapy to the parent/teacher
- Inform parents/teachers of their role in the counseling process
- Describe the rationale of play therapy to the parent/teacher
- Gather information from the parent/teacher about the nature and evolution of the identified problem
- Discuss goals for the child and the parent–teacher in play therapy
- Restate content
- Metacommunicate
- Reflect feelings
- Encourage

Phase 2—Exploring the Parent's/Teacher's Lifestyle

Information provided to the counselor during the first and second phases are additive to his or her understanding and documented on the Lifestyle Conceptualization Forms found in Appendix G. With the adult you gather information about the child's and about the parent or teacher. You will do the following things (see Chapter 4; Appendices B and C).

- Gather information from the adult about the
  –Child's development
  –Child's lifestyle
  –Child's interactions with other children, adults, authority figures
- Explore the adult's assets
- Explore the adult's functioning at life tasks
- Explore the adult's Crucial Cs
- Explore the adult's personality priorities
- Explore the adult's lifestyle convictions and private logic

Phase 3—Helping the Parent/Teacher Gain Insight

In the third phase, the consultations are designed to help the parent/ teacher gain insight into his or her own lifestyle, the child's lifestyle, and the interaction patterns between child and parent/teacher. The following skills and strategies will be used with parents/teachers (see Chapter 4):

- Explaining, to the parent/teacher, the child's
  –Assets
  –Crucial Cs

    –Goals of misbehavior
    –Personality priorities
    –Lifestyle
- Providing feedback to the parent/teacher about his or her:
    –Assets
    –Crucial Cs
    –Personality priorities
    –Lifestyle
- The counselor might use the following strategies to help facilitate insight with the parent/teacher:
    –Metacommunication
    –Metaphoric techniques
    –Sand tray
    –Art techniques
    –Bibliotherapy
    –Discussion
    –Spitting in the parent/teacher's soup about mistaken beliefs, private logic, or self-defeating behaviors

Phase 4—Reorienting and Reeducating the Parent/Teacher

In Phase 4, the Adlerian play therapist provides information and opportunities for the parents/teachers to create new patterns of thinking, feeling, and behaving about and toward his or her self and the child (see Chapter 4).

- Teaching skills that improve the parent/teacher–child interaction
- Teaching the parent/teacher how to discipline, including how to use logical and natural consequences
- Informing the parent/teacher about Adlerian principles such as assets, Crucial Cs, goals of misbehavior, personality priorities, and lifestyles
- Providing resources such as books, articles, videos, or local groups intended to support the parent/teacher and provide useful and relevant information
- Providing opportunities for the parent/teacher to practice the above skills as appropriate, both in the consultations and in interpersonal interactions

Using the Adlerian Play Therapy Parent Consultation Skills Checklist (Appendix I) or the Adlerian Play Therapy Teacher Consultation Skills Checklist (Appendix J), the investigator could ensure that the therapist used the same procedures for all parents or teachers included in the treatment process.

Treatment Resources

Lifestyle Conceptualization Form/Treatment Planning Worksheet (Appendix G)

The Lifestyle Conceptualization Form/Treatment Planning Worksheets guide the counselor through the Adlerian conceptualization process.

Important key principles are outlined on the form that can help counselors to know that they have assessed important areas of functioning of the child. After completing the conceptualization form/treatment planning worksheet, counselors can custom design interventions that meet the child's needs and respond to the child's assets. As with the Session Summary Sheets, this form is used in clinical practice as well as research. We use this form in research to confirm Phase 2 has been established and we can move into Phase 3.

Adlerian Play Therapy Skills Checklists (Appendices I, J, and K)

The Adlerian Play Therapy Skills Checklists (APTSC) were designed as a way to indicate that the play therapist is or is not doing Adlerian play therapy. A list of skills or objectives and an integrity rating system are listed for each of the four phases of Adlerian theory. A trained observer can use these forms as he or she watches a live session (behind a two-way mirror) or watches a recorded session. In either of these scenarios, the counselor has communicated to and obtained consent from the guardian that observers can view the sessions. In research or supervision, the observer can use the checklists to assess whether the play therapist is actually doing Adlerian play therapy by calculating the agreement between the counselor's demonstrated skills and the opportunities to use those skills. The therapist must demonstrate a minimum of 80% of the skills that are appropriate to use with the child to be consistent with Adlerian play therapy. For example, if it is not necessary or appropriate to set limits with a particular child, that skill will not be tallied in the 80% calculation. As covered earlier in this chapter, fidelity is important (albeit a bit cumbersome) in research. It ensures that the interventions children receive are consistent with Adlerian theory and Adlerian play therapy practices.

Session Summary Sheets (Appendix L)

The Session Summary Sheets were intentionally designed to parallel the traditional SOAP notes that collect Subjective, Objective, Assessment, and Plan data. I (TK) developed the summary sheets to satisfy insurance company and community agency standards and auditors and be a relatively easy way to track children's in-session disclosures and play behaviors. The Session Summary Sheets were initially created for regular client sessions but have been used to track progress during research studies as well. As a research tool, this form can be used as evidence for session patterns and use of play or activities throughout the play therapy process.

Progress Forms (Appendix M)

Progress Forms were specifically designed for research purposes. Among other snags we encountered as I (TK) originally developed the treatment protocol and Kristin put it into action was that supervisors or those checking fidelity could not assess change in a child's thinking, feeling, or behaving if they did not observe all of the sessions. After all, we need some sort of baseline to know that something has changed, right? This form allows the play therapist to assess the child's level of functioning after each session. The form is intended to be brief and completed in about 2 minutes. When the person checking fidelity observes the play session, he or she will also have access to the Progress Forms that will provide information that is helpful when determining the counselor's ability to apply Adlerian play therapy principles in Phases 3 or 4. We have also found this form to be a handy piece of additional information in our clinical practices.

Ensuring Integrity of Protocol

To conduct research using Adlerian play therapy, the investigator must ensure the integrity of the Adlerian play therapy protocol. Several steps are recommended to aid in the fidelity check process.

1. All research play therapy sessions are recorded and collected by the principal investigator.
2. The Adlerian play therapist completes the Lifestyle Conceptualization and Treatment Plan form following Phase 2 (Appendix G).
3. The Adlerian play therapist completes the progress forms following each session with the child (Appendix M).
4. Ten percent of all recordings are randomly selected to be reviewed and compared with the Adlerian Play Therapy Skills Checklists (Appendices I, J, and K).
5. The reviewer observes 10 to 15 minutes of each of the selected sessions and uses the APTSC to confirm or deny the counselor's adherence to Adlerian play therapy.
6. The investigator analyzes the completed APTSC forms and calculates an agreement percentage within the response categories. Optimal agreement is between 80% and 100%.
7. Adlerian play therapists maintain regular supervision (biweekly minimum) as an ethical obligation and a strategy to maintain objective client care.
8. Supervision topics include, but are not limited to, client care and the treatment provider's ability to accurately conceptualize a treatment plan according to Adlerian play therapy.

Summary

We've said it throughout this chapter, and we think it's worth repeating . . . this chapter is not intended to provide you with information on how to conduct quality research designs. There is a plethora of important research strategy information that we left out. This chapter is merely to provide you with ideas about how to get started, resources and forms to support your efforts, and an Adlerian treatment protocol with which to strengthen your design. What we hope is that you've (a) stayed awake while reading this chapter, (b) discovered that you can conduct research that helps to promote play therapy and support children and families, and (c) decided to pursue doing research into Adlerian play therapy.

Conclusion

We hope that you have learned a great deal about the theory of Individual Psychology and about practical ways of integrating Adlerian theory into your work with children, parents, and teachers. Remember that your most important tool is who you are and what you believe about people. Be encouraging—to yourself and to the people you encounter, especially the children. Remember to play and have FUN!

Further Resources

http://www.a4pt.org/?page=PlayTherapyPub
http://www.a4pt.org/?page=Research
http://cpt.unt.edu/researchpublications/play-therapy-outcome-research/
http://c.ymcdn.com/sites/www.a4pt.org/resource/resmgr/Publications/Meta-AnalyticLiteratureRevie.pdf
http://www.moplaytherapy.org/uploads/media/Research_The_efficacy_of_play_therapy_with_children.pdf

Appendix A

Selected Fun Things to Do in Play Therapy

This is just a sampling. There are hundreds of books out there . . . go explore!

Adventure/Activity Therapy

Ashby, J. S., Kottman, T., & DeGraaf, D. (2008). *Active interventions for kids and teens: Adding adventure and fun to counseling!* Alexandria, VA: American Counseling Association.

Barber, V. (2011). *Creating children's art games for emotional support.* Philadelphia, PA: Jessica Kingsley.

Delaney, T. (2009). *101 games and activities for children with autism, Asperger's, and sensory processing disorders.* New York, NY: McGraw-Hill eBooks.

Joiner, L. (2012). *The big book of therapeutic activities for children and teens.* Philadelphia, PA: Jessica Kingsley.

Kottman, T., Ashby, J., & DeGraaf, D. (2001). *Adventures in guidance: How to integrate fun into your guidance program.* Alexandria, VA: American Counseling Association.

Kottman, T., Strother, J., & Deniger, M. (1987). Activity therapy: An alternative therapy for adolescents. *Journal of Humanistic Education and Development, 25,* 180–186.

Art Techniques

Darley, S., & Heath, W. (2008). *The expressive arts activity book: A resource for professionals.* Philadelphia, PA: Jessica Kingsley.

Green, E. J., Drewes, A. A., & Kominski, J. M. (2013). Use of mandalas in Jungian play therapy with adolescents diagnosed with ADHD. *International Journal of Play Therapy, 22,* 159–172.

Kellogg, R. (1970). *Analyzing children's art*. Palo Alto, CA: National Press Books.

Knoff, H., & Prout, H. (1985). *Kinetic drawing system for family and school: A handbook*. Los Angeles, CA: Western Psychological Services.

Leibowitz, M. (1999). *Interpreting projective drawings*. New York, NY: Brunner/Mazel.

Lombardi, R. (2014). Art therapy. In E. Green & A. Drewes (Eds.), *Integrating expressive arts and play therapy* (pp. 41–66). Hoboken, NJ: Wiley.

Malchiodi, C. (1998). *Understanding children's art*. New York, NY: Guilford Press.

Malchiodi, C. (2006). *The art therapy sourcebook* (Rev. ed.). New York, NY: McGraw-Hill.

Malchiodi, C. (Ed.). (2014). *Creative interventions with traumatized children* (2nd ed.). New York, NY: Guilford Press.

Malchiodi, C., & Crenshaw, D. (Eds.). (2014). *Creative arts and play therapy for attachment problems*. New York, NY: Guilford Press.

Oaklander, V. (1992). *Windows to our children: A Gestalt approach to children and adolescents*. New York, NY: The Gestalt Journal Press. (Original work published 1978)

O'Connor, K. (1983). The Color Your Life technique. In C. Schaefer & K. O'Connor (Eds.), *Handbook of play therapy* (pp. 251–257). New York, NY: Wiley.

Oster, G., & Gould, P. (1987). *Using drawings in assessment and therapy: A guide for mental health professionals*. New York, NY: Brunner/Mazel.

Steinhardt, L. (1985). Freedom within boundaries: Body outline drawings in art therapy with children. *The Arts in Psychotherapy, 12*, 25–34.

Bibliotherapy

Golding, J. (2006). *Healing stories: Picture books for the big and small changes in a child's life*. New York, NY: Rowman & Littlefield.

Hynes, A., & Hynes-Berry, M. (1986). *Bibliotherapy: The interactive process*. Boulder, CO: Westview Press.

Jackson, S. (2001). Using bibliotherapy with clients. *Individual Psychology, 57*, 289–297.

Malchiodi, C., & Ginns-Gruenberg, D. (2008). Trauma, loss, and bibliotherapy: The healing power of stories. In C. Malchiodi (Ed.), *Creative interventions with traumatized children* (pp. 167–188). New York, NY: Guilford Press.

Myers, J. (1998). Bibliotherapy and DCT: Co-constructing the therapeutic metaphor. *Journal of Counseling & Development, 76*, 243–250. doi:10.1002/j.1556-6676.1998.tb02539.x

Pardeck, J. (1994). Using literature to help adolescents cope with problems. *Adolescence, 29*, 421–427.

Pardeck, J., & Markward, M. (1995). Bibliotherapy: Using books to help children deal with problems. *Early Childhood Development and Care, 106*, 75–90.

Pardeck, J., & Pardeck, J. (1993). *Bibliotherapy: A clinical approach for helping children*. Langhorne, PA: Gordon & Breach Science.

Pardeck, J. (1998). *Using books in clinical social work practice: A guide to bibliotherapy*. Gloucestershire, England: Hawthorn.

Recob, A. (2008). *Bibliotherapy: When kids need books*. Bloomington, IN: iUniverse.

Riordan, R., Mullis, F., & Nuchow, L. (1996). Organizing for bibliotherapy: The science in the art. *Individual Psychology, 52*, 167–180.

Drama Therapy

Gil, E., & Dias, T. (2014). The integration of drama therapy and play therapy in attachment work with traumatized children. In C. Malchiodi & D. Crenshaw (Eds.), *Creative arts and play therapy for attachment problems* (pp. 100–120). New York, NY: Guilford Press.

Irwin, E. (2014). Drama therapy. In E. Green & A. Drewes (Eds.), *Integrating expressive arts and play therapy* (pp. 67–100). Hoboken, NJ: Wiley.

Game Play

Gardner, R. (2004). *Psychotherapeutic use of the Talking, Feeling & Doing game*. Wilkes-Barre, PA: Child's Work/Child's Play.

Jones, A. (2013). *Therapy games: Creative ways to turn popular games into activities that build self-esteem, teamwork, communication skills, anger management, self-discovery, and coping skills*. Lusby, MD: Rec Room.

Metaphoric Storytelling

Gardner, R. (1971). *Therapeutic communication with children: The mutual storytelling technique*. Northvale, NJ: Jason Aronson.

Gardner, R. (1986). *The psychotherapeutic technique of Richard A. Gardner*. Northvale, NJ: Jason Aronson.

Gil, E. (2014). The creative use of metaphor in play and art therapy with attachment problems. In C. Malchiodi & D. Crenshaw (Eds.), *Creative arts and play therapy for attachment problems* (pp. 159–177). New York, NY: Guilford Press.

Kottman, T. (2003). Mutual storytelling: Adlerian style. In H. Kaduson & C. Schaefer (Eds.), *101 favorite play therapy techniques* (Vol. 3, pp. 203–208). Northvale, NJ: Jason Aronson.

Kottman, T., & Ashby, J. (2002). Metaphoric stories. In C. Schaefer & D. Cangelosi (Eds.), *Play therapy techniques* (2nd ed., pp. 133–142). Northvale, NJ: Jason Aronson.

Kottman, T., & Stiles, K. (1990). The mutual storytelling technique: An Adlerian application in child therapy. *The Journal of Individual Psychology, 46*, 148–156.

Lankton, C., & Lankton, S. (1989). *Tales of enchantment: Goal-oriented metaphors for adults and children in therapy*. New York, NY: Brunner/Mazel.

Mills, J., & Crowley, R. (2014). *Therapeutic metaphors for children and the child within* (2nd ed.). New York, NY: Routledge.

Movement and Dance

Devereaux, C. (2014). Moving with the space between us: The dance of attachment security. In C. Malchiodi & D. Crenshaw (Eds.), *Creative arts and play therapy for attachment problems* (pp. 84–99). New York, NY: Guilford Press.

LeFeber, M. (2014). Working with children using dance/movement therapy. In E. Green & A. Drewes (Eds.), *Integrating expressive arts and play therapy* (pp. 125–148). Hoboken, NJ: Wiley.

Music

Hadley, S., & Steele, N. (2014). Music therapy. In E. Green & A. Drewes (Eds.), *Integrating expressive arts and play therapy* (pp. 149–180). Hoboken, NJ: Wiley.

Robarts, J. (2014). Music therapy with children with developmental trauma disorder. In C. Malchiodi & D. Crenshaw (Eds.), *Creative arts and play therapy for attachment problems* (pp. 67–83). New York, NY: Guilford Press.

Prop-Based Play Interventions

Goodyear-Brown, P. (2002). *Digging for buried treasure: 52 prop-based play therapy interventions for treating the problems of childhood*. Franklin, TN: Sundog.

Goodyear-Brown, P. (2005). *Digging for buried treasure 2: 52 more prop-based play therapy interventions for treating the problems of childhood*. Franklin, TN: Sundog.

Guttenberg, R. (2011). *"Funtastic" Adlerian techniques for change*. North Potomac, MD: Author.

Lowenstein, L. (2002). *More creative interventions for troubled children and youth*. Toronto, Ontario, Canada: Champion.

Lowenstein, L. (2010). *Assessment and treatment activities for children, adolescents, and families* (Vol. 2). Toronto, Ontario, Canada: Champion.

Sand Tray

Homeyer, L., & Sweeney, D. (2011). *Sand tray therapy: A practical manual* (2nd ed.). New York, NY: Routledge.

Mitchell, R. R., Friedman, H., & Green, E. (2014). Integrating play therapy and sandplay therapy. In E. Green & A. Drewes (Eds.), *Integrating expressive arts and play therapy* (pp. 101–124). Hoboken, NJ: Wiley.

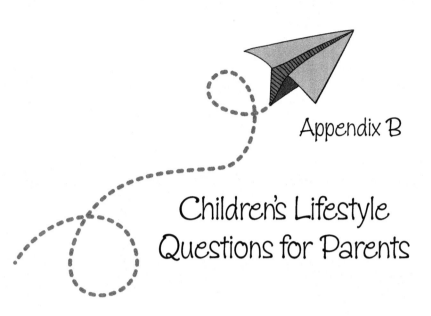

Appendix B

Children's Lifestyle Questions for Parents

Family Atmosphere and Constellation Questions

1. If _____ (the presenting problem) wasn't happening, how would things be different in your family?
2. Describe each person in your family.
3. Which of the child's brothers and sisters is most different from him or her? How is that sibling different from _____? (In a family of just two children, ask how the other sibling is different from the client.)
4. Which of the child's brothers and sisters is most like him or her? How is he or she like _____? (In a family of just two children, ask how the other sibling is like the client.)
5. Which child is mom's favorite? What does mom like about that child?
6. Which child is dad's favorite? What does dad like about that child?
7. Of all the kids in the family, which one is most like dad? How is he or she like dad?
8. Of all the kids in your family, which one is most like mom? How is he or she like mom?
9. Which one of the parents is the client most like? In what ways? (This may have already been answered in Question 7 or 8, but it is a slightly different question, and you may want the parents to elaborate on the answers.)
10. Describe the relationship between the parents. Who makes the decisions? Who is more ambitious for the children? In what way? How do you handle disagreements? What do you disagree about?

11. What is your philosophy on discipline? On what topics related to parenting situations do you have different opinions? What happens when you have different opinions on how to handle parenting situations?
12. What other adults have been important in the child's life? Grandparents? In what way? Other relatives? In what way? Friends or neighbors? In what way?
13. What other children have been important in the child's life? In what way?
14. Do any family members use alcohol or other drugs? To what extent? How does this affect the rest of the family? What is the child's reaction to the use of alcohol or other drugs?
15. If you could change anything about the family, what would you change?
16. How does the client stand out in the family? Positively? (At what activities or experiences has he or she been successful or contributed in positive ways to the family?) Negatively? (What does she or he get into trouble for?)
17. What does the child want to be when he or she grows up?
18. Describe the routine happenings in a typical day for your family.
19. What are the child's responsibilities: Getting up in the morning? Getting off to school? Getting to bed at night? Household chores? Taking care of pets? Does he or she stay home? When? What is mealtime like?
20. Does the child have nightmares? Dreams? What about? How does the child react to nightmares? To other dreams? How do you handle them?
21. What traumatic events have occurred during the child's life (death, divorce, abuse, family violence, etc.)? How did the child react to the trauma? What was done to help the child cope with any trauma he or she experienced?
22. What are your hopes and dreams for the child?
23. Describe your family of origin. What was your birth-order position? What was your parents' discipline style? As a child, what were you known for in your family? What were the most important values in your family as you were growing up?
24. How does your current family resemble your family growing up? How is your current family different from your family growing up?
25. How does your parenting style resemble that of your parents? How is your parenting style different from that of your parents?

School Questions

1. How do things go for _____ at school?
2. What does he or she like best at school?
3. What is his or her favorite subject?
4. What does he or she like least about school?
5. What is his or her least favorite subject?
6. What would he or she be rather doing than going to school?
7. What does he or she do best at school?

8. What does his or her teacher like about him or her?
9. What would he or she like to change about school?
10. What does he or she get in trouble for at school?
11. What happens when he or she gets in trouble at school? (What are the consequences imposed by school personnel? What are the consequences imposed by the family?)
12. How does he or she react to correction or consequences at school?

Social Questions

1. How does _____ get along with adults?
2. Who is his or her favorite adult to be around?
3. What does that adult like about him or her?
4. What does he or she like about that adult?
5. Who is his or her least favorite adult to be around?
6. What doesn't that adult like about him or her?
7. What doesn't _____ like about that adult?
8. How does _____ get along with other kids his or her own age?
9. How does _____ get along with kids younger than him or her?
10. How does _____ get along with kids older than him or her?
11. Who is his or her best friend?
12. Describe the friend.
13. What kinds of activities do they do together?
14. What does this best friend like about _____?
15. What does _____ like about this best friend?
16. What would you like to change about _____'s relationship with other kids?

Goals of Misbehavior

1. What kinds of behaviors that _____ engages in are bothersome to you or other family members?
2. How do you or other family members feel when this behavior occurs?
3. What do you and family members do in response to the bothersome behaviors?
4. What does _____ do when corrected or criticized by you or others in the family?

Sibling Ratings

If you had to rate the children in the family on the following attributes, who would you rate as the highest for each attribute, and who would you rate the lowest for each attribute? If the client is neither highest nor lowest, indicate by an arrow whether she or he would tend toward the higher side or the lower side. If the child is an only child, simply rate him or her as being high or low on each of the attributes as compared to other children who are about the same age.

Attribute	Highest	Lowest
Intelligent		
Hardworking		
Good grades		
Follows rules		
Helps at home		
Complains–critical		
Considerate		
Selfish		
Hard to please		
Hurt feelings		
Temper		
Materialistic		
Friends		
High standards		
Athletic		
Spoiled		
Best looking		
Punished		

Feelings Questions

1. What is _____ most afraid of? What is it about this that scares him or her? How does he or she express fear/how can you tell when he or she is afraid? How do you react when he or she is afraid? What does he or she seem to want you to do when he or she is afraid? What are the coping strategies he or she uses to deal with being afraid? How effective are these coping strategies?

2. What does _____ get angry about? What is there about this (person? relationship? situation? problem?) that angers him or her? How does he or she express anger/how can you tell when he or she is angry? How do you react to this anger? Which of your responses to the child's anger seem to help to optimize his or her coping with anger? What coping strategies does he or she use to manage angry responses? How effective are these coping strategies?

3. What does _____ feel sad about? What is there about this (person? situation? relationship? problem?) that saddens him or her? How does he or she express sadness/how can you tell when he or she is sad? How do you react when he or she is acting sad? Which of your responses to the child's sadness seem to help with the sadness? What coping strategies does he or she use to manage the sadness? How effective are these strategies?

4. What gives _____ joy? What is it about this (person? situation? relationship?) that gives him or her joy? How does he or she express joy/how can you tell he or she is happy? How do you react when he or she is joyful or happy?

5. What hurts _____'s feelings? What is there about this (person? situation? relationship?) that hurts his or her feelings? How does he or she express hurt/how can you tell when he or she has hurt feelings? How do you react when his or her feelings are hurt? What coping strategies does he or she use to manage the hurt feelings? How effective are these strategies?

Note. This interview was adapted by Dr. Terry Kottman from work by Dr. Rudolph Dreikurs, Dr. Don Dinkmeyer Sr., Dr. Don Dinkmeyer Jr., and Dr. Bobbie Wilborn.

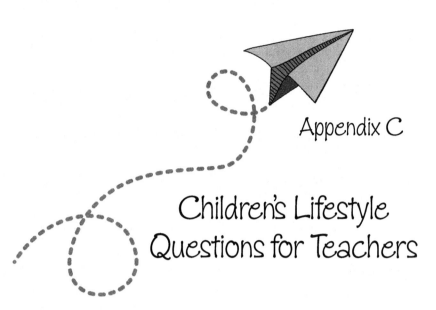

Appendix C

Children's Lifestyle Questions for Teachers

General Questions

1. If _____ (the presenting problem) wasn't happening, how would things be different in your classroom? How would things be different for _____ (child's name) at school?
2. Describe yourself and your style as a teacher.
3. What is your philosophy on discipline?
4. How do you usually handle behavior problems in the classroom?
5. How does _____ stand out in the classroom in positive ways? (At what activities or experiences has he or she been successful or contributed in positive ways to school or the class?)
6. How does _____ stand out in the classroom in negative ways? (What does he or she get into trouble for?)
7. How do you feel when _____ does this?
8. How do you handle discipline when _____ does this?
9. How does _____ react when you discipline?
10. Describe the routine happenings in a typical day in your classroom.
11. How does the child perform academically?
12. How does the child deal with transitions?
13. What does he or she like best at school? What does he or she do best at school?
14. What is his or her favorite subject?
15. What does he or she like least about school?
16. What is his or her least favorite subject?
17. What would he or she be rather doing than going to school?
18. How does recess go for _____?
19. What do you like about him or her?
20. What would he or she like to change about school?

21. Do you know of any traumatic events that have occurred during the child's life (death, divorce, abuse, family violence, etc.)? How did the child react to the trauma? What was done to help the child cope with any trauma he or she experienced?
22. How does _____ get along with other kids his or her own age?
23. How does _____ get along with kids younger than him or her?
24. How does _____ get along with kids older than him or her?
25. Who is his or her best friend at school/in your class?
26. Describe the friend.
27. What kinds of activities do they do together?
28. What does this best friend like about _____?
29. What does _____ like about this best friend?
30. What would you like to change about _____'s relationship with other kids?

Feelings Questions

1. What is _____ most afraid of? What is it about this that scares him or her? How does he or she express fear/how can you tell when he or she is afraid? How do you react when he or she is afraid? What does he or she seem to want you to do when he or she is afraid? What are the coping strategies he or she uses to deal with being afraid? How effective are these coping strategies?
2. What does _____ get angry about? What is there about this (person? relationship? situation? problem?) that angers him or her? How does he or she express anger/how can you tell when he or she is angry? How do you react to this anger? Which of your responses to the child's anger seem to help to optimize his or her coping with anger? What coping strategies does he or she use to manage angry responses? How effective are these coping strategies?
3. What does _____ feel sad about? What is there about this (person? situation? relationship? problem?) that saddens him or her? How does he or she express sadness/how can you tell when he or she is sad? How do you react when he or she is acting sad? Which of your responses to the child's sadness seem to help with the sadness? What coping strategies does he or she use to manage the sadness? How effective are these strategies?
4. What gives _____ joy? What is it about this (person? situation? relationship?) that gives him or her joy? How does he or she express joy/how can you tell he or she is happy? How do you react when he or she is joyful or happy?
5. What hurts _____'s feelings? What is there about this (person? situation? relationship?) that hurts his or her feelings? How does he or she express hurt/how can you tell when he or she has hurt feelings? How do you react when his or her feelings are hurt? What coping strategies does he or she use to manage the hurt feelings? How effective are these strategies?

Note. This interview was adapted by Dr. Terry Kottman from work by Dr. Rudolph Dreikurs, Dr. Don Dinkmeyer Sr., Dr. Don Dinkmeyer Jr., and Dr. Bobbie Wilborn.

Appendix D

Children's Lifestyle Questions

With an only child, for the following questions, you can ask the child to compare himself or herself to friends, cousins, neighbors, "other kids your age," or skip the question (e.g., skip Questions 7, 8, 9, 10). For a single-parent family, skip the questions that do not apply.

Family Atmosphere and Constellation Questions

1. If _____ (the presenting problem) wasn't happening, how would things be different in your life?
2. Describe each person in your family.
3. Which of your brothers and sisters is most different from you? How is he or she different from you? (In a family of just two children, ask how the other sibling is different from the client.)
4. Which of your brothers and sisters is most like you? How is he or she like you? (In a family of just two children, ask how the other sibling is like the client.)
5. What kind of person is your dad?
6. What kind of person is your mom?
7. Of all the kids in the family, which one is most like your dad? How is he or she like your dad?
8. Of all the kids in your family, which one is most like your mom? How is he or she like your mom?
9. Which of the kids is your dad's favorite?
10. Which of the kids is your mom's favorite?
11. Which one of your parents are you most like? How are you like him or her? (This may have already been answered in Question 7 or 8, but it is a slightly different question, and you may want the child to elaborate on her or his answers.)

12. What do you get in trouble for at home?
13. What happens when you get into trouble at home? (What are the consequences, if any?)
14. What do you do (how do you react) when you get into trouble at home?
15. Which of your parents is stricter? What is he/she strict about?
16. What happens when your parents disagree?
17. What do they disagree about?
18. What does your family do for fun together?
19. If you could change anything about your family, what would you change?

School Questions

1. How do things go for you at school?
2. What do you like best at school?
3. What is your favorite subject?
4. What do you like least about school?
5. What is your least favorite subject?
6. What would you be rather doing than going to school?
7. What do you do best at school?
8. What does your teacher like about you? The principal? The school counselor? The custodian?
9. What would you like to change about school?
10. What do you get in trouble for at school?
11. What happens when you get in trouble at school? (What are the consequences, if any?)
12. Who disciplines you at school? How do you feel about that person? How do you react when you get disciplined at school?

Social Questions

1. How do you get along with adults?
2. Who is your favorite adult?
3. What do you like about him or her?
4. What does he or she like about you?
5. Who is your least favorite adult?
6. What don't you like about him or her?
7. How do you get along with other kids your age?
8. How do you get along with kids younger than you?
9. How do you get along with kids older than you?
10. Who is your best friend?
11. Describe him or her.
12. What do you like about him or her?
13. What does he or she like about you?
14. What kinds of things do you do together?
15. Who are your other friends? Where do you see them? What kinds of activities do you do with them?

16. Do you prefer to play with lots of kids all at once, just a few kids, just one other kid, or by yourself?
17. If you could change anything about your relationships with other kids, what would you change?

General Questions

1. If you had three wishes, what would they be?
2. If you could be any animal, what animal would you be? What do you like about that animal? How do you think that animal is like you? What are the qualities of that animal that you wish you could have?
3. If anything in your life could be different, what would you want to change?
4. If you could be any toy in the playroom, what toy would you be? What do you like about that toy?
5. What is your favorite book or story? What do you like about that book or story?
6. Who is your favorite character in a book or story? What do you like about him or her or it?
7. What is your favorite movie? What do you like about that movie?
8. Who is your favorite movie character? What do you like about him or her or it?
9. What is your favorite television show? What do you like about that show?
10. Who is your favorite character on television? What do you like about him or her or it?
11. Do you remember any of the dreams you have at night? Describe them. How do you feel when you wake up? How do your parents and others react when you tell them about your dreams?
12. What are you most afraid of? What is there about _____ that scares you? How do you act when you're afraid/how do you let other people know that you are afraid? How do your parents and other people react when you feel afraid?
13. What do you get the most angry about? What is there about it that angers you? How do you act when you're angry/how do you let other people know when you are angry? How do your parents and other people react when you feel angry?
14. What do you get the most sad about? What is there about it that you feel sad about? How do you act when you're sad/how do you let other people know when you are sad? How do your parents and other people react when you feel sad?
15. What hurts your feelings? What is it about _____ that hurts your feelings? How do you act when your feelings are hurt? How do your parents and other people react when you feel hurt?
16. When you feel afraid (angry, sad, hurt), what can you do to help yourself deal with those feelings? What can other people in your life do to help you deal with those feelings?

17. What gives you joy? What about that gives you joy? How do you act when you are happy or joyful?
18. What are you good at?
19. What do you wish you were better at doing?
20. What do you like about yourself?

Note. This interview was adapted by Dr. Terry Kottman from work by Dr. Rudolph Dreikurs, Dr. Don Dinkmeyer Sr., Dr. Don Dinkmeyer Jr., and Dr. Bobbie Wilborn.

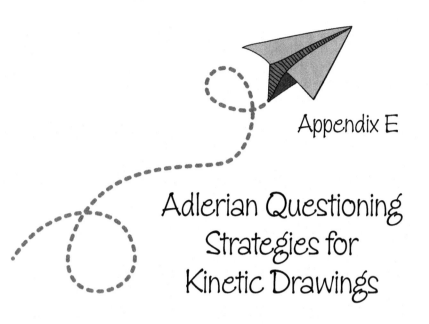

Appendix E

Adlerian Questioning Strategies for Kinetic Drawings

Kinetic Family Drawing (KFD) Lifestyle Questions[1]

"Draw a picture of everyone in your family, DOING something. Try to draw whole people, not cartoons or stick people. Remember, make everyone DOING something—some kind of action." When the child has finished drawing, ask the child the following questions about each of the figures:

1. Who is this person?
2. What is his/her relationship to you?
3. How old is he/she?
4. Can you tell me a little bit about this person?
5. What is this person doing?
6. How does this person feel?
7. What does this person need the most?
8. How do you feel about this person?
9. How does this person get along with other people?

Choose several of these questions to ask about individual figures:

1. What does this person wish for?
2. What is this person thinking?

_____

[1]Terry Kottman adapted the original list of questions for the KFD (Knoff & Prout, 1985) on the basis of work by Dinkmeyer and Dinkmeyer (1977), Eckstein and Kern (2009), Griffith and Powers (2007), and Dr. Bobbie Wilborn, former director of the Child and Family Resource Clinic at the University of North Texas.

3. What do you like about this person?
4. What don't you like about this person?
5. What happened to this person right before the picture?
6. What will happen to this person right after the picture?
7. What will happen to this person in the future?
8. What does this person do well?
9. What does this person get in trouble for?
10. What is this person afraid of?
11. Which of the other children are you most like? How?
12. Which of them is most different from you? How?
13. With which of them do you spend the most time? Doing what?
14. Which of the children is Mom's favorite?
15. Which of the children is Dad's favorite?
16. Which of the children is most like Mom? How?
17. Which of the children is most like Dad? How?
18. Which of your parents are you most like? How?

Choose some of the following questions to ask about the family:

1. What is the family doing?
2. What will happen to this family right after this picture?
3. What happened to this family right before this picture?
4. What will happen to this family in the future?
5. If you could change anything about this family, what would you change?

Kinetic School Drawing (KSD) Lifestyle Questions[2]

Say: "I'd like you to draw a school picture. Put yourself, your teacher, and a friend or two in the picture. Make everybody DOING something. Try to draw whole people and make the best drawing you can. Remember, draw yourself, your teacher, and a friend or two, and make everybody doing something." When the child has finished drawing, ask the child the following questions about each of the figures:

1. Who is this person?
2. Can you tell me a little bit about this person?
3. What is this person doing?
4. How does this person feel?
5. How do you feel about this person?
6. How does this person get along with other people?

Choose several of these questions to ask about individual figures:

1. What does this person wish for?
2. What is this person thinking?

[2]Terry Kottman adapted this list of questions for the original KSD (Knoff & Prout, 1985) on the basis of work by Dinkmeyer and Dinkmeyer (1977), Eckstein and Kern (2009), Griffith and Powers (2007), and Dr. Bobbie Wilborn, former director of the Child and Family Resource Clinic at the University of North Texas.

3. What do you like about this person?
4. What don't you like about this person?
5. What happened to this person right before the picture?
6. What will happen to this person right after the picture?
7. What will happen to this person in the future?
8. What does this person do well?
9. What does this person get in trouble for?
10. What happens when this person gets in trouble?
11. What is this person afraid of?
12. What does this person do for fun?
13. What does this person think about school?
14. Which of these friends are you most like? How?
15. Which of these friends is most different from you? How?
16. With which of these friends do you spend the most time?
17. Which of these friends is the teacher's favorite? Why?
18. Which of these friends doesn't the teacher like? Why?
19. How do things go for you in school?

Choose several of these questions to ask about school interactions:

1. What is the class doing?
2. What will happen to this class right after this picture?
3. What happened to this class right before this picture?
4. What will happen to this class in the future?
5. If you could change anything about this class, what would you change? What would you change about school?

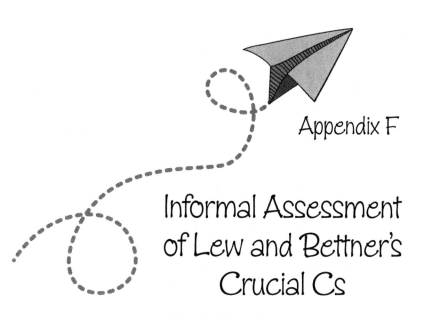

Appendix F

Informal Assessment of Lew and Bettner's Crucial Cs

Assessing a Child's Crucial Cs (Lew & Bettner, 2000)
and Developing Intervention Strategies

Courage: 1 2 3 4 5 6 7 8 9 10

☐ Yes ☐ No Is willing to try new things
☐ Yes ☐ No Gives up easily
☐ Yes ☐ No Is willing to take interpersonal risks
☐ Yes ☐ No Seems to feel inadequate
☐ Yes ☐ No Is willing to take academic risks
☐ Yes ☐ No Tries to avoid challenges
☐ Yes ☐ No Believes he/she can succeed
☐ Yes ☐ No Compares self negatively to others
☐ Yes ☐ No Believes he/she can handle challenges
☐ Yes ☐ No Seems to be hopeful

Situations/relationships in which he/she exhibits courage:

Situations/relationships in which he/she seems to lack courage:

Factors that seem to influence courageous behavior:

Other comments related to courage:

Possible strategies for increasing courage:

Connect: 1   2   3   4   5   6   7   8   9   10

☐ Yes   ☐ No   Makes friends easily
☐ Yes   ☐ No   Seems to feel secure
☐ Yes   ☐ No   Works to keep friends
☐ Yes   ☐ No   Is socially isolated
☐ Yes   ☐ No   Cooperates with others
☐ Yes   ☐ No   Has social network that gets into trouble
☐ Yes   ☐ No   Expresses belief in belonging
☐ Yes   ☐ No   Is socially rejected
☐ Yes   ☐ No   Seeks attention in negative ways

Position in social network (e.g., alpha, beta, scapegoat, worker bee, etc.):

Methods of connecting with friends and in social network:

Situations/relationships in which he/she seems to connect in positive ways:

Situations/relationships in which he/she seems to struggle with connecting:

Factors that seem to influence his/her ability to connect:

Other comments about connecting:

Possible strategies for optimizing connecting:

Capable: 1   2   3   4   5   6   7   8   9   10

☐ Yes   ☐ No   Expresses sense of mastery
☐ Yes   ☐ No   Acknowledges assets
☐ Yes   ☐ No   Exhibits self-control
☐ Yes   ☐ No   Takes responsibility for self
☐ Yes   ☐ No   Exhibits self-discipline
☐ Yes   ☐ No   Has confidence in own ability
☐ Yes   ☐ No   Is responsible
☐ Yes   ☐ No   Tries to show others they cannot be in control
☐ Yes   ☐ No   Tries to control others
☐ Yes   ☐ No   Is dependent on others

Is actually capable in these situations/subjects:

Believes he/she is capable in these situations/subjects:

Struggles with actually being capable in these situations/subjects:

Struggles with believing he/she is capable in these situations/subjects:

Other comments about capability:

Possible strategies for increasing capability OR belief in capability:

Count: 1 2 3 4 5 6 7 8 9 10

☐ Yes   ☐ No   Seems to feel valuable and valued
☐ Yes   ☐ No   Believes he/she makes a difference
☐ Yes   ☐ No   Makes a contribution
☐ Yes   ☐ No   Believes in self without conditions
☐ Yes   ☐ No   Seems to feel insignificant
☐ Yes   ☐ No   Has poor self-image
☐ Yes   ☐ No   Brags, acts superior

Situations/relationships in which he/she believes that he/she counts:

Situations/relationships in which he/she does not believe that he/she counts:

Positive strategies he/she uses to feel important/gain significance:

Negative (self-defeating) strategies he/she uses to feel important/gain significance:

Other comments about count/gaining significance:

Possible strategies for increasing feelings of importance/counting:

Assessing a Parent's Crucial Cs (Lew & Bettner, 2000) and Developing Intervention Strategies

Courage: 1 2 3 4 5 6 7 8 9 10

☐ Yes   ☐ No   Is willing to try unfamiliar things
☐ Yes   ☐ No   Gives up easily
☐ Yes   ☐ No   Is willing to take risk with child
☐ Yes   ☐ No   Seems to feel inadequate
☐ Yes   ☐ No   Tries to avoid challenges
☐ Yes   ☐ No   Is resistant to feedback
☐ Yes   ☐ No   Believes he/she can succeed
☐ Yes   ☐ No   Compares self negatively to others
☐ Yes   ☐ No   Believes he/she can handle challenges
☐ Yes   ☐ No   Seems to be hopeful

Situations/relationships in which he/she exhibits courage in parenting or interacting with spouse:

Situations/relationships in which he/she seems to lack courage in parenting or interacting with spouse:

Factors that seem to influence courageous behavior:

Possible strategies for increasing courage:

Connect: 1 2 3 4 5 6 7 8 9 10

☐ Yes   ☐ No   Builds relationships easily
☐ Yes   ☐ No   Seems to feel secure
☐ Yes   ☐ No   Works to keep relationships
☐ Yes   ☐ No   Is socially isolated
☐ Yes   ☐ No   Cooperates with others
☐ Yes   ☐ No   Connects with children in appropriate ways
☐ Yes   ☐ No   Expresses belief in belonging
☐ Yes   ☐ No   Seeks attention in negative ways
☐ Yes   ☐ No   Is socially rejected

Position in social network (e.g., alpha, beta, scapegoat, worker bee, etc.):

Methods of connecting with his/her child and/or spouse:

Situations/relationships in which he/she seems to connect in positive
   ways:

Situations/relationships in which he/she seems to struggle with connecting:

Factors that seem to influence his/her ability to connect:

Possible strategies for optimizing connecting:

Capable: 1 2 3 4 5 6 7 8 9 10

☐ Yes   ☐ No   Expresses sense of mastery
☐ Yes   ☐ No   Acknowledges assets
☐ Yes   ☐ No   Exhibits self-control
☐ Yes   ☐ No   Takes responsibility for self
☐ Yes   ☐ No   Exhibits self-discipline
☐ Yes   ☐ No   Has confidence in own ability
☐ Yes   ☐ No   Is responsible
☐ Yes   ☐ No   Tries to control others
☐ Yes   ☐ No   Tries to show others they cannot be in control
☐ Yes   ☐ No   Is dependent on others

Is actually capable in these situations with child and/or spouse:

Believes he/she is capable in these situations with child and/or spouse:

Struggles with actually being capable in these parenting/family
   situations:

Struggles with believing he/she is capable in these parenting/family
   situations:

Other comments about capability:

Possible strategies for increasing capability OR belief in capability:

Count: 1 2 3 4 5 6 7 8 9 10

- ☐ Yes ☐ No Seems to feel valuable and valued
- ☐ Yes ☐ No Believes he/she makes a difference
- ☐ Yes ☐ No Makes a contribution
- ☐ Yes ☐ No Believes in self without conditions
- ☐ Yes ☐ No Seems to feel insignificant
- ☐ Yes ☐ No Has poor self-image (related to parenting or generally)
- ☐ Yes ☐ No Brags, acts superior

Situations in which he/she believes that he/she counts with child or other family members:

Situations in which he/she does not believe that he/she counts with child or other family members:

Positive strategies he/she uses to feel important/gain significance:

Negative (self-defeating) strategies he/she uses to feel important/gain significance:

Possible strategies for increasing feelings of importance/counting:

Assessing a Teacher's Crucial Cs (Lew & Bettner, 2000) and Developing Intervention Strategies

Courage: 1 2 3 4 5 6 7 8 9 10

- ☐ Yes ☐ No Is willing to try new techniques
- ☐ Yes ☐ No Gives up easily
- ☐ Yes ☐ No Is willing to take interpersonal risks
- ☐ Yes ☐ No Seems to feel inadequate
- ☐ Yes ☐ No Tries to avoid professional challenges
- ☐ Yes ☐ No Is resistant to constructive feedback
- ☐ Yes ☐ No Believes he/she can succeed
- ☐ Yes ☐ No Compares self negatively to others
- ☐ Yes ☐ No Believes he/she can handle challenges
- ☐ Yes ☐ No Seems to be hopeful

Situations/relationships in which he/she exhibits courage:

Situations/relationships in which he/she seems to lack courage:

Factors that seem to influence courageous behavior:

Possible strategies for increasing courage:

Connect: 1 2 3 4 5 6 7 8 9 10

- ☐ Yes ☐ No Builds relationships easily
- ☐ Yes ☐ No Seems to feel secure

☐ Yes   ☐ No   Works to keep relationships
☐ Yes   ☐ No   Is socially isolated
☐ Yes   ☐ No   Cooperates with others
☐ Yes   ☐ No   Connects with children in appropriate ways
☐ Yes   ☐ No   Expresses belief in belonging
☐ Yes   ☐ No   Seeks attention in negative ways
☐ Yes   ☐ No   Is socially rejected

Position in social network (e.g., alpha, beta, scapegoat, worker bee, etc.):

Methods of connecting with friends and in social network:

Situations/relationships in which he/she seems to connect in positive ways:

Situations/relationships in which he/she seems to struggle with connecting:

Factors that seem to influence his/her ability to connect:

Possible strategies for optimizing connecting:

Capable: 1   2   3   4   5   6   7   8   9   10

☐ Yes   ☐ No   Expresses sense of mastery
☐ Yes   ☐ No   Acknowledges assets
☐ Yes   ☐ No   Exhibits self-control
☐ Yes   ☐ No   Takes responsibility for self
☐ Yes   ☐ No   Exhibits self-discipline
☐ Yes   ☐ No   Has confidence in own ability
☐ Yes   ☐ No   Is responsible
☐ Yes   ☐ No   Tries to show others they cannot be in control
☐ Yes   ☐ No   Tries to control others
☐ Yes   ☐ No   Is dependent on others

Is actually capable in these situations/subjects:

Believes he/she is capable in these situations/subjects:

Struggles with actually being capable in these situations/subjects:

Struggles with believing he/she is capable in these situations/subjects:

Possible strategies for increasing capability OR belief in capability:

Count: 1   2   3   4   5   6   7   8   9   10

☐ Yes   ☐ No   Seems to feel valuable and valued
☐ Yes   ☐ No   Believes he/she makes a difference
☐ Yes   ☐ No   Makes a contribution
☐ Yes   ☐ No   Believes in self without conditions
☐ Yes   ☐ No   Seems to feel insignificant
☐ Yes   ☐ No   Has poor self-image

☐ Yes   ☐ No   Brags, acts superior

Situations/relationships in which he/she believes that he/she counts:

Situations/relationships in which he/she does not believe that he/she counts:

Positive strategies he/she uses to feel important/gain significance:

Negative (self-defeating) strategies he/she uses to feel important/gain significance:

Other comments about count/gaining significance:

Possible strategies for increasing feelings of importance/counting:

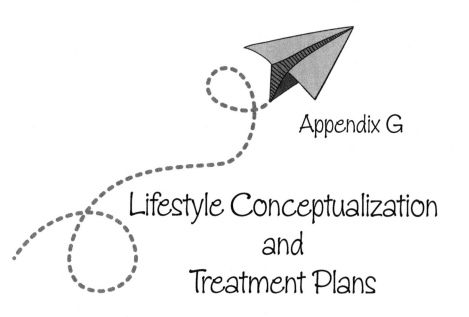

Appendix G

Lifestyle Conceptualization and Treatment Plans

Adlerian Play Therapy Lifestyle Conceptualization for Children

Assets:

Functioning at Life Tasks (can use scaling to indicate how well client is functioning at each life task; if used, 1 = *low* to 10 = *high*):

    School: 1 2 3 4 5 6 7 8 9 10

    Friendship: 1 2 3 4 5 6 7 8 9 10

    Love/family: 1 2 3 4 5 6 7 8 9 10

    Self: 1 2 3 4 5 6 7 8 9 10

    Spirituality/existential: 1 2 3 4 5 6 7 8 9 10

Play Themes:

Family Constellation—Psychological Birth Order (how the child's perception of this position has affected his/her lifestyle):

Family Atmosphere (including parents' lifestyles and parenting styles and how the child's perception of the atmosphere has affected his/her lifestyle):

Early Recollections (themes and what they tell you about the child's lifestyle):

Goal(s) of Misbehavior (manifested in what behavior/how parents deal with problems):

Assessment of Crucial Cs (can use scaling to indicate functioning; if used, 1 = *low* to 10 = *high*):

Connect: 1 2 3 4 5 6 7 8 9 10

Capable: 1 2 3 4 5 6 7 8 9 10

Count: 1 2 3 4 5 6 7 8 9 10

Courage: 1 2 3 4 5 6 7 8 9 10

Personality Priorities (of child and of parents—how do they interact with one another?):

Lifestyle Convictions (Mark those that are mistaken beliefs/faulty convictions with an asterisk [*]):

I am/I must be . . .

Others are/others must be . . .

My relationships with others are/must be . . .

The world is/the world should be . . .

Life is/life must be . . .

Based on these convictions/perceptions/beliefs/feelings, my behavior must be . . .

Private Logic (how did the client get from convictions to behavior?):

Adlerian Play Therapy Treatment Plan for Children

***Assets* you want to encourage:**

Goals for change:

Strategies:

Progress measured by:

Functioning at *life tasks* that needs readjusting/balancing:

Goals for change:

Strategies:

Progress measured by:

Ways to optimize positive qualities and reduce negative aspects of *personality priorities*:

Goals for change:

Strategies:

Progress measured by:

Crucial Cs **that need adjusting:**
  Goals for change:
  Strategies:
  Progress measured by:

Goals of misbehavior **that need readjusting:**
  Goals for change:
  Strategies:
  Progress measured by:

Mistaken beliefs/faulty convictions **(self/others/the world/life) that need readjusting:**
  Goals for change:
  Strategies:
  Progress measured by:

Self-defeating/useless behaviors **you want to change:**
  Goals for change (needed immediately):
  Strategies:
  Progress measured by:

  Goals for change (long-range):
  Strategies:
  Progress measured by:

Skills **the child needs to learn:**
  Goals for change:
  Strategies:
  Progress measured by:

Adlerian Play Therapy Lifestyle Conceptualization for Parents

Assets (both personally and those that relate to parenting):

Functioning at Life Tasks (scaling is optional; if used, 1 = *low* to 10 = *high*):

  Work: 1   2   3   4   5   6   7   8   9   10

  Friendship: 1   2   3   4   5   6   7   8   9   10

  Love/intimacy: 1   2   3   4   5   6   7   8   9   10

  Self: 1   2   3   4   5   6   7   8   9   10

  Spirituality/existential: 1   2   3   4   5   6   7   8   9   10

Functioning in Role as Parent (including assessment of parenting skills, attitudes toward parenting, attitudes toward specific children; scaling is optional; if used, 1 = *low* to 10 = *high*): 1   2   3   4   5   6   7   8   9   10

Family Constellation—Psychological Birth-Order Position (how the parent's perception of family constellation in his/her family of origin has affected his/her lifestyle and functioning as a parent):

Family Atmosphere (how the parent's perception of the atmosphere of his or her family of origin has affected his/her lifestyle; what the parent learned about parenting from his or her parents):

Early Recollections (themes and what they tell you about the parent's lifestyle):

Crucial Cs (scaling is optional; if used, 1 = *low*/10 = *high*):

  Connect: 1   2   3   4   5   6   7   8   9   10

  Capable: 1   2   3   4   5   6   7   8   9   10

  Count: 1   2   3   4   5   6   7   8   9   10

  Courage: 1   2   3   4   5   6   7   8   9   10

Personality Priorities:

Lifestyle Convictions (Mark those that are mistaken beliefs/faulty convictions with an asterisk [*]):

  I am/I must be . . .

  Others are/others must be . . .

  My relationships with others are/must be . . .

  The world is/the world should be . . .

  Life is/life must be . . .

  Based on these convictions/perceptions/beliefs/feelings, my behavior must be . . .

Private Logic:

Adlerian Play Therapy Treatment Plan for Parent Consultation

Personality priorities and Crucial Cs:

Goals for change:

Strategies for consultation:

Progress measured by:

***Assets* you want to encourage:**

Goals for change:

Strategies for consultation:

Progress measured by:

Functioning at *life tasks* that needs readjusting/balancing:

Goals for change:

Strategies for consultation:

Progress measured by:

***Lifestyle elements* that may interfere with parenting:**

Goals for change:

Strategies for consultation:

Progress measured by:

***Parenting skills/information* needed:**

Goals for change:

Strategies for consultation:

Progress measured by:

Adlerian Play Therapy Lifestyle Conceptualization—Teacher

Assets (both personally and those that relate to teaching):

Functioning at Life Tasks (scaling is optional; if used, 1 = *low* to 10 = *high*):

  Work: 1   2   3   4   5   6   7   8   9   10

  Friendship: 1   2   3   4   5   6   7   8   9   10

  Love/intimacy: 1   2   3   4   5   6   7   8   9   10

  Self: 1   2   3   4   5   6   7   8   9   10

  Spirituality/existential: 1   2   3   4   5   6   7   8   9   10

Functioning in Role as Teacher (including assessment of teaching skills, assessment of classroom management skills, attitudes toward teaching, attitudes toward specific "types" of children; philosophy of teaching; scaling is optional; if used, 1 = *low* to 10 = *high*): 1   2   3   4   5   6   7   8   9   10

Family Constellation—Psychological Birth-Order Position (how the teacher's perception of family constellation in his/her family of origin has affected his/her lifestyle and functioning as a teacher; descriptions of siblings who were particularly problematic in his/her growing up):

Family Atmosphere (how the teacher's perception of the atmosphere of his/her family of origin has affected his/her lifestyle; what the teacher learned about discipline from his or her parents):

School Experiences (how the teacher's perception of his or her own experiences in school has affected his/her lifestyle, attitudes, and behavior related to school):

Early Recollections (themes and what they tell you about the teacher's lifestyle—focus especially on those recollections related to school experiences):

Crucial Cs (scaling is optional; if used, 1 = *low* to 10 = *high*):

  Connect: 1   2   3   4   5   6   7   8   9   10

  Capable: 1   2   3   4   5   6   7   8   9   10

  Count: 1   2   3   4   5   6   7   8   9   10

  Courage: 1   2   3   4   5   6   7   8   9   10

Personality Priorities:

Lifestyle Convictions (Mark those that are mistaken beliefs/faulty convictions with an asterisk [*]):

  I am/I must be . . .

  Others are/others must be . . .

  Children are/should be . . .

  My relationships with others are/must be . . .

The world is/the world should be . . .

Life is/life must be . . .

School is/school must be . . .

Based on these convictions/perceptions/beliefs/feelings, my
behavior must be . . .

Private Logic:

Adlerian Play Therapy Treatment Plan for Teacher Consultation

Personality priorities and Crucial Cs:

Goals for change:

Strategies for consultation:

Progress measured by:

***Assets* you want to encourage:**

Goals for change:

Strategies for consultation:

Progress measured by:

***Lifestyle elements* that may interfere with teaching and
interacting with students:**

Goals for change:

Strategies for consultation:

Progress measured by:

***Classroom management skills/information* that might help
relationships with students and improve classroom
atmosphere needed:**

Goals for change:

Strategies for consultation:

Progress measured by:

Appendix H

Research and Anecdotal Support for the Efficacy of Play Therapy With Specific Populations

Academic Achievement

Blanco, P. J., & Ray, D. C. (2011). Play therapy in elementary schools: A best practice for improving academic achievement. *Journal of Counseling & Development, 18,* 235–243. doi:10.1002/j.1556-6678.2011.tb00083x

Sheely-Moore, A., & Ceballos, P. (2015). Child-centered play therapy and school-based problems. In D. Crenshaw & A. Stewart (Eds.), *Play therapy: A comprehensive guide to theory and practice* (pp. 247–261). New York, NY: Guilford Press.

Anger and Aggression

Crenshaw, D. (2015). Play therapy with "children of fury." In D. Crenshaw & A. Stewart (Eds.), *Play therapy: A comprehensive guide to theory and practice* (pp. 217–231). New York, NY: Guilford Press.

Anxiety

Baggerly, J. (2004). The effects of child-centered group play therapy on self-concept, depression, and anxiety of children who are homeless. *International Journal of Play Therapy, 12,* 31–51.

Guerney, L. (2015). Filial therapy with children with anxiety disorders. In D. Crenshaw & A. Stewart (Eds.), *Play therapy: A comprehensive guide to theory and practice* (pp. 428–438). New York, NY: Guilford Press.

Shen, Y. (2002). Short-term group play therapy with Chinese earthquake victims: Effects on anxiety, depression, and adjustment. *International Journal of Play Therapy, 11,* 43–63.

Attachment Disorders

Anderson, S. M., & Gedo, P. M. (2013). Relational trauma: Using play therapy to treat a disrupted attachment. *Bulletin of the Menninger Clinic, 77*, 250–268. doi:10.1521/bumc.2013.77.3.250

Baggerly, J., & Green, E. (2014). Mending broken attachment in displaced children: Finding "home" through play therapy. In C. Malchiodi & D. Crenshaw (Eds.), *Creative arts and play therapy for attachment problems* (pp. 275–293). New York, NY: Guilford Press.

Gil, E. (2014). The creative use of metaphor in play and art therapy with attachment problems. In C. Malchiodi & D. Crenshaw (Eds.), *Creative arts and play therapy for attachment problems* (pp. 159–177). New York, NY: Guilford Press.

Shi, L. (2014). Treatment of reactive attachment disorder in young children: Importance of understanding emotional dynamics. *American Journal of Family Therapy, 42*, 1–13.

Attention-Deficit/Hyperactivity Disorder

Barzegary, L., & Zamini, S. (2011). The effect of play therapy on children with ADHD. *Procedia-Social and Behavioral Sciences, 30*, 2216–2218.

Kaduson, H. (2006). Short-term play therapy for children with attention-deficit/hyperactivity disorder. In H. Kaduson & S. Schaefer (Eds.), *Short-term play therapy for children* (2nd ed., pp. 101–142). New York, NY: Guilford Press.

Kaduson, H. (2015). Play therapy with children with attention-deficit/hyperactivity disorder. In D. Crenshaw & A. Stewart (Eds.), *Play therapy: A comprehensive guide to theory and practice* (pp. 415–427). New York, NY: Guilford Press.

Ray, D., Schottelkorb, A., & Tsai, M. (2007). Play therapy with children exhibiting symptoms of attention deficit hyperactivity disorder. *International Journal of Play Therapy, 16*, 95–111.

Reddy, L., Spencer, P., Hall, T., & Rubel, E. (2001). Use of developmentally appropriate games in a child group training program for young children with attention-deficit/hyperactivity disorder. In A. Drewes, L. Carey, & C. Schaefer (Eds.), *School-based play therapy* (pp. 256–276). New York, NY: Wiley.

Autism

Hess, E. (2012). DIR/Floortime: A developmental/relationship play therapy approach for treating children impacted by autism. In L. Gallo-Lopez & L. Rubin (Eds.), *Play-based interventions for children and adolescents with autism spectrum disorders* (pp. 231–248). New York, NY: Routledge.

Hull, K. (2015). Play therapy with children on the autism spectrum. In D. Crenshaw & A. Stewart (Eds.), *Play therapy: A comprehensive guide to theory and practice* (pp. 400–414). New York, NY: Guilford Press.

Josefi, O., & Ryan, V. (2004). Non-directive play therapy for young children with autism: A case study. *Clinical Child Psychology and Psychiatry, 9*, 533–551. doi:10.1177/1359104504046158

Mittledorf, W., Hendricks, S., & Landreth, G. (2001). Play therapy with autistic children. In G. Landreth (Ed.), *Innovations in play therapy: Issues, process, and special populations* (pp. 257–269). Philadelphia, PA: Taylor & Francis.

Parker, N., & O'Brien, P. (2011). Play therapy: Reaching the child with autism. *International Journal of Special Education, 26,* 80–87.

Ray, D., Sullivan, J., & Carlson, S. (2012). Relational intervention: Child-centered play therapy with children on the autism spectrum. In L. Gallo-Lopez & L. Rubin (Eds.), *Play based-interventions for children and adolescents with autism spectrum disorders* (pp. 159–175). New York, NY: Routledge.

Behavior Problems

Bratton, S., Ceballos, P., Sheely, A., Meany-Walen, K., Pronchenko, Y., & Jones, L. (2013). Child-centered play therapy compared to mentoring as a Head Start mental health intervention: Effects on children exhibiting disruptive behavior in the classroom. *International Journal of Play Therapy, 22,* 28–42. doi:10.1037/a0030318

Fall, M., Navelski, L. F., & Welch, K. K. (2002). Outcomes of a play intervention for children identified for special education services. *International Journal of Play Therapy, 11,* 91–106.

Garza, Y., & Bratton, S. C. (2005). School-based child-centered play therapy with Hispanic children: Outcomes and cultural considerations. *International Journal of Play Therapy, 14,* 51–79.

Meany-Walen, K., Bratton, S., & Kottman, T. (2014). Effects of Adlerian play therapy on reducing students' disruptive behavior. *Journal of Counseling & Development, 92,* 47–56. doi:10.1002/j.1556-6676.2014.00129.x

Meany-Walen, K., & Kottman, T. (2015). Adlerian play therapy with children affected by externalizing behavior disorders. In E. Green & A. Myrick (Eds.), *Play therapy with vulnerable populations: No child forgotten* (pp. 177–194). Lanham, MD: Rowman & Littlefield.

Meany-Walen, K. K., Kottman, T., Bullis, Q., & Dillman Taylor, D. (2015). Adlerian play therapy with children with externalizing behaviors: Single case design. *Journal of Counseling & Development, 93,* 418–428. doi:10.1002/jcad.12040

Muro, J., Ray, D., Schottelkorb, A., Smith, M. R., & Blanco, P. J. (2006). Quantitative analysis of long-term child-centered play therapy. *International Journal of Play Therapy, 15,* 35–58.

Packman, J., & Bratton, S. (2003). A school-based group play/activity therapy intervention with learning disabled preadolescents exhibiting behavior problems. *International Journal of Play Therapy, 12,* 7–29.

Sheely-Moore, A., & Ceballos, P. (2015). Child-centered play therapy and school-based problems. In D. Crenshaw & A. Stewart (Eds.), *Play therapy: A comprehensive guide to theory and practice* (pp. 247–261). New York, NY: Guilford Press.

Swan, K., & Ray, D. (2014). Effects of child-centered play therapy on irritability and hyperactivity behaviors of children with intellectual disabilities. *The Journal of Humanistic Counseling, 53,* 120–133. doi:10.1002/j.2161-1939.2014.00053.x

Bullying

Baron, S. (2015). Play therapy with the spectrum of bullying behaviors. In D. Crenshaw & A. Stewart (Eds.), *Play therapy: A comprehensive guide to theory and practice* (pp. 232–246). New York, NY: Guilford Press.

Chronic Illness

Parson, J. (2015). Holistic mental health care and play therapy for hospitalized chronically ill children. In E. Green & A. Myrick (Eds.), *Play therapy with vulnerable populations: No child forgotten* (pp. 125–138). Lanham, MD: Rowman & Littlefield.

Depression

Baggerly, J. (2004). The effects of child-centered group play therapy on self-concept, depression, and anxiety of children who are homeless. *International Journal of Play Therapy, 12*, 31–51.

Shen, Y. (2002). Short-term group play therapy with Chinese earthquake victims: Effects on anxiety, depression, and adjustment. *International Journal of Play Therapy, 11*, 43–63

Dissociative Identity Disorder

Klein, J., & Landreth, G. (2001). Play therapy with dissociative identity disorder clients with child alters. In G. Landreth (Ed.), *Innovations in play therapy: Issues, process, and special populations* (pp. 323–333). Philadelphia, PA: Taylor & Francis.

Diverse Populations

Baggerly, J., & Abugideiri, S. E. (2010). Grief counseling for Muslim preschool and elementary school children. *Journal of Multicultural Counseling and Development, 38*, 112–124. doi:10.1002/j.2161-1912.2010.tb00119.x

DeHaene, L., Dalgaard, N. T., Montgomery, E., Grietens, H., & Verschueren, K. (2013). Attachment narratives in refugee children: Interrater reliability and qualitative analysis in pilot findings from a two-site study. *Journal of Traumatic Stress, 26*, 413–417. doi:10.1002/jts.21820

Jeong, H. (2014). Considerations of indigenous ethos in psychotherapeutic practices: Pungryu and Korean psychotherapy. *Asia Pacific Journal of Counseling and Psychotherapy, 5*, 10–20. doi:10.1080/21507686.2013.864318

Ojiambo, D., & Bratton, S. C. (2014). Effects of group activity play therapy on problem behaviors of preadolescent Ugandan orphans. *Journal of Counseling & Development, 92*, 355–365. doi:10.1002/j.1556-6676.2014.00163.x.

Divorce and Separation

Gil, E. (2015). Reunifying families after critical separations: An integrative play therapy approach to building and strengthening family ties. In D. Crenshaw & A. Stewart (Eds.), *Play therapy: A comprehensive guide to theory and practice* (pp. 353–369). New York, NY: Guilford Press.

Kenney-Noziska, S., & Lowenstein, L. (2015). Play therapy with children with of divorce: A prescriptive approach. In D. Crenshaw & A. Stewart (Eds.), *Play therapy: A comprehensive guide to theory and practice* (pp. 290–303). New York, NY: Guilford Press.

Fears and Phobias

Knell, S. (2000). Cognitive–behavioral play therapy for childhood fears and phobias. In H. Kaduson & C. Schaefer (Eds.), *Short-term play therapy for children* (pp. 3–27). New York, NY: Guilford Press.

Kottman, T. (2002). Billy, the teddy bear boy. In L. Golden (Ed.), *Case studies in child and adolescent counseling* (3rd ed., pp. 8–20). Columbus, OH: Merrill Prentice Hall.

Foster Care

Crenshaw, D., & Tillman, K. (2015). Trauma narratives with children in foster care. In D. Crenshaw & A. Stewart (Eds.), *Play therapy: A comprehensive guide to theory and practice* (pp. 262–276). New York, NY: Guilford Press.

Drewes, A. (2014). Helping foster care children heal from broken attachments. In C. Malchiodi & D. Crenshaw (Eds.), *Creative arts and play therapy for attachment problems* (pp. 197–214). New York, NY: Guilford Press.

Grief and Loss

Baggerly, J., & Abugideiri, S. E. (2010). Grief counseling for Muslim preschool and elementary school children. *Journal of Multicultural Counseling and Development, 38,* 112–124. doi:10.1002/j.2161-1912.2010.tb00119.x

Pass, S. (2014). The mummy at the door: Play therapy and surviving loss. *Journal of Infant, Child and Adolescent Psychotherapy, 13,* 142–153. doi:10.1080/15289168.2014.905343

Seymour, J. (2014). Integrated play therapy with childhood traumatic grief. In C. Malchiodi & D. Crenshaw (Eds.), *Creative arts and play therapy for attachment problems* (pp. 259–274). New York, NY: Guilford Press.

Steele, W. (2015). Play therapy for children experience grief and traumatic loss. In D. Crenshaw & A. Stewart (Eds.), *Play therapy: A comprehensive guide to theory and practice* (pp. 304–320). New York, NY: Guilford Press.

Homeless Children

Baggerley, J. (2003). Child-centered play therapy with children who are homeless. *International Journal of Play Therapy, 12,* 87–106.

Baggerly, J. (2004). The effects of child-centered group play therapy on self-concept, depression, and anxiety of children who are homeless. *International Journal of Play Therapy, 13,* 31–51.

Baggerly, J., & Jenkins, W. W. (2009). The effectiveness of child-centered play therapy on developmental and diagnostic factors in children who are homeless. *International Journal of Play Therapy, 18,* 45–55. doi:10.1037/a0013878

Sturm, D., & Hill, C. (2015). Play therapy with children experiencing homelessness. In D. Crenshaw & A. Stewart (Eds.), *Play therapy: A comprehensive guide to theory and practice* (pp. 276–289). New York, NY: Guilford Press.

Intellectual Disabilities

Swan, K., & Ray, D. (2014). Effects of child-centered play therapy on irritability and hyperactivity behaviors of children with intellectual disabilities. *The Journal of Humanistic Counseling, 53,* 120–133. doi:10.102/j.2161-1939.2014.00053.x

Intermittent Explosive Disorder

Paone, T. R., & Douma, K. B. (2009). Child-centered play therapy with a seven-year-old boy diagnosed with intermittent explosive disorder. *International Journal of Play Therapy, 18,* 31–44.

Natural Disasters

Baggerly, J., & Allen-Auguston, M. (2015). Disaster response play therapy with vulnerable children. In E. Green & A. Myrick (Eds.), *Play therapy with vulnerable populations: No child forgotten* (pp. 105–123). Lanham, MD: Rowman & Littlefield.

Baggerly, J., & Exum, H. (2008). Counseling children after natural disasters: Guidance for family therapists. *American Journal of Family Therapy, 36,* 79–93.

Dugan, E., Snow, M., & Crowe, S. (2010). Working with children affected by Hurricane Katrina: Two case studies in play therapy. *Child and Adolescent Mental Health, 15,* 52–55.

Jordan, B., Perryman, K., & Anderson, L. (2013). A case for child-centered play therapy with natural disasters and catastrophic event survivors. *International Journal of Play Therapy, 22,* 219–230.

Shen, Y. (2002). Short-term group play therapy with Chinese earthquake victims: Effects on anxiety, depression, and adjustment. *International Journal of Play Therapy, 11,* 43–63

Stewart, A., Echterling, L., & Mochi, C. (2015). Play-based disaster and crisis intervention: Roles of play therapists in promoting recovery. In D. Crenshaw & A. Stewart (Eds.), *Play therapy: A comprehensive guide to theory and practice* (pp. 370–384). New York, NY: Guilford Press.

Self-Concept

Baggerly, J. (2004). The effects of child-centered group play therapy on self-concept, depression, and anxiety of children who are homeless. *International Journal of Play Therapy, 12,* 31–51.

Fall, M., Navelski, L. F., & Welch, K. K. (2002). Outcomes of a play intervention for children identified for special education services. *International Journal of Play Therapy, 11,* 91–106.

Selective Mutism

Shu-Lan, H., Spencer, M. S., & Dronamraju, R. (2012). Selective mutism: Practice and intervention strategies for children. *Children and Schools, 34*, 222–230.

Sexual Abuse

Lilly, J. P. (2015). Jungian analytical play therapy with a sexually abused child. In D. Crenshaw & A. Stewart (Eds.), *Play therapy: A comprehensive guide to theory and practice* (pp. 321–335). New York, NY: Guilford Press.
Prendiville, E. (2015). Healing young children affected by sexual abuse: The therapeutic touchstone. In E. Green & A. Myrick (Eds.), *Play therapy with vulnerable populations: No child forgotten* (pp. 65–83). Lanham, MD: Rowman & Littlefield.

Somatoform Disorders

Dutta, R., & Mehta, M. (2006). Child-centered play therapy in management of somatoform disorders. *Journal of Indian Association for Child and Adolescent Mental Health, 2*, 85–88.

Appendix I

Adlerian Play Therapy Parent Consultation Skills Checklist

Adlerian Play Therapy Parent Consultation Skills Checklist

Phase 1: Building a Relationship

Rating Scale:
1 = No opportunity or not appropriate to do
2 = Had opportunity, appropriate, but did not do
3 = Had opportunity, appropriate, and did adequately

Therapist: _____ Child's name/age: _____/__

Parent's name/age: _____/__

Observer: _____ Date/session #:_____

	1	2	3
Paraphrasing			
Summarizing			
Reflecting feelings			
Encouraging			
Metacommunicating			
Asking questions about child development			
Asking questions about the history of the presenting problem			
Giving information about play therapy			
Giving information about the importance of parental involvement in the process			
Giving information about Adlerian theory/ therapy			
Giving information about logistics of therapy			

Phase 2: Investigating Parent's Lifestyle

Rating Scale:
1 = No opportunity or not appropriate to do
2 = Had opportunity, appropriate, but did not do
3 = Had opportunity, appropriate, and did adequately

Therapist: _____ Child's name/age:_____/___

Parent's name/age: _____/___

Observer: _____ Date/session #:_____

	1	2	3
Paraphrasing			
Summarizing			
Reflecting feelings			
Encouraging			
Metacommunicating			
Asking questions and giving information			
Asking questions (may use art techniques, sand tray, etc.) to gather information about parent's perception of at least one of the following:			
Child's assets			
Child's functioning at life tasks			
Family constellation and how birth order affects child			
Child's goals of misbehavior			
Child's mastery of Crucial Cs			
Child's personality priorities			
Child's lifestyle convictions, mistaken beliefs, and/or private logic			
Asking questions, using art techniques, and/or sand tray to gather information about parent's perceptions of at least one of the following of their own:			
Functioning at life tasks			
Attitude toward child and parenting			
Parenting strategies and skills			
Philosophy of parenting			
Personality priorities			
Mastery of Crucial Cs			
Family-of-origin constellation			
Lifestyle convictions, mistaken beliefs, and private logic			
Family values			
Unresolved dysfunctional patterns across generations			
Spousal/partnered relationship and how it affects child			

(Continued)

Phase 2: Investigating Parent's Lifestyle *(Continued)*

	1	2	3
Asking questions, using art techniques, and/or sand tray to gather information about parent's perceptions of at least one of the following of their own *(Continued)*			
Family structure, boundaries, hierarchy, and power			
Sibling relationships			
Unresolved issues that might interfere with parenting			
Unresolved issues that might negatively affect the child			

Phase 3: Helping Parent Gain Insight Into Child and Self

Rating Scale:

1 = No opportunity or not appropriate to do
2 = Had opportunity, appropriate, but did not do
3 = Had opportunity, appropriate, and did adequately

Therapist: _____ Child's name/age: _____/___

Parent's name/age: _____/___

Observer: _____ Date/session #:_____

	1	2	3
Paraphrasing			
Summarizing			
Reflecting feelings			
Encouraging			
Metacommunicating			
Asking questions and giving information			
Reframing child's behavior			
Spitting in the parent's soup about mistaken beliefs, private logic, or self-defeating behaviors to help parent gain insight			
Using custom-designed therapeutic metaphors, mutual storytelling, Creative Characters, or bibliotherapy			
Using metacommunication, art techniques, metaphor and storytelling, and/or sand tray to help the parent gain insight into at least one of the following:			
How child's functioning at life tasks affects child			
How birth order and family constellation affect child			
How child's goals of misbehavior get played out in the family and other relationships			
How child's mastery of Crucial Cs affects interactions in the family and other relationships			
How child's personality priorities get played out in family and in other relationships			
How child's lifestyle convictions, mistaken beliefs, and private logic affect child and his/her interactions			
How child's mastery of Crucial Cs affects interactions in the family and other relationships			
How parent's functioning at life tasks affects parenting and the child			
How parent's attitudes toward child and parenting affect parenting and the child			

(Continued)

Phase 3: Helping Parent Gain Insight Into Child and Self *(Continued)*

	1	2	3
Using metacommunication, art techniques, metaphor and storytelling, and/or sand tray to help the parent gain insight into at least one of the following *(Continued)*			
How parent's parenting strategies and skills affect parenting and the child			
How parent's philosophy of parenting affects parenting and the child			
How parent's personality priorities affect parenting and the child			
How parent's mastery of Crucial Cs affects parenting and the child			
How parent's family-of-origin constellation and birth order affect parenting and the child			
How parent's lifestyle convictions, mistaken beliefs, and private logic affect parenting and the child			
How family values affect parenting and the child			
How unresolved dysfunctional patterns across generations affect parenting and the child			
How spousal/partnered relationship affects family atmosphere, parenting, and the child			
How family structure, boundaries, power, and hierarchy affect family atmosphere, parenting, and the child			
How sibling relationships affect the child			
How parent's unresolved personal issues affect family atmosphere, parenting, and the child			

Phase 4: Reorienting–Reeducating the Parent

Rating Scale:

1 = No opportunity or not appropriate to do
2 = Had opportunity, appropriate, but did not do
3 = Had opportunity, appropriate, and did adequately

Therapist: _____   Child's name/age: _____/___

Parent's name/age: _____/___

Observer: _____   Date/session #:_____

	1	2	3
Paraphrasing			
Summarizing			
Reflecting feelings			
Encouraging			
Metacommunicating about child's lifestyle patterns, the parent's lifestyle patterns, and the interaction between the two			
Spitting in the parent's soup about mistaken beliefs, private logic, or self-defeating behaviors to help parent change patterns of thinking, feeling, and behaving			
Using brainstorming, discussion, metaphors and storytelling, art techniques, role-playing, and/or didactic teaching to help parents learn at least one of the following skills:			
Encouraging			
Reflective listening			
Setting limits for child			
Defining problem ownership			
Recognizing goals of misbehavior			
Adapting parenting strategies in response to different goals of misbehavior			
Setting logical consequences			
Fostering Crucial Cs			
Fostering improved functioning in child's mastery of life tasks			
Optimizing interaction between parent's personality priorities and child's personality prioritiess			
Refer for personal counseling			
Refer for marital counseling			
Refer for family counseling			

Appendix J

Adlerian Play Therapy Teacher Consultation Skills Checklist

Adlerian Play Therapy Teacher Consultation Skills Checklist

Phase 1: Building a Relationship

Rating Scale:
   1 = No opportunity or not appropriate to do
   2 = Had opportunity, appropriate, but did not do
   3 = Had opportunity, appropriate, and did adequately

Therapist: _____   Child's name/age: _____/___
Teacher's name/age: _____/___
Observer: _____   Date/session #:_____

	1	2	3
Paraphrasing			
Summarizing			
Reflecting feelings			
Encouraging			
Metacommunicating			
Asking questions about child's history at school			
Asking questions about attempts to resolve the presenting problem			
Giving information about play therapy			
Giving information about the importance of teacher involvement in the process			
Giving information about Adlerian theory/ therapy			

Phase 2: Exploring Lifestyles

Rating Scale:

1 = No opportunity or not appropriate to do
2 = Had opportunity, appropriate, but did not do
3 = Had opportunity, appropriate, and did adequately

Therapist: _____   Child's name/age: _____/___

Teacher's name/age: _____/___

Observer: _____   Date/session #:_____

	1	2	3
Paraphrasing			
Summarizing			
Reflecting feelings			
Encouraging			
Metacommunicating			
Asking questions and giving information			
Asking questions (may use art techniques and/or sand tray) to gather information about teacher's perception of at least one of the following:			
Child's assets			
Child's functioning at life tasks			
Child's goals of misbehavior			
Child's mastery of Crucial Cs			
Child's personality priorities and how they get played out in relationships at school			
Child's lifestyle convictions, mistaken beliefs, and/or private logic			
Teacher's functioning at life tasks			
Teacher's attitude toward the child			
Teacher's attitude toward and philosophy of teaching			
Teacher's classroom management skills			
Teacher's personality priorities and how they affect teaching and interaction with the child and other students			
Teacher's mastery of Crucial Cs and how that affects teaching and interaction with the child and other students			
Teacher's lifestyle convictions, mistaken beliefs, and private logic that might be manifested in interactions with child and other students			
Classroom structure, boundaries, power, and hierarchy			

Phase 3: Helping Teacher Gain Insight Into Child and Self

Rating Scale:
1 = No opportunity or not appropriate to do
2 = Had opportunity, appropriate, but did not do
3 = Had opportunity, appropriate, and did adequately

Therapist: _____   Child's name/age: _____/__
Teacher's name/age: _____/__
Observer: _____   Date/session #:_____

	1	2	3
Paraphrasing			
Summarizing			
Reflecting feelings			
Encouraging			
Asking questions and giving information			
Reframing child's behavior			
Spitting in the teacher's soup about mistaken beliefs, private logic, or self-defeating behaviors to help teacher gain insight			
Using metacommunication, art techniques, metaphor and storytelling, and/or sand tray to help the teacher gain insight into at least one of the following:			
How child's functioning at life tasks affects child's school behavior performance			
How child's goals of misbehavior affect child's school behavior and performance			
How child's mastery of Crucial Cs affects child's school behavior and performance			
How child's personality priorities affect child's behavior and performance			
How child's lifestyle convictions, mistaken beliefs, and private logic affect child's school behavior and performance			
How teacher's attitudes toward the child affect child's school behavior and performance			
How teacher's attitudes toward and philosophy of teacher affect child's school behavior and performance			
How teacher's teaching strategies and skills affect child's school behavior and performance			
How teacher's classroom management skills affect child's school behavior and performance			

(Continued)

Phase 3: Helping Teacher Gain Insight Into Child and Self *(Continued)*

	1	2	3
Using metacommunication, art techniques, metaphor and storytelling, and/or sand tray to help the teacher gain insight into at least one of the following *(Continued)*			
How teacher's personality priorities affect child's school behavior and performance			
How teacher's mastery of Crucial Cs affects child's school behavior and performance			
How teacher's lifestyle convictions, mistaken beliefs, and private logic might be manifested in interactions with the child and affect child's school behavior and performance			

Phase 4: Reorienting–Reeducating the Teacher

Rating Scale:
1 = No opportunity or not appropriate to do
2 = Had opportunity, appropriate, but did not do
3 = Had opportunity, appropriate, and did adequately

Therapist: _____   Child's name/age: _____/__

Teacher's name/age: _____/__

Observer: _____   Date/session #:_____

	1	2	3
Paraphrasing			
Summarizing			
Reflecting feelings			
Encouraging			
Asking questions and giving information			
Metacommunicating about child's lifestyle patterns, the teacher's lifestyle patterns, and the interaction between these two patterns			
Spitting in the teacher's soup about mistaken beliefs, private logic, or self-defeating behaviors to help the teacher change patterns of thinking, feeling, and behaving			
Using brainstorming, discussion, metaphors and storytelling, art techniques, role-playing, and/or didactic teaching to help the teacher learn at least one of the following skills:			
Encouraging			
Reflective listening			
Setting limits for child			
Defining problem ownership			
Recognizing goals of misbehavior			
Adapting teaching and classroom management strategies in response to different goals of misbehavior			
Setting logical consequences			
Fostering Crucial Cs in the classroom			
Fostering improved functioning in child's mastery of life tasks relative to school behavior and performance			
Optimizing interaction between teacher's personality priorities and child's personality priorities			

Appendix K

Adlerian Play Therapy Skills Checklist

Adlerian Play Therapy Skills Checklist

Phase 1: Building a Relationship

Rating Scale:
1 = No opportunity or not appropriate to do
2 = Had opportunity, appropriate, but did not do
3 = Had opportunity, appropriate, and did adequately

Therapist: _____ Child's name/age: _____/___

Observer: _____ Date/session #:_____

Therapist's visual attitude:
☐ Yes ☐ No Active involvement
☐ Yes ☐ No Appears interested
☐ Yes ☐ No Relaxed/comfortable
☐ Yes ☐ No Tone and affect congruent with child's affect

	1	2	3
Meeting the child[a]			
Demystifying play therapy process[a]			
Tracking behavior			
Restating content			
Reflecting feelings			
Encouraging			
Asking questions			
Metacommunicating			
Giving explanations and answering questions			
Returning responsibility			
Using the child's metaphor			
Cleaning the room together			
Setting limits			

[a]Generally only happens once in a counseling relationship.

Adlerian Play Therapy Skills Checklist

Phase 2: Investigating Child's Lifestyle

Rating Scale:
1 = No opportunity or not appropriate to do
2 = Had opportunity, appropriate, but did not do
3 = Had opportunity, appropriate, and did adequately

Therapist: _____   Child's name/age: _____/___

Observer: _____   Date/session #: _____

Therapist's visual attitude:
☐ Yes   ☐ No   Active involvement
☐ Yes   ☐ No   Appears interested
☐ Yes   ☐ No   Relaxed/comfortable
☐ Yes   ☐ No   Tone and affect congruent with child's affect

	1	2	3
Tracking behavior			
Restating content			
Reflecting feelings			
Encouraging			
Asking questions			
Metacommunicating			
Giving explanations and answering questions			
Returning responsibility			
Using the child's metaphor			
Cleaning the room together			
Setting limits			
Exploring functioning at life tasks			
Exploring family constellation			
Examining goals of misbehavior			
Exploring Crucial Cs			
Exploring personality priorities			
Exploring lifestyle convictions, mistaken beliefs, and private logic			
Soliciting early recollections			

Adlerian Play Therapy Skills Checklist

Phase 3: Helping the Child Gain Insight

Rating Scale:
1 = No opportunity or not appropriate to do
2 = Had opportunity, appropriate, but did not do
3 = Had opportunity, appropriate, and did adequately

Therapist: _____ Child's name/age: _____/__

Observer: _____ Date/session #:_____

Therapist's visual attitude:
☐ Yes ☐ No Active involvement
☐ Yes ☐ No Appears interested
☐ Yes ☐ No Relaxed/comfortable
☐ Yes ☐ No Tone and affect congruent with child's affect

	1	2	3
Tracking behavior			
Restating content			
Reflecting feelings			
Encouraging			
Asking questions			
Giving explanations and answering questions			
Returning responsibility			
Setting limits			
Using the child's metaphor			
Cleaning the room together			
Metacommunicating as a way to gain insight about the following:			
A single event behavior or interaction			
Meaning about a specific event, behavior, or interaction			
Patterns within a session			
Patterns across sessions			
Patterns that extend into other situations outside of the playroom			
Lifestyle themes, convictions, mistaken beliefs, or private logic			
Assets and strengths			
Functioning at life tasks			
Crucial Cs			
Goals of misbehavior			
Purposes of behavior			
Personality priorities			
Impact of family constellation on child			
Self-defeating behavior patterns			
Play themes			

Adlerian Play Therapy Skills Checklist (APTSC)

Phase 4: Reorienting–Reeducating

Rating Scale:
1 = No opportunity or not appropriate to do
2 = Had opportunity, appropriate, but did not do
3 = Had opportunity, appropriate, and did adequately

Therapist: _____   Child's name/age: _____/__

Observer: _____   Date/session #:_____

Therapist's visual attitude:
☐ Yes ☐ No Active involvement
☐ Yes ☐ No Appears interested
☐ Yes ☐ No Relaxed/comfortable
☐ Yes ☐ No Tone and affect congruent with child's affect

	1	2	3
Tracking behavior			
Restating content			
Reflecting feelings			
Encouraging			
Asking questions			
Metacommunicating			
Giving explanations and answering questions			
Returning responsibility			
Using the child's metaphor			
Cleaning the room together			
Setting limits			
Spitting in the client's soup about mistaken beliefs, private logic, or self-defeating behaviors			
Using custom-designed therapeutic metaphors, mutual storytelling, Creative Characters, or bibliotherapy			
Using brainstorming, discussion, storytelling and metaphoric techniques, art techniques, puppet play, didactic teaching, modeling, and/or role-playing to help the child generate ideas for at least one of the following skills:			
Capitalizing on assets			
Improving functioning at life tasks			
Fostering improvement on Crucial Cs			
Moving toward healthy functioning in personalities priorities			
Shifting from goals of misbehavior to more positive goals			
Substituting positive convictions for mistaken beliefs and common sense for private logic			

(Continued)

Phase 4: Reorienting–Reeducating *(Continued)*

	1	2	3
Using brainstorming, discussion, storytelling, and metaphoric techniques, art techniques, puppet play, didactic teaching, modeling, and/or role-playing to help the child generate ideas for at least one of the following skills *(Continued)*			
Reducing self-defeating behaviors and learning positive behaviors			
Increasing skill such as social skills, negotiating skills, communication skills, assertiveness, taking responsibility for behavior, etc.			
Using brainstorming, problem-solving techniques, discussion, storytelling and metaphoric techniques, art techniques, puppet play, didactic teaching, modeling, and/or role-play to teach the child ideas and/or skills for at least one of the following:			
Capitalizing on assets			
Improving functioning at life tasks			
Fostering improvement on Crucial Cs			
Moving toward healthy functioning in personality priorities			
Shifting from goals of misbehavior to more positive goals			
Substituting positive convictions for mistaken beliefs and common sense for private logic			
Increasing skills such as social skills, negotiation skills, communication skills, assertiveness, taking responsibility for behavior, etc.			
Using storytelling and metaphoric techniques, art techniques, puppet play, role-playing, and/or homework assignments to set up ways for the child to practice at least one of the following:			
Capitalizing on assets			
Improving functioning at life tasks			
Fostering improvement on Crucial Cs			
Moving toward healthy functioning in personality priorities			
Shifting from goals of misbehavior to more positive goals			
Substituting positive convictions for mistaken beliefs and common sense for private logic			
Reducing self-defeating behaviors and learning positive behaviors			

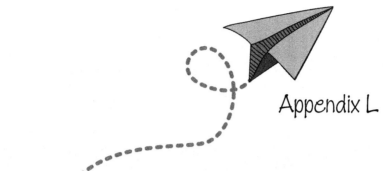

Adlerian Play Therapy Session Summary

Session Summary

Date/session #:_____ Child's name/age: _____/___

Counselor: _____ Diagnosis: _____

Underlying purpose of presenting problem: _____

Specific interventions used:

☐ Tracking ☐ Restating content ☐ Reflecting feelings
☐ Returning responsibility ☐ Asking questions ☐ Limiting
☐ Metacommunicating ☐ Metaphors/storytelling ☐ Bibliotherapy
☐ Spitting in soup ☐ Role-playing
☐ Art activity: _____
☐ Sand tray ☐ Didactic teaching ☐ Modeling
☐ Practicing new skills: _____

I. Subjective (Feelings Expressed). Indicate all that apply and circle the predominant feelings:

Happy: ☐ Relieved ☐ Satisfied ☐ Pleased ☐ Delighted ☐ Excited
☐ Surprised ☐ Silly

Sad: ☐ Disappointed ☐ Hopeless ☐ Pessimistic ☐ Discouraged
☐ Lonely

Angry: ☐ Impatient ☐ Annoyed ☐ Frustrated ☐ Mad ☐ Mean
☐ Jealous ☐ Enraged

Afraid: ☐ Vulnerable ☐ Helpless ☐ Distrustful ☐ Anxious
☐ Fearful ☐ Scared ☐ Terrified

Flat: ☐ Restricted ☐ Contained ☐ Ambiguous

Confident: ☐ Proud ☐ Strong ☐ Powerful ☐ Determined ☐ Free

Hesitant: ☐ Timid ☐ Confused ☐ Nervous ☐ Embarassed
☐ Ashamed

Curious: ☐ Interested ☐ Focused ☐ Intense

(Continued)

II. Objective

A. *Toys/play behavior.* Mark each with a "CH" if the child initiated or "TH" if the therapist initiated:

_____ Sandbox/water/sink	_____ Puppets/theater
_____ Kitchen/cooking/food	_____ Easel/paint/chalkboard/ white board
_____ Bop bag/bean bag	_____ Dress up/jewelry/hats/ masks/wand
_____ Crafts/clay/markers/ paint/scissors/glue	_____ Sheets/blankets/fabric
_____ Doll house/doll family/ bottle/pacifier/baby	_____ Cash register/money/ telephone/camera
_____ Musical instruments	_____ Medical kit/bandages
_____ Games/bowling/balls/ ring toss	_____ Construction toys (Tinker Toys, Legos, blocks)
_____ Vehicles/planes/boats	_____ Animals (domestic, zoo alligator, snake, dinosaur)
_____ Soldiers/weapons/ handcuffs	_____ Sand tray/miniatures

B. *Significant verbalizations:* _____

C. *Set limit(s) on:* _____

D. *Returned responsibility to child when:* _____

E. *Worked to help child gain insight/shift or adjust/move toward more constructive application of:*

☐ Functioning at life tasks (school, friendship, self, spiritual) of: _____

☐ Interpretation of family constellation/family atmosphere: _____

☐ Personality priorities: _____

☐ Crucial Cs: _____

☐ Goals of misbehavior: _____

☐ "Owning" assets: _____

☐ Mistaken beliefs: _____

☐ Self-defeating behaviors: _____

☐ Private logic: _____

(Continued)

III. Assessment

A. *Dynamics of the session.* Indicate the number on the scale that applies to the child's behavior in the session:

Low activity level	1	2	3	4	5	6	7	8	9	10	High activity level
Low degree of self-regulation	1	2	3	4	5	6	7	8	9	10	High degree of self-regulation
Low level of intensity	1	2	3	4	5	6	7	8	9	10	High level of intensity
Little therapist inclusion	1	2	3	4	5	6	7	8	9	10	Much therapist inclusion
Destructive play	1	2	3	4	5	6	7	8	9	10	Constructive play
Chaotic/disorganized	1	2	3	4	5	6	7	8	9	10	Orderly/organized
Aggressive	1	2	3	4	5	6	7	8	9	10	Peaceful
Dependent	1	2	3	4	5	6	7	8	9	10	Independent
Too tight	1	2	3	4	5	6	7	8	9	10	Too loose
Immature/hypermature	1	2	3	4	5	6	7	8	9	10	Age appropriate
Scattered, impulsive, hyper	1	2	3	4	5	6	7	8	9	10	Focused, purposeful, calm

B. *Play themes.* Indicate all that apply and describe the play behaviors that fit into the theme. Circle the predominant theme:

- ☐ Exploratory: _____
- ☐ Relationship: _____
- ☐ Power/control: _____
- ☐ Feelings of inadequacy/helplessness: _____
  _____
- ☐ Aggression/revenge: _____
- ☐ Safety/security/trust: _____
- ☐ Mastery: _____
- ☐ Nurturing: _____
- ☐ Death/loss/grief: _____
- ☐ Trauma: _____
- ☐ Regression: _____
- ☐ Sexualized: _____
- ☐ Other: _____

C. *Plans/recommendations.* Include any consultation with parents or teachers:

Appendix M

Adlerian Play Therapy Progress Form

Session #/Phase: _____

Functioning at Life Tasks (1 = *low* to 10 = *high*)

School	1	2	3	4	5	6	7	8	9	10
Friendship	1	2	3	4	5	6	7	8	9	10
Love/family	1	2	3	4	5	6	7	8	9	10
Self	1	2	3	4	5	6	7	8	9	10
Spirituality	1	2	3	4	5	6	7	8	9	10

Crucial Cs (1 = *low* to 10 = *high*)

Connect	1	2	3	4	5	6	7	8	9	10
Capable	1	2	3	4	5	6	7	8	9	10
Count	1	2	3	4	5	6	7	8	9	10
Courage	1	2	3	4	5	6	7	8	9	10

Goal Misbehavior (1 = *infrequent/low intensity* to 10 = *frequent/high intensity*)

Attention	1	2	3	4	5	6	7	8	9	10
Power	1	2	3	4	5	6	7	8	9	10
Revenge	1	2	3	4	5	6	7	8	9	10
Proving inadequacy	1	2	3	4	5	6	7	8	9	10

Personality Priorities (1 = *healthy* to 10 = *unhealthy*)

Pleasing	1	2	3	4	5	6	7	8	9	10
Superiority	1	2	3	4	5	6	7	8	9	10
Control	1	2	3	4	5	6	7	8	9	10
Comfort	1	2	3	4	5	6	7	8	9	10

Notable changes in lifestyle convictions/mistaken beliefs/private logic:

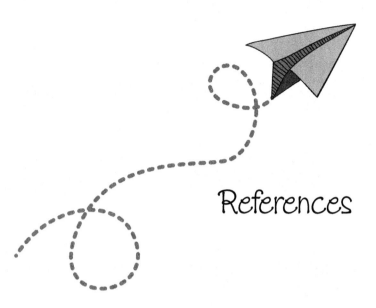

References

Adler, A. (1954). *Understanding human nature* (W. B. Wolf, Trans.). New York, NY: Fawcett Premier. (Original work published 1927)

Adler, A. (1958). *What life should mean to you.* New York, NY: Capricorn. (Original work published 1931)

Adler, A. (1963). *The problem child.* New York, NY: Putnam Capricorn. (Original work published 1930)

Adler, A. (2011). *Social interest: A challenge to mankind.* Mansfield Center, CT: Martino. (Original work published 1938)

Albert, L. (2002). *A teacher's guide to cooperative discipline: How to manage your classroom and promote self-esteem.* Circle Pines, MN: American Guidance Service.

Alizadeh, H. (2012). Individual Psychology and Islam: An exploration of social interest. *The Journal of Individual Psychology, 68,* 216–224.

Ames, L., & Haber, C. (1985). *Your 7-year-old: Life in a minor key.* New York, NY: Delta.

Ames, L., & Ilg, F. (1979). *Your 5-year-old: Sunny and serene.* New York, NY: Delta.

Andreae, G. (1999). *Giraffes can't dance.* New York, NY: Scholastic.

Ansbacher, H., & Ansbacher, R. (Eds.). (1956). *The Individual Psychology of Alfred Adler: A systematic presentation in selections from his writings.* San Francisco, CA: Harper & Row.

Ashby, J., & Kottman, T. (1998, October). *Play therapy applications of Adlerian personality priorities.* Paper presented at the 15th Annual International Play Therapy Conference, Phoenix, AZ.

Ashby, J., Kottman, T., & DeGraaf, D. (2008). *Active interventions for kids and teens: Adding adventure and fun to counseling!* Alexandria, VA: American Counseling Association.

Association for Play Therapy. (2014). *Why play therapy?* Retrieved from http://www.a4pt.org/?page=WhyPlayTherapy

Bang, M. (1999). *When Sophie gets angry—Really, really angry.* New York, NY: Blue Sky.

Barr, C. (2013). *Best books for children, supplement to the 9th edition: Preschool through Grade 6.* Santa Barbara, CA: Libraries Unlimited.

Barr, C., & Gillespie, J. (2010). *Best books for children: Preschool through Grade 6* (9th ed.). Santa Barbara, CA: Libraries Unlimited.

Bartlett, K. (2012). *Encouraging words for kids: What to say to bring out a child's confidence.* Retrieved from http://www.amazon.com/Encouraging-Words-Kids-Kelly-Bartlett-ebook/dp/B009OH52G2/ref=pd_sim_kstore_9?ie=UTF8&refRID=149B1QZRKPY3HSKQ75KB

Beames, T. B. (1992). *A student's glossary of Adlerian terminology* (2nd ed.). Chicago, IL: Adler School of Professional Psychology.

Bettner, B. L., & Lew, A. (1990). *Raising kids who can: Using family meetings to nurture responsible, cooperative, caring, and happy children.* Newton Centre, MA: Connexions Press.

Bettner, B. L., & Lew, A. (1998). *Raising kids who can: Leader's guide.* Newton Centre, MA: Connexions Press.

Bitter, J. (2012). On the essence and origin of character. In J. Carlson & M. Maniacci (Eds.), *Alfred Adler revisited* (pp. 89–95). New York, NY: Taylor & Francis.

Bitter, J. (2014). *Theory and practice of family therapy and counseling* (2nd ed.). Belmont, CA: Brooks/Cole.

Bixler, R. (1949). Limits are therapy. *Journal of Consulting Psychology, 13,* 1–11.

Bordon, B. (1982). Early recollections as a diagnostic technique with primary age children. *Individual Psychology, 38,* 207–212.

Boritzer, E. (1990). *What is God?* Buffalo, NY: Firefly.

Boritzer, E. (2000). *What is death?* Los Angeles, CA: Veronica Lane.

Bottner, B., & Kruglik, G. (2004). *Wallace's lists.* New York, NY: Katherine Tegan.

Bowers, N. R. (2013). *Play therapy with families: A collaborative approach to healing.* Lanham, MD: Jason Aronson.

Brack, G., Hill, M., & Brack, C. (2012). Individual Psychology in South Africa. *The Journal of Individual Psychology, 68,* 294–307.

Bratton, S., Landreth, G., Kellum, T., & Blackard, S. (2006). *CPRT package: Child Parent Relationship Therapy (CPRT) treatment manual: A 10-session filial therapy model for training parents.* New York, NY: Routledge.

Bratton, S., & Ray, D. (2000). What the research shows about play therapy. *International Journal of Play Therapy, 9,* 47–88.

Bratton, S. C., Ray, D., Rhine, T., & Jones, L. (2005). The efficacy of play therapy with children: A meta-analytic review of treatment outcomes. *Professional Psychology: Research and Practice, 36,* 376–390. doi:10.1037/0735-7028.36.4.376

Briggs, N., & Shea, D. (2011). *How to make & keep friends: Tips for kids to overcome 50 common social challenges.* Seattle, WA: CreateSpace.

Brooks, R. (1981). Creative characters: A technique in child therapy. *Psychotherapy, 18,* 131–139.

Brown, S., & Vaughn, C. (2009). *Play: How it shapes the brain, opens the imagination, and invigorates the soul.* New York, NY: Penguin Books.

Bruel, N. (2015). *Bad kitty*. New York, NY: Roaring Brook Press.

Buchalter, S. (2009). *Art therapy techniques and applications*. Philadelphia, PA: Jessica Kingsley.

Buck, J. (1992). *House–Tree–Person projective drawing technique: Manual and interpretive guide* (Revised by W. L. Warren). Los Angeles, CA: Western Psychological Services.

Burke, K. (2008). *What to do with the kid who . . . ? Developing cooperation, self-discipline, and responsibility in the classroom* (3rd ed.). Thousand Oaks, CA: Sage.

Burns, G. (2005). *101 healing stories for kids and teens: Using metaphors in therapy*. Hoboken, NJ: Wiley.

Burns, R. (1990). *A guide to family-centered circle drawings*. New York, NY: Brunner/Mazel.

Cain, J. (2000). *The way I feel*. Seattle, WA: Parenting Press.

Carey, L. (Ed.). (2006). Introduction. In L. Carey (Ed.), *Expressive and creative arts methods for trauma survivors* (pp. 15–19). Philadelphia, PA: Jessica Kingsley.

Carlson, J., & Slavik, S. (Eds.). (1997). *Techniques in Adlerian psychology*. Washington, DC: Accelerated Development.

Carmichael, K. D. (2006). Legal and ethical issues in play therapy. *International Journal of Play Therapy, 15*, 83–99.

Cave, K. (2003). *You've got dragons*. Atlanta, GA: Peachtree.

Chang, C. Y., Ritter, K. B., & Hays, D. G. (2005). Multicultural trends and toys in play therapy. *International Journal of Play Therapy, 14*, 69–85.

Chapman, G., & Campbell, R. (2012). *The 5 love languages of children*. Chicago, IL: Northfield.

Choi, Y. (2003). *The name jar*. Logan, IA: Perfection Learning.

Cocca-Leffler, M. (2002). *Bravery soup*. Morton Grove, IL: Albert Whitman.

Cook, J. (2009). *My mouth is a volcano!—Activity and idea book*. Chattanooga, TN: National Center for Youth Issues.

Cook, J. (2011). *I just don't like the sound of no!* Boys Town, NE: Boys Town Press.

Cook, J. (2012). *Wilma Jean, the worry machine*. Chattanooga, TN: National Center for Youth Issues.

Cook, J. (2014). *Hygiene . . . you stink*. Boys Town, NE: Boys Town Press.

Cooper, S. (2005). *Speak up and get along! Learn the mighty might, thought chop, and more tools to make friends, stop teasing, and feel good about yourself*. Minneapolis, MN: Free Spirit.

Crenshaw, D., & Barker, G. (2008). Sports metaphors and stories in counseling with children. In L. Rubin (Ed.), *Popular culture in counseling, psychotherapy, and play-based interventions* (pp. 297–314). New York, NY: Springer.

Crenshaw, D., Brooks, R., & Goldstein, S. (Eds.). (2015). *Play therapy interventions to enhance resiliency*. New York, NY: Guilford Press.

Crenshaw, D., & Stewart, A. (Eds.). (2015). *Play therapy: A comprehensive guide to theory and practice*. New York, NY: Guilford Press.

Crimi, C. (1999). *Don't need friends*. New York, NY: Random House.

Curtis, J. L. (1998). *Today I feel silly and other moods that make my day*. New York, NY: Harper.

Dean, J., & Dean, K. (2013). *Pete the cat and his magic sunglasses*. New York, NY: HarperCollins.

Dewdney, A. (2005). *Llama llama red pajama*. New York, NY: Penguin.

Dewdney, A. (2007). *Llama llama mad at mama*. New York, NY: Penguin.

Dewdney, A. (2012). *Llama llama time to share*. New York, NY: Penguin.

Dewey, E. (1971). Family atmosphere. In A. Nikelly (Ed.), *Techniques for behavior change* (pp. 41–47). Springfield, IL: Charles C Thomas.

Dewey, E. (1978). *Basic applications of Adlerian psychology for self-understanding and human relationships*. Coral Spring, FL: CMI Press.

Diamond, S. (2011). *Social rules for kids: The top 100 social rules kids need to succeed*. Shawnee Mission, KS: AAPC.

Diesen, D. (2008). *The pout-pout fish*. New York, NY: Farrar, Straus, & Giroux.

Diesen, D. (2010). *The pout-pout fish in the big-big dark*. New York, NY: Farrar, Straus, & Giroux.

Diesen, D. (2014). *The pout-pout fish goes to school*. New York, NY: Farrar, Straus, & Giroux.

Dillman Taylor, D. (2013). *Confirming the constructs of the Adlerian Personality Priority Assessment (APPA)* (Unpublished doctoral dissertation). University of North Texas, Denton, TX.

Dillman Taylor, D., & Meany-Walen, K. K. (2015). *Investigating the effectiveness of Adlerian play therapy with children with disruptive behaviors: A single-case research design*. Manuscript submitted for publication.

Dinkmeyer, D., & Dinkmeyer, D. (1977). Concise counseling assessment: The children's life-style guide. *Elementary School Guidance and Counseling, 12*, 117–124.

Dinkmeyer, D., & Dinkmeyer, D. (1983). Adlerian approaches. In H. T. Prout & D. Brown (Eds.), *Counseling and psychotherapy with children and adolescents: Theory and practice for school and clinic settings* (pp. 289–327). Tampa, FL: Mariner.

Dinkmeyer, D., McKay, G., & Dinkmeyer, D. (2007). *The parent's handbook: Systematic Training for Effective Parenting (STEP)* (Rev. ed.). Circle Pines, MN: American Guidance Service.

Dowd, T., & Tierney, J. (2005). *Teaching social skills to youth* (2nd ed.). Boys Town, NE: Boys Town Press.

Draper, K., White, J., O'Shaughnessy, T., Flynt, M., & Jones, N. (2001). Kinder Training: Play-based consultation to improve the school adjustment of discouraged kindergarten and first grade students. *International Journal of Play Therapy, 10*, 1–30.

Dreikurs, R. (1948). *The challenge of parenthood*. New York, NY: Duell, Sloan & Pearce.

Dreikurs, R. (1967). *Psychodynamics, psychotherapy, and counseling*. Chicago, IL: Alfred Adler Institute.

Dreikurs, R., & Soltz, V. (1964). *Children: The challenge*. New York, NY: Hawthorn/Dutton.

Drewes, A., & Schaefer, C. (Eds.). (2010). *School-based play therapy*. Hoboken, NJ: Wiley.

Duba, J. (2012). The structure of neurosis. In J. Carlson & M. Maniacci (Eds.), *Alfred Adler revisited* (pp. 213–217). New York, NY: Taylor & Francis.

Duba Sauerheber, J., & Bitter, J. R. (2013). An Adlerian approach in pre-marital counseling with religious couples. *The Journal of Individual Psychology, 69*, 305–327.

Duffy, M., & Chenail, R. (2012). Qualitative assessment. In L. Sperry (Ed.), *Family assessment: Contemporary and cutting-edge strategies* (2nd ed., pp. 17–52). New York, NY: Routledge.

Eckstein, D., & Kern, R. (2009). *Psychological fingerprints* (6th ed.). Dubuque, IA: Kendall/Hunt.

Edwards, N., Varjas, K., White, J., & Stokes, S. (2009). Teachers' percep-tions of Kinder Training: Acceptability, integrity, and effectiveness. *International Journal of Play Therapy, 18*, 129–146.

Edwards, P. (2003). *The worrywarts.* New York, NY: Harper Children.

Egan, T. (2007). *The pink refrigerator.* New York, NY: Houghton Mifflin.

Enfield, G., & Grosser, M. (2008). Picking up the coins: The use of video games in the treatment of adolescent social problems. In L. Rubin (Ed.), *Popular culture in counseling, psychotherapy, and play-based interventions* (pp. 181–196). New York, NY: Springer.

Esbaum, J. (2014). *I am cow, hear me moo!* New York, NY: Dial.

Faber, A., & Mazlish, E. (2012). *How to talk so kids will listen and lis-ten so kids will talk* (30th anniversary ed.). New York, NY: Simon & Schuster.

Fallon, M. K. (2004). Adlerian therapeutic techniques for professional school counselors. In B. Erford (Ed.), *Professional school counseling: A handbook of theories, programs, and practices* (pp. 113–122). Austin, TX: PRO-ED.

Ferry, T. (2015). *Stick and stone.* New York, NY: Houghton Mifflin.

Fox, M. (2001). *Whoever you are.* Orlando, FL: Harcourt.

Frey, D. (2006). Video play therapy. In L. Carey (Ed.), *Expressive and cre-ative arts methods for trauma survivors* (pp. 193–206). Philadelphia, PA: Jessica Kingsley.

Frey, D. (2015). Play therapy interventions with adults. In D. Crenshaw & A. Stewart (Eds.), *Play therapy: A comprehensive guide to theory and practice* (pp. 452–464). New York, NY: Guilford Press.

Gallo-Lopez, L., & Schaefer, C. (2005). *Play therapy with adolescents.* Lan-ham, MD: Jason Aronson.

Gardner, B. (2015). Play therapy with adolescents. In D. Crenshaw & A. Stewart (Eds.), *Play therapy: A comprehensive guide to theory and practice* (pp. 439–451). New York, NY: Guilford Press.

Gardner, R. (1993). *Storytelling in psychotherapy with children.* Northvale, NJ: Jason Aronson.

Gardner, R. (2004). *Psychotherapeutic use of the Talking, Feeling & Doing Game and other projective techniques.* Wilkes-Barre, PA: Child's Work/Child's Play.

Garrett, M. (2014). Beyond play therapy: Using the sand tray as an expres-sive arts intervention in counselling adult clients. *Asia Pacific Journal of Counseling & Psychotherapy, 5*, 99–105.

Gassman, J. (2013). *You get what you get.* Mankato, MN: Picture Window Books.

Geras, A. (2002). *Blossom's revenge.* New York, NY: Yearling.

Gil, E. (2006). *Helping abused and traumatized children: Integrating directive and nondirective approaches.* New York, NY: Guilford Press.

Gil, E. (Ed.). (2010). *Working with children to heal interpersonal trauma.* New York, NY: Guilford Press.

Gil, E. (2014). The creative use of metaphor in play and art therapy with attachment problems. In C. Malchiodi & D. Crenshaw (Eds.), *Creative arts and play therapy for attachment problems* (pp. 159–177). New York, NY: Guilford Press.

Gil, E., & Drewes, A. (2005). *Cultural issues in play therapy.* New York, NY: Guilford Press.

Gil, E., & Selekman, M. (2015). *Family play therapy* (2nd ed.). New York, NY: Guilford Press.

Goldblatt, R. (2004). *The boy who didn't want to be sad.* Washington, DC: Magination Press.

Gordon, T. (2000). *Parent effectiveness training* (30th anniversary ed.). New York, NY: Three Rivers.

Gray, C., & Atwood, T. (2010). *The new social story book* (Rev. ed.). Arlington, TX: Future Horizons.

Green, A. (2012). *The monster in the bubble.* Jersey City, NJ: Monsters in My Head.

Green, E., Drewes, A., & Kominski, J. (2013). Use of mandalas in Jungian play therapy with adolescents diagnosed with ADHD. *International Journal of Play Therapy, 22,* 159–172.

Greive, B. (2006). *A teaspoon of courage: The little book of encouragement.* Kansas City, MO: Andrews McMeel.

Griffith, J., & Powers, R. L. (2007). *The lexicon of Adlerian psychology* (2nd ed.). Port Townsend, WA: Adlerian Psychology Associates.

Guerney, L. (2013). *Group filial therapy: The complete guide to teaching parents to play therapeutically with their children.* Philadelphia, PA: Jessica Kingsley.

Hadley, S., & Steele, N. (2014). Music therapy. In E. Green & A. Drewes (Eds.), *Integrating expressive arts and play therapy* (pp. 149–180). Hoboken, NJ: Wiley.

Hanh, T. N. (2012). *A handful of quiet: Happiness in four pebbles.* Berkeley, CA: Plum Blossom.

Hanh, T. N. (2014). *Is nothing something? Kids' questions and Zen answers about life, death, family, friendship, and everything in between.* Berkeley, CA: Plum Blossom.

Hall, M. (2015). *Red: A crayon's story.* New York, NY: Greenwillow.

Hansen, R., & Medius, R. (2009). *Buddha's brain: The practical neuroscience of happiness, love and wisdom.* Oakland, CA: New Harbinger.

Harris, R. (2008). *The day Leo said I hate you!* Boston, MA: Little, Brown.

Henderson, D., & Thompson, C. L. (2011). *Counseling children* (8th ed.). Pacific Grove, CA: Brooks/Cole.

Henkes, K. (1991). *Chrysanthemum.* New York, NY: Greenwillow.

Henkes, K. (1996). *Lilly's purple plastic purse.* New York, NY: Greenwillow.

Henkes, K. (1997). *Chester's way.* New York, NY: Greenwillow.

Henkes, K. (2000). *Wemberly worried.* New York, NY: Greenwillow.

Herring, R., & Runion, K. (1994). Counseling ethnic children and youth from an Adlerian perspective. *Journal of Multicultural Counseling and Development, 22,* 215–226.

Hess, B., Post, P., & Flowers, C. (2005). A follow-up study of Kinder Training for preschool teachers of children deemed at-risk. *International Journal of Play Therapy, 14,* 103–115.

Higgins-Klein, D. (2013). *Mindfulness-based play-family therapy: Theory and practice.* New York, NY: Norton.

Hinman, C. (2003). Multicultural considerations in the delivery of play therapy services. *International Journal of Play Therapy, 12,* 107–122.

Homeyer, L., & Sweeney, D. (2011). *Sand tray therapy: A practical manual* (2nd ed.). New York, NY: Routledge.

Hutchins, H. J. (1996). *Katie's babbling brother.* Toronto, Ontario, Canada: Annick Press.

Jeffers, O. (2004). *How to catch a star.* New York, NY: Philomel.

Joiner, L. (2012). *The big book of therapeutic activities for children and teens.* Philadelphia, PA: Jessica Kingsley.

Jones-Smith, E. (2015). *Theories of counseling and psychotherapy: An integrative approach* (2nd ed.). Thousand Oaks, CA: Sage.

Karges-Bone, L. (2015). *Bibliotherapy.* Dayton, OH: Lorenz Educational Press.

Katz, K. (2002). *The colors of us.* New York, NY: Henry Holt.

Kaufman, D., Chalmers, R., & Rosenberg, W. (2014). Poetry therapy. In E. Green & A. Drewes (Eds.), *Integrating expressive arts and play therapy with children and adolescents* (pp. 205–230). New York, NY: Wiley.

Kfir, N. (1981). Impasse/priority therapy. In R. Corsini (Ed.), *Handbook of innovative psychotherapies* (pp. 400–415). New York, NY: Wiley.

Kfir, N. (1989). *Crisis intervention verbatim.* New York, NY: Hemisphere.

Kfir, N. (2011). *Personality and priorities: A typology.* Bloomington, IN: Author House.

Kim, Y., & Nahm, S. (2008). Cultural considerations in adapting and implementing play therapy. *International Journal of Play Therapy, 17,* 66–77.

Kissel, S. (1990). *Play therapy: A strategic approach.* Springfield, IL: Charles C Thomas.

Klassen, J. (2012). *This is not my hat.* Somerville, MA: Candlewick.

Knoff, H., & Prout, H. (1985). *Kinetic drawing system for family and school: A handbook.* Los Angeles, CA: Western Psychological Services.

Kottman, T. (1999). Using the Crucial Cs in Adlerian play therapy. *Individual Psychology, 55,* 289–297.

Kottman, T. (2003). Mutual storytelling: Adlerian style. In H. Kaduson & C. Schaefer (Eds.), *101 favorite play therapy techniques* (Vol. 3, pp. 203–208). Northvale, NJ: Jason Aronson.

Kottman, T. (2009). *Treatment manual for Adlerian play therapy.* Unpublished manuscript.

Kottman, T. (2011). *Play therapy: Basics and beyond* (2nd ed.). Alexandria, VA: American Counseling Association.

Kottman, T. (with Dougherty, M.). (2013). Adlerian case consultation with a teacher. In A. M. Dougherty (Ed.), *Psychological consultation and collaboration in school and community settings: A casebook* (6th ed., pp. 61–78). Belmont, CA; Brooks/Cole.

Kottman, T., & Ashby, J. (1999). Using Adlerian personality priorities to custom-design consultation with parents of play therapy clients. *International Journal of Play Therapy, 8,* 77–92.

Kottman, T., & Ashby, J. (2002). Metaphoric stories. In C. Schaefer & D. Cangelosi (Eds.), *Play therapy techniques* (2nd ed., pp. 133–142). Northvale, NJ: Jason Aronson.

Kottman, T., & Ashby, J. (2015). Adlerian play therapy. In D. Crenshaw & A. Stewart (Eds.), *Play therapy: A comprehensive guide to theory and practice* (pp. 32–47). New York, NY: Guilford Press.

Kottman, T., Ashby, J., & DeGraaf, D. (2001). *Adventures in guidance: Integrating fun into your guidance program.* Alexandria, VA: American Counseling Association.

Kottman, T., Bryant, J., Alexander, J., & Kroger, S. (2009). Partners in the schools: Adlerian school counseling. In A. Vernon & T. Kottman (Eds.), *Counseling theories: Practical applications with children and adolescents in school settings* (pp. 47–83). Denver, CO: Love.

Kottman, T., & Heston, M. (2012). The child's inner life and a sense of community. In J. Carlson & M. Maniacci (Eds.), *Alfred Adler revisited* (pp. 113–121). New York, NY: Taylor & Francis.

Kottman, T., & Meany-Walen, K. (in press). Adlerian family play therapy. In E. Green, J. Baggerly, & A. Myrick (Eds.), *Integrative family play therapy.* Lanham, MD: Rowman & Littlefield.

Kowalski, B. (2009). *Alexis and Ralph the dragon.* Frederick, MN: American Star Books.

Kronemyer, D. (2009, October 3). Alfred Adler's concept of "social interest." In D. Kronemyer (Ed.), *Phenomenological psychology.* Retrieved from http://phenomenologicalpsychology.com/2009/10/alfred-adlers-concept-of-social-interest/

Landreth, G. (2009, September). *Healing the hurt child: The necessary dimensions of child-centered play therapy.* Paper presented at the meeting of the Iowa Association for Play Therapy, Coralville, IA.

Landreth, G. L. (2012). *Play therapy: The art of the relationship* (3rd ed.). New York, NY: Brunner-Routledge.

Lang, S., & Lang, M. (2015). *Families, families, families.* New York, NY: Random House.

Langenfeld, S., & Main, F. (1983). Personality priorities: A factor analytic study. *Individual Psychology, 39,* 40–51.

La Voy, S. K., Brand, M. J. L., & McFadden, C. R. (2013). An important lesson from our past with significance for our future: Alfred Adler's *Gemeinschaftsgefuhl. The Journal of Individual Psychology, 69,* 280–293.

LeBlanc, M., & Ritchie, M. (2001). A meta-analysis of play therapy outcomes. *International Journal of Play Therapy, 14,* 149–163.

LeFeber, M. (2014). Working with children using dance/movement therapy. In E. Green & A. Drewes (Eds.), *Integrating expressive arts and play therapy* (pp. 125–148). Hoboken, NJ: Wiley.

Leman, K. (2009). *The birth order book* (Rev. ed.). Grand Rapids, MI: Revell.

L'Engle, M. (2001). *The other dog.* San Francisco, CA: Chronicle Books.

Lester, H. (1987). *Score one for the sloths.* New York, NY: Houghton Mifflin.

Lester, H. (2001). *Princess Penelope's parrot.* New York, NY: Houghton Mifflin.

Lester, H. (2012). *All for me and none for all.* New York, NY: Houghton Mifflin.

Lester, J. (2006). *Let's talk about race.* New York, NY: Amistad.

Levine, P., & Kline, M. (2007). *Trauma through a child's eyes: Awakening the ordinary miracle of healing.* Berkeley, CA: North Atlantic Books.

Lew, A. (1999). Parenting education. In R. Watts & J. Carlson (Eds.), *Interventions and strategies in counseling and psychotherapy* (pp. 181–191). Philadelphia, PA: Taylor & Francis.

Lew, A., & Bettner, B. L. (1998). *Responsibility in the classroom: A teacher's guide to understanding and motivating students.* Newton Centre, MA: Connexions Press.

Lew, A., & Bettner, B. L. (2000). *A parent's guide to understanding and motivating children.* Newton Centre, MA: Connexions Press.

Lin, Y., & Bratton, S. (2015). A meta-analytic review of child-centered play therapy approaches. *Journal of Counseling & Development, 93,* 45–58. doi:10.1002/j.1556-6676.2015.00180.x

Lionni, L. (1997). *A color of his own.* New York, NY: Knopf.

Lombardi, R. (2014). Art therapy. In E. Green & A. Drewes (Eds.), *Integrating expressive arts and play therapy* (pp. 41–66). Hoboken, NJ: Wiley.

Lord, B. (1982). On the clinical use of children's early recollections. *Individual Psychology, 38,* 198–206.

Lucado, M. (1997). *You are special.* Wheaton, IL: Crossways Books.

Ludwig, T. (2011). *Better than you.* New York, NY: Knopf.

Ludwig, T. (2013). *The invisible boy.* New York, NY: Knopf.

Malchiodi, C. (Ed.). (2014). *Creative interventions with traumatized children* (2nd ed.). New York, NY: Guilford Press.

Malchiodi, C., & Ginns-Gruenberg, D. (2008). Trauma, loss, and bibliotherapy: The healing power of stories. In C. Malchiodi (Ed.), *Creative interventions with traumatized children* (pp. 167–188). New York, NY: Guilford Press.

Maniacci, M., Sackett-Maniacci, L., & Mosak, H. (2014). Adlerian psychotherapy. In D. Wedding & R. J. Corsini (Eds.), *Current psychotherapies* (10th ed., pp. 55–94). Belmont, CA: Thomson Brooks/Cole.

Manly, L. (1986). Goals of Misbehavior Inventory. *Elementary School Guidance and Counseling, 21,* 160–161.

Manning, J. (2012). *Millie fierce.* New York, NY: Philomel.

Mayer, M. (2000). *I was so mad.* New York, NY: Random House.

McBrien, R. (2012). The problem of distance. In J. Carlson & M. Maniacci (Eds.), *Alfred Adler revisited* (pp. 139–147). New York, NY: Taylor & Francis.

McCloud, C. (2006). *Have you filled a bucket today?* Northville, MI: Nelson.

McCready, A. (2012). *If I have to tell you one more time . . . : The revolutionary program that gets your kids to listen without nagging, reminding, or yelling.* New York, NY: Penguin.

McDonnell, P. (2014). *A perfectly messed-up story.* New York, NY: Little, Brown.

McGinnis, E. (2011). *Skillstreaming the elementary school child: A guide for teaching prosocial skills* (3rd ed.). Champaign, IL: Research Press.

McKay, G. (2005). *Parent group handbook for calming the family storm.* Attascadero, CA: Impact.

McKay, G. (2012). Position in family constellation influences lifestyle. In J. Carlson & M. Maniacci (Eds.), *Alfred Adler revisited* (pp. 71–88). New York, NY: Taylor & Francis.

Meany-Walen, K., Bratton, S., & Kottman, T. (2014). Effects of Adlerian play therapy on reducing students' disruptive behavior. *Journal of Counseling & Development, 92,* 47–56. doi:10.1002/j.1556-6676.2014.00129.x

Meany-Walen, K. K., Bullis, Q., Kottman, T., & Dillman Taylor, D. (2015). Group Adlerian play therapy with children with off-task behavior. *Journal for Specialists in Group Work, 40,* 418–314. doi:10.1080/019339 22.2015.1056569

Meany-Walen, K. K., Kottman, T., Bullis, Q., & Dillman Taylor, D. (2015). Adlerian play therapy with children with externalizing behaviors: Single case design. *Journal of Counseling & Development, 93,* 294–428. doi:10.1002/jcad.12040

Milgrom, C. (2005). An introduction to play therapy with adolescents. In L. Gallo-Lopez & C. Schaefer (Eds.), *Play therapy with adolescents* (pp. 3–17). Lanham, MD: Jason Aronson.

Miller, K. (2001). *Ages and stages: Developmental descriptions and activities, birth through eight years* (Rev. ed.). West Palm Beach, FL: TelShare.

Mills, J. C. (2003). *Gentle willow: A story for children about dying.* Washington, DC: American Psychological Association.

Mills, J., & Crowley, R. (2014). *Therapeutic metaphors for children and the child within* (2nd ed.). New York, NY: Routledge.

Monk, I. (1999). *Hope.* Minneapolis, MN: Carolrhoda Books.

Moore, J. (2011). *When a dragon moves in.* Chicago, IL: Flashlight Press.

Mosak, H. (1971). Life-style. In A. Nikelly (Ed.), *Techniques for behavior change: Applications of Adlerian theory* (pp. 77–81). Springfield, IL: Charles C Thomas.

Mosak, H. (1977). *On purpose.* Chicago, IL: Alfred Adler Institute.

Mulcahy, W. (2012). *Zach gets frustrated.* Minneapolis, MN: Free Spirit.

Nagaraja, D. (2008). *Buddha at bedtime.* London, England: Duncan Baird.

Nash, J. B., & Schaefer, C. (2011). Play therapy: Basic concepts and practices. In C. Schaefer (Ed.), *Foundations of play therapy* (2nd ed., pp. 3–13). Hoboken, NJ: Wiley.

Nelson, J. (2011). *Positive discipline* (Rev. ed.). New York, NY: Ballantine.

Nelson, J., & Erwin, C. (2000). *Parents who love too much: How good parents can learn to love more wisely and develop children of character.* New York, NY: Three Rivers.

Nelson, J., Lott, L., & Glenn, S. (2007). *Positive discipline A–Z: 1001 solutions to everyday parenting problems* (3rd ed.). New York, NY: Harmony Books.

Nelson, J., Lott, L., & Glenn, S. (2013). *Positive discipline in the classroom: Developing mutual respect, cooperation, and responsibility in your classroom* (4th ed.). New York, NY: Three Rivers Press.

Nemiroff, M., & Annunziata, J. (1990). *A child's first book about play therapy.* Washington, DC: American Psychological Association.

Nicoll, W. G., Pelonis, P., & Sperry, L. (2012). Individual Psychology in Greece. *The Journal of Individual Psychology, 68,* 249–259.

Niel, B., & Landreth, G. (2001). Have toys—will travel: A traveling play therapist in the school setting. In G. Landreth (Ed.), *Innovations in play therapy: Issues, process, and special populations* (pp. 349–360). Philadelphia, PA: Taylor & Francis.

Noll, A. (2009). *I need my monster.* Brooklyn, NY: Flashlight.

Nurse, A. R., & Sperry, L. (2012). Standardized assessment. In L. Sperry (Ed.), *Family assessment: Contemporary and cutting-edge strategies* (2nd ed., pp. 53–82). New York, NY: Routledge.

Nystul, M. (1980). Nystulian play therapy: Applications of Adlerian psychology. *Elementary School Guidance and Counseling, 15,* 22–29.

Oaklander, V. (1992). *Windows to our children: A Gestalt approach to children and adolescents.* New York, NY: The Gestalt Journal Press. (Original work published 1978)

Oberst, U., & Stewart, A. (2003). *Adlerian psychotherapy: An advanced approach to Individual Psychology.* New York, NY: Brunner-Routledge.

O'Connor, K. (2000). *The play therapy primer* (2nd ed.). New York, NY: Wiley.

O'Connor, K. (2005). Addressing diversity issues in play therapy. *Professional Psychology: Research and Practice, 36,* 566–573. doi:10.1037/0735-7028.36.5.566

O'Connor, K., & New, D. (2002). The Color-Your-Life technique. In C. Schaefer & D. Cangelosi (Eds.), *Play therapy techniques* (2nd ed., pp. 245–256). Northvale, NJ: Jason Aronson.

Offill, J. (2014). *Sparky!* New York, NY: Schwartz & Wade.

Ojiambo, D., & Bratton, S. C. (2014). Effects of group activity play therapy on problem behaviors of preadolescent Ugandan orphans. *Journal of Counseling & Development, 92,* 355–365. doi:10.1002/j.1556-6676.2014.00163.x

O'Neill, A., & Huliska-Beith, L. (2002). *Recess queen.* New York, NY: Scholastic.

Oryan, S. (2014). The family council: Different styles of family deliberation in two cultures. *The Journal of Individual Psychology, 70,* 128–147.

Oster, G., & Crone, P. (2004). *Using drawings in assessment and therapy: A guide for mental health professionals* (2nd ed.). New York, NY: Brunner-Routledge.

Otoshi, K. (2008). *One.* Mill Valley, CA: KO Kids Books.

Otoshi, K. (2010). *Zero.* Mill Valley, CA: KO Kids Books.

Otoshi, K. (2014). *Two.* Mill Valley, CA: KO Kids Books.

Overholser, J. C. (2010). Psychotherapy that strives to encourage social interest: A simulated interview with Alfred Adler. *Journal of Psychotherapy Integration, 20,* 347–363. doi:10.1037/a0022033

Palmer, P. (2009). *The mouse, the monster and me: Assertiveness for young people* (Rev. ed.). Oakland, CA: Uplift Press.

Parr, T. (2000). *The feelings book.* New York, NY: Little, Brown.

Parr, T. (2003). *The family book.* New York, NY: Little, Brown.

Pepper, F. (1980). Why children misbehave. *Individual Psychologist, 17,* 19–37.

Perrow, S. (2008). *Healing stories for challenging behavior.* Stroud, Gloucestershire, England: Hawthorn Press.

Pett, M. (2011). *The girl who never made a mistake*. Naperville, IL: Source-books Jabberwocky.

Petty, D. (2015). *I don't want to be a frog*. New York, NY: Random House.

Petty, K. (2009). *Developmental milestones of young children*. St. Paul, MN: Redleaf Press.

Pew, W. (1976). The number one priority. In *Monograph of the International Association of Individual Psychology* (pp. 1–24). Munich, Germany: International Association of Individual Psychology.

Piper, W. (2005). *The little engine that could*. New York, NY: Philomel.

Popkin, M. (2014). *Active parenting: A parent's guide to raising happy and successful children* (4th ed.). Atlanta, GA: Active Parenting.

Post, P., & Tillman, K. (2015). Cultural issues in play therapy. In D. Crenshaw & A. Stewart (Eds.), *Play therapy: A comprehensive guide to theory and practice* (pp. 496–510). New York, NY: Guilford Press.

Rathmann, M. (2006). *Ruby, the copycat*. New York, NY: Scholastic.

Ray, D. (2006). Evidence-based play therapy. In C. Schaefer & H. G. Kaduson (Eds.), *Contemporary play therapy: Theory, research, and practice* (pp. 136–157). New York, NY: Guilford Press.

Ray, D. (2011). *Advanced play therapy: Essential conditions, knowledge, and skills for child practice*. New York, NY: Routledge.

Ray, D. (2015). Research in play therapy: Empirical support for practice. In D. Crenshaw & A. Stewart (Eds.), *Play therapy: A comprehensive guide to theory and practice* (pp. 467–482). New York, NY: Guilford Press.

Ray, D. C., Lee, K. R., Meany-Walen, K. K., Carlson, S. E., Carnes-Holt, K. L., & Ware, J. N. (2013). Use of toys in child-centered play therapy. *International Journal of Play Therapy, 22*, 43–57. doi:10.1037/a0031430

Ray, D., Perkins, S., & Oden, K. (2004). Rosebush fantasy technique with elementary school students. *Professional School Counseling, 7*, 277–282.

Recob, A. (2008). *Bibliotherapy: When kids need books*. Bloomington, IN: iUniverse.

Reynolds, P. (2004). *Ish*. Somerville, MA: Candlewick.

Reynolds, P. (2012). *Sky color*. Somerville, MA: Candlewick.

Richmond, M. (2010). *If I could keep you little*. Naperville, IL: Sourcebooks Jabberwocky.

Richmond, M. (2011). *I believe in you*. Naperville, IL: Sourcebooks Jabberwocky.

Riviere, S. (2008). The therapeutic use of popular electronic media with today's teenagers. In L. Rubin (Ed.), *Popular culture in counseling, psychotherapy, and play-based interventions* (pp. 343–364). New York, NY: Springer.

Rotner, S. (2010). *Shades of people*. New York, NY: Holiday House.

Rousaki, M. (2003). *Unique Monique*. San Diego, CA: Kane/Miller.

Rubin, J. (2011). *Introduction to art therapy: Sources and resources*. New York, NY: Routledge.

Rubin, L. (Ed.). (2008). *Popular culture in counseling, psychotherapy, and play-based interventions*. New York, NY: Springer.

Salzberg, B. (2010). *Beautiful oops!* New York, NY: Workman.

Santat, D. (2014). *The adventures of Beckle: The unimaginary friend*. New York, NY: Little, Brown.

Santen, B. (2015). Treating dissociation in traumatized children with body maps. In C. Malchiodi (Ed.), *Creative interventions with traumatized children* (2nd ed., pp. 126–149). New York, NY: Guilford Press.

Schab, L. (2009). *Cool, calm, and confident: A workbook to help kids learn assertiveness skills*. Oakland, CA: New Harbinger.

Schaefer, C. (Ed.). (2003). *Play therapy with adults*. New York, NY: Wiley.

Schaefer, C. (Ed.). (2011). *Foundations of play therapy* (2nd ed.). Hoboken, NJ: Wiley.

Schaefer, C., & DiGeronimo, T. (2000). *Ages and stages: A parent's guide to normal childhood development*. New York, NY: Wiley.

Schaefer, C., & Drewes, A. (2013). *The therapeutic powers of play: 20 core agents of change* (2nd ed.). Hoboken, NJ: Wiley.

Schaefer, C. E., Kelly-Zion, S., McCormick, J., & Ohnogi, A. (2008). *Play therapy for very young children*. Lanham, MD: Jason Aronson.

Schafer, A. (2009). *Honey, I wrecked the kids: When yelling, screaming, threats, bribes, time-outs, sticker charts and removing privileges all don't work*. Ottawa, Ontario, Canada: Wiley.

Schafer, A. (2011). *Ain't misbehavin': Tactics for tantrums, meltdowns, bedtime blues, and other perfectly normal kid behaviors*. Ottawa, Ontario, Canada: Wiley.

Segel, R. (1991, January). *Integrating art, music, creative movement, photo therapy, guided imagery within family therapy*. Paper presented at the Texas Association for Marriage and Family Therapy Annual Conference, Dallas, TX.

Shannon, D. (2004). *A bad case of stripes*. New York, NY: Scholastic.

Shechtman, Z. (2009). *Treating child and adolescent aggression through bibliotherapy*. New York, NY: Springer.

Shragg, K. (2001). *A solstice tree for Jenny*. Amherst, NY: Prometheus Books.

Silver, G. (2009). *Anh's anger*. Berkeley, CA: Plum Blossom.

Simmons, J. (2014). *Seeing red: An anger management and anti-bullying curriculum for kids*. Gabriola Island, British Columbia, Canada: New Society.

Simon, F. (2001). *Horrid Henry's revenge*. London, England: Orion.

Slattery, K. (2010). *If I could ask God anything: Awesome Bible answers for curious kids*. Nashville, TN: Thomas Nelson.

Sobol, B. (2010). "I am an artist": A sexually traumatized girl's self-portraits in paint and clay. In E. Gil (Ed.), *Working with children to heal interpersonal trauma: The power of play* (pp. 240–263). New York, NY: Guilford Press.

Solis, C. M. (2006). Implementing Kinder Training as a preventive intervention: African-American preschool teacher perceptions of the process, effectiveness, and acceptability. *Dissertation Abstract International: Section A. Humanities and Social Sciences, 66*(7-A), 2488.

Spelman, C. (2000). *When I feel angry*. Morton Grove, IL: Albert Whitman.

Sperando, C., & Zimmerman, B. (2007). *Lunch box letters: Writing notes of love and encouragement to your children*. Buffalo, NY: Firefly.

Sperry, L., & Carlson, J. (2012). The global significance of Individual Psychology: An introduction and overview. *The Journal of Individual Psychology, 68,* 205–209.

Spires, A. (2014). *The most magnificent thing.* Tonawanda, NY: Kids Can Press.

Star, F. (Ed.). (2011). *What do you believe? (Big questions).* New York, NY: DK Publishing.

Steinhardt, L. (1985). Freedom within boundaries: Body outline drawings in art therapy with children. *The Arts in Psychotherapy, 12,* 25–34.

Stewart, A., & Green, E. (2015). Integrating play therapy and evidence-informed interventions with vulnerable populations: An overview. In E. Green & A. Myrick (Eds.), *Play therapy with vulnerable populations: No child forgotten* (pp. 3–22). Lanham, MD: Rowman & Littlefield.

Sun, S., & Bitter, J. R. (2012). From China to South Korea: Two perspectives on Individual Psychology in Asia. *The Journal of Individual Psychology, 68,* 233–248.

Sweeney, T. J. (2009). *Adlerian counseling and psychotherapy: A practitioner's approach* (5th ed.). New York, NY: Taylor & Francis.

Tarpley, T. (2015). *My grandma's a ninja.* New York, NY: NorthSouth Books.

Taylor de Faoite, A. (2014). Indirect teaching. In C. Schaefer & A. Drewes (Eds.), *The therapeutic powers of play* (2nd ed., pp. 51–68). Hoboken, NJ: Wiley.

Terr, L. (1990). *Too scared to cry.* New York, NY: Harper & Row.

Trelease, J. (2013). *The read aloud handbook* (7th ed.). New York, NY: Penguin.

Trice-Black, S., Bailey, C. L., & Riechel, M. E. K. (2013). Play therapy in school counseling. *Professional School Counseling, 16,* 303–312.

Vail, R. (2002). *Sometimes I'm bombaloo.* New York, NY: Scholastic.

VanFleet, R. (2009). Filial therapy. In K. O'Connor & L. M. Braverman (Eds.), *Play therapy theory and practice: Comparing theories and techniques* (2nd ed., pp. 163–202). New York, NY: Wiley.

VanFleet, R. (2013). *Filial therapy: Strengthening parent–child relationships through play* (3rd ed.). Sarasota, FL: Professional Resource Press.

VanFleet, R., Sywulak, A., & Sniscak, C. (2010). *Child-centered play therapy.* New York, NY: Guilford Press.

Vaughn, K. M. (2012). *Play therapist's perspectives on culturally sensitive play therapy* (Unpublished doctoral dissertation). University of New Orleans, New Orleans, LA.

Waber, B. (2002). *Courage.* New York, NY: Houghton Mifflin.

Wagenbach, D. (2009). *The grouchies.* Washington, DC: Magination Press.

Walton, F. X., & Stoykova, Z. (2012). Individual Psychology in Bulgaria. *The Journal of Individual Psychology, 68,* 216–224.

Watt, M. (2006). *Scaredy Squirrel.* Tonawanda, NY: Kids Can Press.

Watt, M. (2007). *Scaredy Squirrel makes a friend.* Tonawanda, NY: Kids Can Press.

Watts, R. (2012). On the origin of striving for superiority and of social interest. In J. Carlson & M. Maniacci (Eds.), *Alfred Adler revisited* (pp. 41–56). New York, NY: Taylor & Francis.

Watts, R. (2013). Adlerian counseling. In B. Irby, G. Brown, & S. Jackson (Eds.), *The handbook of educational theories for theoretical frameworks* (pp. 459–472). Charlotte, NC: Information Age.

Weiner, M., & Niemark, J. (2009). *I want your moo*. Washington, DC: Magination Press.

Wells, R. (1988). *Shy Charles*. New York, NY: Penguin.

Wells, R. (1997). *Noisy Nora*. New York, NY: Penguin.

White, J., Flynt, M., & Draper, K. (1997). Kinder Therapy: Teachers as therapeutic agents. *International Journal of Play Therapy, 6*, 33–52.

White, J., Flynt, M., & Jones, N. P. (1999). Kinder Therapy: An Adlerian approach for training teachers to be therapeutic agents through play. *The Journal of Individual Psychology, 55*, 365–382.

White, J., & Wynne, L. (2009). Kinder Training: An Adlerian-based model to enhance teacher–student relationships. In A. Drewes (Ed.), *Blending play therapy with cognitive behavioral therapy: Evidence-based and other effective treatments and techniques* (pp. 281–296). Hoboken, NJ: Wiley.

Willis, J., & Reynolds, A. (2015). *Elephants can't jump*. London, England: Anderson.

Witek, J. (2014). *In my heart: A book of feelings*. New York, NY: Harry N. Abrams.

Wolf, R. (2014). The therapeutic uses of photography in play therapy. In E. Green & A. Drewes (Eds.), *Integrating expressive arts and play therapy* (pp. 181–204). Hoboken, NJ: Wiley.

Wood, C. (2007). *Yardsticks: Children in the classroom ages 4–14* (3rd ed.). Turner Falls, MA: National Foundation for Children.

Wood, D. (2007). *Old turtle*. New York, NY: Scholastic.

Yang, J., Milliren, A., & Blagen, M. (2010). *The psychology of courage: An Adlerian handbook for healthy social living*. New York: NY: Routledge.

Yarlett, E. (2014). *Orion and the dark*. Somerville, MA: Templar.

Yolen, J. (2006). *How do dinosaurs play with their friends?* New York, NY: Scholastic.

Yura, M., & Galassi, M. (1974). Adlerian usage of children's play. *Journal of Individual Psychology, 30*, 194–201.

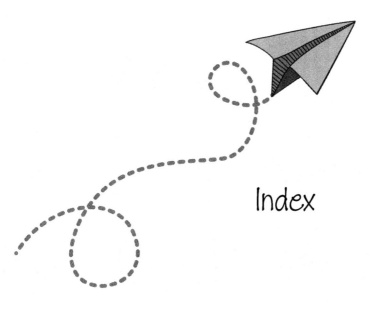

Index

A

Abilities, showing faith in, 138–139
Absolute limits, 148, 152
Abuse
  mandatory reporting of, 54, 108
  revenge-seeking behaviors and, 52
  sexual, 8, 9
Acceptance, unconditional, 137–138
Achievers, 61, 62
Active constructive attention seekers, 45–46
Active destructive attention seekers, 45, 46
Active power seeking, 48
Active revenge seeking, 52–53
ADHD. *See* Attention-deficit/ hyperactivity disorder
Adler, Alfred
  cultural awareness of, 31
  on family constellation, 174
  Individual Psychology developed by, 17
  on nature of people, 18, 23
  on private logic, 25
  "spitting in soup" technique formulated by, 228–229
Adlerian Personality Priority Assessment, 56
Adlerian play therapy
  clients appropriate for, 13–14, 15
  cultural diversity and, 32
  development of, ix, x–xiv

directiveness of therapist in, 295–296
education and training requirements for, 297
egalitarian relationships in. *See* Egalitarian relationship-building
empirical support for, 292
encouragement in. *See* Encouragement
growth and evolution of, ix–x
integrity of protocol in, 304
lifestyle in. *See* Lifestyle; Lifestyle conceptualization
limiting in. *See* Limiting process
logistics of, 107
nature of people and implications for, 21–23, 24, 26–27, 28, 32–33
parent consultations in. *See* Parent consultations
phases of, 28–30, 33. *See also* Information gathering phase; Insight phase; Relationship-building phase; Reorientation–reeducation phase
principles of, ix
research on, xvi, 294–297
session logistics, 297–298
skills used in, 298–302
teacher consultations in. *See* Teacher consultations
therapist's role in, 30–31
toys appropriate for, 6–13
treatment plans in. *See* Treatment plans
uses of, ix

(Continued)

Q

R

U

V

W

Y